Matplotlib 3.0 Cookbook

Over 150 recipes to create highly detailed interactive visualizations using Python

Srinivasa Rao Poladi

BIRMINGHAM - MUMBAI

Matplotlib 3.0 Cookbook

Commissioning Editor: Sunith Shetty
Acquisition Editor: Namrata Patil
Content Development Editor: Unnati Guha
Technical Editor: Sayli Nikalje
Copy Editor: Safis Editing
Project Coordinator: Manthan Patel
Proofreader: Safis Editing
Indexer: Rekha Nair
Graphics: Jisha Chirayil
Production Coordinator: Arvindkumar Gupta

First published: October 2018

Production reference: 2051118

Published by Packt Publishing Ltd.
Livery Place
35 Livery Street
Birmingham
B3 2PB, UK.

ISBN 978-1-78913-571-8

www.packtpub.com

`mapt.io`

Mapt is an online digital library that gives you full access to over 5,000 books and videos, as well as industry leading tools to help you plan your personal development and advance your career. For more information, please visit our website.

Why subscribe?

- Spend less time learning and more time coding with practical eBooks and Videos from over 4,000 industry professionals

- Improve your learning with Skill Plans built especially for you

- Get a free eBook or video every month

- Mapt is fully searchable

- Copy and paste, print, and bookmark content

Packt.com

Did you know that Packt offers eBook versions of every book published, with PDF and ePub files available? You can upgrade to the eBook version at `www.packt.com` and as a print book customer, you are entitled to a discount on the eBook copy. Get in touch with us at `customercare@packtpub.com` for more details.

At `www.packt.com`, you can also read a collection of free technical articles, sign up for a range of free newsletters, and receive exclusive discounts and offers on Packt books and eBooks.

Contributors

About the author

Srinivasa Rao Poladi has been in the IT services industry for over two decades, providing consulting and implementation services in data warehousing, business intelligence, and machine learning areas for global customers.

He has worked with Wipro Technologies for two decades and played key leadership roles in building large technology practices and growing them to multi-million $ business.

He spoke at international conferences, published many blogs and white papers in the areas of big data, business intelligence, and analytics.

He is a co-founder of krtrimaIQ a consulting firm that provides cognitive solutions to create tomorrow's Intelligent Enterprises powered by automation, big data, machine learning, and deep learning.

About the reviewer

Nikhil Borkar holds a CQF designation and a post-graduate degree in quantitative finance. He also holds the Certified Financial Crime Examiner and Certified Anti-Money Laundering Professional qualifications. He is a registered research analyst with the **Securities and Exchange Board of India** (**SEBI**) and has a keen grasp of the Indian regulatory landscape pertaining to securities and investments. He is currently working as an independent FinTech and legal consultant. Prior to this, he worked with **Morgan Stanley Capital International** (**MSCI**) as a Global RFP Project Manager.

Packt is searching for authors like you

If you're interested in becoming an author for Packt, please visit `authors.packtpub.com` and apply today. We have worked with thousands of developers and tech professionals, just like you, to help them share their insight with the global tech community. You can make a general application, apply for a specific hot topic that we are recruiting an author for, or submit your own idea.

Table of Contents

Preface

In the era of big data, finding valuable business insights is akin to finding a needle in a haystack. Visualization plays a critical role in finding those nuggets from an ever-increasing volume and variety of data. Matplotlib, with its rich visualization functionality, makes the process of exploratory data analysis user friendly and more productive.

Matplotlib's core functionality is vast, and it is further enhanced by many in-house and third-party toolkits. Many of the books on the market cover only a small portion of its complete functionality. In this book, we have covered Matplotlib's complete core functionality and many of its popular toolkits.

Matplotlib is popular among machine learning practitioners and researchers who use the Python ecosystem. With its rich functionality, it can be used in business intelligence and operational reporting applications. In this book, we have made an attempt to present examples from these applications.

While a recipe-based cookbook approach makes this book a reference guide for quick solutions, we have covered sufficient theoretical background to make it easy for beginners as well.

Who this book is for

This book is for data analysts, business analysts, data scientists, and Python developers who are looking for quick solutions for a wide variety of visualization applications, such as ad hoc reports, professional dashboards, exploratory data analysis, interactive analysis, embedded visualizations in selected GUI toolkits and web applications, three-dimensional plots, and geographical maps.

Those who are interested in developing business intelligence, machine learning, scientific, or engineering applications will also benefit from the recipes that are relevant for each of these disciplines.

What this book covers

Chapter 1, *Anatomy of Matplotlib*, explains the architecture of Matplotlib, various elements of a figure, interactive and non-interactive modes of operation, and how to customize environmental parameters.

`Chapter` 2, *Getting Started with Basic Plots*, introduces many types of graph that are commonly used in business intelligence and machine learning applications, including line, scatter, bar, stacked, histogram, box, violin, contour plots, heatmaps, and Hinton diagrams.

`Chapter` 3, *Plotting Multiple Graphs, Subplots, and Figures*, shows how to organize graphs into subplots and figures.

`Chapter` 4, *Developing Visualizations for Publishing Quality*, illustrates how to customize various attributes of a figure, including color, fonts, labels, titles, legend, spines, styles, markers, and annotation.

`Chapter` 5, *Plotting with the Object-Oriented API*, introduces the object-oriented API and compares it with the pyplot API. The object-oriented API gives flexibility in designing complex dashboards as required, but requires Python programming experience if you want to write code. The pyplot API comes with pre-packaged graphs that require simple commands to plot, without needing to write much Python code.

`Chapter` 6, *Plotting with Advanced Features*, covers how to develop complex visualization applications by using the advanced customization of legends, artist, and layout, as well as cycling object properties, origin and extent in images, transforms, animations, event handling, and path effects.

`Chapter` 7, *Embedding Text and Expressions*, covers how to add text to plots with regular text, annotations and mathematical expressions.

`Chapter` 8, *Saving the Figure in Different Formats*, explains how to save figures to external output files in PNG, PDF, SVG, and PS formats.

`Chapter` 9, *Developing Interactive Plots*, explains how to develop interactive plots using event handling, animations, and widgets. These features enable the users to perform interactive analysis.

`Chapter` 10, *Embedding Plots in Graphical User Interface*, explains how to embed Matplotlib plots into other graphical user interfaces used for developing applications.

`Chapter` 11, *Plotting 3D Graphs Using the mplot3d Toolkit*, covers how to use the mplot3D toolkit to plot 3D graphs, and the next two chapters cover two more toolkits.

`Chapter` 12, *Using the axisartist Toolkit*, explains that while the standard Matplotlib axes uses a traditional Cartesian coordinate system, it can't handle special features such as curved or floating axes that are useful in plotting geographical or planetary systems. This chapter explains how to create special applications using the `axisartist` toolkit.

`Chapter 13`, *Using the axes_grid1 Toolkit*, covers the `axes_grid1` toolkit. This toolkit enables you to plot images in a grid with an associated color bar that aligns well with the image and also enables anchor images as legends, zoom in/out effects, and more.

`Chapter 14`, *Plotting Geographical Maps Using the Cartopy Toolkit*, explains wide variety of features that cater to many different user communities. We will cover most of the features typically used in business applications.

`Chapter 15`, *Exploratory Data Analysis Using the Seaborn Toolkit*, explains the process of exploratory data analysis using exhaustive features of seaborn toolkit.

To get the most out of this book

Basic knowledge of Python is enough to understand the content in this book, except for `Chapters 9`, *Developing Interactive Plots* and `Chapter 10`, *Embedding Plots in a Graphical User Interface*. These two chapters deal with interactive plotting and embedded applications that need medium-level Python programming experience.

Many Python distributions automatically include Matplotlib, along with all its dependencies. If you have not installed any standard Python distributions, you can follow the installation process at `https://matplotlib.org/users/installing.html` to install Matplotlib and its associated dependencies.

Download the example code files

You can download the example code files for this book from your account at `www.packt.com`. If you purchased this book elsewhere, you can visit `www.packt.com/support` and register to have the files emailed directly to you.

You can download the code files by following these steps:

1. Log in or register at `www.packt.com`.
2. Select the **SUPPORT** tab.
3. Click on **Code Downloads & Errata**.
4. Enter the name of the book in the **Search** box and follow the onscreen instructions.

Once the file is downloaded, please make sure that you unzip or extract the folder using the latest version of:

- WinRAR/7-Zip for Windows
- Zipeg/iZip/UnRarX for Mac
- 7-Zip/PeaZip for Linux

The code bundle for the book is also hosted on GitHub at `https://github.com/PacktPublishing/Matplotlib-3.0-Cookbook`. In case there's an update to the code, it will be updated on the existing GitHub repository.

We also have other code bundles from our rich catalog of books and videos available at `https://github.com/PacktPublishing/`. Check them out!

Download the color images

We also provide a PDF file that has color images of the screenshots/diagrams used in this book. You can download it here: `https://www.packtpub.com/sites/default/files/downloads/9781789135718_ColorImages.pdf`.

Conventions used

There are a number of text conventions used throughout this book.

`CodeInText`: Indicates code words in text, database table names, folder names, filenames, file extensions, pathnames, dummy URLs, user input, and Twitter handles. Here is an example: "We will follow the order of `.txt`, `.csv`, and `.xlsx` files, in three separate sections."

A block of code is set as follows:

```
import matplotlib.pyplot as plt
import pandas as pd
import numpy as np
from matplotlib import cm
```

Bold: Indicates a new term, an important word, or words that you see onscreen. For example, words in menus or dialog boxes appear in the text like this. Here is an example: "When you run the program and click **Next** and **Next**, you will see the following three figures, representing each of the clusters, as shown in the header of each figure."

Warnings or important notes appear like this.

 Tips and tricks appear like this.

Sections

In this book, you will find several headings that appear frequently (*Getting ready, How to do it..., How it works..., There's more...,* and *See also*).

To give clear instructions on how to complete a recipe, use these sections as follows:

Getting ready

This section tells you what to expect in the recipe and describes how to set up any software or any preliminary settings required for the recipe.

How to do it...

This section contains the steps required to follow the recipe.

How it works...

This section usually consists of a detailed explanation of what happened in the previous section.

There's more...

This section consists of additional information about the recipe in order to make you more knowledgeable about the recipe.

See also

This section provides helpful links to other useful information for the recipe.

Get in touch

Feedback from our readers is always welcome.

General feedback: If you have questions about any aspect of this book, mention the book title in the subject of your message and email us at customercare@packtpub.com.

Errata: Although we have taken every care to ensure the accuracy of our content, mistakes do happen. If you have found a mistake in this book, we would be grateful if you would report this to us. Please visit www.packt.com/submit-errata, selecting your book, clicking on the Errata Submission Form link, and entering the details.

Piracy: If you come across any illegal copies of our works in any form on the Internet, we would be grateful if you would provide us with the location address or website name. Please contact us at copyright@packt.com with a link to the material.

If you are interested in becoming an author: If there is a topic that you have expertise in and you are interested in either writing or contributing to a book, please visit authors.packtpub.com.

Reviews

Please leave a review. Once you have read and used this book, why not leave a review on the site that you purchased it from? Potential readers can then see and use your unbiased opinion to make purchase decisions, we at Packt can understand what you think about our products, and our authors can see your feedback on their book. Thank you!

For more information about Packt, please visit packt.com.

Anatomy of Matplotlib 1

This chapter begins with an introduction to Matplotlib, including the architecture of Matplotlib and the elements of a figure, followed by the recipes. The following are the recipes that will be covered in this chapter:

- Working in interactive mode
- Working in non-interactive mode
- Reading from external files and plotting
- How to change and reset default environment variables

Introduction

Matplotlib is a cross-platform Python library for plotting two-dimensional graphs (also called **plots**). It can be used in a variety of user interfaces such as Python scripts, IPython shells, Jupyter Notebooks, web applications, and GUI toolkits. It can be used to develop professional reporting applications, interactive analytical applications, complex dashboard applications or embed into web/GUI applications. It supports saving figures into various hard-copy formats as well. It also has limited support for three-dimensional figures. It also supports many third-party toolkits to extend its functionality.

 Please note that all the examples in this book are tested with Matplotlib 3.0 and Jupyter Notebook 5.1.0.

Architecture of Matplotlib

Matplotlib has a three-layer architecture: **backend**, **artist**, and **scripting**, organized logically as a stack. Scripting is an API that developers use to create the graphs. Artist does the actual job of creating the graph internally. Backend is where the graph is displayed.

Backend layer

This is the bottom-most layer where the graphs are displayed on to an output device. This can be any of the user interfaces that Matplotlib supports. There are two types of backends: **user interface backends** (for use in `pygtk`, `wxpython`, `tkinter`, `qt4`, or `macosx`, and so on, also referred to as **interactive backends**) and **hard-copy** backends to make image files (`.png`, `.svg`, `.pdf`, and `.ps`, also referred to as **non-interactive backends**). We will learn how to configure these backends in later `Chapter 9`, *Developing Interactive Plots* and `Chapter 10`, *Embedding Plots in a Graphical User Interface*.

Artist layer

This is the middle layer of the stack. Matplotlib uses the `artist` object to draw various elements of the graph. So, every element (see elements of a figure) we see in the graph is an artist. This layer provides an **object-oriented API** for plotting graphs with maximum flexibility. This interface is meant for seasoned Python programmers, who can create complex dashboard applications.

Scripting layer

This is the topmost layer of the stack. This layer provides a simple interface for creating graphs. This is meant for use by end users who don't have much programming expertise. This is called a `pyplot` API.

Elements of a figure

The high-level Matplotlib object that contains all the elements of the output graph is called a `figure`. Multiple graphs can be arranged in different ways to form a figure. Each of the figure's elements is customizable.

Figure

The following diagram is the anatomy of a `figure`, containing all its elements:

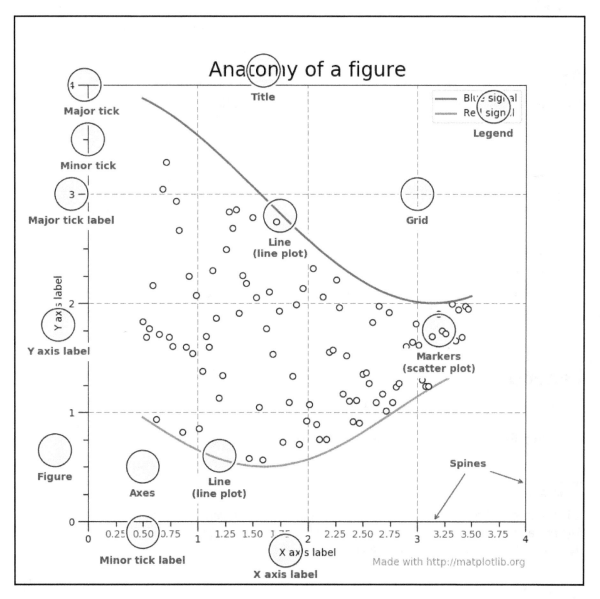

Anatomy of a figure (Source : http://diagramss.us/plotting-a-graph-in-matlab.html)

Axes

`axes` is a sub-section of the figure, where a graph is plotted. `axes` has a **title**, an **x-label** and a **y-label**. A `figure` can have many such `axes`, each representing one or more graphs. In the preceding figure, there is only one `axes`, two line graphs in blue and red colors.

Axis

These are number lines representing the scale of the graphs being plotted. Two-dimensional graphs have an x axis and a y axis, and three-dimensional graphs have an x axis, a y axis, and a z axis.

 Don't get confused between axes and axis. Axis is an element of axes. Grammatically, axes is also the plural for axis, so interpret the meaning of axes depending on the context, whether multiple axis elements are being referred to or an axes object is being referred to.

Label

This is the name given to various elements of the figure, for example, x axis label, y axis label, graph label (blue signal/red signal in the preceding figure *Anatomy of a figure*), and so on.

Legend

When there are multiple graphs in the `axes` (as in the preceding figure *Anatomy of a figure*), each of them has its own label, and all these labels are represented as a legend. In the preceding figure, the legend is placed at the top-right corner of the figure.

Title

It is the name given to each of the `axes`. The `figure` also can have its own title, when the figure has multiple axes with their own titles. The preceding figure has only one axes, so there is only one title for the axes as well as the figure.

Ticklabels

Each axis (*x*, *y*, or *z*) will have a range of values that are divided into many equal bins. Bins are chosen at two levels. In the preceding figure *Anatomy of a figure*, the *x* axis scale ranges from 0 to 4, divided into four major bins (0-1, 1-2, 2-3, and 3-4) and each of the major bins is further divided into four minor bins (0-0.25, 0.25-0.5, and 0.5-0.75). Ticks on both sides of major bins are called **major ticks** and minor bins are called **minor ticks**, and the names given to them are **major ticklabels** and **minor ticklabels**.

Spines

Boundaries of the figure are called **spines**. There are four spines for each axes(top, bottom, left, and right).

Grid

For easier readability of the coordinates of various points on the graph, the area of the graph is divided into a grid. Usually, this grid is drawn along major ticks of the *x* and *y* axis. In the preceding figure, the grid is shown in dashed lines.

Working in interactive mode

Matplotlib can be used in an **interactive** or **non-interactive** modes. In the interactive mode, the graph display gets updated after each statement. In the non-interactive mode, the graph does not get displayed until explicitly asked to do so.

Getting ready

You need working installations of Python, NumPy, and Matplotlib packages.

Using the following commands, interactive mode can be set on or off, and also checked for current mode at any point in time:

- `matplotlib.pyplot.ion()` to set the interactive mode ON
- `matplotlib.pyplot.ioff()` to switch OFF the interactive mode
- `matplotlib.is_interactive()` to check whether the interactive mode is ON (True) or OFF (False)

How to do it...

Let's see how simple it is to work in interactive mode:

1. Set the screen output as the backend:

   ```
   %matplotlib inline
   ```

2. Import the `matplotlib` and `pyplot` libraries. It is common practice in Python to import libraries with crisp synonyms. Note `plt` is the synonym for the `matplotlib.pyplot` package:

   ```
   import matplotlib as mpl
   import matplotlib.pyplot as plt
   ```

3. Set the interactive mode to ON:

   ```
   plt.ion()
   ```

4. Check the status of interactive mode:

   ```
   mpl.is_interactive()
   ```

5. You should get the output as `True`.
6. Plot a line graph:

   ```
   plt.plot([1.5, 3.0])
   ```

   You should see the following graph as the output:

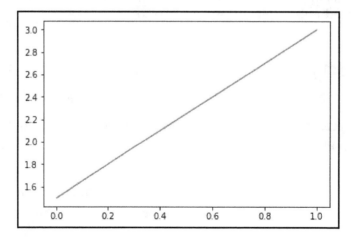

7. Now add the axis labels and a title to the graph with the help of the following code:

```
# Add labels and title
plt.title("Interactive Plot") #Prints the title on top of graph
plt.xlabel("X-axis")          # Prints X axis label as "X-axis"
plt.ylabel("Y-axis")          # Prints Y axis label as "Y-axis"
```

After executing the preceding three statements, your graph should look as follows:

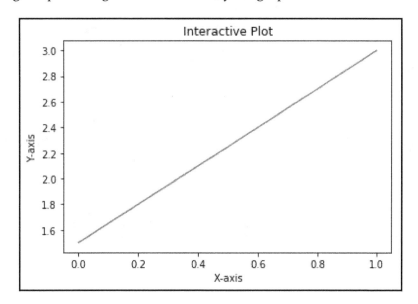

How it works...

So, this is how the explanation goes:

- `plt.plot([1.5, 3.0])` plots a line graph connecting two points (0, 1.5) and (1.0, 3.0).
- The `plot` command expects two arguments (Python list, NumPy array or pandas DataFrame) for the x and y axis respectively.
- If only one argument is passed, it takes it as y axis co-ordinates and for x axis co-ordinates it takes the length of the argument provided.
- In this example, we are passing only one list of two points, which will be taken as y axis coordinates.

- For the *x* axis, it takes the default values in the range of 0 to 1, since the length of the list [1.5, 3.0] is 2.
- If we had three coordinates in the list for *y*, then for *x*, it would take the range of 0 to 2.
- You should see the graph like the one shown in *step 6*.
- plt.title("Interactive Plot"), prints the title on top of the graph as **Interactive Plot.**
- plt.xlabel("X-axis"), prints the *x* axis label as **X-axis.**
- plt.ylabel("Y-axis"), prints the *y* axis label as **Y-axis.**
- After executing preceding three statements, you should see the graph as shown in *step 7*.

If you are using Python shell, after executing each of the code statements, you should see the graph getting updated with title first, then the *x* axis label, and finally the *y* axis label.

If you are using Jupyter Notebook, you can see the output only after all the statements in a given cell are executed, so you have to put each of these three statements in separate cells and execute one after the other, to see the graph getting updated after each code statement.

 In older versions of Matplotlib or certain backends (such as macosx), the graph may not be updated immediately. In such cases, you need to call plt.draw() explicitly at the end, so that the graph gets displayed.

There's more...

You can add one more line graph to the same plot and go on until you complete your interactive session:

1. Plot a line graph:

```
plt.plot([1.5, 3.0])
```

2. Add labels and title:

```
plt.title("Interactive Plot")
plt.xlabel("X-axis")
plt.ylabel("Y-axis")
```

3. Add one more line graph:

```
plt.plot([3.5, 2.5])
```

The following graph is the output obtained after executing the code:

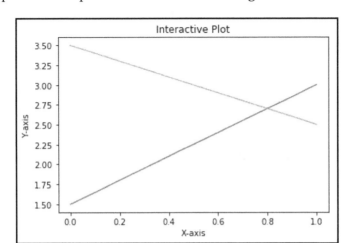

Hence, we have now worked in interactive mode.

Working in non-interactive mode

In the interactive mode, we have seen the graph getting built step by step with each instruction. In non-interactive mode, you give all instructions to build the graph and then display the graph with a command explicitly.

How to do it...

Working on non-interactive mode won't be difficult either:

1. Start the kernel afresh, and import the `matplotlib` and `pyplot` libraries:

    ```
    import matplotlib
    import matplotlib.pyplot as plt
    ```

2. Set the interactive mode to OFF:

    ```
    plt.ioff()
    ```

3. Check the status of interactive mode:

    ```
    matplotlib.is_interactive()
    ```

4. You should get the output `False`.

5. Execute the following code; you will not see the plot on your screen:

```
# Plot a line graph
plt.plot([1.5, 3.0])

# Plot the title, X and Y axis labels
plt.title("Non Interactive Mode")
plt.xlabel("X-axis")
plt.ylabel("Y-axis")
```

6. Execute the following statement, and then you will see the plot on your screen:

```
# Display the graph on the screen
plt.show()
```

How it works...

Each of the preceding code statements is self-explanatory. The important thing to note is in non-interactive mode, you write complete code for the graph you want to display, and call `plt.show()` explicitly to display the graph on the screen.

The following is the output obtained:

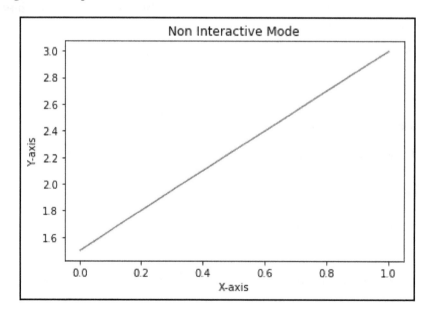

The latest versions of Jupyter Notebook seem to display the figure without calling `plt.show()` command explicitly. However, in Python shell or embedded applications, `plt.show()` or `plt.draw()` is required to display the figure on the screen.

Reading from external files and plotting

By default, Matplotlib accepts input data as a Python list, NumPy array, or pandas DataFrame. So all external data needs to be read and converted to one of these formats before feeding it to Matplotlib for plotting the graph. From a performance perspective, NumPy format is more efficient, but for default labels, pandas format is convenient.

If the data is a `.txt` file, you can use NumPy function to read the data and put it in NumPy arrays. If the data is in `.csv` or `.xlsx` formats, you can use pandas to read the data. Here we will demonstrate how to read `.txt`, `.csv`, and `.xlsx` formats and then plot the graph.

Getting ready

Import the `matplotlib.pyplot`, `numpy`, and `pandas` packages that are required to read the input files:

1. Import the `pyplot` library with the `plt` synonym:

    ```
    import matplotlib.pyplot as plt
    ```

2. Import the `numpy` library with the np synonym. The `numpy` library can manage n-dimensional arrays, supporting all mathematical operations on these arrays:

    ```
    import numpy as np
    ```

3. Import the `pandas` package with pd as a synonym:

    ```
    import pandas as pd
    ```

How to do it...

We will follow the order of `.txt`, `.csv`, and `.xlsx` files, in three separate sections.

Reading from a .txt file

Here are some steps to follow:

1. Read the text file into the `txt` variable:

```
txt = np.loadtxt('test.txt', delimiter = ',')
txt
```

Here is the explanation for the preceding code block:

- The `test.txt` text file has 10 numbers separated by a comma, representing the *x* and *y* coordinates of five points (1, 1), (2, 4), (3, 9), (4, 16), and (5, 25) in a two-dimensional space.
- The `loadtxt()` function loads text data into a NumPy array.

You should get the following output:

```
array([ 1., 1., 2., 4., 3., 9., 4., 16., 5., 25.])
```

2. Convert the flat array into five points in 2D space:

```
txt = txt.reshape(5,2)
txt
```

After executing preceding code, you should see the following output:

```
array([[ 1., 1.], [ 2., 4.], [ 3., 9.], [ 4., 16.], [ 5., 25.]])
```

3. Split the `.txt` variable into x and y axis co-ordinates:

```
x = txt[:,0]
y = txt[:,1]
print(x, y)
```

Here is the explanation for the preceding code block:

- Separate the x and y axis points from the `txt` variable.
- x is the first column in `txt` and y is the second column.
- The Python indexing starts from 0.

After executing the preceding code, you should see the following output:

```
[ 1. 2. 3. 4. 5.] [ 1. 4. 9. 16. 25.]
```

Reading from a .csv file

The .csv file has a relational database structure of rows and columns, and the test.csv file has *x, y* co-ordinates for five points in 2D space. Each point is a row in the file, with two columns: x and y. The same NumPy loadtxt() function is used to load data:

```
x, y = np.loadtxt ('test.csv', unpack = True, usecols = (0,1), delimiter = ',')
print(x)
print(y)
```

On execution of the preceding code, you should see the following output:

```
[ 1. 2. 3. 4. 5.] [ 1. 4. 9. 16. 25.]
```

Reading from an .xlsx file

Now let's read the same data from an .xlsx file and create the x and y NumPy arrays. The .xlsx file format is not supported by the NumPy loadtxt() function. A Python data processing package, pandas can be used:

1. Read the .xlsx file into pandas DataFrame. This file has the same five points in 2D space, each in a separate row with x, y columns:

```
df = pd.read_excel('test.xlsx', 'sheet', header=None)
```

2. Convert the pandas DataFrame to a NumPy array:

```
data_array = np.array(df)
print(data_array)
```

You should see the following output:

```
[[ 1 1] [ 2 4] [ 3 9] [ 4 16] [ 5 25]]
```

3. Now extract the x and y coordinates from the NumPy array:

```
x , y = data_array[:,0], data_array[:,1]
print(x,y)
```

You should see the following output:

```
[1 2 3 4 5] [ 1 4 9 16 25]
```

Plotting the graph

After reading the data from any of the three formats (.txt, .csv, .xlsx) and format it to x and y variables, then we plot the graph using these variables as follows:

```
plt.plot(x, y)
```

Display the graph on the screen:

```
plt.show()
```

The following is the output obtained:

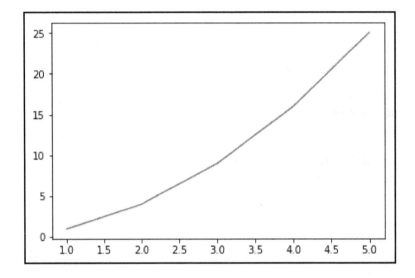

How it works...

Depending on the format and the structure of the data, we will have to use the Python, NumPy, or pandas functions to read the data and reformat it into an appropriate structure that can be fed into the matplotlib.pyplot function. After that, follow the usual plotting instructions to plot the graph that you want.

Changing and resetting default environment variables

Matplotlib uses the matplotlibrc file to store default values for various environment and figure parameters used across matplotlib functionality. Hence, this file is very long. These default values are customizable to apply for all the plots within a session.

You can use the print(matplotlib.rcParams) command to get all the default parameter settings from this file.

The matplotlib.rcParams command is used to change these default values to any other supported values, one parameter at a time. The matplotlib.rc command is used to set default values for multiple parameters within a specific group, for example, lines, font, text, and so on. Finally, the matplotlib.rcdefaults() command is used to restore default parameters.

> The matplotlib.rcsetup() command is used internally by Matplotlib to validate that the parameters being changed are acceptable values.

Getting ready

The following code block provides the path to the file containing all configuration the parameters:

```
# Get the location of matplotlibrc file
import matplotlib
matplotlib.matplotlib_fname()
```

You should see the directory path like the one that follows. The exact directory path depends on your installation:

```
'C:\\Anaconda3\\envs\\keras35\\lib\\site-packages\\matplotlib\\mpl-
    data\\matplotlibrc'
```

How to do it...

The following block of code along with comments helps you to understand the process of changing and resetting default environment variables:

1. Import the `matplotlib.pyplot` package with the `plt` synonym:

   ```
   import matplotlib.pyplot as plt
   ```

2. Load x and y variables from same `test.csv` file that we used in the preceding recipe:

   ```
   x, y = np.loadtxt ('test.csv', unpack = True, usecols = (0,1),
                      delimiter = ',')
   ```

3. Change the default values for multiple parameters within the group `'lines'`:

   ```
   matplotlib.rc('lines', linewidth=4, linestyle='-', marker='*')
   ```

4. Change the default values for parameters individually:

   ```
   matplotlib.rcParams['lines.markersize'] = 20
   matplotlib.rcParams['font.size'] = '15.0'
   ```

5. Plot the graph:

   ```
   plt.plot (x,y)
   ```

6. Display the graph:

   ```
   plt.show()
   ```

The following is the output that will be obtained:

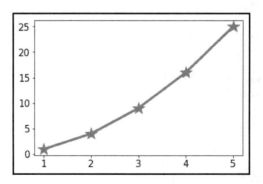

How it works...

The `matplotlib.rc` and `matplotlib.rcParams` commands overwrite the default values for specified parameters as arguments in these commands. These new values will be used by the `pyplot` tool while plotting the graph.

 It should be noted that these values will be active for all plots in the session. If you want different settings for each plot in the same session, then you should use the attributes available with the `plot` command.

There's more...

You can reset all the parameters to their default values, using the `rsdefaults()` command, as shown in the following block:

```
# To restore all default parameters
matplotlib.rcdefaults()
plt.plot(x,y)
plt.show()
```

The graph will look as follows:

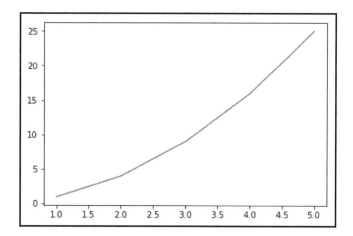

Getting Started with Basic Plots 2

In this chapter, we will cover recipes for plotting the following graphs:

- Line plot
- Bar plot
- Scatter plot
- Bubble plot
- Stacked plot
- Pie plot
- Table chart
- Polar plot
- Histogram
- Box plot
- Violin plot
- Heatmap
- Hinton diagram
- Images
- Contour plot
- Triangulations
- Stream plot
- Path

Introduction

A picture is worth a thousand words, and the visualization of data plays a critical role in finding hidden patterns in the data. Over a period of time, a variety of graphs have been developed to represent different relationships between different types of variables. In this chapter, we will see how to use these different graphs in different contexts and how to plot them using Matplotlib.

Line plot

The line plot is used to represent a relationship between two continuous variables. It is typically used to represent the trend of a variable over time, such as GDP growth rate, inflation, interest rates, and stock prices over quarters and years. All the graphs we have seen in `Chapter 1`, *Anatomy of Matplotlib* are examples of a line plot.

Getting ready

We will use the Google Stock Price data for plotting time series line plot. We have the data (date and daily closing price, separated by commas) in a `.csv` file without a header, so we will use the pandas library to read it and pass it on to the `matplotlib.pyplot` function to plot the graph.

Let's now import required libraries with the following code:

```
import matplotlib.pyplot as plt
import pandas as pd
```

How to do it...

The following code plots the time series chart of the Google Stock Price:

1. Load the `Google Stock Price` file (date and price) into *x*, *y* coordinates:

```
stock = pd.read_csv('GOOG.csv', header=None, delimiter=',')
```

2. Add column names:

```
stock.columns = ['date','price']
```

3. Convert the pandas DataFrame into a time series:

```
stock['date'] = pd.to_datetime(stock['date'], format='%d-%m-%Y')
```

4. Set the date as the index for the pandas DataFrame:

```
indexed_stock = stock.set_index('date')
ts = indexed_stock['price']
```

5. Plot the graph:

```
plt.plot(ts)
plt.xticks(rotation=20)
```

6. Display the graph on the screen:

```
plt.show()
```

How it works...

The following is the explanation of the code:

- `pd.read_csv()` function specifies the following:
    - `header=None`, input file has no header
    - `delimiter=', '`, date and price are separated by a comma (,)
    - Read the data into the `stock` DataFrame
- The `stock.columns` command assigns names for each of the attributes, `date` and `price`, within the `stock` DataFrame.
- The `pd.to_datetime()` function converts the date from the character format to the date time format. The format: `%d-%m-%Y` argument specifies the format of the date in the input file.
- `stock.set_index()` sets the `date` column as the index, so that the `price` column can represent the time series data, which is understood by the `plot` command.
- plt.xticks(rotation=20) prints dates on X axis with 20 degree inclination

The following graph is the output you should get from the preceding code block:

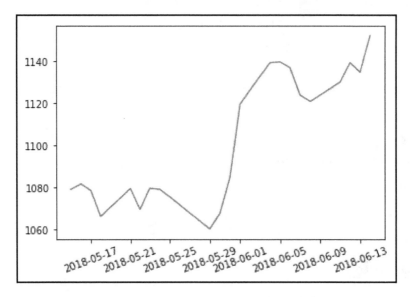

There's more...

Instead of reading the Google Stock Price data from a .csv or .xlsx file, there are standard APIs such as fix_yahoo_finance, pandas_datareader that can read data directly from open databases.

 Standard APIs undergo frequent changes and at times the database websites are not responsive. You need to install these APIs on your machine, as they don't come with standard Python distributions.

Here, we will show an example of using fix_yahoo_finance:

1. Import the required libraries:

```
import matplotlib.pyplot as plt
import pandas as pd
import fix_yahoo_finance as yf
```

2. Download the apple daily closing price from October 1, 2017 to January 1, 2018:

```
data = yf.download('AAPL','2017-10-01','2018-01-01')
```

3. Plot the closing price (`Close`) by date. Please note that `date` is the default *x* axis here, as `yf.download` creates data with `date` index. Hence, we don't need to provide *x* axis co-ordinates for the plot. Please note that here we are using `plot()` command of pandas, not Matplotlib:

```
data.Close.plot()
plt.xticks(rotation=75)
```

4. Display the graph on the screen:

```
plt.show()
```

You should see a graph, like the one depicted here:

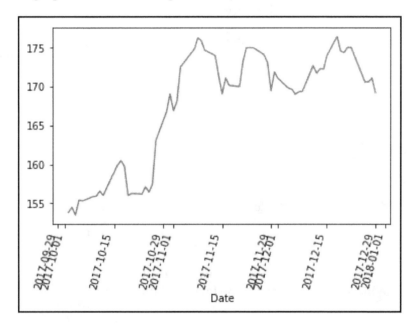

You can try using the `pandas_datareader` API. Please refer to the documentation at `http://pandas-datareader.readthedocs.io/en/latest/` on `pandas_datareader` for more details.

Bar plot

Bar plots are the graphs that use bars to compare different categories of data. Bars can be shown vertically or horizontally, based on which axis is used for a categorical variable. Let's assume that we have data on the number of ice creams sold every month in an ice cream parlor over a period of one year. We can visualize this using a bar plot.

Getting ready

We will use the Python `calendar` package to map numeric months (1 to 12) to the corresponding descriptive months (January to December).

Before we plot the graph, we need to import the necessary packages:

```
import matplotlib.pyplot as plt
import numpy as np
import calendar
```

How to do it...

The following code draws a bar plot:

1. Set up data for the *x* and *y* axes:

```
month_num = [1, 2, 3, 4, 5, 6, 7, 8, 9, 10, 11, 12]
units_sold = [500, 600, 750, 900, 1100, 1050, 1000, 950, 800, 700,
              550, 450]
```

2. Allocate the space and specify the layout of the figure:

```
fig, ax = plt.subplots()
```

3. Set the descriptive month names as *x* axis ticks:

```
plt.xticks(month_num, calendar.month_name[1:13], rotation=20)
```

4. Plot the bar graph:

```
plot = ax.bar(month_num, units_sold)
```

5. Add the data value to the head of the bar:

```
for rect in plot:
    height = rect.get_height()
    ax.text(rect.get_x() + rect.get_width()/2., 1.002*height,'%d' %
    int(height), ha='center', va='bottom')
```

6. Display the graph on the screen:

```
plt.show()
```

How it works...

Here is the explanation of the preceding code blocks:

- Older versions of Matplotlib accept only floating-point data types as their arguments for data. So, the months have to be represented in a numerical format.
- month_num and units_sold are Python lists representing the number of units sold in each month of a year.
- plt.subplots() allows us to define the layout of the figure in terms of the number of graphs and how they should be organized within the figure. We will learn more about it in Chapter 3, *Plotting Multiple Charts, Subplots, and Figures* and Chapter 6, *Plotting with Advanced Features*. In this case, we are using it to get access to the axes on which we are plotting the bar graph so that we can annotate them with the actual data representing the bar. If you recall from Chapter 1, *Anatomy of Matplotlib,* we have seen that axes is the individual plot within the figure.
- Changing the month format from the numerical format to its corresponding month name on the *x* axis. calendar.month_name[1:13] will return January to December, whereas plt.xticks() changes *x* axis tickers from numeric 1 to 12, to January to December, for better readability.

- `ax.text()` within the `for` loop annotates each bar with its corresponding data value. Arguments for this function specify where exactly the data text has to be placed over the bar: first, get the current bar's *x* and *y* coordinates, and then add *bar_width/2* to the *x* co-ordinate with *1.002** height being the *y* co-ordinate; then, using the `va` and `ha` arguments, we align the text centrally over the bar:

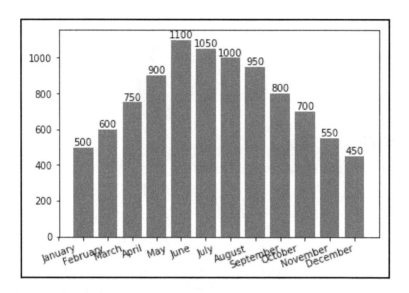

There's more...

The bar graph from the preceding section plots bars vertically. We can also plot a horizontal bar graph, as shown here. Most of the code is the same as the code used in the previous section, except that `plt.xticks()` and `plt.bar()` are replaced with `plt.yticks()` and `plt.barh()` respectively:

```
# matplotlib accepts only floating point data types as its arguments
  for data.

# So months have to be represented in numerical format
month_num = [1, 2, 3, 4, 5, 6, 7, 8, 9, 10, 11, 12]
units_sold = [500, 600, 750, 900, 1100, 1050, 1000, 950, 800, 700, 550,
              450]

fig, ax = plt.subplots()

# change the month number to month name on y axis
plt.yticks(month_num, calendar.month_name[1:13], rotation=20)
```

```
# plot horizontal bar graph
plot = plt.barh(month_num, units_sold)

# Display the graph on the screen
plt.show()
```

Here is how the output graph looks:

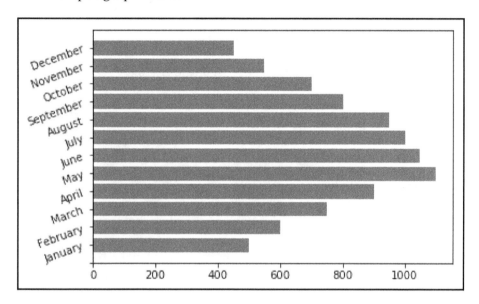

Scatter plot

A scatter plot is used to compare distribution of two variables and see whether there is any correlation between them. If there are distinct clusters/segments within the data, it will be clear in the scatter plot.

Getting ready

Import the following libraries:

```
import matplotlib.pyplot as plt
import pandas as pd
```

We will use pandas to read the Excel files.

How to do it...

The following code block draws a scatter plot that depicts the relationship between the age and the weight of people:

1. Set the figure size (width and height) to (10, 6) inches:

```
plt.figure(figsize=(10,6))
```

2. Read age and weight data from an Excel file:

```
age_weight = pd.read_excel('scatter_ex.xlsx', 'age_weight')
x = age_weight['age']
y = age_weight['weight']
```

3. Plot the scatter plot:

```
plt.scatter(x, y)
```

4. Set *x* and *y* axis labels:

```
plt.xlabel('Age')
plt.ylabel('Weight)
```

5. Display the graph:

```
plt.show()
```

How it works...

The explanation for the code follows:

- `plt.figure(figsize=(10,6))` overwrites the default figure size with size (10, 6).
- `pd.read_excel()` reads the data and assigns values to the *x* and *y* axes coordinates.
- `plt.scatter(x,y)` plots the scatter plot.
- `plt.xlabel()` and `plt.ylabel()` set *x* and *y* axes labels for better readability.

Display the graph on the terminal. You should see the following chart:

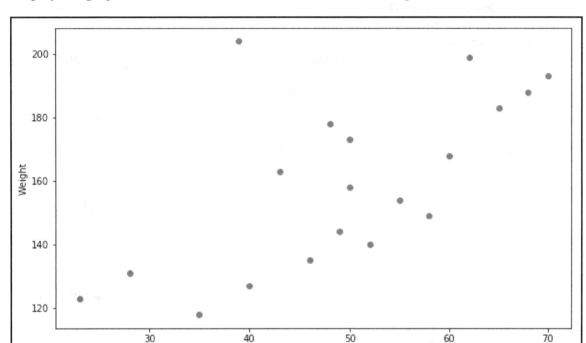

It is clearly visible that there is no relationship between the age and the weight of people, as the points are scattered. If a correlation is present between the two elements depicted, we would observe a pattern of a straight line or a curve.

The previous graphs could have been plotted with the `plt.plot()` method also. The `plt.scatter()` method has a lot more flexibility to customize each of the points with different sizes, colors, and so on, which we will observe in the bubble plot section. However, this flexibility comes at the cost of performance. For larger datasets, the `plt.plot()` method is lot faster than the `plt.scatter()` method.

There's more...

Here, we will see another example of a scatter plot, where we can clearly see distinct segments.

The `Iris` flower dataset is the oldest dataset, introduced in 1936 by Ronald Fisher. The dataset has 50 examples each of three species of Iris, named Setosa, Virginica, and Versicolor. Each example has four attributes, and the length and width in centimeters of both sepals and petals. This dataset is widely used in **machine learning (ML)** for classification and clustering. We will use this dataset to demonstrate how a scatter plot can show different clusters within a dataset.

The following code block plots a scatter plot of the length and width of a petal:

1. Load the `Iris` dataset from a `.csv` file using pandas:

```
iris = pd.read_csv('iris_dataset.csv', delimiter=',')
```

2. In the file, each class of species is defined with descriptive names, which we will map to numeric codes as 0, 1, or 2:

```
iris['species'] = iris['species'].map({"setosa" : 0, "versicolor" :
                    1, "virginica" : 2})
```

3. Plot a scatter plot with the petal lengths on the *x* axis and the petal widths on the *y* axis:

```
plt.scatter(iris.petal_length, iris.petal_width, c=iris.species)
```

4. Label the *x* and *y* axes:

```
plt.xlabel('petal length')
plt.ylabel('petal width')
```

5. Display the graph on the screen:

```
plt.show()
```

Here is the explanation of the code:

- `pd.read_csv()` reads the data into the `iris` DataFrame.
- The `species` attribute in the DataFrame has a descriptive class name, `setosa`, `versicolor`, and `virginica`. However, if we want to plot each class in a different color, the argument we pass should be a numeric code. Hence, we map them to numeric codes.
- `iris['species'] = iris['species'].map()` replaces the descriptive names with 0, 1, and 2 numeric codes.

- `c=iris.species` specifies color mapping to different classes. These argument classes should be numeric, which is what we have done before.
- `plt.scatter()` plots the scatter plot.

You should see the following graph on your screen:

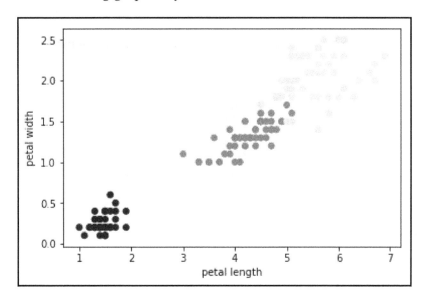

Clearly, we can see three different clusters here. But, it is not clear which color represents setosa, versicolor, and virginica cluster. We will see how to distinguish different clusters using labels in subsequent chapters, where we will learn how to customize the plots.

Bubble plot

A bubble plot is drawn using the same `plt.scatter()` method. It is a manifestation of the scatter plot, where each point on the graph is shown as a bubble. Each of these bubbles can be displayed with a different color, size, and appearance.

Getting ready

Import the required libraries. We will use pandas to read the Excel file:

```
import matplotlib.pyplot as plt
import pandas as pd
```

How to do it...

The following code block plots a bubble plot, for which we have seen a scatter plot earlier:

1. Load the `Iris` dataset:

```
iris = pd.read_csv('iris_dataset.csv', delimiter=',')
```

2. In the file, each class of species is defined as 0, 1, and 2, which we will map to their descriptive names:

```
iris['species'] = iris['species'].map({"setosa" : 0, "versicolor" :
                            1, "virginica" : 2})
```

3. Draw the scatter plot:

```
plt.scatter(iris.petal_length, iris.petal_width,
            s=50*iris.petal_length*iris.petal_width,
            c=iris.species,
            alpha=0.3)
```

4. Label the *x* and *y* axes:

```
plt.xlabel('petal length')
plt.ylabel('petal width')
```

5. Display the graph on the screen:

```
plt.show()
```

How it works...

The following is the explanation for the code:

- `pd.read_csv()` reads the data and replaces the descriptive names with numeric codes, as explained earlier.
- `s = 50 * iris.petal_length * iris.petal_width` specifies the size of the bubble. It essentially represents the area. The constant 50 used in the formula for s is a random number that multiplies the area of every point by this constant. The smaller this constant is, the smaller the relative sizes of all the points will be. Try changing this constant from 25, and then to 50 and then to 100 and see how the sizes of bubbles change. Without this multiplier, the size of some of the points is too small to observe them in the plot.

- c = iris.species specifies different classes (clusters) in the data. The pyplot method uses this to represent each of these classes in different colors.
- alpha=0.3 specifies the appearance of the bubble and decides how transparent the bubble should be. This can range from 0 to 1; if the value is close to zero, the bubble is highly transparent and if it is close to 1, the bubble is highly opaque:

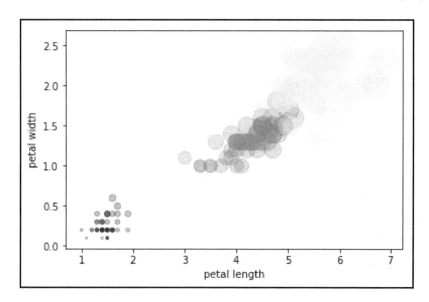

Stacked plot

A stacked plot represents the area under the line plot, and multiple line plots are stacked one over the other. It is used to provide a visualization of the cumulative effect of multiple variables being plotted on the *y* axis.

We will plot the number of product defects by a defect reason code, for three months stacked together to give a cumulative picture for the quarter.

Getting ready

Import the required libraries:

```
import numpy as np
import matplotlib.pyplot as plt
```

How to do it...

The following are the steps to plot a stacked plot:

1. Define the data for the plot:

```
x = np.array([1, 2, 3, 4, 5, 6], dtype=np.int32)
Apr = [5, 7, 6, 8, 7, 9]
May = [0, 4, 3, 7, 8, 9]
June = [6, 7, 4, 5, 6, 8]
```

2. Define the list of `labels` to be used for the legend:

```
labels = ["April ", "May", "June"]
```

3. Define the figure and the axes:

```
fig, ax = plt.subplots()
```

4. Plot the `stackplot` and the `legend`:

```
ax.stackplot(x, Apr, May, June, labels=labels)
ax.legend(loc=2)
```

5. Set the labels and the title:

```
plt.xlabel('defect reason code')
plt.ylabel('number of defects')
plt.title('Product Defects - Q1 FY2019')
```

6. Display the figure on the screen:

```
plt.show()
```

How it works...

Here is the explanation of the code:

- `x = np.array([1, 2, 3, 4, 5, 6], dtype=np.int32)` is the list of product defect codes with the data type as the integer.
- `Apr = [5, 7, 6, 8, 7, 9]` is the list of product defect counts by the defect code for the month of April.
- `May = [0, 4, 3, 7, 8, 9]` is the list of product defect counts by the defect code for the month of May.

- `June = [6, 7, 4, 5, 6, 8]` is the list of product defect counts by the defect code for the month of June.
- `labels = ["April ", "May", "June"]` is the list of labels to be used as the plot legend.
- `fig, ax = plt.subplots()` defines the figure and axes on which the graph is to be plotted.
- `ax.stackplot(x, Apr, May, June, labels=labels)` plots the stacked plot with the given data and labels.
- `ax.legend(loc=2)` specifies the legend to be plotted in the top left of the graph; we will learn more about legend locations in `Chapter 4`, *Developing Visualizations for Publishing Quality*.
- `plt.xlabel('defect reason code')` plots a label for the *x* axis.
- `plt.ylabel('number of defects')` plots the *y* axis label.
- `plt.title('Product Defects - Q1 FY2019')` plots the title for the graph.
- `plt.show()` displays the figure on the screen.

On executing the preceding code, you should see the following figure on your screen:

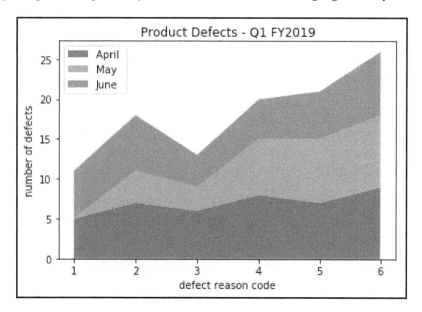

Pie plot

A pie plot is used to represent the contribution of various categories/groups to the total. For example, the contribution of each state to the national GDP, contribution of a movie to the total number of movies released in a year, student grades (A, B, C, D, and E) as a percentage of the total class size, or a distribution of monthly household expenditure on groceries, vegetables, utilities, apparel, education, healthcare, and so on.

Getting ready

Import the required library:

```
import matplotlib.pyplot as plt
```

How to do it...

The following code block plots a pie chart of the genre of movies released in a year:

1. Set up the data for the pie chart:

```
labels = ['SciFi', 'Drama', 'Thriller', 'Comedy', 'Action',
'Romance']
sizes = [5, 15, 10, 20, 40, 10]          # Add upto 100%
```

2. Show one slice slightly outside the circle:

```
explode = (0, 0, 0, 0, 0.1, 0) # only "explode" the 5th slice
(i.e.'Action')
```

3. Plot the pie chart:

```
plt.pie(sizes, labels=labels, explode=explode, autopct='%1.1f%%',
        shadow=True, startangle=90)
```

4. Display the graph on the screen:

```
plt.show()
```

How it works...

The following is the explanation of the code:

- `labels` and `sizes` are Python lists representing genre and the percentage of the total of the movies released in a year. The order of the labels in the input list is plotted counter clockwise in the pie chart.
- The `explode` argument specifies which slice of the chart is to be exploded outwards.
- The `autopct` argument depicts the number of decimal points to be shown in the percentage data points. If this argument is omitted, slices will not show the actual percentage (%) data.
- The `shadow` argument specifies whether each slice should be shown with a shadow.
- The `startangle` arguments specifies the angle in which the first slice should start, and it goes anticlockwise to represent all other slices in the pie chart.
- `plt.pie()` draws the pie plot.

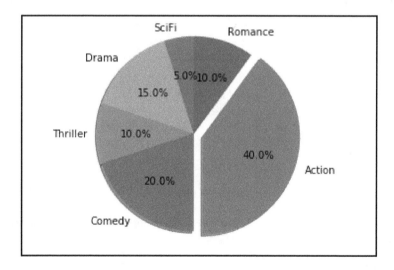

Table chart

A table chart is a combination of a bar chart and a table, representing the same data. So, it is a combination of pictorial representation along with the corresponding data in a table.

Getting ready

We will consider an example of the number of batteries sold in each year, with different **ampere hour** (**Ah**) ratings. There are two categorical variables: year and Ah ratings, and one numeric variable: the number of batteries sold.

Import the required libraries:

```
import numpy as np
import matplotlib.pyplot as plt
```

How to do it...

The following code block draws a table chart for the types of batteries sold in each year:

1. Prepare the data:

```
rows = ['2011', '2012', '2013', '2014', '2015']
columns = ('7Ah', '35Ah', '40Ah', '135Ah', '150Ah')
data = [[75, 144, 114, 102, 108], [90, 126, 102, 84, 126],
        [96, 114, 75, 105, 135], [105, 90, 150, 90, 75],
        [90, 75, 135, 75, 90]]
```

2. Define the range and scale for the y axis:

```
values = np.arange(0, 600, 100)
```

3. Specify the color spectrum to be used. Each year will be represented in a different color:

```
colors = plt.cm.OrRd(np.linspace(0, 0.5, len(rows)))
```

4. Define x axis ticks where the bars are to be plotted:

```
index = np.arange(len(columns)) + 0.3
bar_width = 0.5
```

5. Initialize the vertical offset for the stacked bar chart:

```
y_offset = np.zeros(len(columns))
```

6. Specify the area for the plot in terms of figure and axes:

```
fig, ax = plt.subplots()
```

7. Plot bars and create text labels for the table. Initialize the list in which data for the table is saved:

```
cell_text = []
```

8. Each iteration of the `for` loop plots one year of data for all battery ratings in one color:

```
n_rows = len(data)
for row in range(n_rows):
    plot = plt.bar(index, data[row], bar_width, bottom=y_offset,
                    color=colors[row])
    y_offset = y_offset + data[row]
    cell_text.append(['%1.1f' % (x) for x in y_offset])
    i=0
# Each iteration of this for loop, labels each bar with
  corresponding value for the given year
    for rect in plot:
        height = rect.get_height()
        ax.text(rect.get_x() + rect.get_width()/2, y_offset[i],'%d'
                % int(y_offset[i]),
            ha='center', va='bottom')
        i = i+1
```

9. Add a table to the bottom of the axes:

```
the_table = plt.table(cellText=cell_text, rowLabels=rows,
                rowColours=colors, colLabels=columns, loc='bottom')
plt.ylabel("Units Sold")
```

10. There are n ticks on the *x* axis, since this table covers the labels:

```
plt.xticks([])
plt.title('Number of Batteries Sold/Year')
```

11. Display the plot on the screen:

```
plt.show()
```

How it works...

The following is the explanation of the code:

- `rows` is the list of years and `columns` is the list of battery ratings. They are plotted as rows and columns of the table in the plot.
- `data` is the number of units sold for each rating of the battery, in a given year, for example, 75 units of 7 Ah batteries sold in 2011.
- `values` is the list specifying the scale for the *y* axis with increments of 100, starting with zero, up to six hundred. This being a stacked bar chart, it should cover the sum total of a given battery rating across all years (the maximum in this case is 576).
- `plt.cm.OrRd()` specifies the range of colors with varying intensity; there are pre-defined colormaps in Matplotlib. We will cover these in Chapter 4, *Developing Visualizations for Publishing Quality*. Here, it is used to display each year data in a different color.
- `index` specifies the placement of each bar on the *x* axis, and `bar_width` specifies the width of each bar.
- `y_offset` represents where each year's data should start on the *y* axis, as each year's data is stacked one over the other. Start at the bottom with zero and keep adding for each year.
- When the `for` loop is initiated, each iteration plots bars for all battery ratings for a given year, and then another `for` loop to annotate each bar with the corresponding data label.
- Arguments in the second `for` loop specify the exact location for the data text to be placed over the bar. First, get the current bar *x* and *y* coordinates, then add `bar_width/2` to the *x* coordinate and `y_offset[i]` gives us the *y* coordinate; then, using `va` and `ha`, the arguments align the text over the bar, centrally.
- Then add `Y-label`, title and mask `X-ticks`.

Here is how the plot looks:

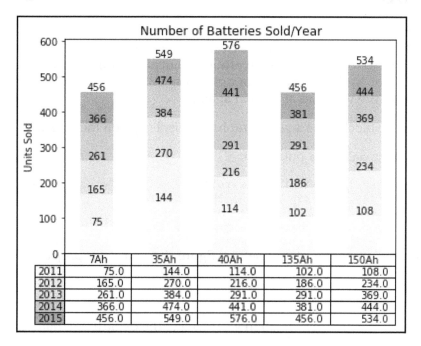

Polar plot

The polar plot is a chart plotted on the polar axis, which has coordinates as angle (in degrees) and radius, as opposed to the Cartesian system of x and y coordinates. We will take the example of planned versus the actual expense incurred by various departments in an organization. This is also known as a **spider web** plot.

Getting ready

Import the required libraries:

```
import numpy as np
import matplotlib.pyplot as plt
```

How to do it...

 Since it is a circular spider web, we need to connect the last point to the first point, so that there is a circular flow of the graph. To achieve this, we need to repeat the first department data point at the end of the list again. Hence, in the following example, 30 and 32 (the first entry in each of the lists) are repeated at the end again.

The following code block plots a polar graph and displays it on the screen:

1. Set up the data for a polar plot:

```
Depts = ["COGS","IT","Payroll","R & D", "Sales & Marketing"]
rp = [30, 15, 25, 10, 20, 30]
ra = [32, 20, 23, 11, 14, 32]
theta = np.linspace(0, 2 * np.pi, len(rp))
```

2. Initialize the spider plot by setting figure size and polar projection:

```
plt.figure(figsize=(10,6))
plt.subplot(polar=True)
```

3. Arrange the grid lines to align with each of the department names:

```
(lines,labels) = plt.thetagrids(range(0,360, int(360/len(Depts))),
                                 (Depts))
```

4. Plot the planned spend graph, which is a line plot on polar coordinates, and then fill the area under it:

```
plt.plot(theta, rp)
plt.fill(theta, rp, 'b', alpha=0.1)
```

5. Plot the actual spend graph, which is a line plot on polar coordinates:

```
plt.plot(theta, ra)
```

6. Add a legend and a title for the plot:

```
plt.legend(labels=('Plan','Actual'),loc=1)
plt.title("Plan vs Actual spend by Department")
```

7. Display the plot on the screen:

```
plt.show()
```

How it works...

The following is the explanation of the code:

- `Depts` is the list of departments in the organization. `rp` and `ra` are lists of planned expenses and actual spending by department.
- `plt.figure(figsize=(10,6))` sets the figure size. `plt.subplot(polar=True)` sets polar projection.
- The `pyplot` method accepts only radians as input, hence we need to divide 2 x `np.pie` (which is equivalent to 360 degrees) radians into number of departments equally, to get the angle coordinates for each of the departments. `np.linspace(0, 2 * np.pi, len(rp))` does this computation.

 While the coordinates need to be given in radians, the degree equivalent is easy for visualization. To convert radians to degrees, you can use `np.degrees(theta)`.

- The default grid lines on a polar projection is 45 degrees (360 degrees divided into eight equal parts of 45 degrees each). Since we have fewer departments (only five), we need to restrict the number of grids to the number of departments.
- `plt.thetagrids(range(0,360, int(360/len(Depts))), (Depts))` function creates the grid and labels them with department names. This function also returns lines and label objects that can be used subsequently, if required.
- `plt.plot(theta, rp)`, plots the planned expense and fills the area with blue using `plt.fill(theta, rp, 'b', alpha=0.1)`.
- `plt.plot(theta, ra)`, plots the actual expense without filling the area under it.

Finally, add a title and a legend to the plot. You should see the following chart:

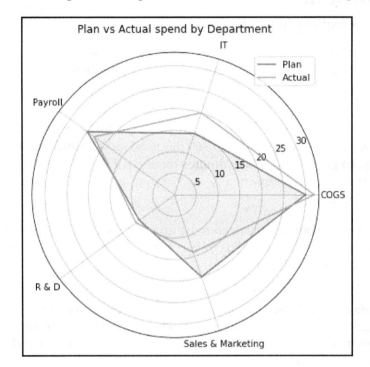

There's more...

In this example, we have used a line plot. A polar projection can also be used with scatter, bubble, and bar plots. It is just another coordinate system and every point needs to be converted into polar co-ordinates.

Histogram

The histogram plot is used to draw the distribution of a continuous variable. Continuous variable values are split into the required number of bins and plotted on the *x* axis, and the count of values that fall in each of the bins is plotted on the *y* axis. On the *y* axis, instead of count, we can also plot percentage of total, in which case it represents probability distribution. This plot is typically used in statistical analysis.

Getting ready

We will use the example of data on prior work experience of participants in a lateral training program. Experience is measured in number of years.

Import the required libraries:

```
import matplotlib.pyplot as plt
import numpy as np
```

How to do it...

The following code draws a histogram of experience data:

1. Create a NumPy array with work experience (in years) of participants in a lateral training class:

```
grp_exp = np.array([12, 15, 13, 20, 19, 20, 11, 19, 11, 12, 19, 13, 12,
                    10, 6, 19, 3, 1, 1, 0, 4, 4, 6, 5, 3, 7, 12, 7, 9,
                    8, 12, 11, 11, 18, 19, 18, 19, 3, 6, 5, 6, 9, 11,
                    10, 14, 14, 16, 17, 17, 19, 0, 2, 0, 3, 1, 4, 6,
                    6, 8, 7, 7, 6, 7, 11, 11, 10, 11, 10, 13, 13, 15,
                    18, 20, 19, 1, 10, 8, 16, 19, 19, 17, 16, 11, 1,
                    10, 13, 15, 3, 8, 6, 9, 10, 15, 19, 2, 4, 5, 6, 9,
                    11, 10, 9, 10, 9, 15, 16, 18, 13])
```

2. Plot the distribution of group experience:

```
nbins = 21
n, bins, patches = plt.hist(grp_exp, bins = nbins)
```

3. Add axis labels and title for the plot:

```
plt.xlabel("Experience in years")
plt.ylabel("Frequency")
plt.title("Distribution of Experience in a Lateral Training
          Program")
```

4. Draw the red vertical line in the graph at the average experience:

```
plt.axvline(x=grp_exp.mean(), linewidth=2, color = 'r')
```

5. Display the plot on the screen:

```
plt.show()
```

How it works...

The following is the explanation of the code:

- grp_exp is a NumPy array containing experience data in number of years.
- This data is divided into 21 bins of equal size, by specifying nbins = 21.
- plt.hist() plots the histogram with grp_exp and nbins as arguments. It returns three parameters, n, bins, and patches. n is the list containing the number of items in each bin, bins is another list specifying starting point of the bin, and patches is the list of objects for each bin. These can be used for any other purpose later in the program.
- Add the title, and the *x* and *y* axis labels, before displaying the histogram on the screen.
- plt.axvline() plots a vertical line at the mean value of the data, just to represent how the data is distributed on either side of the mean value. Here is how the output looks:

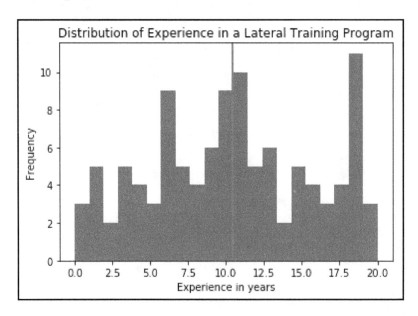

There's more...

On the *y* axis, instead of plotting frequency, you can plot the percentage of the sum of all the entries in the `grp_exp` list in each bin, by specifying `density=1` in `plt.hist()`. You can also plot approximate normal distribution using the mean and standard deviation of this data to see how well this distribution follows a normal distribution:

1. Create a NumPy array with work (years) of participants of a lateral training class:

```
grp_exp = np.array([12, 15, 13, 20, 19, 20, 11, 19, 11, 12, 19, 13,
                    12, 10, 6, 19, 3, 1, 1, 0, 4, 4, 6, 5, 3, 7, 12,
                    7, 9, 8, 12, 11, 11, 18, 19, 18, 19, 3, 6, 5, 6,
                    9, 11, 10, 14, 14, 16, 17, 17, 19, 0, 2, 0, 3,
                    1, 4, 6, 6, 8, 7, 7, 6, 7, 11, 11, 10, 11, 10,
                    13, 13, 15, 18, 20, 19, 1, 10, 8, 16, 19, 19,
                    17, 16, 11, 1, 10, 13, 15, 3, 8, 6, 9, 10, 15,
                    19, 2, 4, 5, 6, 9, 11, 10, 9, 10, 9, 15, 16, 18,
                    13])
```

2. Plot the distribution of experience:

```
nbins = 21
n, bins, patches = plt.hist(grp_exp, bins = nbins, density=1)
```

3. Add axis labels:

```
plt.xlabel("Experience in years")
plt.ylabel("Percentage")
plt.title("Distribution of Experience in a Lateral Training
          Program")
```

4. Compute the mean (`mu`) and the standard deviation (`sigma`) for `grp_exp` data:

```
mu = grp_exp.mean()
sigma = grp_exp.std()
```

5. Add a best-fit line for normal distribution with `mu` and `sigma` computed:

```
y = ((1 / (np.sqrt(2 * np.pi) * sigma)) * np.exp(-0.5 * (1 / sigma
          * (bins - mu))**2))
plt.plot(bins, y, '--')
```

6. Display the plot on the screen:

```
plt.show()
```

Here is how the output plot looks:

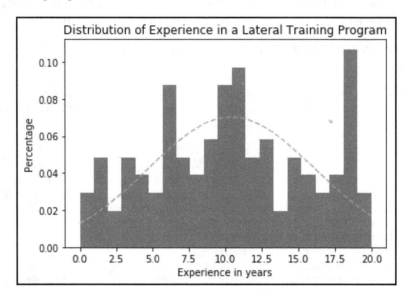

Clearly, the data is not following a normal distribution, as there too many bins way above or way below the best fit for a normal curve.

Box plot

The box plot is used to visualize the descriptive statistics of a continuous variable. It visually shows the first and third quartile, median (mean), and whiskers at 1.5 times the **Inter Quartile Range (IQR)**—the difference between the third and first quartiles, above which are outliers. The first quartile (the bottom of rectangular box) marks a point below which 25% of the total points fall. The third quartile (the top of rectangular box) marks a point below which 75% of the points fall.

If there are no outliers, then whiskers will show min and max values.

This is again used in statistical analysis.

Getting ready

We will use an example of wine quality dataset for this example. We will consider three attributes: `alcohol`, `fixed acidity`, and `quality`. Usually, the same attribute is plotted against different dimensions, such as geography or time, to compare the data distribution along these dimensions. Here, we are drawing box plots for three different attributes:

```
import matplotlib.pyplot as plt
import pandas as pd
```

How to do it...

The following is the code block that plots three box plots, one for each of the attributes:

1. Read the data from a CSV file into a pandas DataFrame:

   ```
   wine_quality = pd.read_csv('winequality.csv', delimiter=';')
   ```

2. Create a `data` list with three attributes of the `Wine Quality` dataset:

   ```
   data = [wine_quality['alcohol'], wine_quality['fixed acidity'],
           wine_quality['quality']]
   ```

3. Plot the boxplot:

   ```
   plt.boxplot(data)
   ```

4. Display the plot on the screen:

   ```
   plt.show()
   ```

How it works...

- `plt.boxplot()` is the method to plot a boxplot. The `data` argument can be a list of one or more attributes. The yellow line in each box represents the median value of the attribute by default (it can be changed to mean too). The bottom whisker is at 1.5 IQR from the bottom line of the box, the upper whisker is at 1.5 IQR above the upper line of the box. The bottom line of the box is at the first quartile, and the upper line of the box is at the third quartile of the data.
- Points above and below whiskers are outliers. In the first and second box plots, there are no outliers below the bottom whisker, whereas all three of them have outliers above the upper whisker:

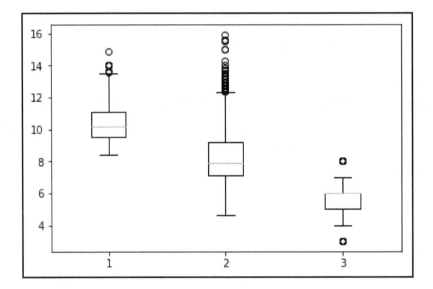

There's more...

In `plt.boxplot()`, by specifying the `showfliers=False` argument, you can suppress the outliers, so it plots only up to the whiskers on both sides. By specifying the `vert=False` argument, you can plot the box plots horizontally, and outliers can also be customized with different shapes and colors:

```
plt.boxplot(data, vert=False, flierprops=dict(markerfacecolor='r',
            marker='D'))
plt.show()
```

You should see the following output:

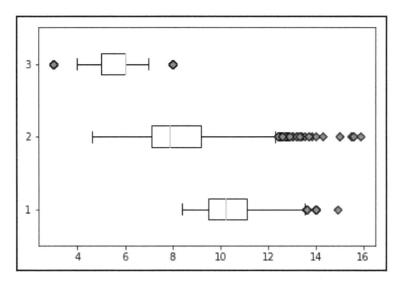

Violin plot

The violin plot is a combination of histogram and box plot. It gives information on the complete distribution of data, along with mean/median, min, and max values.

Getting ready

We will use the same data that we used for the box plot for this example also.

Import the required libraries:

```
import matplotlib.pyplot as plt
import pandas as pd
```

How to do it...

The following is the code block that draws violin plots:

1. Read the data from a CSV file into a pandas DataFrame:

```
wine_quality = pd.read_csv('winequality.csv', delimiter=';')
```

2. Prepare the list of three attributes of `wine_quality`:

```
data = [wine_quality['alcohol'], wine_quality['fixed acidity'],
        wine_quality['quality']]
```

3. Plot the violin plot:

```
plt.violinplot(data, showmeans=True)
```

4. Display the plot on the screen:

```
plt.show()
```

How it works...

Here is the explanation for the code:

- `plt.violinplot()` draws the violin plot. The bottom whisker is the minimum value, the top whisker is the maximum value, and the horizontal line is at the mean value. On both sides of the vertical line is the histogram of the data representing the actual distribution of the data. By replacing `showmeans=True` with `showmedian=True`, we can have a horizontal line representing the median of the data instead of the mean:

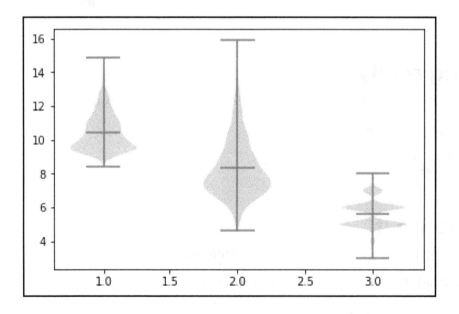

Reading and displaying images

`Matplotlib.pyplot` has features that enable us to read `.jpeg` and `.png` images and covert them to pixel format to display as images.

Getting ready

Import the required library:

```
import matplotlib.pyplot as plt
```

How to do it...

Here is the code block that reads a JPEG file as a pixel-valued list and displays it as an image on the screen:

1. Read the image `louvre.jpg` into a three-dimensional array (color images have three channels, whereas black and white images have one channel only):

```
image = plt.imread('louvre.jpg')
```

2. Print the dimensions of the image:

```
print("Dimensions of the image: ", image.shape)
```

3. Plot the image:

```
plt.imshow(image)
```

4. Display the image on the screen:

```
plt.show()
```

How it works...

- The `plt.imread()` method reads the image into an array of pixels.
- The `plt.imshow()` method displays the image on the screen.

- `image.shape` gives the dimensions of the list into which the image was read.
- `print()` displays the dimensions of the image on the screen:

Heatmap

A heatmap is used to visualize data range in different colors with varying intensity. Here, we take the example of plotting a correlation matrix as a heatmap. Elements of the correlation matrix indicate the strength of a linear relationship between the two variables, and the matrix contains such values for all combinations of the attributes in the given data. If the data has five attributes, then the correlation matrix will be a 5 x 5 matrix.

Getting ready

We will use the Wine Quality dataset for this example also. It has 12 different attributes. We will first get a correlation matrix and then plot it as a heatmap. There is no heatmap function/method as such, so we will use the same `imshow` method that we used to read and display the images.

Import the required libraries:

```
import matplotlib.pyplot as plt
import pandas as pd
```

How to do it...

The following is the code block that plots a heatmap of the correlation matrix:

1. Read the data from a CSV file into a pandas DataFrame:

```
wine_quality = pd.read_csv('winequality.csv', delimiter=';')
```

2. Get the correlation matrix of all attributes of `wine_quality`:

```
corr = wine_quality.corr()
```

3. Specify the figure size:

```
plt.figure(figsize=(12,9))
```

4. Plot the heatmap:

```
plt.imshow(corr, cmap='hot')
```

5. Plot the colorbar to map which color represents which data values:

```
plt.colorbar()
```

6. Label the *x* and *y* axis ticks. Show the *x* axis labels with 20 degrees of rotation:

```
plt.xticks(range(len(corr)),corr.columns, rotation=20)
plt.yticks(range(len(corr)),corr.columns)
```

7. Display the plot on the screen:

```
plt.show()
```

How it works...

The following is the explanation for the code:

- The `wine_quality.corr()` method returns a correlation matrix for all the attributes in the dataset.
- The correlation values range from -1 (highly negative) to +1 (highly positive). Negative values are represented from red to black, and positive values are represented from dark yellow to white. Pure white is +1, which is the highest positive correlation, and pure black is the highest negative correlation.

- As expected, all diagonal boxes are white, as they are a correlation with themselves, which has to be +1. The correlation between the pH and fixed acidity values is black, which means highly negative, close to -1

We get the output as follows:

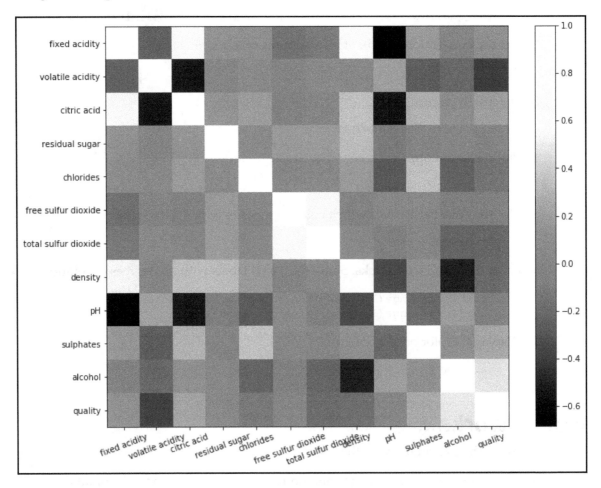

Hinton diagram

The Hinton diagram is a 2D plot for visualizing weight matrices in deep-learning applications. Matplotlib does not have a direct method to plot this diagram. So, we will have to write code to plot this. The weight matrix for this is taken from one of the machine learning algorithms that classifies images.

Getting ready

Import the required libraries:

```
import numpy as np
import matplotlib.pyplot as plt
import pandas as pd
```

How to do it...

The following code block defines the function and makes a call to the function to plot the Hinton diagram:

1. Read the weight matrix data from an Excel file:

```
matrix = np.asarray((pd.read_excel('weight_matrix.xlsx')))
```

2. Instantiate the figure and axes:

```
fig, ax = plt.subplots()
```

3. Set up the parameters for the axes:

```
ax.patch.set_facecolor('gray')
ax.set_aspect('equal', 'box')
ax.xaxis.set_major_locator(plt.NullLocator())
ax.yaxis.set_major_locator(plt.NullLocator())
```

4. Plot the Hinton diagram:

```
max_weight = 2 ** np.ceil(np.log(np.abs(matrix).max()) / np.log(2))
for (x, y), w in np.ndenumerate(matrix):
        color = 'white' if w > 0 else 'black'
        size = np.sqrt(np.abs(w) / max_weight)
        rect = plt.Rectangle([x - size / 2, y - size / 2], size,
size, facecolor=color, edgecolor=color)
        ax.add_patch(rect)
ax.autoscale_view()
```

5. Display it on the screen:

```
plt.show()
```

How it works...

Here is the explanation for the code:

- `pd.read_excel()` reads the Excel file into a pandas DataFrame.
- `np.asarray()` converts a DataFrame into a NumPy array, as required for further processing. It is a 20 x 7 matrix.
- `np.abs()` returns absolute values of the matrix that is given as input.
- `np.abs(matrix).max()` returns the maximum value from an absolute matrix.
- `np.log()` returns a natural logarithmic value of the argument that is passed.
- `np.ceil()` rounds up the argument to the next highest value for a given floating point number, for example *np.ceil(2.2) = 3.0*.
- `ax.patch.set_facecolor('gray')` sets the color of each of the box points to gray.
- `ax.set_aspect('equal', 'box')` specifies the aspect ratio (the ratio of width to height) and shape of the points on the graph to be a box.
- `ax.xaxis.set_major_locator(plt.NullLocator())` sets the *x* axis ticks to nulls so that there are no ticks marked, and no ticklabels placed.
- Initiate a `for` loop to go over each of the elements of the weight matrix, and set the color to white for positive values, black for negative values, and size proportional to `max_weight`. Finally, `ax.autoscale_view()` arranges all the boxes neatly and plots the Hinton diagram.

You should get the output as follows:

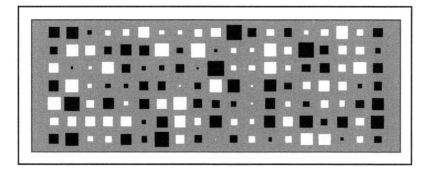

Contour plot

The contour plot is typically used to display how the error varies with varying coefficients that are being optimized in a machine learning algorithm, such as linear regression. If the linear regression coefficients are theta0 and theta1, and the error between the predicted value and the actual value is a Loss, then for a given Loss value, all the values of theta0 and theta1 form a contour. For different values of Loss, different contours are formed by varying the values of theta0 and theta1.

Getting ready

The data for Loss, theta0, theta1, and theta (optimal values of theta0 and theta1 that give the lowest error) are taken from one of the regression problems for plotting the contour plot. If theta0 and theta1 are vectors of size 1 x n, then the Loss will be in the form of an n x n matrix.

Import the required libraries. We will introduce one more library for color mapping from Matplotlib:

```
import matplotlib.pyplot as plt
import pandas as pd
import numpy as np
from matplotlib import cm
```

We also need to understand the concept of a mesh grid, since the contour, surface, and stream plots also use this concept:

- A mesh grid is a grid in a geometric space, derived from two vectors. Each data item in the vectors acts as a coordinate, and a combination of coordinates from the two vectors form points in a 2D geometric space. The area spread by all possible combinations of these vector coordinates is defined in the form of a mesh grid, for example:
  - $x = [-3.0, 0., 3.0]$ and $y = [-2.0, 2.0]$. Vector x has three data points and vector y has two. Hence, we will have total of six points (3 * 2) in 2D geometric space, and those six points are (-3.0, -2), (-3.0, 2.0), (0., -2.0), (0., 2.0), (3.0, -2.0), and (3.0, 2.0). Now, these six points and 12 data items (6 * 2) are again represented as two matrices x and y, where the following applies:
    - X = [[-3.0, 0., 3.0], [-3.0, 0., 3.0]], a 2 x 3 matrix (the number of rows is equal to the length of Y), and Y = [[-2.0, 2.0], [-2.0, 2.0], [-2.0, 2.0]] a 3 x 2 matrix (the number of rows is equal to the length of X). NumPy has a function, `np.meshgrid(x, y)`, used to create these X and Y matrices using x and y vectors. This is what we will use for all our requirements.

How to do it...

The following is the code to draw a contour plot of loss function in the given regression problem:

1. Read the `Loss`, `theta0`, and `theta1` values from saved files:

```
Loss = pd.read_excel('Loss.xlsx')
theta0_vals = pd.read_excel('theta0.xlsx')
theta1_vals = pd.read_excel('theta1.xlsx')
```

2. Specify the figure size:

```
fig = plt.figure(figsize=(12,8))
```

3. Create the mesh grid for the X and Y coordinates:

```
X, Y = np.meshgrid(theta0_vals, theta1_vals)
```

4. Draw the contour plot and label contours with their corresponding loss values:

```
CS = plt.contour(X, Y, Loss, np.logspace(-2,3,20),
cmap=cm.coolwarm)
                plt.clabel(CS, inline=1, fontsize=10)
```

5. Display the contour plot on the screen:

```
plt.show()
```

How it works...

Here is the explanation for the code:

- `theta0 = np.linspace(-10, 10, 100)` and `theta1 = np.linspace(-1, 4, 100)` help us compute the `Loss`, which is the error for the ranges of `theta0` and `theta1` values. All this data is available in the form of Excel files, so we read them all using `pd.read_excel()`.
- `np.meshgrid()` creates the mesh grid between `theta0` and `theta1` to get X and Y, then passes on X, Y, and `Loss` to plot the contour plot.
- `CS = plt.contour()` draws the contour plot.
- `np.logspace(-2,3,20)` specifies the range of values on a logarithmic scale for the `Loss` attribute, which needs to be drawn on a contour plot. On a linear scale, this range will be from 0.01 (10 to the power of -2) to 1,000 (10 to the power of 3). And 20 is the number of samples it draws in this range, using which contours are plotted.
- `plt.clabel()` specifies that actual loss values to be plotted on the contour as labels. As can be seen in the plot, the value of loss (error) goes all the way to 545.559 from zero!

We get the output as follows:

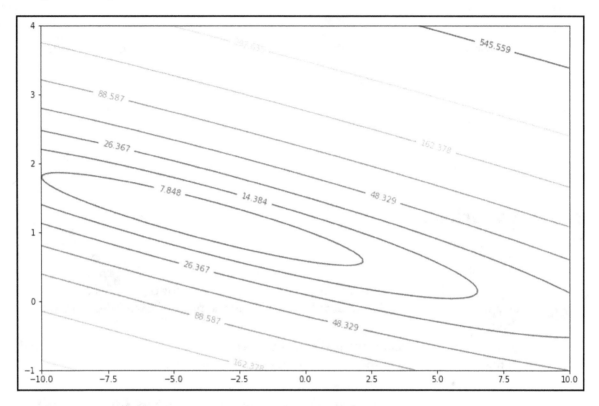

There's more...

The previous screenshot only represents various contours of the Loss function for a given set of theta0 and theta1. We can also plot the optimal values of theta0 and theta1 on the same plot to represent minimum loss:

```
# Plot the minimum point(Theta at Minimum cost)
plt.plot(theta[0], theta[1], 'rx', markersize=15, linewidth=2)
plt.show()
```

Here is how the plot looks. The red cross position depicts the optimal theta that gives lowest error for this regression problem:

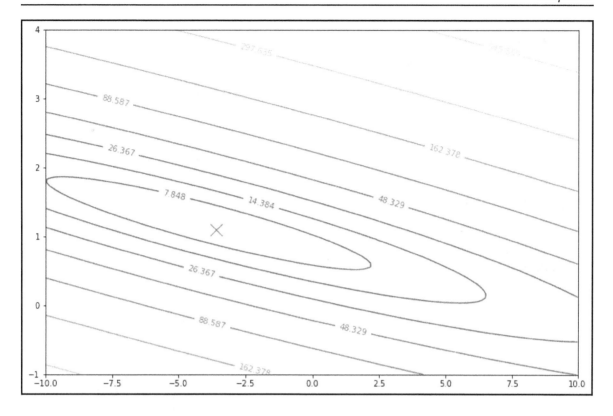

Triangulations

Triangulations are used to plot geographical maps, which help with understanding the relative distance between various points. The longitude and latitude values are used as x, y coordinates to plot the points. To draw a triangle, three points are required; these are specified with the corresponding indices of the points on the plot. For a given set of coordinates, Matplotlib can compute triangles automatically and plot the graph, or optionally we can also provide triangles as an argument.

Getting ready

Import the required libraries. We will introduce the `tri` package for triangulations:

```
import numpy as np
import matplotlib.pyplot as plt
import matplotlib.tri as tri
```

How to do it...

The following code block generates 50 random points, creates triangles automatically, and then plots the triangulation plot:

```
data = np.random.rand(50, 2)
triangles = tri.Triangulation(data[:,0], data[:,1])
plt.triplot(triangles)
plt.show()
```

How it works...

We first generate 50 random points using np.random.rand function, which generates numbers between 0 and 1. The tri.Triangulation() function creates triangles automatically, whereas plt.triplot() plots the triangulation plot.

This is how the output plot looks:

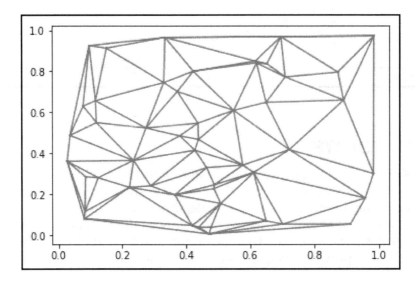

There's more...

In the previous plot, we generated triangles automatically. Here, we will learn how to add triangles manually:

1. Set up data for longitude and latitude in radians:

```
xy = np.array([[-0.101, 0.872], [-0.080, 0.883], [-0.069, 0.888],
               [-0.054, 0.890], [-0.045, 0.897], [-0.057, 0.895],
               [-0.073, 0.900], [-0.087, 0.898],
               [-0.090, 0.904], [-0.069, 0.907]])
```

2. Convert xy from radians to degrees:

```
x = np.degrees(xy[:, 0])
y = np.degrees(xy[:, 1])
```

3. Choose the points to form triangles from xy coordinates converted to degrees:

```
triangles = np.array([[1, 2, 3], [3, 4, 5], [4, 5, 6], [2, 5, 6],
                      [6, 7, 8], [6, 8, 9], [0, 1, 7]])
```

4. Plot the triangulation:

```
plt.triplot(x, y, triangles, 'go-', lw=1.0)
```

5. Plot labels and the title:

```
plt.title('triplot of user-specified triangulation')
plt.xlabel('Longitude (degrees)')
plt.ylabel('Latitude (degrees)')
```

6. Display the plot on the screen:

```
plt.show()
```

Here is how it works:

- xy is an array of coordinates in radians.
- np.degrees() converts radians to degrees; x and y are in radians and are then converted to degrees, where x and y stand for the longitude and latitude values, respectively.

A triangle is an array of three point tuples for each triangle to be plotted. Numbers are indices of the points in x and y (0 to 9, a total of 10 points). The output looks as follows:

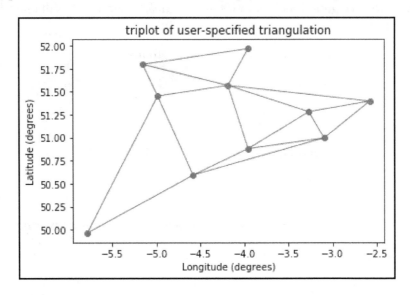

Stream plot

Stream plots, also known as **streamline plots** are used to visualize vector fields. They are mostly used in the engineering and scientific communities. They use vectors and their velocities as a function of base vectors to draw these plots.

Getting ready

Import the required libraries:

```
import numpy as np
import matplotlib.pyplot as plt
import matplotlib.gridspec as gridspec
```

How to do it...

The following code block creates a stream plot:

1. Prepare the data for the stream plot:

```
x, y = np.linspace(-3,3,100), np.linspace(-2,4,50)
```

2. Create the mesh grid:

```
X, Y = np.meshgrid(x, y)
```

3. Compute velocities, U and V, as a function of X and Y respectively:

```
U = 1 - X**2
V = 1 + Y**2
```

4. Plot the stream plot:

```
plt.streamplot(X, Y, U, V)
```

5. Set the title for the plot:

```
plt.title('Basic Streamplot')
```

6. Display the graph on the screen:

```
plt.show()
```

How it works...

- `np.linspace(-3, 3, 100)` creates 100 data points in the range of -3 to 3 with equal gaps between consecutive points. x and y are randomly generated vectors of length 100 and 50 with ranges -3 to 3 and -2 to 4, respectively.
- `np.meshgrid(x, y)` creates the mesh grid as explained earlier in the chapter.

- U and V are velocity vectors as a function of x and y. A stream plot is a combination of vectors x, y and velocities U and V. `plt.streamplot(X, Y, U, V)` plots the stream plot and it looks as shown here:

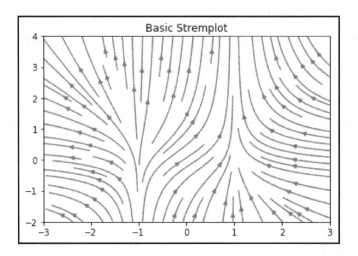

There's more...

We have seen a basic stream plot in the previous section. We can control the density and thickness as functions of the speed and color of the stream lines. Here is the code and its output:

```
# Define the speed as a function of U and V
speed = np.sqrt (U*U + V*V)

# Varying line width along a streamline
lw = 5 * speed / speed.max()

strm = plt.streamplot(X, Y, U, V, density=[0.5, 1], color=V,
                      linewidth=lw)
plt.colorbar(strm.lines)

plt.title('Varying Density, Color and Line Width')

plt.show()
```

`np.sqrt(U*U + V*V)` defines the speed; line width (`lw`) is defined as a function of speed.`plt.streamplot()` draws the stream plot using the parameters supplied. `density=[0.5, 1]` specifies density values to be used, `color=V` specifies how the color of streamlines should change based on the values of `V`, and `linewidth` specifies how the width of streamlines should change:

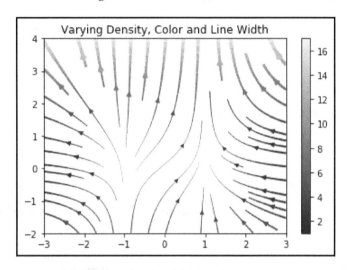

Path

`Path` is a method provided by Matplotlib for drawing custom charts. It uses a helper function patch that is provided by Matplotlib. Let's see how this can be used to draw a simple plot.

Getting ready

Import the required libraries. Two new packages, `Path` and `patches`, will be introduced here:

```
import matplotlib.pyplot as plt
from matplotlib.path import Path
import matplotlib.patches as patches
```

How to do it...

The following code block defines points and associated lines and curves to be drawn to form the overall picture:

1. Define the points along with the first curve to be drawn

```
verts1 = [(-1.5, 0.),       # left, bottom
          (0., 1.),         # left, top
          (1.5, 0.),        # right, top
          (0., -1.0),       # right, bottom
          (-1.5, 0.)]       # ignored
```

2. Plot the graph connecting the points defined in *step 1*:

```
codes1 = [Path.MOVETO,      # Go to first point specified in vert1
          Path.LINETO,      # Draw a line from first point to second
                            point
          Path.LINETO,      # Draw another line from current point to
                            next point
          Path.LINETO,      # Draw another line from current point to
                            next point
          Path.CLOSEPOLY]   # Close the loop
```

3. Create the complete path with points and lines/curves defined in *step 1* and *step 2*:

```
path1 = Path(verts1, codes1)
```

4. Repeat the same for the second curve:

```
verts2 = [(-1.5, 0.),       # left, bottom
          (0., 2.5),        # left, top
          (1.5, 0.),        # right, top
          (0., -2.5),       # right, bottom
          (-1.5, 0.)]       # ignored

codes2 = [Path.MOVETO,  # Move to the first point
          Path.CURVE3,  # Curve from first point along the control
                          point and terminate on end point
          Path.CURVE3,  # Curve from current point along the control
                          point and terminate on end point
          Path.CURVE3,
          Path.CURVE3]  # close by the curved loop

path2 = Path(verts2, codes2)
```

5. Define the figure and the axes:

```
fig = plt.figure()
ax = fig.add_subplot(111)
```

6. Create the first patch and add it to the axes:

```
patch1 = patches.PathPatch(path1, lw=4, zorder=2)
ax.add_patch(patch1)
```

7. Create the second patch and add it to the axes:

```
patch2 = patches.PathPatch(path2, facecolor='orange', lw=2,
                            zorder=1)
ax.add_patch(patch2)
```

8. Set the limits for x and y axes:

```
ax.set_xlim(-2,2)
ax.set_ylim(-2,2)
```

9. Display the plot on the screen:

```
plt.show()
```

How it works...

- `verts1` and `verts2` define the points along which the curves have to be drawn. `path1` and `path2` define the complete path for each of the curves to be drawn.
- `Path.MOVETO` takes the starting point of the curve to the specified first point in `verts`.
- `Path.LINETO` draws a line from the current position to the next point specified.
- `Path.CLOSEPOLY` closes the polynomial curve loop.
- `Path.CURVE3` draws a curve from a given point, along a control point, and then terminates at the third point.
- `Path.CURVE4` (not used in this example) does the same, but over two control points instead of one.
- `patches.PathPatch` is a helper function that draws the curve along the given path.

- The `zorder` parameter overrides the default order of plotting different patches. In this case, we want the second patch to be plotted first and then the first patch so that both are visible. Otherwise, the smaller patch would be hidden behind the larger one.
- `lw` specifies the line width and `facecolor` specifies the color to be filled inside the patch, overriding the default color.

Here is the output from the code:

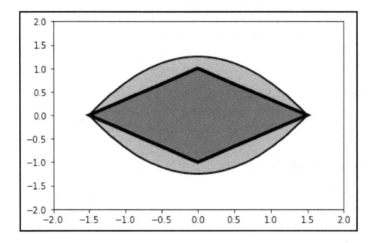

3
Plotting Multiple Charts, Subplots, and Figures

In this chapter, we will cover the following recipes:

- Plotting multiple graphs in the same axis
- Plotting subplots in the same figure
- Plotting multiple figures in a session
- Using the logarithmic scale
- Using units of measurement

Introduction

In the last chapter, we saw how to plot various graphs individually. In this chapter, we will learn how to plot multiple graphs in the same axes, multiple axes/plots in the same figure, and multiple figures in a session. We will also learn how to use a logarithmic scale and units of measurement, such as centimeters, inches, and so on.

Plotting multiple graphs on the same axes

As we learned from the first chapter, axes are the space where we plot a graph, and all the elements we typically see in the plot are part of the axes. We can have multiple axes in one figure. In this recipe, we will learn how to plot multiple charts on the same axes.

Getting ready

We will use an example of an **Receiver Operating Characteristics** (**ROC**) curve, using which multiple **machine learning** (**ML**) algorithms are compared to a given classification problem, and the best performing algorithm is chosen for that problem. An ROC curve is plotted with a **True Positive Rate** (**TPR**) and a **False Positive Rate** (**FPR**) for a range of threshold probabilities. The objective is to see the sensitivity of the TPR and the FPR as the threshold probability changes. The algorithm whose ROC curve covers the maximum **area under the curve** (**AUC**) is considered to be the best performing algorithm in terms of classification accuracy.

We are using TPR and FPR data for a set of algorithms, the **k-nearest neighbor algorithm** (**k-NN**), **multilayer perceptron** (**MLP**), **Stochastic Gradient Descent** (**SGD**), **random forest** (**RF**), and **decision tree** (**DT**), run on a classification problem to plot the graphs. This dataset is provided as part of the code library for this book.

Import the required libraries:

```
import matplotlib.pyplot as plt
import pandas as pd
```

How to do it...

Here is the code block that plots multiple ROC curves on the same axes:

1. Read the FPR and TPR data for various algorithms from their respective Excel sheets using `pandas`:

```
# K-nearest neighbor (KNN)
fpr_KNN = pd.read_excel('ROC_Curves.xlsx', 'fpr_KNN')
tpr_KNN = pd.read_excel('ROC_Curves.xlsx', 'tpr_KNN')

# Multilayer Perceptron(MLP)
fpr_MLP = pd.read_excel('ROC_Curves.xlsx', 'fpr_MLP')
tpr_MLP = pd.read_excel('ROC_Curves.xlsx', 'tpr_MLP')

# Stochastic Gradient Descent (SGD)
fpr_SGD = pd.read_excel('ROC_Curves.xlsx', 'fpr_SGD')
tpr_SGD = pd.read_excel('ROC_Curves.xlsx', 'tpr_SGD')

# Random Forest (RF)
fpr_RF = pd.read_excel('ROC_Curves.xlsx', 'fpr_RF')
tpr_RF = pd.read_excel('ROC_Curves.xlsx', 'tpr_RF')
```

```
# Decision Trees (DT)
fpr_DT = pd.read_excel('ROC_Curves.xlsx', 'fpr_DT')
tpr_DT = pd.read_excel('ROC_Curves.xlsx', 'tpr_DT')
```

2. Plot the line graphs, including the black threshold line, using `fpr` and `tpr` data, read for each of the five algorithms in the previous step:

```
plt.plot([0, 1], [0, 1], 'k--')
plt.plot(fpr_KNN, tpr_KNN, label='KNN',color='green')
plt.plot(fpr_DT, tpr_DT, label='DecisionTree', color='orange')
plt.plot(fpr_RF, tpr_RF, label='Random Forest',color='purple')
plt.plot(fpr_MLP, tpr_MLP, label='MLP',color='red')
plt.plot(fpr_SGD, tpr_SGD, label='SGD', color='pink')
```

3. Print the labels, the title, and the legend:

```
plt.xlabel('False Positive Rate')
plt.ylabel('True Positive Rate')
plt.title('ROC curve')
plt.legend(loc='best')
```

4. Display the plot on the screen:

```
plt.show()
```

How it works...

Here is the explanation of how the code works:

- The `pd.read_excel()` statements read TPR and FPR data for five algorithms (KNN, MLP, SGD, RF, and DT).
- `plt.plot([0, 1], [0, 1], 'k--')` plots a black dashed line at a 45 degree angle. This is the base performance level (reference line), and an algorithm whose ROC curve is above this line and covers the largest area under it, compared to all other curves, is supposed to be the best-performing algorithm.
- Subsequent `plt.plot()` statements plot the ROC curve for each of the five chosen algorithms. Each plot statement is drawing a graph on the same axes. You can plot as many graphs as required, before `plt.show()`, which displays the graph on the screen.
- Parameter labels and colors differentiate each of these algorithms on the graph. We will learn more about these parameters in subsequent chapters.
- `plt.xlabel()`, `plt.ylabel()`, and `plt.title()` are the labels on the plot, and the legend is where these graph labels are placed on the graph.

You should see the following plot:

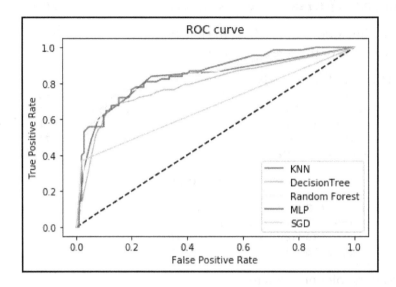

From the plot, it is clear that the SGD Classifier algorithm is performing poorly compared to all others, as the area under that chart is the lowest (or it is closest to the reference block dashed line). The MLP algorithm is the best among these five algorithms for this specific classification problem, since the area under this curve is the highest (or it is farthest from the reference block dashed line).

Plotting subplots on the same figure

Matplotlib provides many different methods and helper functions that leverage the axes method for drawing multiple plots on the same figure and arrange them in a variety of grid formats. This allows us to develop sophisticated dashboard applications.

Getting ready

We will use the same Wine Quality and Iris datasets that were introduced in Chapter 2, *Getting Started with Basic Plots*, for the examples in this chapter.

Multiple plots in the figure are arranged in an *m x n* grid, where *m* is the number of rows, and *n* is the number of columns. If we have six plots to be arranged in the figure, we can either arrange all of them in one row (each of them is identified by 161, 162, 163, 164, 165, or 166) or 3 x 2 (321, 322, 323, 324, 325, and 326) or 2 x 3 (231, 232, 233, 234, 235, and 236) or one column (611, 612, 613, 614, 615, and 616). The first two digits represent the number of rows and columns, and the last digit represents the sequential numbers 1 to 6 (total number of plots), and reads from left to right,and then from the top down.

The plots can also be specified as (3, 2, 1) instead of (321). When there are more than nine plots in the grid, the later notation is confusing, and Matplotlib does not accept it. In such cases, we must use (3, 4, 10), (3, 4, 11), or (3, 4, 12) instead of (3410), (3411), or (3412), when you have a 3 x 4 grid with a total of 12 plots.

We can also plot fewer plots than the maximum allowed in the grid, for example, three plots in a 2 x 2 grid (four is the maximum).

Import the required libraries:

```
import pandas as pd
import matplotlib.pyplot as plt
```

How to do it...

The following code block draws three plots in one figure:

1. Define the figure and its layout with three axes:

```
fig = plt.figure()
ax1 = plt.subplot(221)
ax2 = plt.subplot(222)
ax3 = plt.subplot(212)
```

2. Plot the line graphs on each of the axes:

```
ax1.plot([1,2])
ax2.plot([2,1])
ax3.plot([2,4])
```

3. Display the plot on the screen:

```
plt.show()
```

How it works...

Here is the explanation for the code:

- `plt.figure()` creates the object for the figure and allocates space for it.
- `plt.subplot(221)` creates the axes for the first plot in a 2 x 2 grid.
- `plt.subplot(222)` creates one more axis for the second plot in a 2 x 2 grid, which is placed in the same first row.
- `plt.subplot(212)` creates one more axes for the third plot, but this is part of another 2 x 1 grid (the first two digits of 212) and it is the second plot in this 2 x 1 grid, so it will be placed in the second row. Since the first 2 x 2 grid did not use the second row, this grid will occupy the full space.

We get the output as follows:

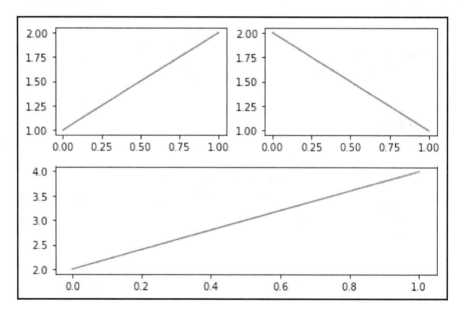

If we had coded `plt.subplot(211)` for the third plot, it would have overwritten the first two plots, because 211 means the first plot in the 2 x 1 grid, which will start in the first row! If we want to draw the same three plots, but arrange two in the first column and one in the second column, as opposed to the current first two in the first row, and the third one in the second row, then we will have to specify a plot sequence of 221, 223, and 122. Try this out as an exercise!

There's more...

Since there are many such possible grids, we will see one more example with four different plots in a 2 x 2 grid, each one with a different type of graph, histogram, line, scatter, and bar graph. In the last example, we kept adding axes one by one, with the `plt.subplot()` method. In this example, we will define all axes in the grid at once, and then use indexing to access each of them and plot different graphs:

1. Read `Wine Quality` and `Iris` datasets from `.csv` files and compute the mean and standard deviation for each of the attributes:

```
wine_quality = pd.read_csv('winequality.csv', delimiter=';')
iris = pd.read_csv('iris_dataset.csv', delimiter=',')
iris_mean = iris.mean()
iris_std = iris.std()
```

2. This defines the figure and its layout:

```
fig, axs = plt.subplots(2, 2, figsize=(8, 8))
```

3. Plot the histogram with the `alcohol` attribute of the `Wine Quality` dataset on the first axis:

```
axs[0, 0].hist(wine_quality['alcohol'])
axs[0, 0].set_title('Histogram')
axs[0, 0].set_xlabel('Alcohol Bins')
axs[0, 0].set_ylabel('Frequency')
```

4. Plot the line graph of `sepal_length` and `sepal_width` on the second axis:

```
axs[0, 1].plot(iris['sepal_length'], iris['sepal_width'])
axs[0, 1].set(title='Line', xlabel='Sepal Length', ylabel='Sepal
             Width')
```

5. Plot a scatter plot with the `petal_length` and the `petal_width` attributes on the third axis:

```
axs[1, 0].scatter(iris['petal_length'], iris['petal_width'])
axs[1, 0].set(title='Scatter', xlabel='Petal Length', ylabel='Petal
             Width')
```

6. Plot a bar graph on the fourth axis:

```
axs[1, 1].bar(['sepal_l','sepal_w', 'petal_l', 'petal_w'],
             iris_mean, yerr=iris_std)
axs[1, 1].set(title='Bar', xlabel='Category', ylabel='Category
             Mean')
```

7. Set the title for the overall figure:

```
plt.suptitle('Subplots Demo')
```

8. Adjust the space in between the plots:

```
plt.tight_layout(pad=3, w_pad=1.0, h_pad=1.0)
```

9. Display the plot on the screen:

```
plt.show()
```

Here is the explanation of how the code works:

- `iris.mean()` and `iris.std()` compute the mean and standard deviation for all four attributes in the `Iris` dataset. These will be used to plot the bar plot on the fourth axis of this figure.
- `fig, axs = plt.subplots(2, 2, figsize=(8, 8))` defines 2 x 2 grid and assigns them to the axis list, which will be accessed with respective indexes while plotting the graph on each of these axes.
- `axs[0, 0].hist(wine_quality['alcohol'])` plots the histogram plot for the alcohol attribute in the `Wine Quality` dataset. `axes[0,0]` represents the first plot on the first row and the first column (Python indexing starts with 0).
- `axs[0, 0].set_title('Histogram')` sets the title for the first plot.
- `axs[0, 0].set_xlabel('Alcohol Bins')` sets the label for the *x* axis and `axs[0, 0].set_ylabel('Alcohol Bins')` sets the label for the *y* axis.
- `axs[0, 1]` represents the second plot, placed in the first row and the second column, and a line plot is drawn on this axis. `axs[0, 1].set()` sets title, `xlabel`, and `ylabel` with one command instead of three separate commands.
- `axs[1, 0]` represents the third plot, placed in the second row and the first column, and a scatter plot is drawn on this axis.
- Finally, `axs[1, 1]` represents the fourth plot, placed in the second row and the second column, and a bar plot is drawn on this axes.
  The `yerr` attribute represents the standard deviation for the group represented by the bar, and it is shown as a black vertical line on top of each bar. The length of the line is relative to all other lines on the bars; the longer the line, the higher the standard deviation for that group (or bar).

- `plt.suptitle('Subplots Demo')` sets the title for the figure (a combination of all four plots together).
- `plt.tight_layout(pad=3, w_pad=1.0, h_pad=1.0)` ensures that the labels on the four plots are not overlapping with one another. The `pad` parameter controls the space at the top of the figure; the higher the number, the larger the gap between the title of the figure and the headers of the two plots below it. `w_pad` controls the space between two plots in a row, and `h_pad` controls the space between two plots in a column.

You should see the output plots as shown in the following figure:

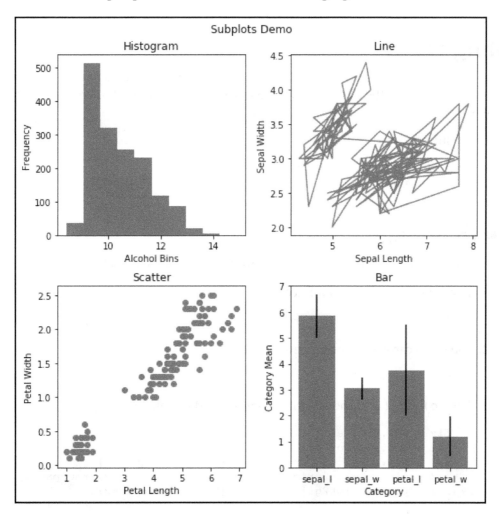

In this index-based axes approach, all the plots will be the same size, so we can't manage different sized plots the way we did in the example at the beginning of this recipe.

Plotting multiple figures in a session

So far, we have learned how to plot multiple plots on a single axes and multiple axes in a figure. In this recipe, we will learn how to plot multiple figures in a given session.

Getting ready

We will use same Iris dataset in this example also. We will plot two figures, and multiple plots in each of them. In the first figure, we will use another method to create a grid with different-sized plots.

Import the required libraries:

```
import matplotlib.pyplot as plt
import pandas as pd
```

How to do it...

The following code block plots two figures with multiple plots in each:

1. Read the Iris data from Excel:

```
iris = pd.read_csv('iris_dataset.csv', delimiter=',')
```

2. Clear the canvas to start a new figure:

```
plt.close('all')
```

3. Define *figure 1* and the associated layout and subplots:

```
fig = plt.figure(1, figsize=(12, 9))
ax1 = plt.subplot2grid((3, 3), (0, 0))
ax2 = plt.subplot2grid((3, 3), (0, 1), colspan=2)
ax3 = plt.subplot2grid((3, 3), (1, 0), colspan=2, rowspan=2)
ax4 = plt.subplot2grid((3, 3), (1, 2), rowspan=2)
```

4. Plot the graphs on each of the four axes defined in *step 3*:

```
ax1.hist(iris['petal_width'])
ax2.scatter(iris['petal_length'], iris['petal_width'],
s=50*iris['petal_length']*iris['petal_width'], alpha=0.3)
ax3.scatter(iris['sepal_length'], iris['sepal_width'])
ax4.violinplot(iris['petal_length'])
```

5. Set the title and adjust the space between the plots:

```
plt.suptitle('Figure 1: Grid Plotting Demo', fontsize=20)
plt.tight_layout(pad=5, w_pad=0.5, h_pad=1.0)
```

6. Define the *figure 2* and its size:

```
plt.figure(2, figsize=(12, 5))
```

7. Set up the data for the bar plot:

```
names = ['group_a', 'group_b', 'group_c', 'group_d', 'group_e']
values = [1, 10, 50, 100, 500]
```

8. Define the first axis and plot the bar graph:

```
plt.subplot(131)
plt.bar(names, values, color='orange')
```

9. Define the second axis and plot a scatter plot:

```
plt.subplot(132)
plt.scatter(names, values, color='orange')
```

10. Define the third axis and a line graph:

```
plt.subplot(133)
plt.plot(names, values, color='orange')
```

11. Set the title for the overall figure and adjust the space between the plots in the figure:

```
plt.suptitle('Figure 2: Row Plotting Demo', fontsize=20)
plt.tight_layout(pad=5, w_pad=0.5, h_pad=1.0)
```

12. Display the figure on the screen:

```
plt.show()
```

How it works...

Here is the explanation of the code:

- `plt.close('all')` clears the space before starting a new figure.
- `fig = plt.figure(1, figsize=(12, 9))` defines *figure 1* with a size equal to `(12, 9)`.
- `ax1 = plt.subplot2grid((3, 3), (0, 0))` creates `ax1` axes, where the first plot will be drawn, and `ax1` is the first axes in a 3 x 3 grid of 9 axes. Python indexing starts from 0, 1, and 2, which represent the first, second, and third row or column.
- `ax2 = plt.subplot2grid((3, 3), (0, 1), colspan=2)` creates `ax2` axes, which spans two columns of the 3 x 3 grid, starting at the first row and the second column.
- `ax3 = plt.subplot2grid((3, 3), (1, 0), colspan=2, rowspan=2)` creates an`ax3` axes, which spans two columns and two rows, starting at the second row and the first column.
- `ax4 = plt.subplot2grid((3, 3), (1, 2), rowspan=2)` creates an `ax4` axis, which spans two rows and one column, starting at the second row and the third column.
- As with the last recipe, we now plot a histogram, bubble plot, scatter plot, and a violin plot on each of the four axes respectively.
- `plt.suptitle('Figure 1: Grid Plotting Demo', fontsize=20)` sets the title for *figure 1*, with a font size of `20`.
- `plt.tight_layout(pad=5, w_pad=0.5, h_pad=1.0)` adjusts the space between the plots so that there is no overlapping of labels.
- `plt.figure(2, figsize=(12, 5))` starts the second figure with a size of `(12, 5)`.
- The names and the values are Python lists of data to be plotted on the *x* and the *y* axis respectively for three plots to be drawn.
- As in the previous example, we plot three plots in a 1 x 3 grid, and plot one bar plot, one scatter plot and one line plot. Then, we set the title for the figure and adjust the space between the plots so that there is no overlap, just as with any other subplot.

You should see the output figures as shown here:

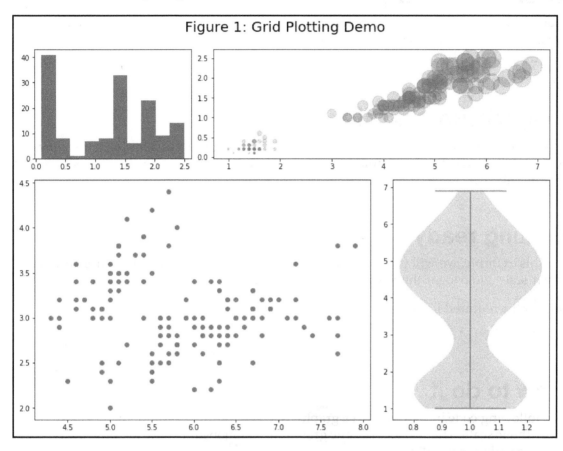

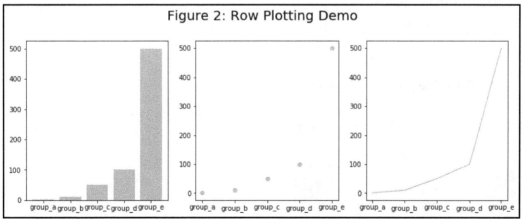

There's more...

Matplotlib also provides one more toolkit, called AxesGrid, which covers even more advanced grid options, including images in a grid. We will cover this in Chapter 13, *Using the axes_grid1 Toolkit.*

Logarithmic scale

When the data ranges from very small values to very large values, plotting it on a linear scale may not give the right intuition of the relative size of the data points. In such cases, a logarithmic scale is used.

Getting ready

For this example, we will use some dummy data to demonstrate the difference between a linear scale and a logarithmic scale.

Import the required library:

```
import matplotlib.pyplot as plt
```

How to do it...

The following code block plots three graphs, one on a linear scale and the other two on a logarithmic scale. The two logarithmic graphs also demonstrate how the physical size and the data scale can be adjusted:

1. Define the figure and its layout:

```
fig, (ax1, ax2, ax3) = plt.subplots(1, 3)
```

2. Plot a line graph on a linear scale on axis ax1:

```
ax1.plot([0.1, 5, 10, 500], [0.01, 25, 100, 10000], "x-")
ax1.set(title="Linear Scale", xlim=(1e1, 1e3), ylim=(1e2, 1e4))
```

3. Draw an empty plot with a logarithmic scale on both *x* and *y* axes:

```
ax2.set(title="adjustable = box", xscale="log", yscale="log", xlim=
        (1e1, 1e3), ylim=(1e2, 1e3), aspect=2)
```

4. Plot a line graph on `ax3` with a logarithmic scale on both the *x* and the *y* axis:

```
ax3.plot([0.1, 5, 10, 500], [0.01, 25, 100, 10000], "o-")
ax3.set(title="adjustable = datalim", xscale="log", yscale="log",
        adjustable="datalim", xlim=(1e-1, 1e3),
        ylim=(1e-2, 1e4), aspect=1)
```

5. Adjust the space in between the plots and display the figure on the screen:

```
plt.tight_layout()
plt.show()
```

How it works...

Here is the explanation for the code:

- `fig, (ax1, ax2, ax3) = plt.subplots(1, 3)` defines the layout of the figure with three axes objects to be plotted in one row.
- On the `ax1` axes, a simple line chart is plotted with the *x* and *y* axis limits set. Due to the very large range of data, not all the points are clearly visible, and the relative gap between them is not easy to visualize.
- On `ax2`, a logarithmic scale is demonstrated without any chart in it. `ax2.set()` sets all the parameters for the plot. `xscale="log"` and `yscale="log"` set the *x* and the *y* axis to logarithmic scale. `aspect=2` sets the ratio of the *y*-scale data to be twice the size of the *x*-scale data. As you can see, the distance between 10^2 to 10^3 on the *y* axis is twice that on the *x* axis.
- On `ax3`, a logarithmic scale and the same line chart that was plotted on `ax1` are plotted here, to show the difference. Here, we can see all four points clearly and we can also see the relative distance among them. `adjustable="datalim"` adjusts/extends the *x* or the *y* limits to accommodate the aspect ratio specified. This attribute was omitted in the second plot (`ax2`), so it took the default argument of `box`, which adjusts the physical object size (instead of data scale) to accommodate the aspect ratio.

You should see the output figure as follows:

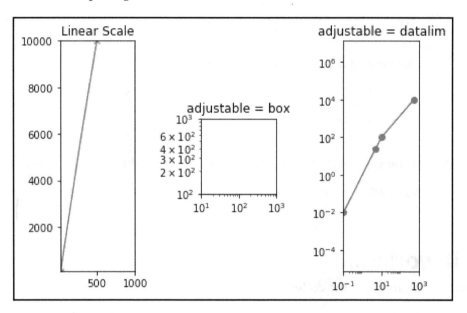

There's more...

Let's take one more example of how the logarithmic scale can be used. Let's say that within an organization, employees are classified into five categories based on their position. Each of these five categories is further split into men and women. For each of these 10 categories (five men and five women), we have the average salary and the standard deviation. This data is plotted to see how salary data is distributed across groups of men and women.

Here is the code and how it works:

- Import the required libraries:

```
import matplotlib.pyplot as plt
import numpy as np
```

- Define Python lists containing mean and standard deviation data for men and women:

```
menMeans = [3, 10, 100, 500, 50]
menStd = [0.75, 2.5, 25, 125, 12.5]

womenMeans = [1000, 3, 30, 800, 1]
womenStd = [500, 0.75, 8, 200, 0.25]
```

- Define the figure layout, the *index* list where the menMeans bars are to be placed on the *x* axis, and the width of each bar, and then plot the bar graph for men data in red with a black line on the head of the bar, indicating the size of the standard deviation for the group:

```
fig, ax = plt.subplots()
ind = np.arange(len(menMeans))
width = 0.35
p1 = ax.bar(ind, menMeans, width, color='lightblue', bottom=0,
            yerr=menStd)
```

- Similarly, plot the womenMeans bar chart in yellow, adjacent to the menMeans bars, then set the title, xticks placement on the *x* axis, and their labels:

```
p2 = ax.bar(ind + width, womenMeans, width, color='orange',
            bottom=0, yerr=womenStd)
ax.set_title('Scores by category and gender')
ax.set_xticks(ind + width / 2)
ax.set_xticklabels(('C1', 'C2', 'C3', 'C4', 'C5'))
```

- Finally, ax.set_yscale('log') sets the *y* axis scale to logarithmic and ax.legend((p1[0], p2[0]), ('Men', 'Women')) sets the legend for the plot. Then, plt.show() displays the plot on the screen.

Here is how the output bar plot looks:

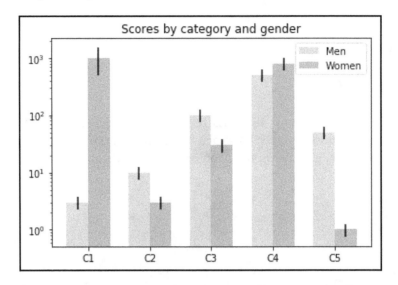

 Matplotlib supports four different scales. The default is *linear,* and we have covered *log* in this recipe. You can refer to the Matplotlib documentation for the other two scales: *symlog* and *logit* (`https://matplotlib.org/examples/scales/scales.html`).

Using units of measurement

Sometimes, we may have data using one unit of measurement but want to draw the plot using a different unit of measurement, or sometimes we may want to use different units of measurement on the *x* and *y* axis, say *centimeters* on the *x* axis and *inches* on the *y* axis. The same is true for degrees and radians when we are plotting angles. Matplotlib does not have these functions built in, but there is an extension utility, `basic_units.py`, available on GitHub, which enables these different units of measurement. This Python module currently supports only centimeters/inches and radians/degrees. For other units of measurement, such as kg/lb, km/miles, and so on, we will have to update this utility module.

 `basic_units.py` is not a standard package to be installed like all other Python packages. It is a user-defined Python program that needs to be copied into your working directory. Then, in the main program, import the functions from this program similar to the way we import any other package or user-defined programs.

Getting ready

Once you have copied `basic_units.py` into your working directory, you can start using all the functions available there.

Import the required libraries. Here, we are introducing two other features of Matplotlib, `lines`, which has objects for drawing lines, and `text`, which is used to annotate objects on the chart:

```
import matplotlib.lines as lines
import matplotlib.text as text
from basic_units import cm, inch
import matplotlib.pyplot as plt
```

How to do it...

The following code block draws two plots, one with centimeters and the other with inches, to demonstrate the difference between two units of measurement:

1. Define a figure with two plots in a row:

    ```
    fig, ax = plt.subplots(1,2)
    ```

2. Define `line` and the `text` artists to be added to the first axis:

    ```
    line = lines.Line2D([0*cm, 1.5*cm], [0*cm, 2.5*cm], lw=2,
                        color='black', axes=ax[0])
    t = text.Text(3*cm, 2.5*cm, 'text label', ha='left', va='bottom',
                axes=ax[0])
    ```

3. Add the artists to axis 0, and set the limits, units of measurement, and the grid:

    ```
    ax[0].add_line(line)
    ax[0].add_artist(t)
    ax[0].set_xlim(-1*cm, 10*cm)
    ax[0].set_ylim(-1*cm, 10*cm)
    ax[0].xaxis.set_units(cm)
    ax[0].yaxis.set_units(cm)
    ax[0].grid(True)
    ```

4. Define the `line` and `text` artists to be added to the second axis:

```
line = lines.Line2D([0*cm, 1.5*cm], [0*cm, 2.5*cm], lw=2,
                     color='black', axes=ax[1])
t = text.Text(3*cm, 2.5*cm, 'text label', ha='left', va='bottom',
              axes=ax[1])
```

5. Add the artists to axes 1 and set limits, units of measurement, and grid:

```
ax[1].add_artist(line)
ax[1].add_artist(t)
ax[1].set_xlim(-1*cm, 10*cm)
ax[1].set_ylim(-1*cm, 10*cm)
ax[1].xaxis.set_units(inch)
ax[1].yaxis.set_units(inch)
ax[1].grid(True)
```

6. Set the title for the figure and adjust the space between the plots:

```
plt.suptitle("Demonstration of Units Of Measurement")
plt.tight_layout(pad=3)
```

7. Display the figure on the screen:

```
plt.show()
```

How it works...

Here is the explanation of how the code works:

- `fig, ax = plt.subplots(1,2)` defines the figure with two axis objects on the same row. Since it is only one row with two plots, `ax` is a one-dimensional vector, so we will access them with `ax[0]` and `ax[1]`.
- `line = lines.Line2D([0*cm, 1.5*cm], [0*cm, 2.5*cm], lw=2, color='black', axes=ax[0])` plots a black line segment on axis `ax[0]`, with *line width* 2, and input data, in centimeters.
- Similarly, `t = text.Text(3*cm, 2.5*cm, 'text label', ha='left', va='bottom', axes=ax[0])` defines a `text label` object to `ax[0]` at the specified position (3, 2.5) in centimeters with the left alignment horizontally and a bottom alignment vertically.

It should be noted that Matplotlib does not support sharing objects across different axes; we need to explicitly specify for each object in which axes it is to be included. We specified `axes=ax[0]` for the line plot, since the same line is plotted again on `ax[1]`, and we had to tell Matplotlib on which axis it is plotting the line at any given time. This also means that if the same line or text is to be drawn on two different axis, then it will have to be repeated twice.

- `ax[0].add_line(line)` and `ax[0].add_artist(t)` add the line and text objects on `ax[0]`. Remember, artist is an object that actually draws the object on the canvas/chart. In fact, `add_line` can also be replaced with `add_artist`, as we have done for `ax[1]` later.
- `ax[0].xaxis.set_units(cm)` and `ax[0].yaxis.set_units(cm)` set the units of measurement for the *x* axis and the *y* axis for actual display. For `ax[0]`, this is set to centimeters, and for `ax[1]`, this is set to inches. For both axes, the input data is in centimeters.
- `ax[0].grid(True)` shows the grid, along with the major ticks on both the *x* and the *y* axis. This helps in visualizing the exact coordinate values anywhere on the graph.
- `plt.suptitle()` sets the title for the figure, `plt.tight_layout(pad=3)` adjusts the space between the plots, and `pad=3` ensures that the figure title sufficiently precedes the figure.
- Exactly the same steps are repeated for `ax[1]`, the only the difference being that `ax[1].xaxis.set_units(inch)` and `ax[1].yaxis.set_units(inch)` are specified in inches instead of `cm`.

Here is how the figure looks:

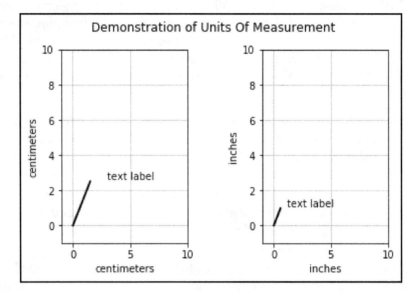

Since the scales are the same on both of the plots, the size of the line is smaller in inches than in centimeters, as expected.

There's more...

Here is another example of using a mix of centimeters and inches on the *x* and *y* axis. We have four bar plots with the same input data, plotted on a 2 x 2 grid.

Import the required libraries:

```
import numpy as np
from basic_units import cm, inch
import matplotlib.pyplot as plt
```

The following code plots the figure with four bar plots in a 2 x 2 grid:

1. Define the data and the units of measurement:

```
cms = cm * np.arange(0, 21, 3)
bottom = 0 * cm
width = 0.8 * cm
```

2. Define the figure and its layout:

```
fig, axs = plt.subplots(2, 2)
```

3. Plot a bar chart on the first axes, and set xticks in centimeters:

```
axs[0, 0].bar(cms, cms, bottom=bottom)
axs[0, 0].set_xticks(cm * np.arange(0, 21, 3))
```

4. Plot a bar chart on the second axes with the *x* axis in centimeters and the *y* axis in inches:

```
axs[0, 1].bar(cms, cms, bottom=bottom, width=width, xunits=cm,
              yunits=inch)
axs[0, 1].set_xticks(cm * np.arange(0, 21, 3))
```

5. Plot a bar chart on the third axes with the *x* axis in inches and the *y* axis in centimeters:

```
axs[1, 0].bar(cms, cms, bottom=bottom, width=width, xunits=inch,
              yunits=cm)
axs[1, 0].set_xticks(cm * np.arange(0, 21, 3))
axs[1, 0].set_xlim(2, 6)
```

6. Plot a bar chart on the fourth axes with both the *x* and the *y* axis in inches:

```
axs[1, 1].bar(cms, cms, bottom=bottom, width=width, xunits=inch,
              yunits=inch)
axs[1, 1].set_xticks(cm * np.arange(0, 21, 3))
axs[1, 1].set_xlim(2 * cm, 6 * cm)
```

7. Adjust the space between the plots and display the figure on the screen:

```
fig.tight_layout()
plt.show()
```

Here is the explanation of how it works:

- Prepare the input data for both the *x* and the *y* coordinates, set the bottom offset for the bars, and the width of the bar.
- `fig, axs = plt.subplots(2, 2)` defines the figure layout in a 2 x 2 grid.
- `axs[0, 0].bar(cms, cms, bottom=bottom)` plots a bar plot on `axs[0, 0]` and the input data is in centimeters. `axs[0, 0].set_xticks(cm * np.arange(0, 21, 3))` sets the tick lines on the *x* axis so that they are aligned with the bars.

- The bar plot on axs[0, 1] is exactly same as axs[0, 0], except that the units for the *y* axis changed from centimeters to inches, which is visible on the plot.
- The bar plot on axs[1, 0] is again similar to the one on axs[0, 0], but the units on the *x* axis changed to inches, and axs[1, 0].set_xlim(2, 6) sets the *x* axis limits to be (2, 6). Here, only scalars are used to set the limits, without any unit of measurement, which means whatever the *x* axis unit of measurement is, the same would be applicable for the limits, which in this case range from two to six inches.
- The bar plot on axs[1,1] uses inches as the unit of measurement for both the *x* and the *y* axis and sets the *x* axis limits in centimeters (2, 6), which will be converted to inches in alignment with the unit of measurement for the *x* axis. So it would be converted to inches, which in this case translates to 0.79 to 2.362 inches.

You should see a figure like the following:

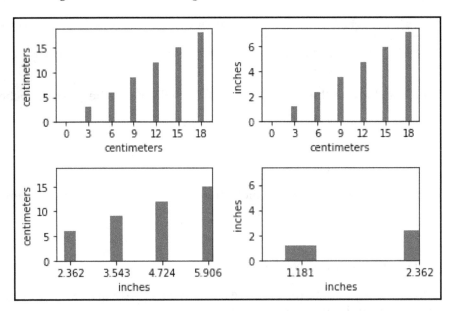

4
Developing Visualizations for Publishing Quality

In this chapter, we will cover the following recipes:

- Color, line style, and marker customization
- Working with standard colormaps
- User-defined colors and colormaps
- Working with legends
- Customizing labels and titles
- Using autoscale and axis limits
- Customizing ticks and ticklabels
- Customizing spines
- Twin axes
- Using hatches
- Using annotation
- Using style sheets

Introduction

Matplotlib provides many features to customize all the attributes of a figure. It also offers many different ways to achieve the same feature that gives maximum flexibility and a variety of choices. In this chapter, we will cover the standard features available with each of the figure attributes, such as colors, labels, titles, legends, ticks, spines, styles, hatches, and annotation. Advanced topics such as property cycles, transforms, GridSpec, and Path effects will be covered in `Chapter 6`, *Plotting with Advanced Features*.

Color, line style, and marker customization

Matplotlib supports many different ways of specifying the color, line style, and markers. In this recipe, we will learn how to use these features.

Getting ready

Import the following required libraries:

```
import numpy as np
import matplotlib.pyplot as plt
```

How to do it...

The following code block draws five different plots to demonstrate most of the possible combinations for specifying the colors, line styles, and markers:

1. Define the figure layout, as follows:

```
fig = plt.figure(figsize=(12,6))
```

2. Define axes names for each of the plots:

```
ax1 = plt.subplot(321)
ax2 = plt.subplot(322)
ax3 = plt.subplot(323)
ax4 = plt.subplot(324)
ax5 = plt.subplot(325)
ax6 = plt.subplot(326)
```

3. Set up data for x co-ordinates:

```
x = np.linspace(0, 10, 20)
```

4. Following is the demonstration of many color specifications:
    - `xkcd:sky blue`: Name from `xkcd` color survey
    - `green`: CSS4 color name
    - `1F1F1F1F`: Hexadecimal value in RGBA format; digits range from 0-F
    - `b`: CSS4 color abbreviation
    - `1C0B2D`: Hexadecimal value in RGB format
    - `pink`: Tableau color
    - `C4`: Color from property cycle; this is case-sensitive, and C has to be capitalized

We represent them in code format as follows:

```
color_list = ['xkcd:sky blue', 'green', '#1F1F1F1F', 'b',
'#1C0B2D',
                'pink', 'C4']
for i, color in enumerate(color_list):
    y = x - (-5*i + 15)
    ax1.plot(x, y, color)
ax1.set_title('colors demo')
```

5. The following is a demonstration of the many line styles:

```
line_style = ['-', '--', '-.', ':', '.']
for i, ls in enumerate(line_style):
    y = x - (-5*i + 15)
    line, = ax2.plot(x, y, ls)
ax2.set_title('line style demo')
plt.setp(line, ls='steps')
```

6. Here is a demonstration of the many marker specifications:

```
marker_list = ['.', ',', 'o', 'v', '^', 's', 'p', '*', 'h', 'H',
                'D']
for i, marker in enumerate(marker_list):
    y = x - (-5*i + 15)
    ax3.plot(x, y, marker)
ax3.set_title('marker demo')
```

7. The following is a demonstration of specifying combinations of color, line styles, and markers:

```
y = x              # reset y to x
ax4.plot(x, y-10, 'k-d')
ax4.plot(x, y-5, 'c--')
ax4.plot(x, y, '|')
ax4.plot(x, y+5, '-.')
ax4.plot(x, y+10, color='purple', ls=':', marker='3')
ax4.plot(x, y+15, color='orange', linestyle=':', marker='1')
ax4.set_title('combination demo')
```

8. The following is a demonstration of specifying colors and sizes of lines and markers:

```
ax5.plot(x, y-10, 'y-D', linewidth=2, markersize=4,
         markerfacecolor='red',
         markeredgecolor='k',markeredgewidth=1)
ax5.plot(x, y-5, 'm-s', lw=4, ms=6, markerfacecolor='red',
         markeredgecolor='y', markeredgewidth=1)
ax5.set_title('Line and Marker Sizes Demo')
```

9. The following is a demonstration of cap styles for dashed lines:

```
dash_capstyles = ['butt','projecting','round']
for i, cs in enumerate(dash_capstyles):
    y = x - (-5*i + 15)
    ax6.plot(x, y, ls='--', lw=10, dash_capstyle=cs)
ax6.set_title('dash capstyle demo')
```

10. Use just the space in between the plots, and display the figure on the screen:

```
plt.tight_layout()
plt.show()
```

How it works...

The following is the output from the code followed by an explanation of how it works:

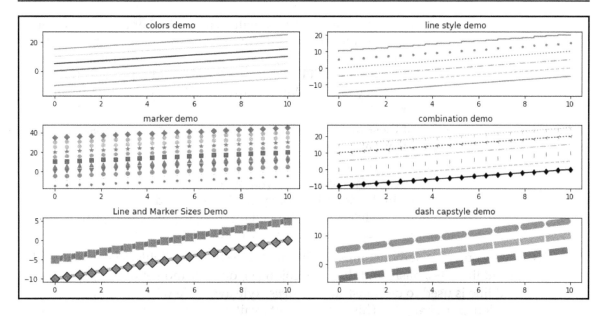

- `np.linspace(0, 10, 20)` creates 20 values in the range from 0 to 20, which are mapped to the *x* axis.
- `fig = plt.figure(figsize=(12,6))` defines the figure with a size of (12, 6), followed by six subplots using `plt.subplot()`.
- The first plot demonstrates various ways a color can be specified in the plots. `color_list` is the list of colors for which line plots are drawn. The `for` loop that follows plot lines for each of the colors in the list. `enumerate` in for loop allows two variables: one for an index starting at zero, and the other for actual items in the list:
  - `xkcd:sky blue`—This is one of the colors from the `xkcd` color survey. `xkcd:` has to precede the actual color code. Please find the full list of colors at this site (`https://blog.xkcd.com/2010/05/03/color-survey-results/`).
  - Color codes (b, g, r, c, m, y, k, w) and their expanded names (`blue`, `green`, `red`, `cyan`, `magenta`, `yellow`, `black`, `white`).
  - (`tab:blue`, `tab:orange`, `tab:green`, `tab:red`, `tab:purple`, `tab:brown`, `tab:pink`, `tab:gray`, `tab:olive`, `tab:cyan`) which are the tableau colors from `T10` categorical palette (which is also the default color cycle). We can specify these colors by using `tab:` before them or without using `tab`. Both of them are acceptable.

- We can specify hexadecimal values in an RGB or an RGBA format as well. Hexadecimal values for any channel range from 00 to FF. So, RBG ranges from 000000 to FFFFFF, and RGBA ranges from 00000000 to FFFFFFFF. A stands for alpha and represents the transparency of the color; towards 00 is highly transparent and towards FF is highly opaque.
- All of these are case insensitive, so we can use uppercase or lowercase alphabets.
- One more option is CN, where C is case-sensitive and has to be an uppercase character, followed by a number, which is the index of colors in the default color cycle. As described, the first color in the default cycle is blue, followed by orange, green, red, purple, and so on. So, C0 represents blue, C1 represents orange, and so on.

- The second plot demonstrates six different line styles available. They are dash (-), solid line (--), dash, and dot (-.), colon (:), dot (.), and solid (' '). The last solid line is used to demonstrate the *steps* style available with the set property function, plt.setp(). This option is not available directly like other line styles.
- The third plot demonstrates various markers. Not all the available markers are plotted here. For a complete list of markers, please refer to the Matplotlib documentation here (https://matplotlib.org/api/markers_api.html?highlight=list%20markers).
- The fourth plot demonstrates how we can specify a combination of color, line style, and marker with their abbreviations or full names. Either we can specify all three parameters in a string such as g-^, we can specify even one or two of them only such as g or --, or D, in which case it uses default values for other attributes not specified here. We can also specify individually, for instance color is purple, linestyle is :, marker >, and so on.
- Plot five demonstrates how to specify the size and color parameters for the line width, marker size, edge, and face colors for markers.
- Finally, plot six demonstrates cap styles in the case of dashed line styles.

Working with standard colormaps

In the last recipe, we have seen how colors can be used when plotting the graphs. If we want to visualize a data range with visual perceptual colors to get a sense of patterns in the data, it will be tedious to create color combinations that match with data changes in the range we are looking for. Matplotlib provides a range of pre-defined colormaps that can be leveraged to meet any specific requirement. Matplotlib also enables user-defined colormaps that will be covered in the next recipe.

 In Python notebooks, you can type `matplotlib.pyplot.cm.` and press *Tab* or type `help (matplotlib.pyplot.cm)` to get a complete list of the available colormaps.

Getting ready

We will be using the familiar `Iris` dataset for this example. We will first create a correlation matrix and apply a standard colormap to see how it looks. We saw the same correlation matrix plotted as a heatmap in `Chapter 2`, *Getting Started with Basic Plots*. There, we used the *hot* colormap, but we did not go into the details regarding colormaps. We will explain that here.

Import the following required libraries:

```
import matplotlib.pyplot as plt
import pandas as pd
import numpy as np
```

How to do it...

The following code block plots a correlation matrix with a `Blues` colormap:

1. Read the `winequality` data from the Excel file:

    ```
    wine_quality = pd.read_csv('winequality.csv', delimiter=';')
    corr = wine_quality.corr()
    ```

2. Define the figure and its size:

```
plt.figure(figsize=(12,8))
```

3. Plot the correlation map, the associated x and y ticks, and the colorbar:

```
plt.imshow(corr, cmap='Blues')
plt.colorbar()
plt.xticks(range(len(corr)),corr.columns, rotation=45)
plt.yticks(range(len(corr)),corr.columns)
```

4. Display the figure on the screen:

```
plt.show()
```

How it works...

Here is the explanation of how it works:

- `pd.read_csv()` reads the `winequality` data, and `wine_quality.corr()` computes the correlation matrix.
- `plt.imshow(corr, cmap='Blues')` displays the correlation matrix as an image and applies one of the standard colormaps: `Blues`.
- `plt.colorbar()` displays the color scale indicating which color share represents which data range.
- `plt.xticks()` and `plt.yticks()` plot the tickers (one for each attribute in the dataset) and the corresponding ticker labels for the x and the y axis. Argument `rotation=45` in `plt.xticks()` indicates that ticker lables should be placed at 45 degrees to the corresponding axis.

You should see the following heatmap. As expected, the data ranges from -0.6 to 1.0 (correlations can range only between -1.0 and 1.0). 1.0 is represented with a `dark blue` color at one end, and on the other end a `white` color represents -1, and dark to lighter shades in between dark blue and white colors, represent numbers between 1.0 and -1.0:

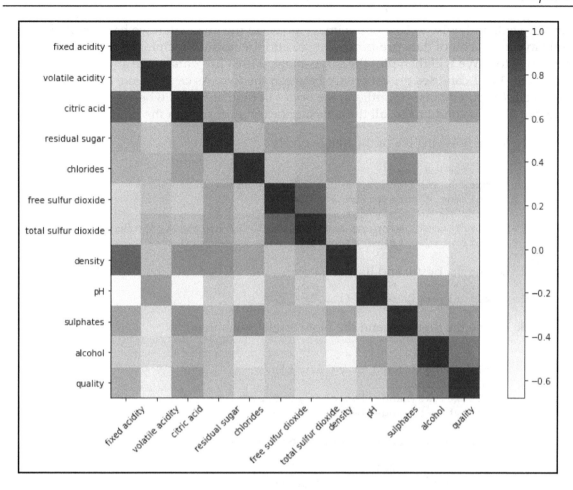

There's more...

In the preceding plot, we displayed the complete data range available in the input data. However, we can limit the the data range we want to color code using the `plt.clim()` method. This is useful when there are outliers (a few entries of the variable are too large or too small compared to rest of the data), and then by default the colormap extends color codes for the complete range of data. When there are outliers, because of the larger range, the majority of the values get blurred and outliers stand out with extreme colors. If we want to suppress the impact of outliers, we can limit the data range that excludes the outliers and plot the desired range with a complete list of colors in the colorbar. This gives a true picture of the data distribution. Here is how we can accomplish this.

First, we will add noise to 10% of the image pixels to the image that we have created. We will have to do a bit of data pre-processing to add the noise, which increases the data range beyond -1 to 1. We will then plot the same image with a full data range and a data range limited to -1 to 1 , and see the difference between the two. As can be seen, in the first image, a few cells (imputed noise or outliers) are bright in blue or white, where as all others are blur, but in the second image, all the cell colors vary uniformly in the range of -1 to 1:

1. Make noise in 10% of the image pixels:

```
np.random.seed(0)
mask = (np.random.random(corr.shape) < 0.1)
columns = corr.columns
corr1 = np.array(corr)
corr1[mask] = np.random.normal(0, 5, np.count_nonzero(mask))
corr = pd.DataFrame(corr1, columns=columns)
```

2. Define the figure and its size:

```
plt.figure(figsize=(12, 5))
```

3. Define the first axes and the plot correlation map on it:

```
plt.subplot(121)
plt.imshow(corr, cmap='Blues')
plt.colorbar()
plt.xticks(range(len(corr)),corr.columns, rotation=75)
plt.yticks(range(len(corr)),corr.columns)
```

4. Define the second axes and plot the correlation map, with limits on data:

```
plt.subplot(122)
plt.imshow(corr, cmap='Blues')
plt.clim(-1,1)
plt.colorbar(extend='both')
plt.xticks(range(len(corr)),corr.columns, rotation=75)
plt.yticks(range(len(corr)),corr.columns)
```

5. Adjust the space in between the plots, and display the figure on the screen:

```
plt.tight_layout()
plt.show()
```

Here is the explanation of the code and how it works:

- `np.random.seed(0)` sets the seed so that every time we run the random number generator we get the same data. This ensures repeatability of results, when we run the same code multiple times.
- `mask = (np.random.random(corr.shape) < 0.1)` creates a matrix of the same size of `corr`, with entries as `True` for all values less than 0.1; otherwise they are `False`.
- `columns = corr.columns` extracts the column names from the `corr` pandas DataFrame for later use.
- `corr1 = np.array(corr)` creates a NumPy array for our `corr` data frame, as the next statement works well with the NumPy array rather than data frame.
- `corr1[mask] = np.random.normal(0, 5, np.count_nonzero(mask))` replaces entries in `corr1`, corresponding to the `True` entries in the mask, by generating random normal values for 10% of the entries, and this distribution would have a mean of zero mean and a standard deviation of five. The idea is to replace 10% of the entries with larger values representing noise.
- `corr = pd.DataFrame(corr1, columns=columns)` creates the data frame for the noise-imputed correlation matrix.
- `plt.subplot(1, 2, 1)` creates the axes for the first plot, where we would display the noise-imputed image.
- `plt.imshow(corr, cmap='Blues')` plots the image in `plot1`, followed by colorbar, ticks, and ticklabels.
- `plt.subplot(1, 2, 2)` creates the axes for the second plot, in which we limit the data range between -1 and 1.
- `plt.clim(-1, 1)` limits the colors (actually the data range) to between -1 and 1.
- `plt.colorbar(extend='both')` plots the colorbar with arrows on both ends, indicating that the range extends beyond what is displayed.

You should see following plots:

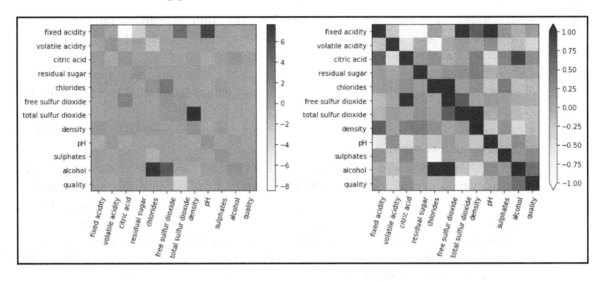

User-defined colors and colormaps

In the previous recipe, we learned how to leverage pre-defined colors and colormaps and how to customize them for specific needs. In this recipe, we will learn how to create our own colormaps. We will use the `Iris` dataset for this example.

Getting ready

We will first learn how to create discrete colormaps, followed by continuous colormaps.

Import the following required libraries:

```
import matplotlib.pyplot as plt
import pandas as pd
import numpy as np
from matplotlib.colors import LinearSegmentedColormap
```

How to do it...

The following code block displays three plots; the first one uses the standard colormap, `coolwarm`, and the other two use user-defined discrete colormaps. Of the two user-defined ones, the first one uses pure RED (1, 0, 0), GREEN (0, 1, 0), and BLUE (0, 0, 1) colors, and the other uses a mix of RGB colors [(1, 0.5, 0), (0.25, 1, 0), (0, 0.5, 1)] to generate three discrete colors. Please note in the first colormap tuple (1, 0, 0), only red is 1; green and blue are zeros. In the second one, the first and second colors are (1, 0.5, 0), and (0.25, 1, 0) means they are a combination of red and green, and the third color is a combination of green and blue.

We are using three discrete colors here, since we have three clusters in the input dataset. We should have as many colors as the number of clusters:

1. Read the `Iris` data from Excel and replace text class names with numeric values:

```
iris = pd.read_csv('iris_dataset.csv', delimiter=',')
iris['species'] = iris['species'].map({"setosa" : 0, "versicolor" :
                    1, "virginica" : 2})
```

2. Define the figure and its layout:

```
fig, axs = plt.subplots(1,3, figsize=(9,6))
fig.subplots_adjust(left=0.0, bottom=0.05, right=0.9, top=0.95,
                    wspace=0.6)
```

3. Define a function to plot the graph:

```
def plot_graph(axes, cm, cbaxs):
    im = axes.scatter(iris.petal_length, iris.petal_width,
        s=10*iris.petal_length*iris.petal_width, c=iris.species,
            cmap = cm)
    caxs = plt.axes(cbaxs)
    fig.colorbar(im, caxs, ticks=range(3), label='clusetr #')
```

4. Plot the `Iris` dataset clusters with three colors chosen from the pre-defined colormap, `coolwarm`:

```
cbaxs = [0.24, 0.05, 0.03, 0.85] # left, bottom, width and height
plot_graph(axs[0], plt.cm.get_cmap('coolwarm', 3), cbaxs)
```

5. Plot the `Iris` data clusters with custom-defined colors that are pure red, green, and blue:

```
colors = [(1, 0, 0), (0, 1, 0), (0, 0, 1)] # R -> G -> B
cm = LinearSegmentedColormap.from_list('custom_RGB_cmap', colors,
```

```
                                                         N=3)
cbaxs = [0.58, 0.05, 0.03, 0.85]
plot_graph(axs[1], cm, cbaxs)
```

6. Plot `Iris` data clusters with custom-defined colors that are a mixed combination of colors:

```
colors = [(1, 0.5, 0), (0.25, 0.5, 0.25), (0, 0.5, 1)] # R -> G -> B
cm = LinearSegmentedColormap.from_list('dummy', colors, N=3)
cbaxs = [0.95, 0.05, 0.03, 0.85]
plot_graph(axs[2], cm, cbaxs)
```

7. Display the figure on the screen:

```
plt.show()
```

How it works...

The following is the explanation of the code and how it works:

- `fig, axs = plt.subplots(1,3, figsize=(9,6))` defines the figure layout with three plots in a row, with a figure size of (9, 6).
- `fig.subplots_adjust(left=0.0, bottom=0.05, right=0.9, top=0.95, wspace=0.6)` defines the bounding box for the figure leaving space on all four directions as defined on the left, bottom, right, and top of the figure. `wspace` defines the amount of space to be left in between the plots in a row so that there is no overlap between their labels or plots. `hspace` is another parameter that controls the space between the plots in a column. We have not used it in this example, as we are plotting all the graphs in one row only.
- `plot_graph()` is a user-defined function to plot the graph with the given arguments, axes, colormap, and color bar axes.
- `axs.scatter()` plots a scatter plot using the given arguments. `caxs = plt.axes(cbaxs)` defines the color bar at the given axes, co-ordinates. `fig.colorbar()` plots the color bar with three ticks for each of the clusters with a defined color, and labels the color bar with `cluster #`.
- We plot the first graph on `axes[0]`, the first three colors of the pre-defined colormap `coolwarm`, and colorbar axes `cbaxs =[0.24, 0.05, 0.03, 0.85]`. These are the fractions of the figure from `left` and `bottom`, and the `width` and the `height` of the bar. We will learn more about co-ordinate systems in `Chapter 6`, *Plotting with Advanced Features*.

- We plot the second graph on `axes[1]`, with custom colors `colors = [(1, 0, 0), (0, 1, 0), (0, 0, 1)]`, which are pure red, green, and blue.
- `cmap_name = 'custom_RGB_cmap'` defines the name for the first user-defined colormap. This will be useful if we have to register it to be included in the standard colormaps library.
- `cm = LinearSegmentedColormap.from_list(cmap_name, colors2, N=3)` defines the colormap with the list of three colors defined previously.
- For the second graph, we place the color bar at these co-ordinates: `cbaxs = [0.58, 0.05, 0.03, 0.85]`.
- Similarly, we plot the third graph with `colors = [(1, 0.5, 0), (0.25, 0.5, 0.25), (0.8, 0.8, 0.25)]` and place them at co-ordinates `cbax = [0.95, 0.05, 0.03, 0.85]`. The colors in each of the red, green, and blue channels are again mixed with a combination of red, green, and blue of different values to create new custom colors.

You should see the following plots:

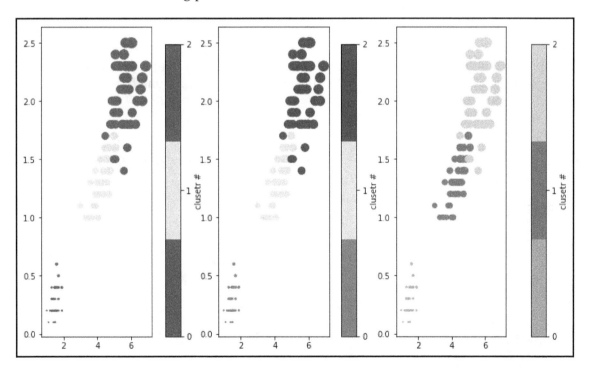

There's more...

Previously, we have learned how to create discrete user-defined colormaps. Now let's see how to create user-defined continuous colormaps. The difference is in the color specification. In discrete colormaps, we will have as many RGB tuples as the number of clusters we have in data, so that each color represents one cluster. However, in continuous colormaps, the color has to move gradually from one end of the spectrum to the other, along the complete data range.

As we know, each color is represented with a tuple of three numbers: R, G, and B channels. In some cases, the fourth channel, `alpha`, is also used to represent the transparency (or opaqueness) of the colors. Here is how we need to specify the colors. Let's take an example:

```
cdict1 = {'red':    ((0.0, 0.0, 0.25), (0.5, 0.4, 0.4), (1.0, 0.8,
                     1.0)),
          'green': ((0.0, 0.0, 0.25), (0.25, 0.5, 0.5), (0.75, 0.75,
                     0.75), (1.0, 0.9, 1.0)),
          'blue':  ((0.0, 0.0, 0.25), (0.5, 0.5, 0.5), (1.0, 0.75,
                     1.0))}
```

Let's say the first item in each of the tuples is *x*, and the second one is *y0*, and the third one is *y1*. In each color combination, *x* has to move from 0.0 to 1.0 gradually. Transition from the top to bottom rows has to happen gradually from *y1* (top row) to *y0* (next row), *y0* to *y1* on the same row, and again *y1* to *yo* of the next row should be gradual. In the case of red, *x* moved from 0.0, to 0.5 and then to 1.0. Similarly, *y1* moved from 0.25 to 0.4, 0.4, 0.8, which again is gradual. We can have as many tuples as we want in each of the colors. In this case, red and blue colors have three each, whereas green has four.

Similarly, we have defined three other color dictionaries including one with `alpha` as well, just to demonstrate all possible combinations:

```
cdict2 = {'red' : ((0.0, 0.0, 0.0), (0.5, 0.0, 1.0), (1.0, 0.1, 1.0)),
          'green': ((0.0, 0.0, 0.0), (1.0, 0.0, 0.0)),
          'blue': ((0.0, 0.0, 0.1), (0.5, 0.5, 0.5), (1.0, 0.8, 0.8)) }
cdict3 = {'red': ((0.0, 0.0, 0.0), (0.25, 0.0, 0.0), (0.5, 0.8, 1.0),
                  (0.75, 1.0, 1.0),(1.0, 0.4, 1.0)),
          'green': ((0.0, 0.0, 0.0), (0.25, 0.0, 0.0), (0.5, 0.9, 0.9),
                    (0.75, 0.0, 0.0), (1.0, 0.0, 0.0)),
          'blue': ((0.0, 0.0, 0.4), (0.25, 1.0, 1.0), (0.5, 1.0, 0.8),
                   (0.75, 0.0, 0.0), (1.0, 0.0, 0.0))}
cdict4 = {'red': ((0.0, 0.0, 0.5), (0.5, 0.8, 1.0), (0.75, 1.0, 1.0),
                  (1.0, 0.9, 1.0)),
          'green': ((0.0, 0.0, 0.5), (0.25, 0.75, 0.0), (0.5, 0.9,
                     0.9), (1.0, 0.0, 0.0)),
          'blue': ((0.0, 0.0, 0.4), (0.25, 1.0, 1.0), (0.75, 0.0, 0.0),
```

```
                    (1.0, 0.0, 0.0)),
        'alpha': ((0.0, 1.0, 1.0), (0.5, 0.4, 0.4), (1.0, 0.7, 1.0)) }
```

The following code block plots four colormaps, using four color dictionaries as defined previously. It is similar to what we have seen in the case of discrete colormaps.

Read the `Iris` dataset and the map class names of the numeric codes:

```
iris = pd.read_csv('iris_dataset.csv', delimiter=',')
iris['species'] = iris['species'].map({"setosa" : 0, "versicolor" : 1,
                                "virginica" : 2})
```

Define the figure, layout, size, and adjust the space in between the plots:

```
fig, axs = plt.subplots(1,4, figsize=(16,6))
fig.subplots_adjust(left=0.0, bottom=0.0, right=0.95, top=0.94,
                wspace=0.4)
```

Define a function to plot the charts:

```
def plot_graph(name, dictionary, axs, cbaxs):
    custom = LinearSegmentedColormap(name, dictionary)
    im = axs.scatter(iris.petal_length, iris.petal_width,
s=100*iris.petal_length*iris.petal_width,
                    c=iris.species, cmap=custom)
    caxs = plt.axes(cbaxs) # left, bottom, width and height
    fig.colorbar(im, caxs)
```

Plot the graphs for each of the color combinations, and display it on the screen:

```
plot_graph('custom1', cdict1, axs[0], [0.2, 0.01, 0.01, 0.93])
plot_graph('custom2', cdict2, axs[1], [0.45, 0.01, 0.01, 0.93])
plot_graph('custom3', cdict3, axs[2], [0.7, 0.01, 0.01, 0.93])
plot_graph('custom4', cdict4, axs[3], [0.97, 0.01, 0.01, 0.93])
plt.show()
```

Here is what the output plots look like:

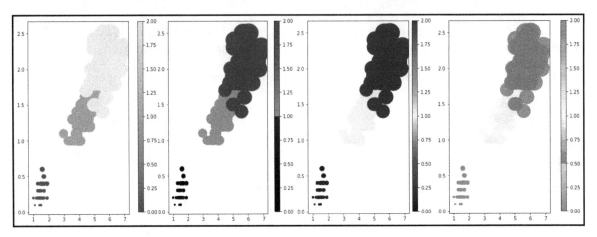

Working with legend

The legend is the description of each of the graphs on a given axes. Each axis has its own legend. Matplotlib provides many different ways in which a legend can be specified. We will cover as many combinations as possible, though we wont be able to cover a complete set of possibilities in this book.

Getting ready

Import the following required libraries:

```
import matplotlib as plt
import numpy as np
import matplotlib.patches as mpatches
from numpy.random import randn
```

How to do it...

The following code block plots 11 different ways a legend can be specified:

1. Set the seed for repeatability and define the figure with its size:

```
np.random.seed(19681211)
plt.figure(figsize=(15, 10))
```

2. Plot the first graph with an inline label:

```
plt.subplot(3,4,1)
line, = plt.plot([1, 2, 3], label='Inline label')
plt.legend()
```

3. Plot the second graph with the legend, using the `set_label` method:

```
plt.subplot(3,4,2)
line, = plt.plot([1, 2, 3])
line.set_label('Label via method')
plt.legend()
```

4. Plot the third graph with two lines, and the legend with a list of labels:

```
plt.subplot(3,4,3)
plt.plot([1, 2, 3])
plt.plot([3, 2, 1])
plt.legend(['Positive Slope', 'Negative Slope'])
plt.title('List of Labels')
```

5. Plot the fourth graph with three lines, and the legend with handles and labels:

```
plt.subplot(3,4,4)
line1, = plt.plot([1, 2, 3])
line2, = plt.plot([3, 2, 1])
line3, = plt.plot([2,2])
plt.legend((line3, line2, line1), ('Zero Slope', 'Negative Slope',
            'Positive Slope'),title='Legend', title_fontsize=15,
            fontsize='x-small', loc=9)
plt.title('Handles and Labels')
```

6. Plot the fifth graph with three lines and legend with a partial list of handles:

```
plt.subplot(3,4,5)
line_up, = plt.plot([1,2,3], label='Line 2')
line_down, = plt.plot([3,2,1], label='Line 1')
line_3, = plt.plot([2,3,4], label='no label')
plt.legend(handles=[line_up, line_down])
plt.title('Labels for given handles')
```

7. Plot the sixth graph with three lines and a partial list of handles and labels:

```
plt.subplot(3,4,6)
line_up, = plt.plot([1,2,3], label='Line 2')
line_down, = plt.plot([3,2,1], label='Line 1')
line_3, = plt.plot([2,3,4], label='no label')
plt.legend([line_up, line_down], ['Line Up', 'Line Down'])
plt.title('partial handles & labels')
```

8. Plot the seventh graph with a patch as a label:

```
plt.subplot(3,4,7)
red_patch = mpatches.Patch(color='red', label='The red data')
plt.legend(handles=[red_patch])
plt.title('Patch as a label')
```

9. Plot the eighth graph with category labels in the legend:

```
plt.subplot(3,4,8)
z = randn(10)
blue_dot, = plt.plot(z, "bo", markersize=15)

# Put a white cross over some of the data.
white_cross, = plt.plot(z[:5], "w+", markeredgewidth=3,
                        markersize=15)
plt.legend([blue_dot, (blue_dot, white_cross)], ["Attr A", "Attr
          A+B"])
plt.title('category labels')
```

10. Plot the ninth graph with the legend on top of the figure in two columns:

```
plt.subplot(3,4,9)
plt.plot([1, 2, 3], label="test1")
plt.plot([3, 2, 1], label="test2")

# Place a legend above this subplot, expanding itself to
# fully use the given bounding box.
plt.legend(bbox_to_anchor=(0, 1.02, 1., .102), #left, bottom,
width,
                                              height
          ncol=2, mode="expand", borderaxespad=0.5)
ax = plt.gca()
ax.set_title('Legend on top', pad=20)
```

11. Plot the tenth graph with the legend on the right side of the figure:

```
plt.subplot(3,4,10)
plt.plot([1, 2, 3], label="test1")
plt.plot([3, 2, 1], label="test2")

# Place a legend to the right of this smaller subplot.
plt.legend(bbox_to_anchor=(1.02, 1.0), borderaxespad=0)
plt.title('Legend on right')
```

12. Plot the eleventh graph with the legend split into multiple places on the figure:

```
plt.subplot(3,4,11)
line1, = plt.plot([1, 2, 3], label="Line 1", linestyle='--')
line2, = plt.plot([3, 2, 1], label="Line 2", linewidth=4)

# Create a legend for the first line.
first_legend = plt.legend(handles=[line1], loc=1)

# Add the legend manually to the current Axes. Repeated calls to
plt.legend()
# will overwrite previous calls, so only last one remains
ax = plt.gca().add_artist(first_legend)

# Create another legend for the second line.
plt.legend(handles=[line2], loc=4)
plt.title('Split Legend')
```

13. Blank out the twelfth plot space:

```
plt.subplot(3,4,12)
plt.axis('off')
```

14. Adjust the space in between the plots, and display the figure on the screen:

```
plt.tight_layout(w_pad=5, h_pad=5)
plt.show()
```

How it works...

Here is the explanation for each of the eleven plots:

- **Plot1**: Label is specified as part of the line plot itself.
- **Plot2**: Label is specified as a method on the line axes, after the line object is created.

- **Plot3**: Labels are defined as a list on the `plt.legend()` command itself.
- **Plot4**: Handles (axes objects) and labels are passed on as tuples to the `plt.legend()` function. Latest 3.0.0 version allows to include legend title, fontsize for title as well as label text, which we have used in this case
- **Plot5**: Only two out of three handles are passed on to `plt.legend()`, so `line_3` is not shown in the legend.
- **Plot6**: Similar to plot five, but both handles and labels are passed on to the `plt.legend()`.
- **Plot7**: A patch is used as a label. `mpatches.Patch()` creates a red patch.
- **Plot8**: Plots two different categories of data and labels them separately.
- **Plot9**: Plots the legend on top of the plot, with labels spreading from left to right, and not overlapping with the title. `plt.legend(bbox_to_anchor=(0, 1.02, 1., .102), ncol=2, mode="expand", borderaxespad=0.5)` places labels on top of the plot using `bbox_to_anchor` (0 from left, 1.02 from bottom, 1.0 is the width, and 0.102 is height, in proportion to the plot's dimensions). `ncol=2` specifies that labels should be placed in two columns, as opposed to two rows, which is the default.
- **Plot10**: Legend is placed on the right side of the plot, again using `bbox_to_anchor()` co-ordinates.
- **Plot11**: Splits the label into two parts and places them at different locations. Multiple calls to `plt.legend()` will overwrite previous legends; only the last one will prevail, so it can't be used to split and place the labels at different locations. One of them has to be placed manually with `ax=plt.gca().add_artist(first_legend).plt.gca()` getting the current axes, and then `add_artist()` adding the label on to this axis. For the second label, use the standard `plt.legend()`.
- **Plot12**: Since there is no twelfth part, we have to clean up spines, ticks, and ticklabels. Otherwise, they will show up without any plot! We will learn about spines and ticks soon in this chapter.

Here are how the plots look with the respective legends:

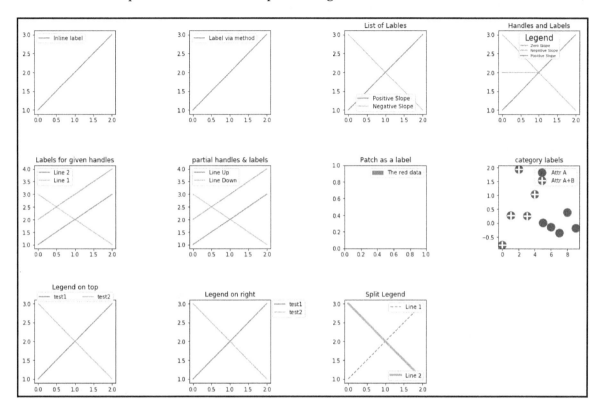

There's more...

One more very common option to use the legend is with `loc` argument on `plt.legend()`. This argument can take the codes 0 to 10 to specify different locations on the plot. Each of them also has a text description, which can be found on the Matplotlib documentation (https://matplotlib.org/api/legend_api.html?highlight=legend#module-matplotlib. legend).

The following is the sample code for two of the possible options:

```
plt.legend(loc='best') or plt.legend(loc=0)
plt.legend(loc='upper right') or plt.legend(loc=1)
```

Customizing labels and titles

In this recipe, we will learn how to customize axis labels, ticklabels, plots, and figure titles. For some of these customizations, we will set the `plt.rcParams` default parameters. However, these settings will be active and apply for all the plots in the session.

Getting ready

Let's import the required libraries and set up `plt.rcParams()`, which is also required for this recipe. These settings will be applicable to all the plots drawn in this session:

```
import matplotlib.pyplot as plt
import numpy as np

plt.rcParams['figure.titlesize'] = 15
plt.rcParams['legend.fontsize'] = 12
plt.rcParams['axes.labelsize'] = 12
plt.rcParams['axes.labelweight'] = 'bold'
plt.rcParams['xtick.labelsize'] = 12
plt.rcParams['ytick.labelsize'] = 12
```

How to do it...

The following code block draws three plots with various labels to demonstrate how these can be customized:

1. Define the figure, layout, and size, with adequate space in between the plots:

```
fig, ax = plt.subplots(1, 3, figsize=(10,4))
fig.subplots_adjust(wspace=0.7)
```

2. Plot a histogram on the first axis with customized labels and title:

```
ax[0].hist(np.random.randn(1000))
ax[0].set(xlabel='Bins', ylabel='Frequency')
atitle = ax[0].set_title('Histogram', fontstyle='italic',
                         fontsize=14)
plt.setp(atitle,color='blue')
```

3. Plot a bar graph on the second axis:

```
# Plot the bars for men's data
menMue = [3, 10, 100, 500, 50]
menSigma = [0.75, 2.5, 25, 125, 12.5]
index = np.arange(len(menMue)) # the x locations for the groups
width = 0.35                    # the width of the bars
p1 = ax[1].bar(index, menMue, width, color='r', bottom=0,
               yerr=menSigma)

# Plot the bars for women's data
womenMue = [1000, 3, 30, 800, 1]
womenSigma = [500, 0.75, 8, 200, 0.25]
p2 = ax[1].bar(index + width, womenMue, width, color='y', bottom=0,
               yerr=womenSigma)

# customize title and labels for the figure
atitle = ax[1].set_title('Scores by category and gender',
                         fontstyle='italic', fontsize=14)
plt.setp(atitle,color='blue')
ax[1].set(xticks=(index + width / 2), xticklabels=('C1', 'C2',
'C3',
                 'C4', 'C5'), yscale='log')
ax[1].legend((p1[0], p2[0]), ('Men', 'Women'), bbox_to_anchor=
             (1.05,1))
```

4. Plot a scatter plot on the third axis:

```
ax[2].scatter(np.random.rand(100),np.random.rand(100),
              s=100*np.random.rand(100)*np.random.rand(100))
atitle = ax[2].set_title('Scatter Plot', fontstyle='italic',
                         fontsize=14)
plt.setp(atitle,color='blue')
```

5. Set the title for the figure:

```
ftitle= plt.suptitle('Figure Title', fontname='arial', fontsize=20,
                     fontweight='bold')
plt.setp(ftitle,color='green')
```

6. Adjust the space between the plots and display the figure on the screen:

```
plt.tight_layout(pad=3, w_pad=5)
plt.show()
```

How it works...

Here is the explanation of how it works:

- `fig, ax = plt.subplots(1, 3, figsize=(10,4))` defines the figure layout.
- `fig.subplots_adjust(wspace=0.5)` adjusts the space in between the subplots.
- `ax[0].hist(np.random.randn(1000))` plots the histogram on axes 0, followed by labels for the X and Y axes, then title for the plot.
- `ax[0].set_title()` includes font style and size arguments apart from the title text, but it does not have the color argument; hence, we use `plt.setp(atitle,color='blue')` to set the color for the title.
- `plt.rcParams['axes.labelsize'] = 10` and `plt.rcParams['axes.labelweight'] = 'bold'` set the font size and weight for x and y axes labels for all the plots. Here, we have labels only for the first plot, hence, they are shown in bold with a `fontsize` of 10.
- `p1` and `p2` are the bar plots on axis one for men and women. `ax[1].set_xticks(ind + width / 2)` sets the ticks followed by `ax[1].set_xticklabels(('C1', 'C2', 'C3', 'C4', 'C5'))`, setting `ticklabels` on the x axis. For the y axis, we are using default ticks and `ticklabels` as applicable for a logarithmic scale. Typically, we override `ticklables` for categorical variables to give meaningful names.
- Finally, `plt.suptitle()` and `plt.setp()` define the title for the overall figure for a given font name, size, and color.
- `plt.tight_layout(pad=3)` adjusts the space between plots, and `pad=3` adjusts the space between the figure title and the individual plot titles so that there is no overlap between them.

We get the output as follows:

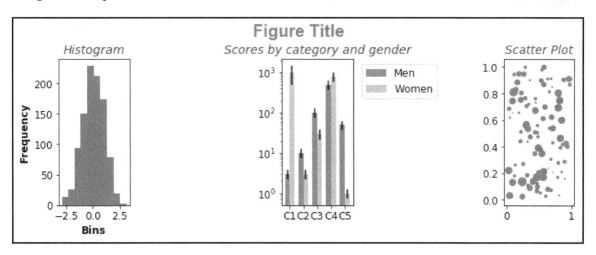

There's more...

There are quite a number of possibilities with various combinations of options available for fonts, `fontstyle`, `fontsize`, `fontweight`, and the font color applied to axes labels, ticklabels, axes titles, and the figure title. Taking advantage of all these features, we can plot professional quality visualizations.

Using autoscale and axis limits

Matplotlib automatically fits the complete data range in the input data for both the x and the y axis, splits it into bins, and displays ticks and ticklabels accordingly. At times, we may want to see a specific range of data more closely on either of the axes, instead of a complete range of data. In this recipe, we will learn how to do this.

Getting ready

Let's import the required libraries:

```
import numpy as np
import matplotlib.pylab as plt
from matplotlib.ticker import FuncFormatter
```

How to do it...

The following code displays two plots for the same input data, but the first one uses default settings so it displays a full range of data on both the x and the y axes, whereas the second plot limits both the x and y axes range:

1. Prepare the data for the graph:

```
x = np.linspace(-50,50,500)
y = x**2 + np.cos(x)*100
```

2. Define a function to format numeric data before printing on the plot:

```
def Num_Format(x, pos):
    """The two arguments are the number and tick position"""
    if x >= 1e6:
        string = '${:1.1f}M'.format(x*1e-6)
    else:
        string = '${:1.0f}K'.format(x*1e-3)
    return string
```

3. Apply the function defined earlier to the `formatter`, and define the figure with size and layout:

```
formatter = FuncFormatter(Num_Format)
fig, axs = plt.subplots(1,2, figsize=(8,5))
```

4. Plot a line graph on the first axis with autoscale:

```
axs[0].plot(x, y**2)
axs[0].yaxis.set_major_formatter(formatter)
axs[0].set_title('Full Data/Autoscale')
```

5. Plot the same graph again with limits applied on both the x and y axis:

```
axs[1].plot(x, y**2)
axs[1].set(xlim=(-5,5), ylim=(0,10000), title='X and Y limited')
axs[1].yaxis.set_major_formatter(formatter)
```

6. Display the figure on the screen:

```
plt.show()
```

How it works...

- `x = np.linspace(-50,50,500)` creates 500 points with equal distance between them ranging from -50 to +50 for *x* axis co-ordinates.
- `def Num_Format(x, pos)` is a function to format large numeric numbers into $K or $M based on whether the number is in the thousand or the millions. `FuncFormatter(Num_Format)` is a matplotlib function that takes the user-defined function currency as an argument, and this `FuncFormatter` is then applied to the *x* or *y* axis on which numbers are to be formatted, using `axs[0].yaxis.set_major_formatter(formatter)`.
- `axs[0].plot(x, y**2)` plots the graph on axes 0, using default settings for the *x* and *y* axes, so it displays a full range of data from the input.
- `axs[1].plot(x, y**2)` plots the same graph again on axis one.
- `axs[1].set_xlim(-5,5)` sets the data limit from -5 to +5 on the *x* axis, and `axs[1].set_ylim(0,10000)` sets the data limit from *0 to 10,000* on the *y* axis. These limits are set to the plot on axis one.

You should get the two plots as shown here:

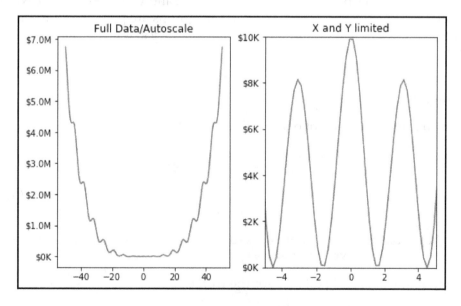

Customizing ticks and ticklabels

So far, we have seen Matplotlib automatically placing ticks and ticklabels based on input data. In this recipe, we will learn how to customize these default settings on both the *x* and *y* axes for categorical and numerical variables.

Getting ready

Let's import the required libraries:

```
import numpy as np
import matplotlib.pyplot as plt
from matplotlib.ticker import (MultipleLocator, FormatStrFormatter,
                               AutoMinorLocator)
from matplotlib.ticker import FuncFormatter
```

How to do it...

The following code blocks plot two bar graphs for men and women. On the *y* axis, the average salary is plotted, and on the *x* axis, various groups are plotted within the men and women categories. So, we have a numeric variable on the *y* axis and a categorical variable on the *x* axis.

The following code block uses default settings for ticks and ticklabels on the *y* axis, but uses custom settings for the *x* axis:

1. Set up the data and plot bars for the men's data:

```
menMue = [3, 10, 100, 500, 50]
menSigma = [0.75, 2.5, 25, 125, 12.5]

fig, ax = plt.subplots()
ind = np.arange(len(menMue)) # the x locations for the groups
width = 0.35                  # the width of the bars
p1 = ax.bar(ind, menMue, width, color='lightblue', bottom=0,
            yerr=menSigma)
```

2. Set up the data and plot bars for the women's data:

```
womenMue = [1000, 3, 30, 800, 1]
womenSigma = [250, 0.75, 8, 200, 0.25]
p2 = ax.bar(ind + width, womenMue, width, color='orange', bottom=0,
            yerr=womenSigma)
```

3. Set the title, labels, and legend for the figure:

```
ax.set_title('Scores by group and gender')
ax.set(xticks=(ind + width / 2), xticklabels=('C1', 'C2', 'C3',
                              'C4', 'C5'), yscale='log')
ax.legend((p1[1], p2[1]), ('Men', 'Women'), bbox_to_anchor=(1.3,1))
```

4. Display the figure on the screen:

```
plt.show()
```

How it works...

Here is the explanation for the code:

- `ax.set_xticks(ind + width / 2)` sets where exactly each tick is to be placed on *x* axis. Since `ind` is defined based on the men's data, it would place the ticks in the middle of the men's bars (light blue), and by adding *width/2* to each of those indices we are moving the ticks to in-between the two bars.
- `ax.set_xticklabels(('C1', 'C2', 'C3', 'C4', 'C5'))` sets ticklabels on the *x* axis:

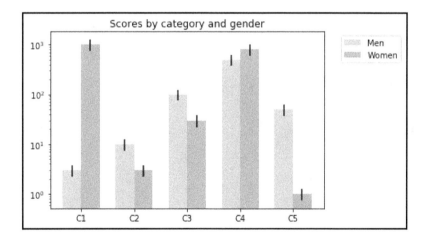

There's more...

Let's take one more example of how to customize the size, length, and color of ticks. The following code block displays three plots; the first one uses default settings for ticks and ticklabels, and the second one is customized to display major and minor ticks, and the third one is customized to specify the length, thickness, and color of the major and minor ticks:

1. Define the function for formatting numeric data:

```
def Num_Format(x, pos):
 """The two arguments are the number and tick position"""
 if x >= 1e6:
     string = '${:1.1f}M'.format(x*1e-6)
 else:
     string = '${:1.0f}K'.format(x*1e-3)
 return string
```

2. Define a function to plot the graph:

```
def plot_graph(axes, axis, major_step_size, minor_step_size):
    majorLocator = MultipleLocator(major_step_size)
    minorLocator = MultipleLocator(minor_step_size)
    if axis == 'x':
        axes.xaxis.set_major_locator(majorLocator)
        axes.xaxis.set_minor_locator(minorLocator)
    else:
        axes.yaxis.set_major_locator(majorLocator)
        axes.yaxis.set_minor_locator(minorLocator)
```

3. Set up the data for the plot:

```
x = np.linspace(-50,50,500)
y = x**2 + np.cos(x)*100
```

4. Define the figure, layout, and size with adjustment for space in between the plots:

```
fig, axs = plt.subplots(1,3, figsize=(15,5))
fig.subplots_adjust(wspace=0.25)
```

5. Plot the graph with the `formatter` applied to the y axis:

```
formatter = FuncFormatter(Num_Format)
axs[0].plot(x, y**2)
axs[0].set_title('Default Ticks and Ticklabels')
axs[0].yaxis.set_major_formatter(formatter)
```

6. Plot the line graph on the second axis with major and minor ticks:

```
axs[1].plot(x, y**2)
plot_graph(axs[1], 'y', 500000, 250000)
plot_graph(axs[1], 'x', 10, 2)
axs[1].set_title('Major and Minor Ticks')
axs[1].ticklabel_format(style='sci', scilimits=(3, 3), axis='y')
```

7. Plot the line graph on axis three with customized ticks and ticklabels:

```
axs[2].plot(x, y**2)
plot_graph(axs[2], 'x', 10, 2)
minorLocator = AutoMinorLocator()
axs[2].xaxis.set_minor_locator(minorLocator)
axs[2].ticklabel_format(style='sci', scilimits=(6, 6), axis='y')
axs[2].tick_params(which='major', length=10, color='g')
axs[2].tick_params(which='minor', length=4, color='r')
axs[2].tick_params(which='both', width=2)
axs[2].set_title('Customised Ticks')
axs[2].grid(True)
```

8. Display the figure on the screen:

```
plt.show()
```

Here is the explanation of the code and how it works:

- The first plot on axis zero, uses default settings, and it automatically chooses one million bins for the *y* axis, and 20 unit bins for the *x* axis, and places ticks and ticklabels accordingly.
- `formatter = FuncFormatter(Num_Format)` defines the custom formatting function for large numbers, and `axs[0].yaxis.set_major_formatter(formatter)` applies this custom defined function to first plot y axis
- The second plot on axis one, `majorLocator = MultipleLocator(500000)`, specifies that major ticks should be placed at `500000` intervals, and `axs[1].yaxis.set_major_locator(majorLocator)` sets this interval on the *y* axis major tick.
- `axs[1].ticklabel_format(style='sci', scilimits=(3, 3), axis='y')` sets formatting options given by Matplotlib 3.0.0 for y axis. `scilimits=(3,3)` specifies that units should be displayed in thousands(1e3)
- The same process is repeated for the *x* axis with `10` unit bins for major ticks and `2` units for minor ticks.

- `axs[2].ticklabel_format(style='sci', scilimits=(6, 6), axis='y')` sets predefined formatting options. Units should be displayed in millions(1e6) on y axis.
- The third plot is similar to the second one, limiting minor ticks only to the *x* axis, and the addition of setting length, width, and color for both major and minor ticks. `tick_params()` sets these parameters, with the argument `which=` specifying major, minor, or both ticks to be applied.

Here is the generated output for the preceding code:

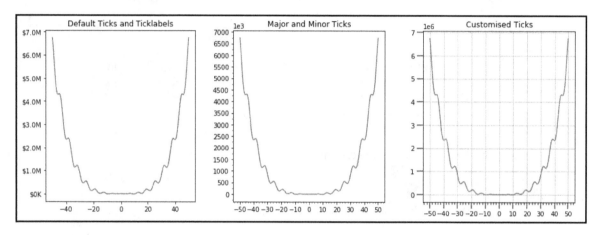

Customizing spines

Matplotlib, by default, displays all four spines at the top, bottom, left and right of the plot, creating a boundary box around it. It displays ticks and ticklabels only on the left (*y* axis) and the bottom (*x* axis). However, it allows us to customize their placement and also omit any of the spines, as required.

Getting ready

We will plot six graphs with the same data, but setting various options for spines.

Import the following required libraries:

```
import numpy as np
import matplotlib.pyplot as plt
```

How to do it...

The following code block displays six plots with the same data, but with different options for spines:

1. Set up the data for the plot:

```
theta = np.linspace(0, 2*np.pi, 128)
y = np.sin(theta)
```

2. Define the figure with its size:

```
fig = plt.figure(figsize=(8,6))
```

3. Define the first axes and plot the sin wave with default spines:

```
ax1 = fig.add_subplot(2, 3, 1)
ax1.plot(theta, np.sin(theta), 'b-*')
ax1.set_title('default spines')
```

4. Define the function to plot a graph:

```
def plot_graph(axs, title, lposition, bposition):
    ax = fig.add_subplot(axs)
    ax.plot(theta, y, 'b-*')
    ax.set_title(title)
    ax.spines['left'].set_position(lposition)
    ax.spines['right'].set_visible(False)
    ax.spines['bottom'].set_position(bposition)
    ax.spines['top'].set_visible(False)
    ax.xaxis.set_ticks_position('bottom')
    ax.yaxis.set_ticks_position('left')
```

5. Plot five graphs with different position of spines:

```
plot_graph(232, 'centered spines', 'center', 'center')
plot_graph(233, 'zeroed spines', 'zero', 'zero')
plot_graph(234, 'spines at axes [0.25, 0.75]', ('axes', 0.25),
           ('axes', 0.75))
plot_graph(235, 'spines at data [1.0, -1.0]', ('data', 1.0),
           ('data', -1.0))
plot_graph(236, 'adjusted spines',('outward', 10),('outward', 10))
```

6. Adjust space in between the plots and display the figure on the screen:

```
plt.tight_layout()
plt.show()
```

How it works...

- Plot 1 uses default settings for spines. So, it displays all four spines, with the left and bottom ones representing the y and x axes with appropriate ticks and ticklabels.
- In plot 2, the top and right spines are made invisible using the `set_visible(False)` method. `set_position('center')` positions the x and y axes in between the corresponding data range. In this case, data on the y axis ranges from -1 to +1, so the center point is 0, and the x axis data ranges from 0 to 6, so the center point is 3. So, the intersection point is (3, 0).
- Plot 3 places left and bottom spines in such a way that they intersect at (0, 0).
- Plot 4 places left and bottom spines in such a way that they intersect at 0.25* range on x axis and 0.75* range on y axis. [0.25, 0.75] is 0.25 * x-range = 0.25 *(0 to 6) = 1.5, 0.75 * y-range = 0.75 * (-1 to 1) = 0.5. So, the intersection point is (1.5, 0.5). The `axes` option basically sets the bottom 25% (first quartile) on the x axis and the bottom 75% (third quartile) on y axis.
- In plot 5, we use the `data` option to specify the position in the input data. So, it places the left and bottom spines to intersect at (1, -1).
- In plot 6, we place the spines away from the graph using the `outward` argument by a specified number of units; here, it is 10:

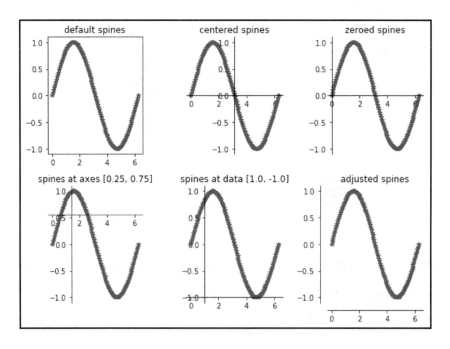

Twin axes

Sometimes, we may want to plot two charts on the same axes, but have a different scale of data. If we use a standard plot with the same scale on the left and right spines, charts may not look right due to a large difference in their scale of data. In such cases, we can use the twin axes feature provided by Matplotlib. We will learn how to use it in this recipe.

We will use product defects data for a month in a manufacturing plant for this example. We will draw a bar plot of the number of defects by reason code (for example 0 to 5, representing various reasons for producing defective products) and cumulative percentage line graph (sum total of defective products aggregated over reason codes).

There are three options for twinning the axes:

- `twinx`: Shares the *x* axis for both the graphs, while the left and right axes denote two different scales
- `twiny`: Shares the *y* axis for both the graphs, while the top and bottom axis denote two scales
- `no sharing`: Where the bottom and the left axis are used by one graph, and the top and right axis are used by the second graph

We will learn how to implement all three possibilities in this recipe.

Getting ready

We will use product defects data in a manufacturing plant for a given month. It has a defect reason code and a number of defects. So, we will plot a bar graph for the number of defects by the defect reason code, and a line plot for cumulative defects as a percentage of the total defects. Obviously, the range of data for number of defects and cumulative percentage will vary significantly, so a common *y* axis does not give the right picture of data. Twinning the axes comes to the rescue in such situations.

We will plot two different plots; one using `twinx()` and the other using `twiny()` in this section. We will learn how to plot the third option of `no sharing` of any axis in the *There's more...* section of this recipe.

Import the required libraries:

```
import matplotlib.pyplot as plt
from matplotlib.ticker import MultipleLocator
```

How to do it...

Here are the steps involved in plotting the required graphs:

1. Prepare the data for the plots:

```
x = [0, 1, 2, 3, 4, 5]
y = [19, 12, 6, 4, 3, 2]
y1 = [41, 67, 80, 89, 96, 100]
```

2. Define the figure and required axes, including twin axes:

```
fig = plt.figure(figsize=(10,6))

ax1 = plt.subplot(121)        # first plot
ax2 = ax1.twinx()             # share x axis

ax3 = plt.subplot(122)        # second plot
ax4 = ax3.twiny()             # share y axis
```

3. Plot the bar and line graphs using the `twinx()` option:

```
b = ax1.bar(x, y, label='Number of Defects')
l, = ax2.plot(x, y1, color='g', lw=5, label='Cumulative Defects as
          %')
```

4. Set the labels and legend for the first plot:

```
majorLocator = MultipleLocator(2)
ax1.yaxis.set_major_locator(majorLocator)
ax1.set(xlabel='Defect Reason Codes', ylabel='Number of Defects')
ax2.set(ylabel='Cumulative Defects as %')
ax1.legend([b, l],['Number of Defects','Cumulative Defects as %'],
          loc=5)
```

5. Plot the bar and line graphs using the `twiny()` option:

```
b1 = ax3.barh(x, y, label='Number of Defects')
l1, = ax4.plot(y1, x, color='g', lw=5, label='Cumulative Defects as
          %')
```

6. Set the labels and legend for the second plot:

```
ax3.xaxis.set_major_locator(majorLocator)
ax3.set(xlabel='Number of Defects', ylabel='Defect Reason Codes')
ax4.set(xlabel='Cumulative Defects as %')
ax3.legend([b1, l1], ['Number of Defects', 'Cumulative Defects as
                       %'], loc=1)
ax3.set_ylim(-1,6)
```

7. Print the title for the figure and adjust the space in between the two plots:

```
plt.suptitle('Product Defects - August 2018', fontname='arial',
             fontsize=20,
             fontweight='bold')
plt.tight_layout(w_pad=5, pad=3)
```

8. Display the figure on the screen:

```
plt.show()
```

How it works...

Here is the explanation for the preceding code:

- `x = [0, 1, 2, 3, 4, 5]` is the list of product defect codes, `y = [19, 12, 6, 4, 3, 2]` is the list of number of defects for each of the defect codes in a given month, and `y1 = [41, 67, 80, 89, 96, 100]` is the list of cumulative defects as a percentage of total defects.
- `ax1 = plt.subplot(121)` defines the main axes for the first plot, and `121` represents that it is the first plot in the 1 x 2 grid.
- `ax2 = ax1.twinx()` defines the twin axes for the first plot. It does not create another axis physically, but uses the main axes only, and uses the right spine as the *y* axis for this new logical axes `ax2`, sharing the bottom spine as the *x* axis for both `ax1` and `ax2`.
- `ax3 = plt.subplot(121)` defines the main axes for the second plot, and `122` represents that it is the second plot in a 1 x 2 grid.
- `ax4 = ax3.twinx()` defines the twin axes for the second plot. Again, it does not create another axes physically, but uses the main axes only, and uses the right spine as the *y* axis for this new logical axes `ax4`, sharing the bottom spine as the *x* axis for both `ax3` and `ax4`.

- `b = ax1.bar(x, y, label='Number of Defects')` plots the bar graph, defect codes versus the number of defects.
- `l, = ax2.plot(x, y1, color='g', lw=5, label='Cumulative Defects as %')` plots a line graph: defect codes versus cumulative defects %.
- `majorLocator = MultipleLocator(2)` defines the major ticks to have step of 2.
- `ax1.yaxis.set_major_locator(majorLocator)` applies the major locator to y axis of the main axis of the first plot.
- `ax1.set(xlabel='Defect Reason Codes', ylabel='Number of Defects')` sets x and y axis labels for the main axes.
- `ax2.set(ylabel='Cumulative Defects as %')` sets the `ylabel` for twin axes and since x axis is shared; no label here again.
- `ax1.legend([b, l], ['Number of Defects', 'Cumulative Defects as %'], loc=5)` sets the legend for the main axes:
  - `[b,l]` is the list of handles for bar graph and line graph, respectively.
  - `['Number of Defects', 'Cumulative Defects as %']` is the list of labels for the bar graph and line graph, respectively.
  - `loc=5` specifies that the legend should be placed at the center of the axis with right alignment.
- `b1 = ax3.bar(x, y, label='Number of Defects')` plots the bar graph, defect codes versus the number of defects.
- `l1, = ax4.plot(x, y1, color='g', lw=5, label='Cumulative Defects as %')` plots the line graph, defect codes versus the cumulative defects %.
- `majorLocator = MultipleLocator(2)` defines the major ticks to have a steps of 2.
- `ax3.yaxis.set_major_locator(majorLocator)` applies the major locator to the y axis of main axes of the first plot.
- `ax3.set(xlabel='Defect Reason Codes', ylabel='Number of Defects')` sets the x and y axis labels for the main axes.
- `ax4.set(ylabel='Cumulative Defects as %')` sets the `ylabel` for twin axes and, since the x axis is shared, there is no label here again.
- `ax3.legend([b1, l1], ['Number of Defects', 'Cumulative Defects as %'], loc=1)` sets the legend for the main axes of the second plot.

- `ax3.set_ylim(-1,6)` sets the lower and upper limits for the *y* axis of the main axes of the second plot.
- `plt.suptitle('Product Defects - August 2018', fontname='arial', fontsize=20, fontweight='bold')` plots the title for the overall figure with various attributes such as font name, size, and weight.
- `plt.tight_layout(w_pad=5, pad=3)` adjusts the space between the plots so that there are no overlaps:
  - `w_pad=5` specifies the amount of gap between two plots.
  - `pad=3` specifies the amount space at the top of the figure to make room for the title.
- `plt.show()` displays the figure on the screen.

Upon running the preceding code, you should see the following figure on your screen:

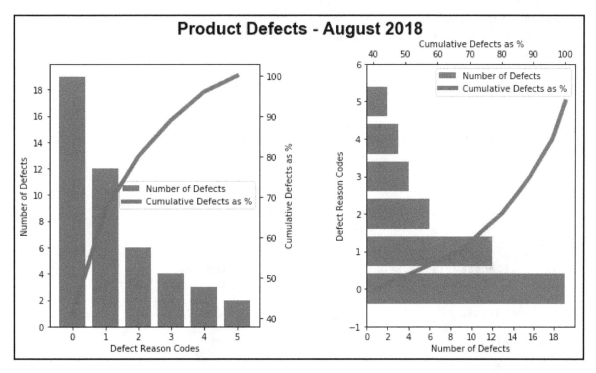

There's more...

We have learned how to use twin axes features for sharing the x and y axes individually. Now, let's look at the option of not sharing either of the axes, but using the left and bottom spines for one graph and the top and right spines for the other graph. All four spines use different scales, so there are different `ticks` and `ticklabels`.

We will use the familiar `Iris` dataset for this example. As we know, there are four attributes: `petal_width`, `petal_leangth`, `sepal_width`, and `sepal_length`. So, as we have seen many times in this book, when we plot a scatter plot with `petal_width` and `petal_length`, we see three distinct clusters, but when we plot a scatter plot using `sepal_length` and `sepal_width`, we don't observe any such clusters.

Here is the code required to plot this. Since we have seen this many times earlier, we will not explain it here line by line. The only difference here is `ax1 = ax.twinx().twiny()`. Instead of using `twinx()` or `twiny()`, we use both so that the top and right axes will be used for this new logical axes (`ax1`), whereas the left and bottom axes will be used by the main axes (`ax`):

```python
import matplotlib.pyplot as plt
import pandas as pd

iris = pd.read_csv('iris_dataset.csv', delimiter=',')
iris['species'] = iris['species'].map({"setosa" : 0, "versicolor" : 1,
                                        "virginica" : 2})

plt.figure(figsize=(8,6))
ax = plt.subplot(111)
h1 = ax.scatter(iris.petal_width, iris.petal_length,
s=5*iris.petal_width*iris.petal_length, c='b')

ax1 = ax.twinx().twiny()
h2 = ax1.scatter(iris.sepal_width, iris.sepal_length,
                 s=5*iris.sepal_width*iris.sepal_length, c='g')

ax.legend([h1, h2], ['petals', 'sepals'], loc='best')

plt.show()
```

Upon running the preceding code, you should see the following figure on your screen:

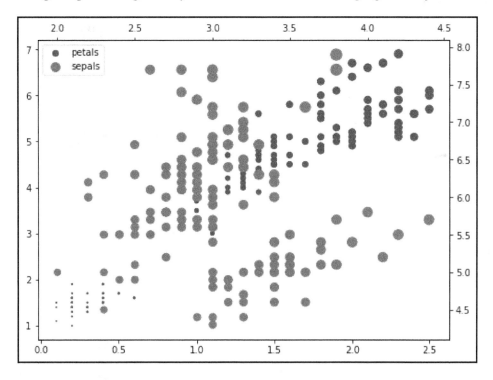

As can be seen from the plot, blue dots that are plotted using petal width and length do form three distinct clusters, whereas green dots plotted with sepal width and length scatter all over without any specific pattern!

Please also note the scale of data on each of the four axes. All of them have a different scale!

Using hatch

Hatch is used to fill a pattern in a specified area. We will learn how to use it in this recipe.

Getting ready

Import the required libraries:

```
import matplotlib.pyplot as plt
import numpy as np
```

How to do it...

The following code block creates five charts that represent a tie, with different colors and patterns printed on them:

```
# Set up the data
x = np.array([0.2, 0.4, 0.6, 0.8, 0.5])
y = [1, 6, 6, 1, 0]

# Plot a tie graph 5 times with different colors and hatches
plt.fill(x+1, y, facecolor='g', edgecolor='k', hatch='+*')
plt.fill(x+2, y, facecolor='b', edgecolor='k', hatch='-o')
plt.fill(x+3, y, facecolor='y', edgecolor='k', hatch='+x')
plt.fill(x+4, y, facecolor='r', edgecolor='k', hatch='\\')
plt.fill(x+5, y, facecolor='m', edgecolor='k', hatch='Ox')
plt.title('Hatch Demo')

plt.show()
```

How it works...

x and y are lists representing five points on two-dimensional space. The area covered by these five points creates a tie. It is filled with a color and a pattern using a hatch argument in the plt.fill() method:

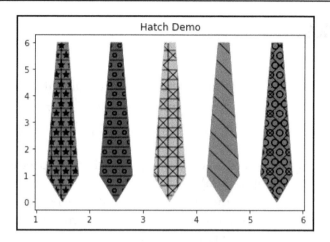

Using annotation

Annotation is used to describe specific details on the plot, by pointing to the area being described in text. We will cover a simple example in the recipe. A more elaborate description is covered in later chapters.

Getting ready

Import the required libraries:

```
import matplotlib.pyplot as plt
import numpy as np
```

How to do it...

The following code block displays a plot on which a point (3, 0) is annotated with an arrow:

```
plt.plot(theta, np.sin(theta), 'b-*')
a = plt.annotate("(3,0)", xy=(3, 0), xycoords='data', xytext=(4.0,
               0.5), textcoords='data',
          arrowprops=dict(arrowstyle="->", color="green", lw=5,
          connectionstyle=("arc3,rad=0.")))
plt.setp(a, size=25)
plt.show()
```

How it works...

Here is the explanation of the code:

- The `plt.annotate()` method annotates the graph with specified details.
- `(3, 0)` specifies the text to be displayed as description.
- `xy = (3, 0)` specifies the co-ordinates of the point to be annotated on the graph.
- `xycoords='data'` specifies that the `xy` co-ordinates specified are with respect to the data (points in input data).
- `arrowprops()` specifies the `style, linewidth, color, connectionstyle` of the arrow to be used from the text to the point being annotated.
- `plt.setp()` sets the font size of the text `(3, 0)` to 25.

We get the following output by running the preceding code:

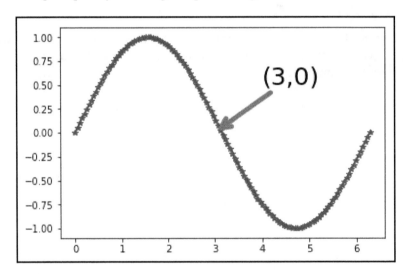

Using style sheets

We have learned how to use various attributes of the figure to create professional graphics. However, it is very time consuming to figure out so many different combinations and to arrive at good-looking graphics. Matplotlib provides a list of ready-made templates called **style sheets** that use pre-defined combinations of various attributes. In this recipe, we will learn how to use these pre-defined style sheets.

> You can use `print(plt.style.available)` to get the list of all the available style sheets.

Getting ready

Import the required libraries:

```
import matplotlib.pyplot as plt
import numpy as np
```

How to do it...

The following code block plots four different types of graphs, all with the same style sheet, to demonstrate how to use a style sheet:

1. Define the style to be applied for all the graphs in this session:

   ```
   plt.style.use('seaborn-bright')
   ```

2. Define the figure, size, and adjust the space between the plots:

   ```
   fig, ax = plt.subplots(1, 4, figsize=(10,5))
   fig.subplots_adjust(wspace=0.5)
   ```

3. Plot a histogram on the first axis:

   ```
   ax[0].hist(np.random.randn(1000))
   ```

4. Plot three line graphs on the second axis:

```
for i in range(3):
    ax[1].plot(np.random.rand(10))
ax[1].legend(['a', 'b', 'c'], loc='lower left')
```

5. Plot a scatter plot on the third axis:

```
ax[2].scatter(np.random.rand(100),np.random.rand(100),
              s=100*np.random.rand(100)*np.random.rand(100))
```

6. Plot a pie chart on the fourth axis:

```
labels = ['SciFi', 'Drama', 'Thriller', 'Comedy', 'Action',
          'Romance']
sizes = [5, 15, 10, 20, 40, 10] # Add upto 100%
explode = (0, 0, 0, 0, 0.1, 0)
ax[3].pie(sizes, explode=explode, labels=labels, autopct='%1.0f%%',
          pctdistance=0.7,
          shadow=True, startangle=90)
ax[3].axis('equal') # Equal aspect ratio ensures that pie is drawn
                    as a circle.
```

7. Set the title for the figure and display it on the screen:

```
plt.suptitle('seaborn-bright', color='b', weight='bold')
plt.show()
```

How it works...

Here is the explanation of the code just given:

`plt.style.use('seaborn-bright')` sets the specific style sheet to be used. The same style sheet will be applied for all the plots in this session. In this example, we are using the `seaborn-bright` style sheet.

The remaining code plots four graphs, as we have seen earlier.

As you can see, we have not specified any specific parameters to any of the figure attributes; all of them are borrowed from the style sheet we supplied in the beginning:

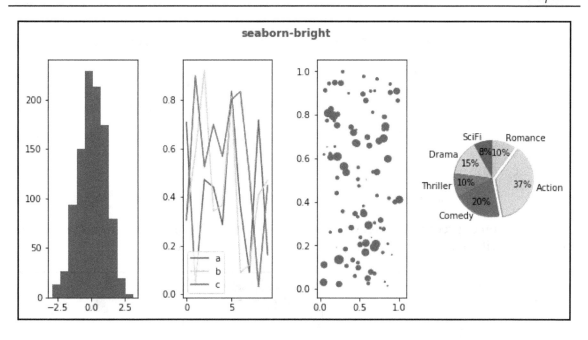

There's more...

Just to demonstrate a few more style sheets, the following code block uses the same four plots as before, but applies a list of style sheets as specified in `style_list`.

Since the same code is to be repeated multiple times, we define a function and call it in a for loop with a different `style` parameter each time:

```
style_list = ['classic', 'dark_background', 'ggplot', 'grayscale',
              'seaborn']
def plot_the_graph(style):
    np.random.seed(0)
    fig, ax = plt.subplots(1, 4, figsize=(12,5))
    fig.subplots_adjust(wspace=0.5)
    ax[0].hist(np.random.randn(1000))
    for i in range(3):
        ax[1].plot(np.random.rand(10))
    ax[1].legend(['a', 'b', 'c'], loc='lower left')
    ax[2].scatter(np.random.rand(100),np.random.rand(100),
                  s=100*np.random.rand(100)*np.random.rand(100))
    labels = ['SciFi', 'Drama', 'Thriller', 'Comedy', 'Action',
              'Romance']
    sizes = [5, 15, 10, 20, 40, 10] # Add upto 100%
    explode = (0, 0, 0, 0, 0.1, 0) # only "explode" the 2nd slice (i.e.
```

```
                                                        'Hogs')
    ax[3].pie(sizes, explode=explode, labels=labels, autopct='%1.0f%%',
            pctdistance=0.7,
            shadow=True, startangle=90)
    ax[3].axis('equal') # Equal aspect ratio ensures that pie is drawn
                    as a circle.

    plt.suptitle(style)
    plt.show()

for style in style_list:
    with plt.style.context(style):
        plot_the_graph(style)
```

Upon execution of preceding code, you should see following five separate figures on your screen, each with a different style as specified in the `style_list`:

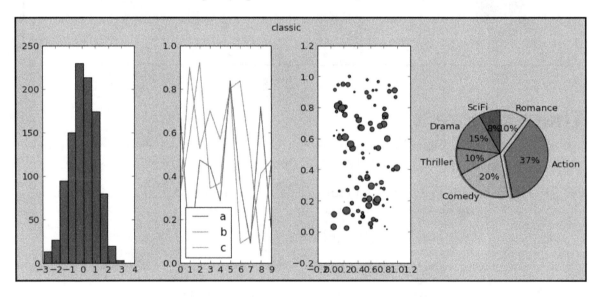

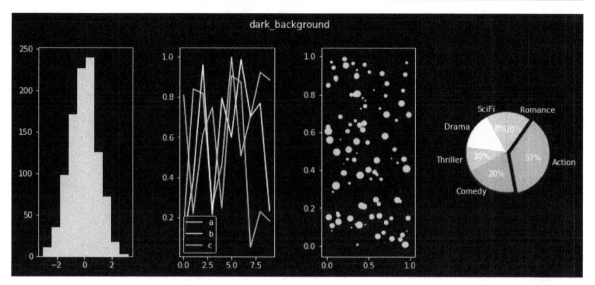

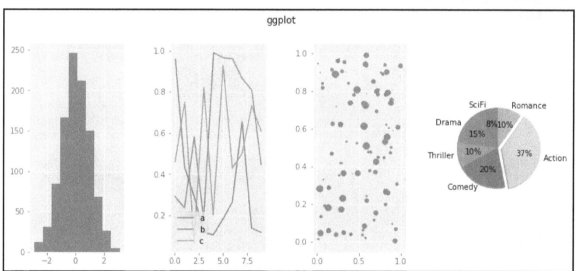

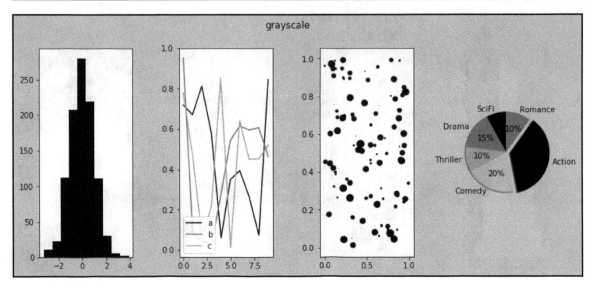

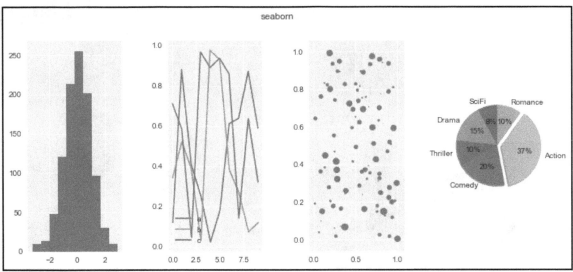

5
Plotting with Object-Oriented API

In this chapter, we will learn the differences between the `pyplot` API and an object-oriented API with the use of following recipes:

- Plotting a correlation matrix using `pyplot` and an object-oriented API
- Plotting patches using an object-oriented API
- Plotting collections using an object-oriented API

Introduction

As described in `Chapter 1`, *Anatomy of Matplotlib*, Matplotlib has a three-layer architecture. The top layer is called the **scripting layer**, and is implemented with `pyplot()` API. This API has been designed for users without much programming experience, so it shields the user from the complexities of creating and rendering the plots using the bottom two layers (artist and backend). For complex applications that use advanced features, such as patches, collections, interactive plotting using events, callbacks, animation, and widgets, we will have to use an object-oriented API. However, it requires quite a bit of Python coding experience to leverage full potential of this API. As new versions of Matplotlib get released, more and more of these features are moving into the `pyplot` API, reducing the dependence on an object-oriented API.

The name object-oriented API is a bit confusing, as it may give the impression that the `pyplot` API is not an object-oriented, which is not true. It only means that an object-oriented API uses artist and backend layers directly, bypassing the scripting layer (without using the `pyplot` API). This gives the flexibility to use complete functionality offered by Matplotlib, whereas the `pyplot` API offers a subset of it.

It should be noted that for any plot or figure, it need not be the `pyplot` API or an object-oriented API; it can be a mix of both. In fact, many graphs we have developed so far use a mix of both. When we had to use a complex grid structure to place plots in a figure, we used an object-oriented API. When plotting each graph individually and creating figure objects and underlying canvas, we used the `pyplot` API. Once we see the differences between the two APIs, you will understand this combined use of both the APIs.

Plotting a correlation matrix using pyplot and object-oriented APIs

In this recipe, we will learn the difference between `pyplot` and an object-oriented APIs. We will plot the same correlation matrix, first with the `pyplot` API and then with an object-oriented API. We will use the same `Wine Quality` dataset for plotting the correlation matrix.

Getting ready

Import the following libraries for the `pyplot` API:

```
import pandas as pd
import matplotlib.pyplot as plt
```

Import the following libraries for an object-oriented API:

```
import pandas as pd
from matplotlib.backends.backend_agg import FigureCanvasAgg as FigureCanvas
from matplotlib.figure import Figure
from IPython.core.display import display
```

`matplotlib.backends` has a set of backends that it supports. Here, we are importing `FigureCanvasAgg`, which provides the space for plotting the figure and maps it to the defined backend device.

`IPython.core.display` enables displaying the plot onto the output device.

How to do it...

The following code block reads the data using pandas and plots the correlation matrix using the `pyplot` API. This is the same as what we did to plot the heat map in `Chapter 2`, *Getting Started with Basic Plots*:

1. Read the data from a CSV file into pandas DataFrame:

```
wine_quality = pd.read_csv('winequality.csv', delimiter=';')
```

2. Get a correlation matrix of all attributes of `wine_quality`:

```
corr = wine_quality.corr()
```

3. Define the figure with its size, and plot the image and associated color bar:

```
plt.figure(figsize=(12,9))
plt.imshow(corr,cmap='hot')
plt.colorbar()
```

4. Set the title and ticks for the figure and display it on the screen:

```
plt.title('Correlation Matrix')
plt.xticks(range(len(corr)),corr.columns, fontsize=10,
fontweight='bold',rotation=45)
plt.yticks(range(len(corr)),corr.columns)

plt.show()
```

All the commands in the preceding code block are familiar to us, as we have already learned them in `Chapter 2`, *Getting Started with Basic Plots* and `Chapter 4`, *Developing Visualizations for Publishing Quality*.

The following code block plots the same correlation map using an object-oriented API (without using the `pyplot` API):

1. Read the data from a CSV file into pandas DataFrame:

```
wine_quality = pd.read_csv('winequality.csv', delimiter=';')
```

2. Get a correlation matrix of all attributes of `wine_quality`:

```
corr = wine_quality.corr()
```

3. Define the figure with its size:

```
fig = Figure(figsize=(12,9))
```

4. Attach the figure to the canvas:

```
FigureCanvas(fig)
```

5. Define the axes on the figure, where we need to plot a correlation map, and plot the correlation map and colorbar:

```
axs = fig.add_subplot(111)
corimage = axs.imshow(corr,cmap='hot')
fig.colorbar(corimage)
```

6. Set `ticks` and `ticklabels`:

```
axs.set(xticks=range(len(corr)), yticks=range(len(corr)),
        title='Correlation Matrix')
fontd = {'fontsize': 10,
        'fontweight': 'bold',
        'rotation': 45}
axs.set_xticklabels(corr.columns, fontdict=fontd)
axs.set_yticklabels(corr.columns)
```

7. Display the figure on the screen:

```
display(fig)
```

How it works...

The `pyplot` API code block is self-explanatory. Here is the output chart:

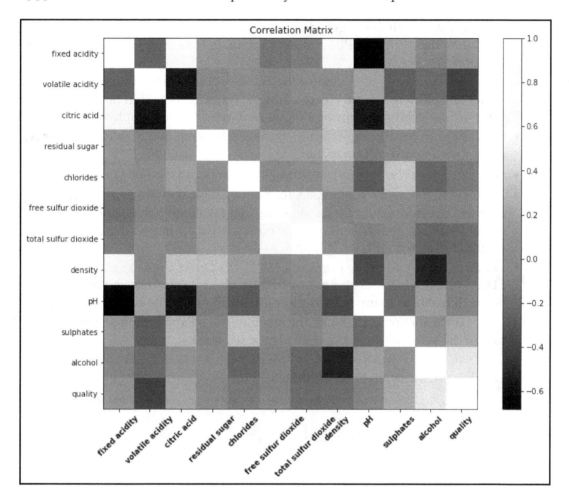

Here is the explanation for the object-oriented API code block:

- `Figure(figsize=(12,9))` instantiates the figure object with a size of `(12, 9)`.
- `FigureCanvas(fig)` attaches the canvas (area where the figure needs to be plotted, which ultimately gets displayed on the connected backend device). In the case of the `pyplot` API, we don't have to do this, as the `pyplot` API takes care of it.
- `fig.add_subplot(111)` creates the axis object within the figure object created earlier. Please note we can create multiple axes objects within one figure object. Here, we are creating only one axis, as we have only one graph to plot.
- `axs.imshow(corr, cmap='hot')` creates the correlation matrix as an image, using the standard colormap, `hot`.
- `fig.colorbar(corimage)` attaches the color bar to the image created before.
- To create `ticks` and `ticklabels` for both *x* and *y* axes, the `pyplot` API has the `plt.xticks` and `plt.yticks` methods that take both tick positions and ticklables as arguments, and manage both with one command. But, in the case of an object-oriented API, we will have to do it separately.
- `axs.set(xticks=range(len(corr)), yticks=range(len(corr)), title='Correlation Matrix')` defines *x* and *y* axis ticks and title for the figure. It needs as many ticks as there are attributes in the correlation matrix.
- `fontd` is the dictionary with all the attributes to be applied on `xticklabels`. We can do the same for `yticklabels` also, if we want.
- `axs.set_xticklabels(corr.columns, fontdict=fontd)` sets the `xticklabels` with defined attributes.
- `axs.set_yticklabels(corr.columns)` sets `ticklabels` for the *y* axis.

You should see the following plot after executing the preceding code:

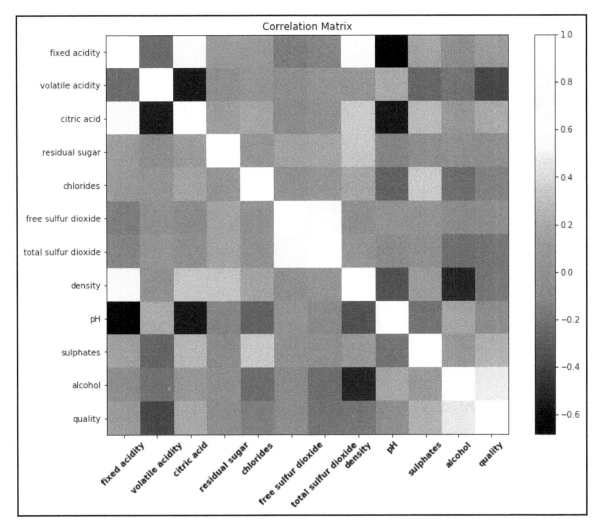

Plotting patches using object-oriented API

Matplotlib offers some special types of plots using patches and collections classes. In this recipe, we will learn how to use `patches` using the object-oriented API. In the next recipe, we will learn about `collections`.

Getting ready

We will need to import the following libraries for this recipe:

```
from IPython.core.display import display
from matplotlib.backends import backend_agg
from matplotlib.patches import Ellipse, Polygon
```

How to do it...

The following code block plots two patches as separate plots in the same figure:

1. Define the figure with its size using `figure_manager`, and attach it to the canvas:

```
figure_manager = backend_agg.new_figure_manager(1, figsize=(12,6))
fig = figure_manager.canvas.figure
```

2. Define the first axis and plot an ellipse patch on it:

```
axs1 = fig.add_subplot(121)
axs1.add_patch(Ellipse((3, 1.0), 4, 1.0, hatch='/', facecolor='g'))

# centre=(3, 1.0), width=4, height=1.0
axs1.set_xlim((0, 6))
axs1.set_ylim((0, 2.5))
```

3. Define the second axis and plot a polygon patch on it:

```
axs2 = fig.add_subplot(122)
axs2.add_patch(Polygon([[0, 0], [4, 1.1], [6, 2.5], [2, 1.4]],
lw=5,
               facecolor='k', edgecolor='skyblue', hatch='+*'))
axs2.set_xlim((0, 6))
axs2.set_ylim((0, 2.5))
```

4. Display the figure on the screen:

```
display(fig)
```

How it works...

Here is the explanation for the preceding code and how it works:

- To define the figure and canvas, we are using another method, `new_figure_manager()`, in this recipe just to demonstrate the multiple options Matplotlib provides. We could have used the same methods as in the previous recipe as well. This approach is more suitable for batch processing of multiple figures in a loop. It takes the arguments as figure number and figure size.
- `fig.add_subplot(121)` instantiates the first axis for the first patch.
- `axs1.add_patch(Ellipse((3, 1.0), 4, 1.0, hatch='/', facecolor='g'))` adds the ellipse patch on `axs1`. `(3, 1.0)` defines the co-ordinates of the center of the ellipse; `4` is the width and `1.0` is height of the ellipse. `facecolor` specifies which color to fill the patch and `hatch` specifies the hatch design inside the ellipse.
- `axs1.set_xlim((0, 6))` and `axs1.set_ylim((0, 2.5))` define the limits for the *x* and *y* axes. Without these limits defined, the patch will not be plotted as it would not know exactly where to place the patch in the co-ordinate system.
- `axs2.add_patch(Polygon([[0, 0], [4, 1.1], [6, 2.5], [2, 1.4]], lw=5, facecolor='k', edgecolor='skyblue', hatch='+*'))` plots the polygon patch on `axs2`:
  - It is specified by *x,y* co-ordinates of four points
  - `facecolor='k'` specifies that the area inside the patch should be filled with black color
  - `edgecolor='skyblue'` is used for plotting edges of Polygon and hatches with skyblue color
  - `lw=5`specifies the linewidth of Polygon
  - Here, we are using +* characters for `hatch`

Here is the output figure:

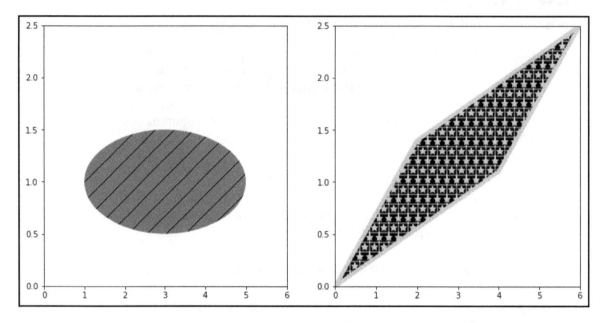

Plotting collections using object-oriented API

collections is a container of similar objects that share many properties.

Getting ready

Import the required libraries:

```
from matplotlib import collections
from IPython.core.display import display
from matplotlib.backends import backend_agg
import numpy as np
```

How to do it...

The following code block plots a collection of polygons that cycle through a given number of sizes and a given list of colors:

1. Define the data for plotting a collection of polygons:

```
nsizes = 50   #number of different sizes to be used to plot the
items in the collection
npts = 100    # number of items in the collection
r = np.arange(nsizes)
theta = np.linspace(0, 2*np.pi, nsizes)
xx = r * np.sin(theta)
```

2. Offset co-ordinates where the items of the collection would be plotted:

```
rs = np.random.RandomState([125])
xo = rs.randn(npts)
yo = rs.randn(npts)
xyo = list(zip(xo, yo))
```

3. Define the figure size and attach it to the canvas, and also define an axis on this figure:

```
figure_manager = backend_agg.new_figure_manager(1, figsize=(8,6))
fig = figure_manager.canvas.figure
axs1 = fig.add_subplot(111)
```

4. Plot six-sided regular polygons as a collection:

```
col = collections.RegularPolyCollection(6, sizes=np.fabs(xx) * 20,
        offsets=xyo, transOffset=axs1.transData)
axs1.add_collection(col, autolim=True)
```

5. Make a list of `colors` to cycle:

```
colors = ['b', 'g', 'r', 'c', 'm', 'y', 'k', 'w', 'tab:blue',
          'tab:orange', 'tab:green', 'tab:red',
          'tab:purple', 'tab:brown', 'tab:pink', 'tab:gray',
          'tab:olive', 'tab:cyan']
col.set_color(colors)
```

6. Set the title and `autoscale_view` for adjusting the scale on both axes:

```
axs1.autoscale_view()
axs1.set_title('RegularPolyCollection')
```

7. Display the figure on the screen:

```
display(fig)
```

How it works...

Here is the explanation for the code:

- `nsizes` and `npts` specifies the number of sizes and number of items in the collection. If `nsizes` is less than `npts` for the remaining points, `nsizes` would start from the beginning and the cycle goes on. The same holds true for colors as well.
- `xx = r * np.sin(theta)` computes the actual size for all `nsizes`.
- `xyo = list(zip(xo, yo))` computes *x* and *y* co-ordinates for each of the items in the collection. `zip` is a Python function that takes items from two or more lists and creates tuples of two or more each.
- `col = collections.RegularPolyCollection()` creates the collection of polygons. Number 6 is the number of sides of the polygon, and `np.fabs()` converts all the numbers in `xx` to their absolute values (since size can't be negative), and `offsets=xy0` specifies the actual co-ordinates where the polygons are to be plotted. `axs1.transData` is the internal representation of the co-ordinate system, whose explanation is beyond the scope of this book.
- `axs1.add_collection(col, autolim=True)` connects the collection object to the defined axis `axs1`, `autolim=True` ensures the axes limits are adjusted in such a way that the entire collection fits within the range.
- `col.set_color(colors)` specifies the list of colors to cycle through to cover all the items in the collection.

Here is how the output plot looks:

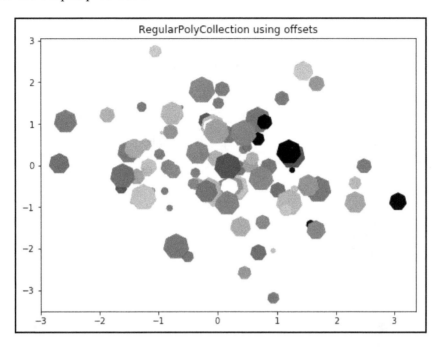

6
Plotting with Advanced Features

In this chapter, we will learn the following recipes:

- Using property cycler
- Plotting path effects
- Using transforms
- Taking control of axes positions
- Using gridspec
- Using `gridspec_kw` with `pyplot.subplots`
- Aligning the plots gridspec
- Using constrained layout
- Using origin and extent for image plotting
- Geographical plotting using geopandas

Using property cycler

We learned in `Chapter 4`, *Developing Visualizations for Publishing Quality*, that Matplotlib has a default color cycle that gets repeated as we plot more graphs in a given axis. The property cycler enables us to define such cyclers for multiple attributes in a single function. If you want to plot an axis with repetitive patterns, we can achieve it with the property cycler.

Getting ready

We will use the object-oriented API here. In Chapter 4, *Developing Visualizations for Publishing Quality,* we used the pyplot API for this example. Import the required libraries:

```
from cycler import cycler
import numpy as np
from matplotlib.backends.backend_agg import FigureCanvasAgg as FigureCanvas
from matplotlib.figure import Figure
from IPython.core.display import display
```

How to do it...

The following code block plots six tie objects; the last two are repeats of the first two. It repeats the cycle after every four objects in this example:

1. Define the figure and attach it to the canvas:

   ```
   fig = Figure()
   FigureCanvas(fig)
   ```

2. Set facecolor, edgecolor, and alpha for the figure and add an axis:

   ```
   fig.set(facecolor='grey', alpha=0.2, edgecolor='m')
   ax = fig.add_subplot(111)
   ```

3. Set the data for plotting the graphs:

   ```
   x = np.array([0.2, 0.4, 0.6, 0.8, 0.5])
   y = [1, 6, 6, 1, 0]
   ```

4. Define a custom_cycler for the color and hatch attributes, and set it for the axis:

   ```
   custom_cycler = cycler('color', ['g', 'blue', 'y', 'c']) + \
                   cycler('hatch', ['+*', 'xx', '+x', '+O.'])
   ax.set_prop_cycle(custom_cycler)
   ```

5. Plot the graphs for six tie objects:

```
ax.fill(x+1, y)
ax.fill(x+2, y)
ax.fill(x+3, y)
ax.fill(x+4, y)
ax.fill(x+5, y)
ax.fill(x+6, y)
```

6. Display the figure on the screen:

```
display(fig)
```

How it works...

The following is an explanation of the code:

- `fig = Figure()` defines the figure object.
- `FigureCanvas(fig)` attaches the figure object to the canvas on which the figure will be drawn.
- `fig.set(facecolor='grey', alpha=0.2, edgecolor='m')` sets various attributes of the figure. More often, we use these attributes at the axis level for the individual plot. But here, we are using them at the figure level. `ax = fig.add_subplot(111)` instantiates the axes.
- `x` and `y` define the data co-ordinates where the tie objects are plotted.
- `cycler()` defines the property cycle with two properties, and four values for each. If we give more values to each of the properties, the cycle will be repeated after all the values in the list are covered.
- `ax.set_prop_cycle(custom_cycler)` activates the previously defined custom property cycler.
- `fill()` plots tie objects using the data co-ordinates and properties defined in the property cycler.
- `display(fig)` displays the figure on the screen.

You should get the following figure as output on your screen:

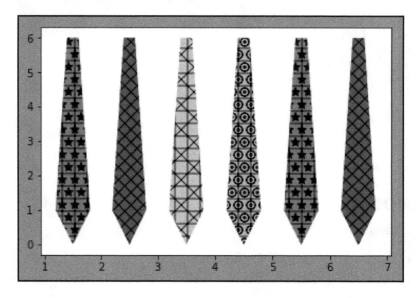

There's more...

We can also set the property cycler in the global parameters `rcParams` file, which then becomes the default cycler for a given session.

Here is the code to achieve this:

```
import matplotlib as mpl
from cycler import cycler
mpl.rc('axes', prop_cycle=cycler('color', ['r', 'orange', 'c', 'y']) +\
                    cycler('hatch', ['x', 'xx-', '+O.', '*']))
```

Using Path effects

We learned how to use the `Path` method to draw custom plots in `Chapter 2`, *Getting Started with Basic Plots*. Here, we will learn how to create effects such as a simple shadow and a hatch shadow using the `path_effetcts` attribute on various plotting objects.

Getting ready

Import the required libraries:

```
import matplotlib.pyplot as plt
import numpy as np
from matplotlib.patheffects import PathPatchEffect, SimpleLineShadow, Normal
```

How to do it...

The following code block plots a sigmoid curve and text object on the graph, with the `path_effects` attributes:

1. Define the style to be used for all the plots in this session:

   ```
   plt.style.use('seaborn-darkgrid')
   ```

2. Define the figure and figure size:

   ```
   plt.subplots(figsize=(10,6))
   ```

3. Define the data for the plot:

   ```
   x = np.linspace(-10, 10, 50)
   y = 1.0 / (1 + np.exp(-x))
   ```

4. Define the text to be printed on the plot with the desired path effects:

   ```
   t = plt.text(-10., 1.15, 'Sigmoid with Path Effects', fontsize=40,
               weight=50, va='center',
   path_effects=[PathPatchEffect(offset=(3, -3),
               hatch='xxxx', facecolor='gray'),
               PathPatchEffect(edgecolor='white', linewidth=1.1,
               facecolor='black')])
   ```

5. Plot the sigmoid curve with the specified path effects and display the figure on the screen:

```
plt.plot(x, y, linewidth=8, color='blue', path_effects=
                              [SimpleLineShadow(), Normal()])
plt.show()
```

How it works...

Here is an explanation of the code:

- `plt.style.use('seaborn-darkgrid')` specifies the style to be used as the background of the figure.
- `plt.subplots()` instantiates the figure object to specify the size of the figure. If we want to use the default size, then this statement is not required.
- x and y define the data for plotting the sigmoid curve.
- `plt.text()` creates a text object and places it at the specified co-ordinates:
    - `(-10., 1.15)` are the co-ordinates on the axes where this text object is to be placed.
    - `Sigmoid with Path Effects` is the text.
    - `weight` is the same as font weight (depth of bold)
    - `va` is vertical alignment.
    - `path_effects[]` specifies a list of `PathPatchEffects` to be applied to the text object.
    - `PathPatchEffect()` enables a custom path effect with various attributes.
- `plt.plot()` draws a sigmoid curve again with `path_effects[]`. Here, we are using the predefined path effects `SimpleLineShadow()` and `Normal()`.

Here is how the output looks:

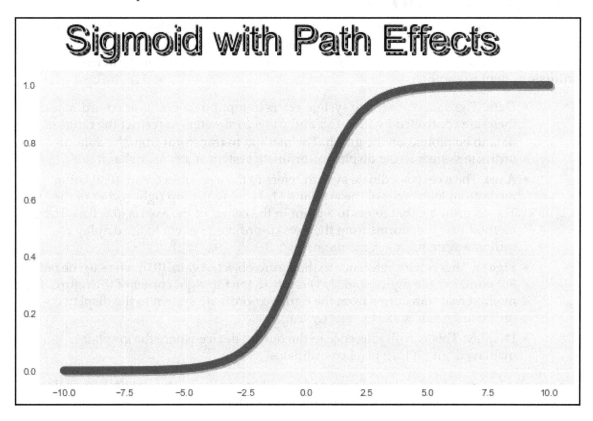

There's more...

We have demonstrated how to use predefined and custom path effects in this recipe.
However, there are many predefined path effects available in Matplotlib. For a full list of
possibilities, please refer to the Matplotlib documentation (https://matplotlib.org/api/
patheffects_api.html).

Using transforms

To refer to a specific point on the graph, we need its co-ordinates. There are four different co-ordinate systems used by Matplotlib with reference to data, axes, figures, and display. In this recipe, we will learn how to use these co-ordinate systems and transform from one co-ordinate system to another:

- **Data**: The data co-ordinate system refers to input data points as co-ordinates, and these are controlled by the `xlim` and `ylim` parameters to restrict the range of data to be plotted on the graph. The method to transform from the data co-ordinate system to the display co-ordinate system is `ax.transData`.
- **Axes**: The axes co-ordinate system refers to the axes object, with (0,0) being the bottom left corner of the axes and (1, 1) being the top right corner of the axes. The co-ordinate that refers to a point in the center of the axes is (0.5, 0.5). The method that transforms from the axes co-ordinate system to the display co-ordinate system is `ax.transAxes`.
- **Figure**: This is with reference to the figure object. Again, (0,0) refers to the bottom left corner of the figure, and (1, 1) refers to the top right corner of the figure. The method that transforms from the figure co-ordinate system to the display co-ordinate system is `ax.transFigure`.
- **Display**: This is with reference to the output device where the graph is displayed, and it is in pixel co-ordinates.

We can also use the blended co-ordinate system, where one axis uses the data co-ordinate system and the other axis uses the axes co-ordinate system.

The display and figure co-ordinates are rarely used; the data and axes co-ordinate systems are used more frequently.

We will have two recipes, one to demonstrate the transformation of data co-ordinates to display co-ordinates, and the other to demonstrate the axes and blended co-ordinate systems.

Transforming data co-ordinates to display co-ordinates

In this recipe, we will demonstrate how we can transform data co-ordinates to display co-ordinates.

Getting ready

Import the required libraries:

```
import matplotlib.pyplot as plt
import numpy as np
```

How to do it...

The following code plots a sine wave and annotates a point on the graph in both data and display co-ordinates:

1. Define the figure and add an axis to it:

   ```
   fig = plt.figure()
   ax = fig.add_subplot(111)
   ```

2. Define the data for the sine curve and plot it:

   ```
   theta = np.linspace(0, 2*np.pi, 128)
   y = np.sin(theta)
   ax.plot(theta, y, 'r-*')
   ```

3. Define the point on the data co-ordinate system and transform it to the display co-ordinate system:

   ```
   xdata, ydata = 3, 0
   xdisplay, ydisplay = ax.transData.transform_point((xdata, ydata))
   ```

4. Define the attributes of the bounding box to be used around the text description:

   ```
   bbox = dict(boxstyle="round", fc="1.0")
   ```

5. Define the arrow properties to be used in the annotation:

   ```
   arrowprops = dict(arrowstyle="->", color='green', lw=5,
             connectionstyle="angle,angleA=0,angleB=90,rad=10")
   ```

6. Define the offset to be used to specify the co-ordinates where the text description is to be placed on the plot:

   ```
   offset = 72
   ```

7. Define the annotation for the point in the data co-ordinate system:

```
data = ax.annotate('data = (%.1f, %.1f)' % (xdata, ydata),
                   (xdata, ydata), xytext=(-2*offset, offset),
                   textcoords='offset points', bbox=bbox,
                   arrowprops=arrowprops)
```

8. Define the annotation for the point in the display co-ordinate system:

```
disp = ax.annotate('display = (%.1f, %.1f)' % (xdisplay, ydisplay),
                   (xdisplay, ydisplay), xytext=(0.5*offset, -
                   offset),
                   xycoords='figure pixels', textcoords='offset
                   points',bbox=bbox, arrowprops=arrowprops)
```

9. Display the figure on the screen:

```
plt.show()
```

How it works...

Here is an explanation of the code:

- `theta` and `y` are the data points for plotting the sine wave. Zero to 2*pi covers one cycle of the wave.
- `xdata` and `ydata` are the co-ordinates in the data co-ordinate system; in this case, their values are 3 and 0. We will see where this specific point is on the plot.
- `xdisplay` and `ydisplay` are the co-ordinates for the same point in display format. We have converted them using `ax.transData.transform_point((xdata, ydata))`.
- `bbox` specifies the bounding box style in which text will be displayed.
- `arrowprops` specifies the style of connection between the text describing the point and the actual point on the graph. We will learn more about text annotation in the next chapter.
- `offset=72` is used to specify the co-ordinates where the text box is to be placed. This offset is from the xy co-ordinates of the point that is being annotated. A positive offset for the x co-ordinate means to the right of the point, and negative means to the left of the point. Similarly, a positive offset for the y co-ordinate means above the point, and negative means below the point.

- `ax.annotate()` plots the annotation (text describing the point in observation) pointing to the observation and giving a text description of the observation. The first `annotate()` statement plots the annotation for the data co-ordinate system and the second one plots it for the display co-ordinate system:

  - The first argument in `annotate()` is the text description of the annotation
  - `(xdata, ydata)` are the co-ordinates of the point being annotated
  - `xycoords` (not provided in the first annotation, as it uses the default data co-ordinate system) specifies which co-ordinate system to use for `xy`
  - `xytext` specifies the co-ordinates of where the text description is to be placed
  - `textcoords` specifies the co-ordinate system for text co-ordinates
  - Point in *offset point* is a unit of length and equal to 1/72 inches, so when we specify `72` offset points, it is equal to 1 inch

- In the second `annotate()` statement, we specify `xycoords='figure pixels'` explicitly, as we don't want to use default, but use `figure pixels` co-ordinates.

The following is the output plot:

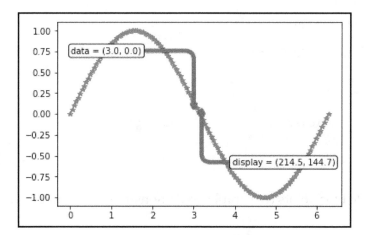

Please note that the arrows are not exactly aligned to the same point. That is because of the variation in default settings for various output devices. This is the reason why display co-ordinates are not used often. They are useful only in interactive plotting where we need to capture keyboard or mouse events.

There's more...

There are many options to specify co-ordinates for a point on the plot, in the context of annotation. For a complete list of options, please refer to Matplotlib documentation (https://matplotlib.org/api/_as_gen/matplotlib.axes.Axes.annotate.html).

Using axes and blended co-ordinate system transforms

In this recipe, we will learn how to use the axes and blended co-ordinate systems.

Getting ready

Import the required libraries:

```
import matplotlib.pyplot as plt
import numpy as np
import matplotlib.patches as patches
import matplotlib.transforms as transforms
from scipy.stats import norm
from matplotlib.ticker import MultipleLocator
```

How to do it...

The following code block plots two graphs to demonstrate axes and blended co-ordinate systems:

1. Fix the random state for repeatability and set the style to be used in this session:

```
np.random.seed(19681211)
plt.style.use('ggplot')
```

2. Define the figure with size and add an axis to it:

```
fig = plt.figure(figsize=(12,5))
ax1 = fig.add_subplot(121)
```

3. Define the data for a scatter plot and plot it using the `plot` method, instead of the `scatter` method:

```
x, y = 50*np.random.rand(2, 500)
ax1.plot(x, y, 'cH')
```

4. Define an ellipse patch and add it to the axes:

```
ellipse = patches.Ellipse((0.5, 0.5), 0.6, 0.3,
                          transform=ax1.transAxes,
                          facecolor='blue', alpha=0.3)

ax1.add_patch(ellipse)

# remove the comment below to check if Ellipse remains at the same
place,
# since it is on axes co-ordinates
#ax.set_xlim(10,40)
```

5. Define the second axes and on it, plot two normal distributions with different means but the same standard deviation:

```
ax2 = fig.add_subplot(122)

mu1, mu2 = 0, 0.3
sigma = 0.1
x1 = np.linspace(mu1 - 3*sigma, mu1 + 3*sigma, 100)
            ax2.plot(x1, norm.pdf(x1, mu1, sigma))
x2 = np.linspace(mu2 - 3*sigma, mu2 + 3*sigma, 100)
            ax2.plot(x2, norm.pdf(x2, mu2, sigma))
```

6. Set the title and `xaxis_major_locator` for the second axes:

```
ax2.set_title(r'$\sigma=0.05 \/ \dots \/ \sigma=0.25$',
fontsize=16)
            ax2.xaxis.set_major_locator(MultipleLocator(0.1))
```

7. Transform the *y* co-ordinates to axes co-ordinates and keep the *x* co-ordinates as data co-ordinates:

```
trans = transforms.blended_transform_factory(ax2.transData,
ax2.transAxes)
```

8. Highlight the 0.05 to 0.25 `stddev` region with a rectangular box that shows the *x* co-ordinates in the data and the *y* co-ordinates in the axes:

```
rect = patches.Rectangle((0.05, 0), width=0.2,
height=1,transform=trans, color='green', alpha=0.3)
ax2.add_patch(rect)

plt.show()
```

How it works...

Here is an explanation of the code:

 `np.random.seed()` is required to ensure that we get the same data points from any `np.random.*` function we may use subsequently. This ensures repeatability of the graph.

- `plt.style.use('ggplot')` specifies the style to be used for the figure.
- `ax1.plot(x, y, 'cH')` plots 500 random points on `ax1` patches.
  - `Ellipse()` adds an ellipse patch to `ax1` at the center of the axes.
    - `(0.5, 0.5)` are the co-ordinates for the center of the ellipse, 0.6 is the width and 0.3 is the height.
    - `transform=ax1.transAxes` specifies that co-ordinates in the axes co-ordinate system need to be transformed to display co-ordinates before displaying the picture on the screen.
- On `ax2`, we plot two normal distributions with different mean (`mu`) and standard deviation (`sigma`), using the `norm` function of `scipy.stats`.
- `ax2.set_title(r'$\sigma=0.05 \/ \dots \/ \sigma=0.25$', fontsize=16)` sets the title using regular expressions. We will learn more about it in the next chapter on text and mathematical expressions.
- `ax2.xaxis.set_major_locator(MultipleLocator(0.1))` ensures that ticks are placed at 0.1 intervals on the *x* axis instead of using default ticks.
- `trans = transforms.blended_transform_factory(ax2.transData, ax2.transAxes)` defines the co-ordinate system to be used for *x* and *y* axis.

- `rect = patches.Rectangle((0.05, 0), width=0.2, height=1, transform=trans, color='green', alpha=0.3)` defines a rectangular patch:
    - `(0.05, 0)` are the co-ordinates of the bottom left corner of the rectangle
    - `width=0.2` is the width in the data co-ordinate system, so translates to 0.25 on x axis (from 0.05)
    - `height=1` is the height of the rectangle in the axes co-ordinate system, so spans the complete height (100 percent) of the axes
    - `transform=trans` is the co-ordinate system (defined in the previous step) to be used

Here is how the output looks:

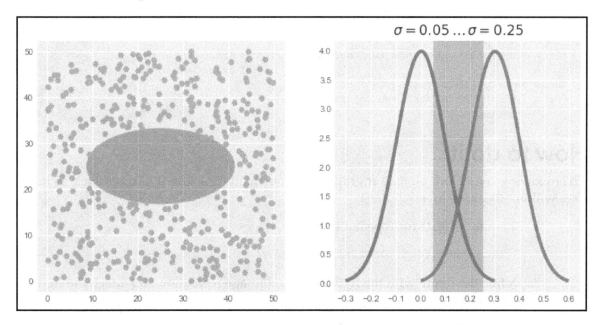

Taking control of axes positions

In Chapter 3, *Plotting Multiple Charts, Subplots and Figures*, we learned about `plt.subplot()`, `plt.subplots()`, and `plt.subplot2grid()` features, used to create various figure layouts. We will learn one more feature, `GridSpec()`, a little later in this chapter. Each of them gives an additional level of flexibility to design the required figure layouts. However, they all come with predefined parameters, using which axes positions in the figure are controlled. The ultimate flexibility a user can get is the ability to specify exact co-ordinates and the size of the axes to place within the figure layout. This is what we will learn in this recipe.

Getting ready

We will use the object-oriented API for this recipe. Import the required libraries:

```
import numpy as np
from matplotlib.backends.backend_agg import FigureCanvasAgg as
                                           FigureCanvas
from matplotlib.figure import Figure
from IPython.core.display import display
```

How to do it...

The following code block plots four graphs, the fourth one is a subset of three axes, so it is axes within other axes (overlapping):

1. Fix random state for repeatability:

    ```
    np.random.seed(19681211)
    ```

2. Define the figure with the figure size and image resolution and attach the figure to a canvas:

    ```
    fig = Figure(figsize=(10,6), dpi=100)
    FigureCanvas(fig)
    fig.set(facecolor='c', alpha=0.1, edgecolor='m')
    ```

3. Define the first axes and set the `title` and `ylabel`:

```
ax1 = fig.add_axes([0.0, 0.55, 0.4, 0.4])
ax1.set_ylabel('volts')
ax1.set_title('a sine wave')
```

4. Define the data for the sine wave and plot it on the first axes:

```
t = np.arange(0.0, 1.0, 0.01)
s = np.sin(2*np.pi*t)
line, = ax1.plot(t, s, color='blue', lw=2)
```

5. Define the second axes and plot a histogram on it:

```
ax2 = fig.add_axes([0.0, 0.1, 0.4, 0.4])
n, bins, patches = ax2.hist(np.random.randn(1000), 50,
                            facecolor='yellow', edgecolor='blue')
ax2.set_xlabel('time (s)')
```

6. Define data for the next two plots:

```
x = np.linspace(0, 10, 20)
y = (x+5)*(x-7)*(x-9) - 150
```

7. Define the outer axes, (left, bottom, width, height) and plot the curve defined by x and y:

```
ax3 = fig.add_axes([0.5, 0.1, 0.4, 0.85])
ax3.plot(x, y, 'g--')
ax3.set(xlabel='x', ylabel='y', title='outer axes')
```

8. Define the four axes and plot the same curve by reversing x and y:

```
ax4 = fig.add_axes([0.575, 0.6, 0.2, 0.25])
ax4.plot(y, x, 'r-*')
ax4.set(xlabel='y', ylabel='x', title='inset axes')
```

9. Display the figure on the screen:

```
display(fig)
```

How it works...

Here is an explanation of the code:

- `ax1 = fig.add_axes([0.0, 0.55, 0.4, 0.4])` adds a new axis to the figure object:
    - Co-ordinates are in the figure co-ordinate system, and specify the starting point of the axes from left, bottom, the width and height of the axes.
    - The first co-ordinate `0.0` means the axes starts at the extreme left
    - The second co-ordinate `0.55` means that the axes starts at 55 percent of the height of the figure from the bottom
    - The third co-ordinate `0.4` specifies that the width of this axes is 40 percent of the width of the figure
    - The fourth co-ordinate `0.4` specifies that the height of the axes is 40 percent of the height of the figure
    - A sine graph is plotted on this axes
- `ax2 = fig.add_axes([0.0, 0.1, 0.4, 0.4])` is the second axes, this is also same size as the first one, starts from the extreme left, and is 10 percent of the height of the figure from the bottom. A histogram is plotted on this axes.
- `ax3 = fig.add_axes([0.5, 0.1, 0.4, 0.85])` is the third axes. It starts at 50 percent of the figure on the left, 10 percent of the figure from the bottom, the width is 40 percent of the figure width, and the height is 85 percent of the figure height. A green polynomial is drawn on this axes.
- `ax4 = fig.add_axes([0.575, 0.6, 0.2, 0.25])` is the fourth axes in the figure with title inset axes. This axes starts at 57.5 percent of the width of the figure from the left, and 60 percent of the height of the figure from the bottom, with a width of 20 percent of the figure's width and 25 percent of the figure's height. The same polynomial is drawn from the previous axes, but in red with the x and y axis swapped.

As can be seen in the output here, axes four is within axes three; it is an axes inside another axes:

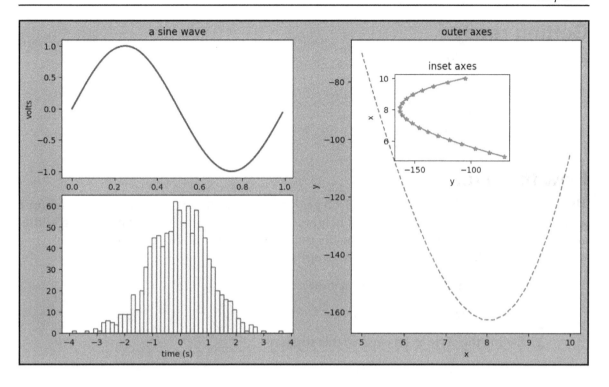

GridSpec for figure layout

GridSpec() is another powerful feature for complex figure layouts. plt.subplot() and plt.subplot2grid() add plots one at a time after instantiating the figure, and figure layout is specified in the number of rows and columns in each subplot, followed by the sequence number of the plot from left to right and top to bottom. But plt.subplots() defines the entire figure layout, in terms of number of rows and columns, in one go, then each plot/axes is accessed using the corresponding index. GridSpec() enables multiple grids to be created in the figure layout, with each grid similar to plt.subplots(). In this recipe, we will learn about how to use GridSpec() and how GridSpec() keyword parameters can be used with plt.subplots().

Using GridSpec

In this recipe, we will learn about how to use GridSpec() for the figure layout.

Getting ready

Import the required libraries:

```
import numpy as np
import matplotlib.pyplot as plt
import matplotlib.patches as patches
from matplotlib.gridspec import GridSpec
```

How to do it...

The following code block defines two 3 x 3 grids using GridSpec(). In grid1, we plot four graphs, each with different widths and heights. In grid2, we plot nine graphs, using width and height ratios, in such a way that the height is the same for all the graphs in a row, whereas the width is the same for all the graphs in a column:

1. Fix random state for reproducibility:

```
np.random.seed(19681211)
```

2. Define the style to be used in this session:

```
plt.style.use('seaborn')
```

3. Define the figure's size and define the layout:

```
fig = plt.figure(figsize=(14,10))
gs1 = GridSpec(ncols=3, nrows=3, left=0.05, right=0.5, wspace=0.2,
               hspace=0.1)
```

4. Define an axes on the gs1:

```
ax1 = fig.add_subplot(gs1[0, 0])
```

5. Define an ellipse patch and add it to the ax1 axes:

```
ellipse = patches.Ellipse((0.5, 0.5), 0.7, 0.3,
transform=ax1.transAxes, facecolor='blue', alpha=0.3)
ax1.add_patch(ellipse)
```

6. Define a second axes on gs1 and plot a histogram on it:

```
ax2 = fig.add_subplot(gs1[0, 1:])
ax2.hist(np.random.randn(1000), 50, facecolor='yellow',
         edgecolor='blue')
```

7. Define a third axis on `gs1` and plot a scatter plot on it:

```
ax3 = fig.add_subplot(gs1[1:, 0])
x, y = 50*np.random.rand(2, 500)
ax3.plot(x, y, 'cH', alpha=0.3)
```

8. Define a fourth axes on `gs1` and plot a `polar` plot:

```
ax4 = fig.add_subplot(gs1[1:, 1:], projection='polar')
N = 30
theta = np.linspace(0.0, 2 * np.pi, N, endpoint=False)
radii = 10 * np.random.rand(N)
width = np.pi / 4 * np.random.rand(N)
bars = ax4.bar(theta, radii, width=width, bottom=0.0)
```

9. Use custom colors and transparency for the bars on the polar plot:

```
for r, bar in zip(radii, bars):
    bar.set_facecolor(plt.cm.BuPu(r / 10.))
    bar.set_alpha(0.5)
```

10. Define a second `GridSpec` `gs2` with width and height ratio arguments:

```
widths = [2, 3, 1.5]
heights = [1, 3, 2]
gs2 = GridSpec(ncols=3, nrows=3, left=0.55, right=0.95, wspace=0.2,
        hspace=0.1, width_ratios=widths, height_ratios=heights)
```

11. Define data for another `polar` plot, plot nine polar plots, and display the whole figure on the screen:

```
theta = np.arange(0., 2., 1./180.)*np.pi
for row in range(3):
    for col in range(3):
        ax = fig.add_subplot(gs2[row, col], projection='polar')
        ax.plot((col+2)*theta, theta/(row+6))
        ax.plot(theta, np.cos((row+5)*theta))
        ax.plot(theta, [1.25]*len(theta))
plt.show()
```

How it works...

Here is how the code works:

- `plt.style.use('seaborn')` specifies the seaborn style is to be used.
- `gs1 = GridSpec(ncols=3, nrows=3, left=0.05, right=0.5, wspace=0.2, hspace=0.1)` creates the first grid:
  - `ncols` and `nrows` specify the grid layout, a 3 x 3 grid in this case
  - `left` and `right` co-ordinates are in the figure co-ordinate system and specify where the grid starts from the `left` and where it ends on the `right`
  - `wspace` controls the space between plots in a row
  - `hspace` controls the space between plots in a column
- `ax1 = fig.add_subplot(gs1[0, 0])` creates an axes instance for the first cell in the `gs1` grid.
- `patches.Ellipse()` defines an ellipse patch whose co-ordinates are specified in the axes co-ordinate system. `ax1.add_patch(ellipse)` adds the ellipse patch to axes `ax1`.
- `ax2 = fig.add_subplot(gs1[0, 1:])` creates the axes instance `ax2` for the second and third cells in the first row of `gs1`. A histogram is plotted on this axes.
- `ax3 = fig.add_subplot(gs1[1:, 0])` creates an axes instance `ax3` for the second and third cells in the first column of `gs1`. A scatter plot of 500 random numbers is plotted on this axes.
- `ax4 = fig.add_subplot(gs1[1:, 1:], projection='polar')` creates a polar axes instance `ax4` for the first and second rows, and the first and second columns. It occupies 2 x 2 cells of `gs1`. A polar bar plot is drawn on this axes.
- `gs2 = GridSpec(ncols=3, nrows=3, left=0.55, right=0.95, wspace=0.2, hspace=0.1, width_ratios=widths, height_ratios=heights)` creates the second grid, again a 3 x 3 grid:
  - Here also, the `left` and `right` co-ordinates are in the figure co-ordinate system
  - `width_ratios` and `height_ratios` specify relative width and height in a row and column respectively
  - Nine polar plots are drawn in this grid with different `widths` and `heights`, as specified in the width and height ratio arguments

You should see the following figure as output of the preceding code:

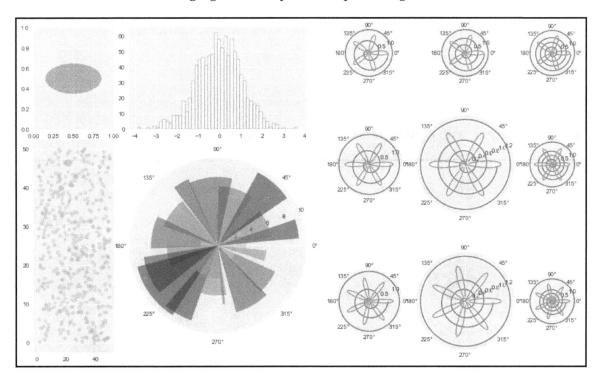

There's more...

In the preceding example, we used `width_ratios` and `height_ratios` arguments to define the required grid using `GridSpec()`. The same arguments can be passed on to `plt.subplots()` to plot a similar grid that we created in the preceding example. Here is the code:

```
widths = [2, 3, 1.5]
heights = [1, 3, 2]
t = np.arange(0.0, 1.0, 0.01)
s = np.sin(2*np.pi*t)

### Passing keyword specs to plt
gs_kw = dict(width_ratios=widths, height_ratios=heights)

fig, axes = plt.subplots(ncols=3, nrows=3, figsize=(10,8),
gridspec_kw=gs_kw)
for r, row in enumerate(axes):
```

```
for c, ax in enumerate(row):
    ax.plot(t, s)
    label = 'Width: {}\nHeight: {}'.format(widths[c], heights[r])
        ax.annotate(label, (0.1, 0.5), xycoords='axes
        fraction', va='center')

fig.tight_layout()

plt.show()
```

Here is the output, with exactly the same layout that we saw before using `GridSpec()`:

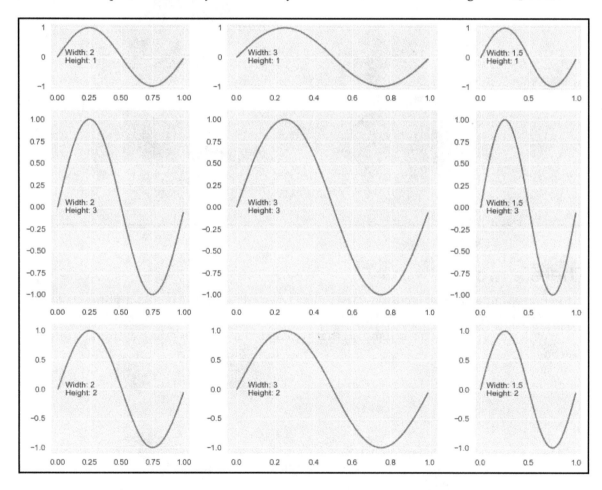

GridSpec alignment

When we create multiple grids and place them side by side in the figure, they are sometimes likely to be misaligned at the top, bottom, or both. In this recipe, we will learn how to avoid such alignment issues.

Getting ready

We will use an error bar plot example for this recipe. We will also learn how to create a constant error bar, symmetric and asymmetric error bar, and error bar sampling.

Let's import the required libraries:

```
import matplotlib.pyplot as plt
from matplotlib.gridspec import GridSpec
```

How to do it...

The following code block plots five graphs with three in the first grid and two in the second grid. We plot a constant error bar and a symmetric and asymmetric error bar on the first grid, and all error bars and sampled error bars on the second grid:

1. Define the figure with its size and set the style to be used in this session:

```
fig = plt.figure(figsize=(8,8))
plt.style.use('seaborn-deep')
```

2. Define the function to plot a graph:

```
def plot_errorbar(axs, x, y, xerr=None, yerr=None, errevery=1,
                  title=None, xlabel=None, ylabel=None, fmt=None):
    ax = fig.add_subplot(axs)
    ax.errorbar(x, y, xerr=xerr, yerr=yerr, errorevery=errevery,
                fmt=fmt)
    ax.set(title=title, xlabel=xlabel, ylabel=ylabel)
```

3. Define the first grid `gs1` with a 3 x 1 layout using `GridSpec`:

```
gs1 = GridSpec(3, 1)
```

4. Define the data for an exponential curve:

```
x = np.arange(0.1, 5, 0.5)
y = np.exp(-x)
```

5. Plot the error bar with constant errors on both *x* and *y* axes:

```
plot_errorbar(gs1[0], x, y, xerr=0.8, yerr=0.3, title='Constant
            Errors', xlabel='X', ylabel='Y', fmt='-o')
```

6. Define the varying error as a function of *x*, then plot only `yerror`:

```
error = 0.1 + 0.25 * x
plot_errorbar(gs1[1], x, y, yerr=error, title='Variable Symmetric
            Error', xlabel='X', ylabel='Y', fmt='-o')
```

7. Define the bounded error to create an asymmetrical error bar:

```
lower_error = 0.5 * error
upper_error = error
asymmetric_error = [lower_error, upper_error]
plot_errorbar(gs1[2], x, y, xerr=asymmetric_error, title='Variable
            Asymmetric Error', xlabel='X', ylabel='Y', fmt='o')
```

8. Adjust the space between the plots on the first grid, `gs1`:

```
gs1.tight_layout(fig, rect=[0, 0, 0.5, 1])
```

9. Define the data with a smaller interval for an exponential curve:

```
x = np.arange(0.1, 5, 0.1)
y = np.exp(-x)
```

10. Define the second grid `gs2` with a 2 x 1 layout:

```
gs2 = GridSpec(2, 1)
```

11. Define the varying error as a non-linear function of *x*, and plot all error points in the error bar:

```
yerr = 0.1 + 0.1 * np.sqrt(x)
plot_errorbar(gs2[0], x, y, yerr=yerr, title='All Errorbars',
            xlabel='X', ylabel='Y', fmt='-')
```

12. Plot only every fifth sample error:

```
plot_errorbar(gs2[1], x, y, yerr=yerr, errevery=5, title='only
every
                5th errorbar',
                xlabel='X', ylabel='Y', fmt='-')
```

13. Adjust the space between the plots on `gs2`:

```
gs2.tight_layout(fig, rect=[0.5, 0, 1, 1], h_pad=0.5)
```

14. If the two grids are not aligned on the top or bottom, try to match them to align properly:

```
top = min(gs1.top, gs2.top)
bottom = max(gs1.bottom, gs2.bottom)

gs1.update(top=top, bottom=bottom)
gs2.update(top=top, bottom=bottom)

plt.show()
```

How it works ...

Here is an explanation of the code:

- `plot_errorbar()` is a user-defined function to plot the error graph with the given parameters such as `axes`, `data` to be plotted, and other parameters that control the plot.
- `gs1 = GridSpec(3, 1)` defines a 3 x 1 grid, `gs1`.
- `plot_errorbar()` plots the error bar on axes `gs1[0]` with constant error on both the x and y axis:
    - The length of the horizontal line in the plot indicates the magnitude of error in X.
    - The length of the vertical line represents the magnitude of error in Y.
    - In the first plot, both of them look the same size, but their values are quite different, at 0.8 and 0.3. That is because the scale on the x and y axis are different. If we want to get them onto the same scale, we should set `aspect=1` on the plot.

- `plot_errorbar()` plots the second error bar only for a `yerror` that is varying with x, but symmetric, where the error on both sides of the curve is equal.
- The third error bar is plotted for an `xerror` that is also varying, but asymmetrical where the value on the two sides of the average are not equal. This happens when the error is limited within certain boundaries of lower and upper limits, as in this case.
- `gs1.tight_layout(fig, rect=[0, 0, 0.5, 1])` ensures the boundaries for `gs1` are set with the figure co-ordinate system, from the bottom left corner of the figure to half way through the figure in terms of width and full height. This also ensures that there is sufficient gap between the plots within the grid, as we learned about with `tight_layout()` in Chapter 3, *Plotting Multiple Charts, Subplots, and Figures*.
- `gs2 = GridSpec(2, 1)` defines the second grid, which is 2 x 1.
- On this grid, we again plot a standard error bar for only `yerror`, which varies with x on the first axes, and on the second axes we plot another error bar, but sampled every five errors, rather than plotting every error item as we did on the first axes.
- When we have two grids of unequal plot sizes, it is likely that they are not aligned well at the top, bottom, or both. One of them may go up or down relative to the other grid. In such cases, you compute the min or max of the two grids at the top and bottom, and force both the grids to follow these min/max values so that they are both aligned.
- `top = min(gs1.top, gs2.top)` computes the min from both tops.
- `bottom = max(gs1.bottom, gs2.bottom)` computes the max from both bottoms.
- `gs1.update(top=top, bottom=bottom)` and `gs2.update(top=top, bottom=bottom)` force both the grids to have common top and bottom positions so that they are aligned.

Upon execution of the preceding code, you should see the following figure on your screen:

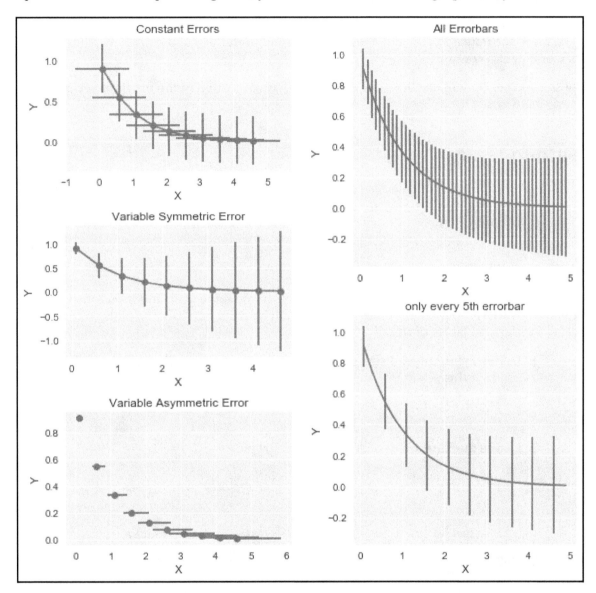

Constrained layout

Constrained layout is similar to tight layout, but uses a different algorithm that is supposed to be more accurate and efficient. However, it is still under test at the time of writing so this may or may not continue.

For this recipe, we will use the same error bars that we plotted in the previous recipe, but use a single grid with a constrained layout.

Getting ready

Import the required libraries:

```
import matplotlib.pyplot as plt
from matplotlib.gridspec import GridSpec
```

How to do it...

The following code block plots five error bar plots in the same grid, and uses constrained layout to ensure proper alignment and appropriate spacing between the plots so that there are no overlaps on labels or ticks:

1. Define the figure and size, and set a constrained layout, then set the style to be used for this session:

```
fig = plt.figure(figsize=(8,8), constrained_layout=True)
plt.style.use('bmh')
```

2. Define the function to plot an error bar graph:

```
def plot_errorbar(ax, x, y, xerr=None, yerr=None, errevery=1,
                  title=None, xlabel=None, ylabel=None, fmt=None):
    ax.errorbar(x, y, xerr=xerr, yerr=yerr, errorevery=errevery,
                fmt=fmt)
    ax.set(title=title, xlabel=xlabel, ylabel=ylabel)
```

3. Define the data for an exponential curve:

```
x = np.arange(0.1, 5, 0.5)
y = np.exp(-x)
```

4. Define the grid `gs` with a 6 x 2 layout using `GridSpec` and add an axes to it:

```
gs = GridSpec(6, 2, figure=fig)
ax = fig.add_subplot(gs[0:2, 0])
```

5. Plot an error bar with constant error on both x and y:

```
plot_errorbar(ax, x, y, xerr=0.1, yerr=0.3, title='Constant
Errors',
              xlabel='X', ylabel='Y', fmt='-o')
```

6. Plot an error bar with error as a function of x and symmetric error on y:

```
error = 0.1 + 0.2 * x
ax = fig.add_subplot(gs[2:4, 0])
plot_errorbar(ax, x, y, yerr=error, title='Variable Symmetric
              Error', xlabel='X', ylabel='Y', fmt='-o')
```

7. Define a bounded error on x, resulting in an asymmetric error bar, and plot the error bar:

```
lower_error = 0.4 * error
upper_error = error
asymmetric_error = [lower_error, upper_error]
ax = fig.add_subplot(gs[4:, 0])
plot_errorbar(ax, x, y, xerr=asymmetric_error, title='Variable
              Asymmetric Error', xlabel='X', ylabel='Y', fmt='o')
```

8. Define the data with a smaller interval for an exponential curve:

```
x = np.arange(0.1, 5, 0.1)
y = np.exp(-x)
```

9. Define the error again as a function of x, but non-linear, and plot the error bar:

```
yerr = 0.1 + 0.1 * np.sqrt(x)
ax = fig.add_subplot(gs[:3, 1])
plot_errorbar(ax, x, y, yerr=yerr, title='All Errorbars',
              xlabel='X', ylabel='Y', fmt='-')
```

10. Add an axes to the grid and plot the error bar with every fifth error item, instead of plotting all of them, to create a sample error bar:

```
ax = fig.add_subplot(gs[3:, 1])
plot_errorbar(ax, x, y, yerr=yerr, errevery=5, title='only every
5th
              errorbar', xlabel='X', ylabel='Y', fmt='-')
```

11. Adjust the space between the plots and display the figure on the screen:

```
fig.set_constrained_layout_pads(w_pad=2./72., h_pad=2./72.,
                                hspace=0.2, wspace=0.2)
plt.show()
```

How it works...

Most of the explanation was already given in the previous recipe:

- `fig = plt.figure(figsize=(8,8), constrained_layout=True)` specifies the figure size, sets `constrained_layout`, and instantiates the figure.
- `fig.set_constrained_layout_pads(w_pad=2./72., h_pad=2./72., hspace=0.2, wspace=0.2)` ensures the proper alignment and spacing between the plots in the grid:
  - It has four arguments, which we can set to control the spacing between the plots.
  - `w_pad` and `h_pad` are specified in inches and are fixed in the data co-ordinate system, so even if the figure size changes, the space between the plots does not change as it is a fixed space.
  - When we specify `wspace` and `hspace`, which are in the figure co-ordinate system, if the figure size changes, then the space between the plots also changes proportionally.
  - `w_pad` and `wspace` control the space between the plots in the same row, whereas `h_pad` and `hspace` control the space between the plots in a column.

Here is how the output looks. The background is different from the previous recipe because we used a different style in this case:

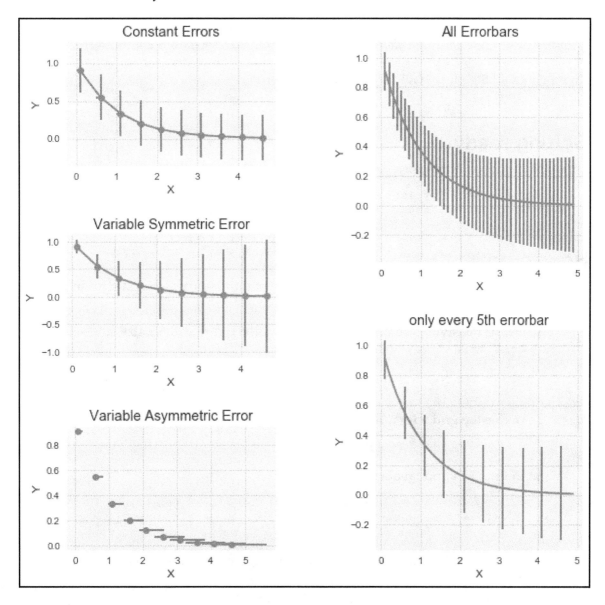

Using GridSpecFromSubplotSpec

`GridSpecFromSubplotSpec()` is one more method available for figure layout in multiple grids. This is somewhat similar to the `subplot2grid()` method that we learned in Chapter 3, *Plotting Multiple Charts, Subplots and Figures*. We will also see how a complex grid created by `GridSpecFromSubplotSpec()` can leverage `constrained_layout` for better alignment of all the plots in all the grids within the figure.

Getting ready

Import the required libraries:

```
import matplotlib.pyplot as plt
from matplotlib.gridspec import GridSpec, GridSpecFromSubplotSpec
```

How to do it...

The following code block plots three grids of different numbers of cells and sizes in one figure:

1. Define the style to be used for this session, the figure with its size, and set `constrained_layout`:

   ```
   plt.style.use('ggplot')
   fig = plt.figure(figsize=(12,6), constrained_layout=True)
   ```

2. Define the grid with a 1 x 3 layout, which contains three grids in a row:

   ```
   gs0 = GridSpec(1, 3, figure=fig)
   ```

3. Define each grid layout:

   ```
   gs00 = GridSpecFromSubplotSpec(2, 2, subplot_spec=gs0[0])
   gs01 = GridSpecFromSubplotSpec(3, 2, subplot_spec=gs0[1])
   gs02 = GridSpecFromSubplotSpec(3, 3, subplot_spec=gs0[2])
   ```

4. Plot each cell within each of the grids, using a for loop for each of the grids:

   ```
   for a in range(2):
       for b in range(2):
           fig.add_subplot(gs00[a, b])

   for a in range(3):
   ```

```
        for b in range(2):
            fig.add_subplot(gs01[a, b])

    for a in range(3):
        for b in range(3):
            fig.add_subplot(gs02[a, b])
```

5. Adjust the space between the plots and display the figure on the screen:

```
fig.set_constrained_layout_pads()
plt.show()
```

How it works...

In this example, we are not plotting any graphs, just plotting cells to demonstrate how the GridSpecFromSubplotSpec() method is used:

- fig = plt.figure(figsize=(12,6), constrained_layout=True) defines and instantiates the figure object with constrained_layout set to True. It is important to set the constrained_layout flag to True here, otherwise, it will not recognize the fig.set_constrained_layout_pads() statement at the end of the code. This is a difference compared to tight_layout(), which works even without setting this flag to true at the time of figure instantiation, as we saw earlier.
- gs0 = GridSpec(1, 3, figure=fig) defines the structure of the grid in the figure. Here, we are defining three grids, all in one row:
  - figure=fig, reference to figure instance in GridSpec() is required, if we want to use constrained_layout option. For tight_layout(), this argument need not be specified.
- gs00 = GridSpecFromSubplotSpec(2, 2, subplot_spec=gs0[0]) defines the layout within the grid. Here, we are using a 2 x 2 layout for the first grid.
- Similarly, we are using 3 x 2 for the second grid, and 3 x 3 for the third grid.
- fig.set_constrained_layout_pads() applies the constrained layout for proper alignment and spacing between the plots within and across grids. We are using all the default parameters for this method here.

Here is how the figure looks:

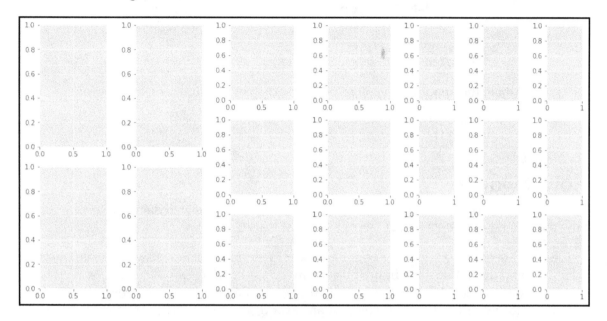

 As an exercise, you can try replacing the constrained layout option with tight layout(). Even with any level of optimization of all the available parameters, such as pad, w_pad, h_pad, you may not get as clean alignment and spacing than you get with constrained_layout.

Using origin and extent for image orientation

We have learned how to use the imshow() method to plot two-dimensional color images. By default, imshow() uses the top left corner of the axes as the origin (0, 0) in data co-ordinates and fills the image with respect to these co-ordinates. If we want to change this to the lower left corner, and also extend the data limits along each of the axis, then the origin and extent arguments of the imshow() method help.

Getting ready

Import the required libraries:

```
import numpy as np
import matplotlib.pyplot as plt
from matplotlib.ticker import MultipleLocator
```

How to do it...

The following code block plots an image of a bird six times in two figures, with the default parameters as well as the optional arguments of origin and extent, with different options for each to demonstrate how these arguments influence the orientation of the image:

1. Read the image of a bird (adapted from the *Machine Learning* course on Coursera: https://www.coursera.org/learn/machine-learning?action= enroll):

```
img = plt.imread('bird_small.png')
```

2. Define a function to plot the image:

```
def plot(ax, origin, extent, title):
    ax.imshow(img, origin=origin, extent=extent)
    ax.xaxis.set_major_locator(MultipleLocator(25))
    ax.yaxis.set_major_locator(MultipleLocator(25))
    ax.set_title(title)
```

3. Define the figure, its size, and its layout:

```
fig1, axs1 = plt.subplots(1, 3, figsize=(12,6))
```

4. Plot three images of the same picture, with different options for the origin argument:

```
plot(axs1[0], None, None, title='default')
plot(axs1[1], 'upper', None, title='origin=upper')
plot(axs1[2], 'lower', None, title='origin=lower')
plt.tight_layout()
```

5. Define the second figure with size and layout:

```
fig2, axs2 = plt.subplots(1, 3, figsize=(12,6))
```

6. Plot three images of the same picture with different options for the extent argument:

```
plot(axs2[0], None, None, title='default')
plot(axs2[1], 'upper', (-25, 150, 150, -25), title='origin=upper \n
    extent=(-25, 150, 150, -25)')
plot(axs2[2], 'lower', (-25, 150, -25, 150), title='origin=lower \n
    extent=(-25, 150, -25, 150)')
```

7. Adjust the space between the plots and display the figure on the screen:

```
plt.tight_layout()
plt.show()
```

How it works...

Here is an explanation of how this code works:

- `img = plt.imread('bird_small.png')` reads the image into a NumPy array, which is understood by Matplotlib.
- To avoid repeating the code for each plot, we defined a `plot` function that plots a graph for a given set of parameters.
- `ax.xaxis.set_major_locator(MultipleLocator(25)` sets ticks at intervals of 25 on the *x* axis. We repeat the same for the *y* axis as well.
- In *figure 1*, first row, we plot using the default parameters of `origin` and `extent`, then with `origin='upper'` and `origin='lower'` using the default for the extent parameter. Please note that the default and `origin='upper'` are the same. When `origin='lower'` is used, the image turns upside down, because the *y* co-ordinates change from top down to bottom up (0 to 125). You can now see (0, 0) co-ordinates at the bottom left corner of the picture.
- In *figure 2*, we set different extent options from the default one to see the difference:
    - The extent parameters are set (left, right, bottom, top) in the data co-ordinate system.
    - For the first image, we use the default parameters.
    - For the second image we use (-25, 150, 150, -25), which means -25 at the left, 150 at the right, 150 at the bottom and -25 at the top. This is setting the bounding box in which the image fits. If these co-ordinates go beyond the original image data limits, then it will fill additional pixels using the interpolation options; if they are lower, then it will use re-sampling options to reduce the size.

Here is how the figure looks:

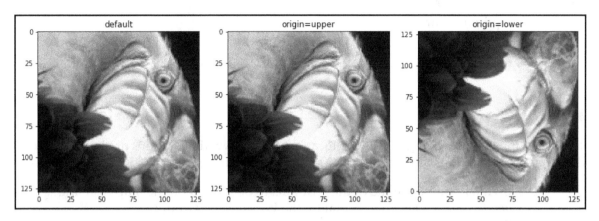

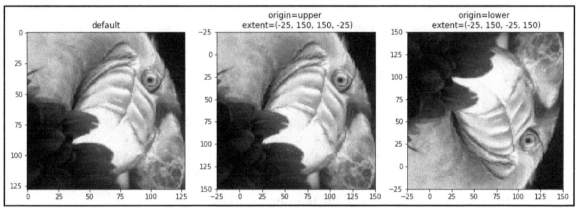

Geographical plotting using geopandas

In this recipe, we will learn how to plot geographical maps using the geopandas package that comes packaged with Matplotlib. There are third party packages supported by Matplotlib for advanced geographical maps, such as Basemap (being sunset in 2020) and Cartopy (replacing Basemap). We will learn to use Cartopy in Chapter 14, *Plotting Geographical Maps Using Cartopy*.

Getting ready

Import the required libraries:

```
import geopandas as gpd
import matplotlib.pyplot as plt
```

How to do it...

The following code block highlights the locations where weather stations are located across the globe. These stations monitor weather and climate changes:

1. Download the shape file of the locations to be plotted on the map from the *Climate Change Knowledge* portal by the World Bank Group:

```
world_wc = gpd.read_file('GRDC.shp')
world_wc.head() # View the first 5 rows of the data, it is a pandas
                function
```

Source URL: `http://climate4development.worldbank.org/open/#precipitation`
The shape file contains places where Global Weather Stations are located, which monitor weather changes across the globe. Although we use a `.shp` file here, it requires the corresponding `.shx`, `.sbx`, and so on. All the files that are part of the ZIP file should be unzipped and placed in a working directory. Otherwise, this code fails. This is true with all shape files.

2. Download the shape file of the boundaries of the world from `thematicmapping.org`:

```
world_borders = gpd.read_file('TM_WORLD_BORDERS_SIMPL-0.3.shp')
world_borders.head()
```

Source URL: `http://thematicmapping.org/downloads/world_borders.php`

3. Initialize a figure and axes, and set the style to be used for this session:

```
plt.style.use('dark_background')
fig,ax = plt.subplots(figsize=(12,9))
```

4. Plot the *Global Weather Change* data on `ax`:

```
world_wc.plot(ax=ax)
```

5. Draw the simple world map borders:

```
world_borders.boundary.plot(ax=ax,color='#cccccc',linewidth=0.6)
```

6. Display the figure on the screen:

```
plt.show()
```

How it works...

Here is an explanation of the code:

- Download shape files (`.shp`) from the URLs mentioned in the code.
- The first one has the locations of weather stations and the second one has the boundaries of the world.
- These files come in a ZIP file containing multiple different files with different file extensions. We should extract all of them and put them in a working directory. Although we use only a `.shp` file in the code to read, it internally calls other files in the ZIP file.
- `gpd.read_file()` reads the contents of the `.shp` file. The first read loads the weather station location data and the second read loads the borders data.
- `world_wc.plot(ax=ax)` plots weather station locations on the map.

- `world_borders.boundary.plot()` plots boundary information. Please note that we are using the pandas `plot` function here, not the Matplotlib `plot` function. That is why you don't see the usual format of the plot method here!

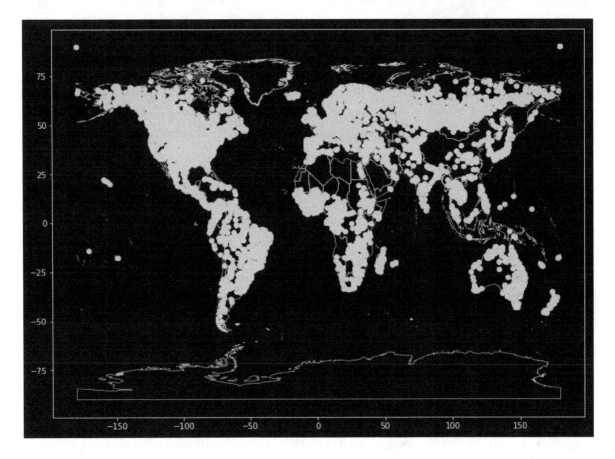

Blue dots represent the locations where weather stations are located.

7
Embedding Text and Expressions

In this chapter, we will learn how to embed text and mathematical expressions on the plot using the following recipes:

- Using mathematical expressions with a font dictionary
- Annotating a point on a polar plot
- Using `ConnectionPatch`
- Using a text box
- Plotting the area under an integral curve
- Defining custom markers
- Using fractions, regular mathematical expressions, and symbols
- Word embeddings in a two-dimensional space

Introduction

Annotations and text come in handy when you want to draw the user's attention to specific areas of the plot, want to provide additional information, or provide an explanation for certain parts of the plot. They also help in creating a story line, and providing additional insights into your data for any formal presentations. In this chapter, we will learn how to use these features.

Using mathematical expressions with a font dictionary

In this recipe, we will learn how to embed mathematical expressions in a text using a font dictionary to apply the same attributes to all the text on the plot, including the title, labels, and text expressions.

Getting ready

Import the required libraries:

```
import numpy as np
import matplotlib.pyplot as plt
```

How to do it...

The following code block plots a decaying exponential function. First, we define the font dictionary with all the required attributes, and then we apply the same to every text element on the graph, including the title and the x and y labels. This ensures that the text on the graph looks and feels consistent:

1. Define the `font` dictionary to be applied to all the text in the plot:

```
font = {'family': 'DejaVu Sans', 'name': 'Times New Roman',
        'style': 'italic', 'color': 'orange',
        'weight': 'bold', 'size': 16}
```

2. Define the data for an exponentially decaying curve and plot it:

```
t = np.linspace(0.0, 5.0, 100)
y = np.sin(2*np.pi*t) * np.exp(-t/2)
plt.plot(t, y, 'm')
```

3. Define the text, title, and labels, and print them on the plot:

```
plt.text(2, 0.65, r'$\sin(2 \pi t) \exp(-t/2)$', fontdict=font)
plt.title('Damped exponential decay', fontdict=font)
plt.xlabel('time (s)', fontdict=font)
plt.ylabel('voltage (mV)', fontdict=font)
```

4. Adjust the space to prevent clipping of `ylabel` and display the figure on the screen:

```
plt.subplots_adjust(left=0.15)
plt.show()
```

How it works...

Here is the explanation of the code:

- `font` is the dictionary of various text attributes that we want to apply to every text item:
    - `family` and `name` represent the font family and font name
    - `style` represents whether it is italic or normal
    - `weight` represents whether it is bold
    - `size` represents the font size
- `t = np.linspace(0.0, 5.0, 100)` defines 100 points in the range of 0.0 to 5.0 with equal spacing in between them
- `y` is defined as a function of `sin`, `exponential`, and `t`
- `plt.title()`, `plt.xlabel()`, and `plt.ylabel()` all are familiar to you by now, but we are adding an additional `fontdict` argument that provides specific parameters to defined attributes in the dictionary
- `plt.text(2, 0.65, r'$\sin(2 \pi t) \exp(-t/2)$', fontdict=font)` prints text at coordinates (2, 0.65) on a data coordinate system:
    - `text` is expressed in a regular expression format; hence, it is enclosed within in `r'.....'`
    - When the text includes mathematical symbols/expressions such as `sin` or `pi`, then it has to be enclosed within `$....$`
    - Characters with special meaning should be preceded by back slash(\) so that their special meaning will appear on the graph, such as `pi`

You should get the following output graph after executing the code:

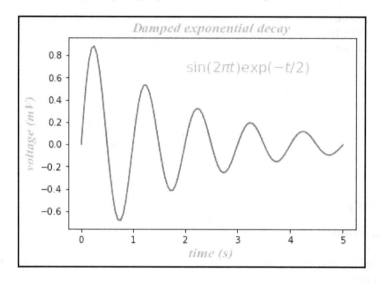

Annotating a point on a polar plot

In this recipe, we will learn how to annotate a specific point on a polar plot.

Getting ready

Import the required libraries:

```
import numpy as np
import matplotlib.pyplot as plt
```

How to do it...

The following code block plots a polar graph and annotates a point on it:

1. Define the figure and axes on it, and declare the polar projection:

```
fig = plt.figure()
ax = fig.add_subplot(111, projection='polar')
```

2. Define the data for the polar plot and plot it:

```
r = np.arange(0,1,0.001)
theta = 2 * 2*np.pi * r
ax.plot(theta, r, color=[0.9,0.4,0.7], lw=3)
```

3. Plot a point with diamond marker at the 600 point on the polar curve:

```
ind = 600
pointr, pointtheta = r[ind], theta[ind]
ax.plot([pointtheta], [pointr], 'D', markersize=10)
```

4. Define the annotation for the diamond point and display the figure on the screen:

```
ax.annotate('a polar annotation',
            xy=(pointtheta, pointr), xytext=(1.0, 0.75),
            textcoords='figure
            fraction', arrowprops=dict(facecolor='red',
            shrink=0.05),
            horizontalalignment='right',
            verticalalignment='bottom')
plt.show()
```

How it works...

Here is the explanation of the code:

- `fig.add_subplot(111, projection='polar')` defines the axes and declares it as a polar plot. In place of `projection='polar'`, you can also use `polar=True`
- `r` and `theta` set the data for radius and angle for the plot of the polar coordinates
- `ax.plot(theta, r, color=[0.9,0.4,0.7], lw=3)` plots the polar chart with `theta` and `r`:
  - Color is specified with R, G, and B color values to create a custom color. R, G, and B values vary from 0 (dark) to 1 (bright).
  - `lw=3` specifies a line width of 3 for the polar chart.

- `ax.plot([pointtheta], [pointr], 'D', markersize=10)` plots a point in a diamond shape on the polar chart, with coordinates `pointtheta` and `pointr`; it is denoted by its index (600) in the list of data points used to plot the polar chart:
- `ax.annotate()` annotates the point with its text description (`'a polar annotation'`):
  - `xy` specifies the coordinates of the point to be annotated (polar coordinates)
  - `xytext` specifies the coordinates where the text description should be placed
  - `textcoords` specifies the co-ordinate system for text co-ordinates specified, in this case it is figure coordinates
  - `arrowprops` specifies the attributes for the arrow between text and the point on the plot

You should see the following graph on your screen:

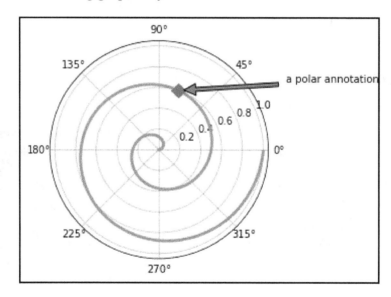

Using ConnectionPatch

In this recipe, we will learn how to use the `ConnectionPatch()` method to connect two points on the same plot or two different plots on the same figure. This comes in handy when trying to show a relationship between two points on the plot(s).

Getting ready

Import the required libraries:

```
from matplotlib.patches import ConnectionPatch
import matplotlib.pyplot as plt
```

How to do it...

The following code block plots two axes, four points, and the connectivity between them. This is a kind of annotation without any text:

1. Define the figure, size, layout, and axes:

```
fig, (ax1, ax2) = plt.subplots(1, 2, figsize=(6, 3))
```

2. Define two points on the data coordinate system and declare the coordinate system for them:

```
pointA = (0.2, 0.2)
pointB = (0.8, 0.8)
coordsA = "data"
coordsB = "data"
```

3. Define the connection between the two points:

```
con = ConnectionPatch(pointA, pointB, coordsA, coordsB,
                      arrowstyle="fancy",
                      shrinkA=5, shrinkB=5, fc="k")
```

4. Plot two points with marker "o" on `ax1`:

```
ax1.plot([pointA[0], pointB[0]], [pointA[1], pointB[1]], "o")
```

5. Add the connection artist to `ax1`:

```
ax1.add_artist(con)
```

6. Print the text for points A, B, and C on ax1 and set the *x* and *y* axis limits:

```
ax1.text(0.06, 0.18, 'A', size=25, weight=50)
ax1.text(0.83, 0.8, 'B', size=25, weight=50)
ax1.text(0.3, 0.15, 'C', size=25, weight=50)
ax1.set_xlim(0, 1)
ax1.set_ylim(0, 1)
```

7. Define two more points, C and D, and assign the coordinate system; both are the same coordinates but on two different axes:

```
pointC = (0.3, 0.2)
coordsC = "data"
coordsD = "data"
```

8. Define the connection between C and D, add it to ax2, add text annotation and set limits for the *x* and *y* axes:

```
con = ConnectionPatch(xyA=pointC, xyB=pointC, coordsA=coordsC,
                      coordsB=coordsD, axesA=ax2, axesB=ax1,
                      arrowstyle="wedge", shrinkB=5)
ax2.add_artist(con)
ax2.text(0.3, 0.15, 'D', size=25, weight=50)
ax2.set_xlim(0, .5)
ax2.set_ylim(0, .5)
```

9. Display the figure on the screen:

```
plt.show()
```

How it works...

Here is the explanation of the code:

- `fig, (ax1, ax2) = plt.subplots(1, 2, figsize=(6, 3))` defines the figure with the size of (6, 3) and two axes in a row on the figure.
- `pointA` and `pointB` are the coordinates of two points.
- `coordsA` and `coordsB` are the respective coordinate system.

- `ConnectionPatch()` defines the connection between `pointA` and `pointB`:
  - `arrowstyle` specifies a `"fancy"` arrow.
  - `shrinkA` and `shrinkB` specify how far away the arrow tip should be from the point they are pointing to, the higher the `shrink` the longer the distance.
  - `fc='k'` specifies the face color to be black.
- `ax1.add_artist(con)` plots the connection path defined previously on axes 1
- Then plot points A, B, and C on axes 1, using `ax1.text()` at appropriate coordinates.
- `pointC` and `pointD` have exactly the same coordinates on the data coordinate system, but on two different axes.
- As we did earlier, plot the connection between `pointC` and `pointD`, the only difference being `arrowstyle="wedge"`

We get the following output:

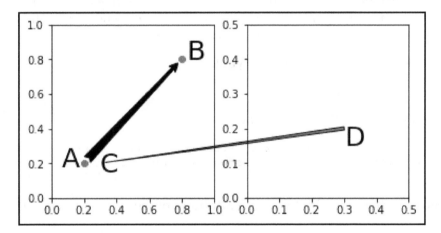

You can replace A, B, C, and D with any text that describes the relationship between the points being connected!

Using a text box

In this recipe, we will learn how to embed a text box to identify different clusters in the plot. We will use a familiar `Iris` dataset that has three clusters of data.

Getting ready

Import the required libraries:

```
import numpy as np
import pandas as pd
import matplotlib.pyplot as plt
```

How to do it...

The following code block plots `Iris` data twice on two different axes. One uses regular legend to indicate three different clusters with different colors and labels. The other uses a textbox within the cluster of points to indicate the class:

1. Define the figure, size, and its layout:

```
fig, ax = plt.subplots(1,2, figsize=(10,6))
```

2. Read the `Iris` dataset with pandas:

```
iris = pd.read_csv('iris_dataset.csv', delimiter=',')
iris['species1'] = iris['species'].map({"setosa" : 0, "versicolor"
                                        : 1, "virginica" : 2})
```

3. Plot a scatter plot with two of the attributes of the `Iris` dataset:

```
ax[0].scatter(iris.petal_length, iris.petal_width,
              s=10*iris.petal_length*iris.petal_width,
              c=iris.species1)
```

4. Define the bounding box properties for the text box to be embedded into the graph:

```
bbox_props = dict(boxstyle="round", fc="w", ec="0.25", alpha=0.9)
```

5. Define the text boxes and plot them on the first axis:

```
ax[0].text(2.75, 0.25, "Setosa", ha="center", va="center", size=15,
           color='m', bbox=bbox_props)
ax[0].text(5.5, 1.0, "Versicolor", ha="center", va="center",
           size=15,color='g', bbox=bbox_props)
ax[0].text(6.0, 2.0, "Virginica", ha="center", va="center",
           size=15, rotation=45, color='y', bbox=bbox_props)
```

6. Use another approach to distinguish clusters using labels and a legend:

```
x,y = iris['petal_length'], iris['petal_width']
classes = sorted(set(iris['species']))
for name in classes:
    index = iris['species'] == name
    ax[1].scatter(x[index], y[index], marker='o', label=name)
plt.legend()
plt.show()
```

How it works...

Here is the explanation of the code:

- As we did earlier, first read the data using pandas, and create another new species1 attribute in the same Iris dataset to hold the numeric class of 0, 1, and 2 for the respective text classes as given in the map function.
- ax[0].scatter() plots a scatter plot of petal_length and petal_width, since there are three classes the data points form three clusters as shown in different colors.
- bbox_props = dict(boxstyle="round", fc="w", ec="0.25", alpha=0.9) defines the text box with:
  - boxstyle as rounded edges
  - face color as white
  - edge color as light gray
  - lower transparency
- ax[0].text() plots the text box, one for each cluster. It is similar to plotting text as we learned earlier, except that now text sits inside bbox as defined earlier. The entire text box is placed at defined coordinates in the data coordinate system which is the default.

- The first two text boxes are horizontal, but the third one is a 45 degree rotation as specified in the arguments.
- Then we plot the same graph using label and legend attributes, just to show a different way of achieving the same output. When we introduced a scatter plot in `Chapter 2`, *Getting Started with Basic Plots*, we did not explain the legend to indicate which cluster/color belongs to which class name. Here, we will learn how to do that:
    - `x,y = iris['petal_length'], iris['petal_width']` gets `petal_length` and `petal_width` into *x* and *y* coordinates
    - `classes = sorted(set(iris['species']))` gets unique classes in the dataset, and sorts them in ascending order
- The `for` loop plots the scatter plot for each class at a time:
    - `index = iris['species'] == name` gets indices of a given class name
    - `ax[1].scatter(x[index], y[index])` plots the scatter plot for given indices

The following is the output graph you should get after executing the code:

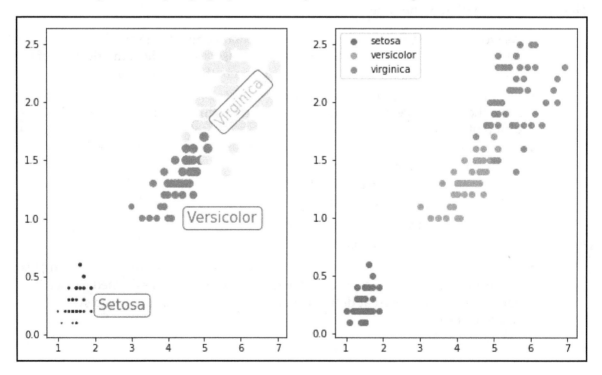

There's more...

In this example, we have used predefined "round" boxstyle. There are many predefined options, such as "circle", "darrow", "larrow", "rarrow", "square", "sawtooth", and "roundtooth".

We can also custom develop these boxstyles as shown as follows:

1. Import the required libraries:

```
import matplotlib.pyplot as plt
from matplotlib.path import Path
```

2. Define a function to plot a custom text box:

```
def tbox_custom_style(x0, y0, width, height, size,
mutation_aspect=1):
    pad = 0.5 * size
    x0, y0 = x0 - pad, y0 - pad
    width, height = width + 2 * pad, height + 2 * pad
    x1, y1 = x0 + width, y0 + height

    # Define the points along with first curve to be drawn
    verts = [(x0, y0), (x1, y0),(x1 + 2*pad, y0 + 2*pad),(x1, y1),
            (x0, y1), (x0, y0)]

    # How to draw the plot along above points
    codes = [Path.MOVETO, # Go to first point specified in verts
            Path.LINETO, # Draw a line from first point to
                            second point
            Path.LINETO,
            Path.LINETO, # Draw another line from current point to
                            next point
            Path.LINETO, # Draw another line from current point to
                            next point
            Path.CLOSEPOLY]     # Close the loop
    # Create complete path with points and lines/curves
    path = Path(verts, codes)
    return path
```

3. Define the figure and add a text box and text labels to the four corners of the text box:

```
fig, ax = plt.subplots()
ax.text(0.5, 0.5, 'Text Box', size=25, va="center", ha="center",
        rotation=25,
        color='b', bbox=dict(boxstyle=tbox_custom_style,
```

```
            alpha=0.25,
                  fc='r',ec='k'))
ax. text(0.35, 0.22, '(x0,y0)', size=15)
ax. text(0.7, 0.5, '(x1,y0)', size=15)
ax. text(0.6, 0.75, '(x1,y1)', size=15)
ax. text(0.15, 0.45, '(x0,y1)', size=15)

plt.show()
```

Here is how it works:

- `tbox_custom_style(x0, y0, width, height, size, mutation_aspect=1)` is a user defined function to draw the box:
  - It takes a size argument provided on the `ax.text()` method and computes internally `width` and `height` proportionate to the size.
  - It takes (`x0, y0`) as (0,0), a reference point.
  - `mutation_aspect` is the scaling factor proportional to the size we provide.
  - This custom `boxstyle` function requires all these arguments in the definition. We can draw any custom object in this function using these parameters.
- To draw a boxed arrow, we need five points to connect. We define these five points using size, `x0, y0, width`, and `height`. Then we use the `path` method to connect these five points as we learned in `Chapter 2`, *Getting Started with Basic Plots*.
- We provide this custom defined function as an argument to `boxstyle=tbox_custom_style` in the `ax.text()` call:
  - `size=25` specifies the font size of the text, which is proportional to the box size
  - `va` and `ha` specify the alignment of the text vertically and horizontally
  - `rotation` specifies the angle of rotation for a text box
  - `color` specifies the color of the text
  - `fc` specifies the face color
  - `ec` specifies the edge color
  - `alpha` specifies transparency of the text box

You should see the following as output of the code:

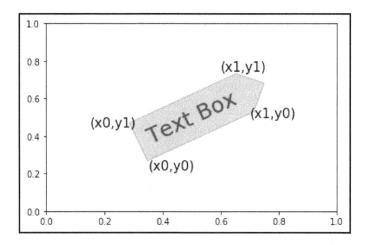

Plotting area under an integral curve

In this recipe, we will learn how to plot a defined area under a curve and embed the equation as text on the plot.

Getting ready

Import the required libraries:

```
import numpy as np
import matplotlib.pyplot as plt
from matplotlib.patches import Polygon
```

How to do it...

The following code block plots a polynomial of the third $y = x ** 3$ order and plots the area under this curve between two points on the x axis, which is the integral of the function limited by the two points:

1. Define two points a and b that are the limits of integral being plotted and the data for the integral function:

```
a, b = 5, 9 # integral limits in which the area to be plotted
x = np.linspace(0, 10)
y = x ** 3 # 3rd order Polynomial curve
```

2. Define the figure and axes and plot the integral function, set the y axis limit to 0 on the lower bound:

```
fig, ax = plt.subplots()
plt.plot(x, y, 'r', linewidth=2)
plt.ylim(0)
```

3. Plot the shaded region between the two bounds of a and b:

```
intx = np.linspace(a, b)
inty = intx ** 3
verts = [(a, 0)] + list(zip(intx, inty)) + [(b, 0)]
poly = Polygon(verts, facecolor='0.9', edgecolor='0.5')
ax.add_patch(poly)
```

4. Embed the integral function on the plot as text:

```
plt.text(0.5 * (a + b), 60, r"$\int_a^b f(x)\mathrm{d}x$",
         horizontalalignment='center', fontsize=20)
```

5. Plot the x and y axis symbols: x and y:

```
plt.figtext(0.9, 0.1, 'x', size=20)
plt.figtext(0.1, 0.9, 'y', size=20)
```

6. Make the right and top spines invisible:

```
ax.spines['right'].set_visible(False)
ax.spines['top'].set_visible(False)
```

7. Set the ticks and ticklabels for the *x* axis and set no ticks for the *y* axis:

```
ax.set_xticks((a, b))
ax.set_xticklabels(('a=5', 'b=9'), size=15)
ax.set_yticks([])
plt.show()
```

How it works...

Here is the explanation of the code:

- a and b are the limits of integral for which we need to plot the area.
- x is an array of 50 (default) values spread equally in between 0 and 10, and y is a third-order polynomial of x.
- `plt.plot(x, y, 'r', linewidth=2)` plots the polynomial curve, and `plt.ylim(0)` sets the lower limit for the *y* axis to 0.
- intx is an array of 50 points spread equally between a and b.
- inty is an array of 50 points corresponding to 50 points in intx, which fall on the polynomial curve between a and b.
- verts is a list of points that form the polynomial from point (a, 0) to all the points formed by intx and inty, followed by (b, 0).
- `poly = Polygon(verts, facecolor='0.9', edgecolor='0.5')` defines the polygon formed by all the points in the verts array with facecolor=0.9 (closer to white) and edgecolor=0.5 (gray).
- `ax.add_patch(poly)` adds the poly patch on to the axes.
- `plt.text()` adds the text at the `(0.5*(a+b), 60)` coordinates, with a fontsize of 20.
- In a regular expression, the following applies:
    - int is the integral sign
    - _a is the subscript a that goes as the lower limit of the integral
    - ^b is the superscript that goes as the upper limit of the integral
    - f(x) goes as is
    - mathrm{d} specifies that *d* is to be printed in roman font
    - x is to be printed as is
- `plt.figtext(0.9, 0.1, 'x', size=20)` is the text plotted on the figure coordinate system, and it plots the *x* axis with a size of 20. Similarly, the *y* axis is plotted at (0.1, 0.9) on the figure coordinate system.

- `ax.spines['right'].set_visible(False)` sets the right spine as invisible, and `ax.spines['top'].set_visible(False)` sets the top spine as invisible.
- `ax.set_xticks((a, b))` sets ticks at a and b.
- `ax.set_xticklabels(('a=5', 'b=9'), size=15)` sets `xticklabels` with a `fontsize` of 15.

We get the output as follows:

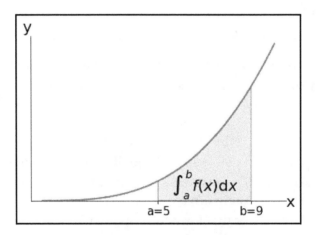

Defining custom markers

In `Chapter 2`, *Getting Started with Basic Plots*, we have learned how to use predefined markers as supplied by Matplotlib. Here we will learn how to define our own markers and use them to plot a sine curve.

Getting ready

Import the required libraries:

```
import matplotlib.pyplot as plt
import numpy as np
```

How to do it...

Here is the code that plots the sine curve for each of the markers:

1. Define the data for plotting a sine curve:

```
x = np.arange(1, 2.6, 0.1)
y = np.sin(2 * np.pi * x)
```

2. Define the figure and size:

```
plt.subplots(figsize=(10,8))
```

3. Define the list of custom markers:

```
custom_markers = ['$'+x+'$' for x in
                 ['£','\$','\%','\clubsuit','\diamondsuit',
                  '\spadesuit','\heartsuit','\sigma', '😃" />']]
```

4. Plot the sine curve for each of the markers:

```
for i,marker in enumerate(custom_markers):
    plt.plot(x, 2*(i+2)*y, marker=marker, markersize=15)
```

5. Display the figure on the screen:

```
plt.show()
```

How it works...

Here is the explanation of the preceding code:

- x and y are the data points for plotting a sine curve.
- custom_markers is the list of custom defined markers; it supports all mathematical symbols and unicode supported emojis. That is why they need to be enclosed within '$....$'.
- The for loop plots the sine curve for each of markers in the custom_markers list, with markersize of 15.

Here is how the output looks:

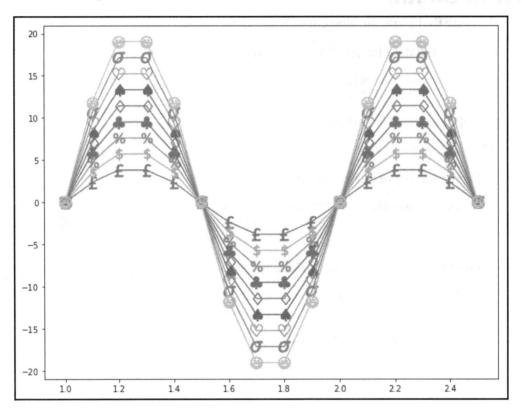

Fractions, regular mathematical expressions, and symbols

In this recipe, we will learn how to embed fractions, binomials, symbols, and mathematical expressions on the plot and the attributes such as labels and title. Functions plotted on each of the plots have no relevance to various text elements embedded within them. They all are meant to demonstrate how various text elements can be printed on a plot.

Getting ready

Import the required libraries:

```
import matplotlib.pyplot as plt
import numpy as np
```

How to do it...

The following code block plots two charts in a row, two functions in each plot, and various text elements on each of them:

1. Define the figure, size, and layout:

   ```
   fig, ax = plt.subplots(1,2, figsize=(12,6))
   ```

2. Define the data for curves to be plotted:

   ```
   x = np.linspace(0, 9, 10)
   y = 10*np.sqrt(x**2)
   y1 = x ** 2
   ```

3. Plot the curves and legend with regular expressions and mathematical symbols:

   ```
   ax[0].plot(x, y, 'g', label=r'$y=10*\sqrt{x^2}$')
   ax[0].plot(x, y1, 'b',label=r'$y={x^2}$')
   ax[0].legend()
   ```

4. Set x and y labels and title with regular expressions and mathematical symbols:

   ```
   ax[0].set_xlabel(r'$\Theta_i^j$', fontsize=20, color='#800080')
   ax[0].set_ylabel(r'$\Theta_{i+1}^j$', fontsize=20, color='#800080')
   ax[0].set_title(r'$\Delta_i^j \hspace{0.4} \mathrm{versus}
   \hspace{0.4} '
        r'\Delta_{i+1}^j$', fontsize=20, color='m')
   ```

5. Set the y axis limits from 0 to 100 so that there is enough space for the legend and all other text to be embedded:

   ```
   ax[0].set_ylim(0,100)
   ```

6. Define three text objects and embed them on to the same axes:

```
text1 = r'$\frac{2}{3} \binom{2}{3} \stackrel{2}{3}$'
text2 = r'$\left(\frac{3 - \frac{1}{x}}{2}\right)$'
text3 = r'$\mathcal{R}\prod_{i=\alpha_{i+1}}^\infty
\gamma_i\/\sin(2 \pi f x_i)$'
ax[0].text(1.5, 60, text1, fontsize=20, va='bottom', color='b')
ax[0].text(1.5, 40, text2, fontsize=20, va='bottom', color='g')
ax[0].text(3.5, 0, text3, fontsize=20, va='bottom', color='r')
```

7. Define the data for curves to be drawn on the second axes:

```
A, B = 1, 2
t = np.arange(0.0, 4.0, 0.01)
s = A*np.sin(np.pi*t)
c = B*np.cos(np.pi*t)
```

8. Plot sin and cosine curves with their functions as labels:

```
ax[1].plot(t,s, label=r'$\mathcal{A}\mathrm{sin}(2 \omega t)$')
ax[1].plot(t,c, label=r'$\mathcal{B}\mathrm{cos}(2 \mathit{\omega}
t)$')
```

9. Set the title and the x and y axis labels and legend using mathematical symbols:

```
ax[1].set_title(r'$\alpha_i > \beta_i$', fontsize=20,
color='#A1F92F')
ax[1].set_xlabel('time (s)', labelpad=20, color=(0.25, 0.5, 0.9))
ax[1].set_ylabel('Amplitude', color=(0.25, 0.5, 0.9))
ax[1].legend(bbox_to_anchor=(1.02, 1.05), borderaxespad=2)
```

10. Embed the text with regular expression and mathematical symbols:

```
ax[1].text(1.9, -0.6, r'$\sum_{i=0}^\infty x_i$', fontsize=20,
color='#808080')
```

11. Adjust the space in between the plots and display the figure on the screen:

```
plt.tight_layout()
plt.show()
```

How it works...

Let's now see how this code works:

- x, y , and y1 define the data for two curves to be plotted on the first chart
- label=r'$y=10*\sqrt{x^2}$' defines the label for first curve plotted in *green*
  - It is a regular expression, so it is enclosed within r'......'
  - sqrt is a mathematical symbol, so the whole expression is enclosed within $ ..... $
- Similarly, label for the second curve, plotted in blue color, is printed
- In Theta_i^j, Theta represents the uppercase Greek letter Θ, '_' represents subscript, '^' represents superscript.
- In r'$\Delta_i^j \hspace{0.4} \mathrm{versus} \hspace{0.4} and r'\Delta_{i+1}^j$', ' connects two regular expressions spanning to two lines:
  - Delta_i^j represents the uppercase Greek letter Δ with *subscript i* and *superscript j*
  - hspace{0.4} represents white space in between
  - mathrm{versus} prints versus in roman font (rm in mathrm stands for roman)
  - Delta_{i+1}^j is Δ with *subscript i+1* and *superscript j*
- In r'$\frac{2}{3} \binom{2}{3} \stackrel{2}{3}$':
  - frac{2}{3} prints 2 over 3 with a horizontal line between them and frac stands for fraction
  - binom{2}{3} prints 2 over 3 within parenthesis
  - stackrel{2}{3} prints 2 over 3 in a stack
- In r'$\left(\frac{3 - \frac{1}{x}}{2}\right)$':
  - 'left(' prints left open bracket "(" spanning entire expression
  - "right)" prints right closing bracket ")"
  - frac is the fraction and works the same way as explained earlier

- In `r'$\mathcal{R}\prod_{i=\alpha_{i+1}}^\infty \gamma_i\/\sin(2 \pi f x_i)$'`, the following applies
  - `mathcal{R}` prints "R" in a calligraphy font (`cal` in `mathcal` stands for calligraphy):
  - `prod` prints the uppercase Greek letter Π in large font
  - "_" after `prod` is the subscript, but it works a little differently when used with large symbols like `prod` and `sum`, and goes under the symbol
  - `alpha` is the lowercase Greek letter α
  - `infty` prints the infinity symbol ∞
  - `gamma` prints lowercase Greek letter γ
  - `\/` prints a white space(similar to `hspace`)
  - `sin` stands for sine function
  - `pi` prints the lowercase Greek letter π.
- `ax[0].text()` prints the text on axes `ax[0]` at x and y coordinates given as the first two arguments, followed by text to be printed on the plot with specified font size, alignment, and color.
- On axes `ax[1]`, we plot sine and cosine curves with amplitude A and B respectively.
- `mathcal` prints *calligraphy* font, `mathrm` prints *roman* font, and `mathit` prints *italics* font.
- `omega` prints the lowercase Greek letter ω, `alpha` prints the lowercase Greek letter α, and `beta` prints the lowercase Greek letter β.
- `sum` prints the uppercase Greek letter in large font Σ.

We get the following output:

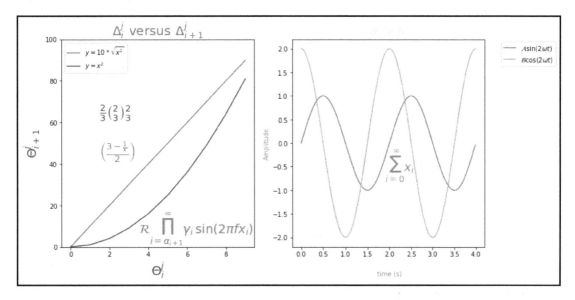

There's more...

Let's take a real-life example of using the combination of a text box and mathematical symbols.

Let's generate random numbers for a normal distribution and plot a histogram. Then let's embed the descriptive statistics of this histogram as a text box on the plot. The following code block does this for us:

1. Import the required libraries:

```
import numpy as np
import matplotlib.pyplot as plt
from scipy.stats import kurtosis, skew
```

2. Set the seed for repeatability, define the figure with size and axes:

```
np.random.seed(19681211)
fig, ax = plt.subplots(figsize=(8,5))
```

3. Define the data for a histogram, and compute the descriptive statistics for this distribution:

```
x = np.random.normal(25, 5, 25000)
mu = x.mean()
median = np.median(x)
sigma = x.std()
minimum = x.min()
maximum = x.max()
kurt = kurtosis(x)
skw = skew(x)
```

4. Define a text string containing all the descriptive statistical measures:

```
textstr =
'$\mathrm{min}=%.2f$\n$\mathrm{max}=%.2f$\n$\mathrm{median}=%.2f$\n
$\mathcal{   \mu=%.2f}$\n
$\mathcal{\sigma=%.2f}$\n\$\mathit{kurtosis}=%.2f$\n$\mathit{skew}=
%.2f$\n'
               % (minimum, maximum, median, mu, sigma, kurt, skw)
```

5. Plot the histogram:

```
ax.hist(x, 50)
```

6. Define the properties of the bounding box in which the descriptive statistics are to be placed:

```
props = dict(boxstyle='round', facecolor='wheat', alpha=0.5)
```

7. Place a text box upper left in the axis coordinates:

```
ax.text(0.05, 0.95, textstr, transform=ax.transAxes, fontsize=14,
        verticalalignment='top', bbox=props)
```

8. Display the figure on the screen:

```
plt.show()
```

You should get the following as an output from this code block:

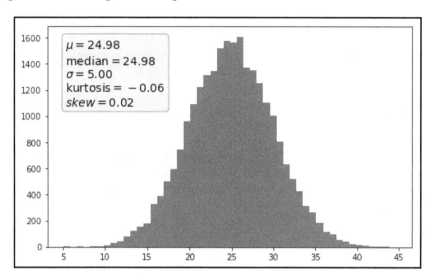

Word embeddings in two dimensions

For **natural language processing** (**NLP**) applications, words need to be represented in numerical format as machines can only process numeric data. Representing words in arrays of numbers is known as "Word embedding", as each of these arrays (word representations) is a point in an n-dimensional space, where "n" is the number of dimensions/features (length of the array) that represents each word.

Depending on the type of NLP application, a **machine learning** (**ML**) algorithm is trained to learn the word representations. The typical length of the word representations can vary from 50 to 300 dimensions, which is impossible to visualize or comprehend. Using dimensionality reduction techniques such as PCA or t-SNE, this high-dimensional space is reduced to a two- or three-dimensional space so that it can be plotted on a graph to visualize whether similar words are coming closer to one another or not. If they are, then our machine-learning algorithm is working fine; otherwise, it is not.

For this example, I have taken the word representations learned using a skip gram algorithm, and reduced it to a two-dimensional space using the t-SNE algorithm. The final two-dimensional output is plotted in this recipe.

For the same example, we will also see a three-dimensional representation and corresponding plot in `Chapter 11`, *3D Plots Using the mplot3d Toolkit*.

Getting ready

Import the required libraries. Note that `pickle` is a Python package used to save and retrieve files in binary format. We will use it here to load previously saved two-dimensional word representations and a word dictionary that maps number representations to textual words that will be displayed on the plot:

```
import matplotlib.pyplot as plt
import pickle
```

How to do it...

The following steps implement the required logic:

1. Load the data using `pickle`:

```
twod_embeddings = pickle.load(open('twod_embeddings','rb'))
reverse_dictionary =
pickle.load(open('word_reverse_dictionary','rb'))
```

2. Set the figure parameters using `rcParams`:

```
plt.rcParams['axes.labelsize'] = 20
plt.rcParams['axes.labelweight'] = 'bold'
plt.rcParams['xtick.labelsize'] = 15
plt.rcParams['ytick.labelsize'] = 15
```

3. Define the figure and axes:

```
fig, ax = plt.subplots(figsize=(20,20))
```

4. Draw the scatter plot and embed words using `annotate`:

```
num_points = 400
words = [reverse_dictionary[i] for i in range(1, num_points+1)]
for i, label in enumerate(words):
    x, y = twod_embeddings[i,:]
    ax.scatter(x, y)
    ax.annotate(label, xy=(x, y), xytext=(5, 3), textcoords='offset
points',ha='right', va='bottom')
```

5. Set labels:

```
ax.set_xlabel('X')
ax.set_ylabel('Y')
```

6. Display the plot on the screen:

```
plt.show()
```

How it works...

Here is the explanation of the preceding code:

- `twod_embeddings = pickle.load(open('twod_embeddings','rb'))`
  loads two-dimensional word representations. As explained earlier, `pickle` is the
  Python package to save and retrieve files in binary format. We are loading the
  data from the `twod_embeddings` file, and `'rb'` represents read in binary format.
- `reverse_dictionary =`
  `pickle.load(open('word_reverse_dictionary','rb'))` loads the word
  dictionary that is used to map numbers to corresponding textual words, which
  will be displayed on the plot.
- `plt.rcParams['axes.labelsize'] = 20` sets the *x* and *y* axes `labelsize`.
- `plt.rcParams['axes.labelweight'] = 'bold'` sets the *x* and *y*
  `labelweight`.
- `plt.rcParams['xtick.labelsize'] = 15` sets the *x-axis* tick value's size.
- `plt.rcParams['ytick.labelsize'] = 15` sets the *y-axis* tick value's size.

- `fig, ax = plt.subplots(figsize=(20,20))` defines and instantiates the figure and axes on which the plot is drawn.
- `num_points = 400`, we are plotting only first 400 words. We had set this limit while reducing the dimensions using the t-SNE algorithm, since more than this count may lead to overlapping words in the plot.
- `words = [reverse_dictionary[i] for i in range(1, num_points+1)]` creates the list of 400 words, and `reverse_dictionary` stores these words with their indices starting from 1 to 400+ (the total vocabulary of training set).
- `x, y = twod_embeddings[i, :]` reads the coordinates of the word from the `twod_embeddings` reduced dimensionality array and maps them to x and y.
- `ax.scatter(x, y)` plots the word represented by x and y coordinates.
- `ax.annotate(label, xy=(x, y), xytext=(5, 3), textcoords='offset points',ha='right', va='bottom')` plots the corresponding word next to the point plotted, and `label` represents the word. Furthermore, `xy` represents the coordinates of the point being annotated, and `xytext` represents the coordinates where the word text is to be plotted; `textcoords` specifies the coordinate system for `xytext` , and finally `ha` and `va` specify horizontal and vertical alignment of the text.
- `ax.set_xlabel('X')` sets the x-axis label.
- `ax.set_ylabel('Y')` sets the y-axis label.
- `plt.show()` displays the plot on the screen.

On running the preceding code, you should get the plot shown below. Groups of words marked in red circles are added to the plot later on to denote similar words showing up close to one another, which indicates that the learning algorithm has done reasonably well:

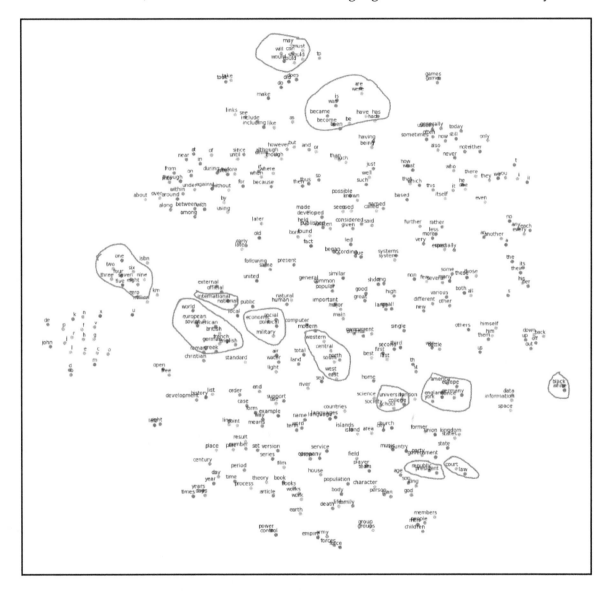

Saving the Figure in Different Formats

8

In this chapter, we will learn how to save the figure in various formats that can be printed or embedded in other applications using the following recipes:

- Saving the figure in various formats
- Avoiding truncation while saving the figure
- Saving partial figures
- Managing image resolution
- Managing transparency for web applications
- Creating multi-page PDF reports

Introduction

Reports and dashboards created by Matplotlib can be consumed in different ways. They can be consumed in upstream web applications, they can be distributed as PDF files, they can be embedded into GUI toolkits, or they can be consumed online interactively.

In this chapter, we will learn how to save reports in various formats so that they can be distributed to consumers for direct consumption as in the case of PDF formats, or embedded into another application, such as GUI toolkits.

Saving the figure in various formats

Matplotlib supports PNG, SVG, SVGZ, PDF, PS, and EPS formats for saving figures. We need to have the respective readers on our computer to be able to view these output formats. In this recipe, we will learn how to save a histogram plot in all these formats.

Getting ready

Import the required libraries:

```
import matplotlib.pyplot as plt
import numpy as np
```

How to do it...

The following code block plots a histogram and saves it in all Matplotlib-supported formats:

1. Set the seed for repeatability and define the figure with the size:

    ```
    np.random.seed(19681211)
    plt.figure(figsize=(6,4))
    ```

2. Define the data for the histogram, plot it, and set ylabel to histogram:

    ```
    nd = np.random.normal(25, 5, 10000)
    plt.hist(nd)
    plt.ylabel('histogram')
    ```

3. Create a list of all the supported file extensions:

    ```
    file_ext = ['png', 'pdf', 'svg', 'svgz','eps','ps']
    ```

4. Save the figure to each of these file formats using a for loop, and display the figure on the screen:

    ```
    for extension in file_ext:
        print('saving Histogram.%s ' % (extension))
        plt.savefig('Histogram.%s' % (extension), dpi=300)
    plt.show()
    ```

How it works...

Here is the explanation of the code:

*   plt.hist(nd) plots the histogram with randomly generated nd data.
*   plt.ylabel('histogram') labels the *y* axis as histogram.
*   file_ext is the list of all supported file formats.

- The `for` loop displays the format being saved for all formats.
- `plt.savefig()` saves the figure with the name `Histogram.file_ext` such as `Histogram.png`, `Histogram.pdf`, and so on.
- `plt.savefig()` is similar to `plt.show()` that displays the figure on the screen, whereas `plt.savefig()` sends the figure to the working directory in the specified format.

You can use both the methods in the same session, as we have done here, so that it saves the file in the specified format to the working directory and also displays it on your screen.

While you can open the files saved in the working directory and see how the saved figures look, we have cropped the images from PDF, SVG, and PNG formats and displayed them here for your reference. When you open and see the respective files, you should see the following screenshot:

 Please note that titles are not part of the figure saved; they have been added over the image to show which image belongs to which output format.

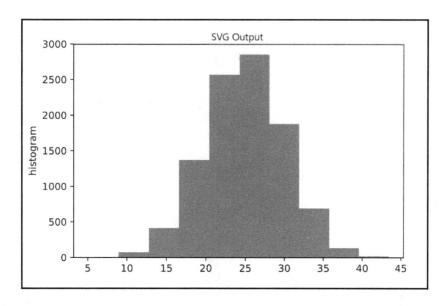

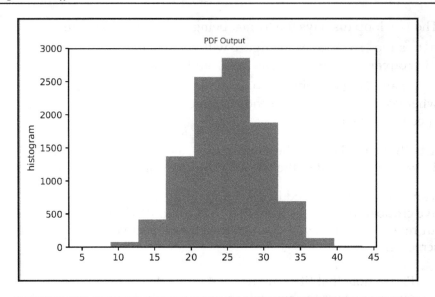

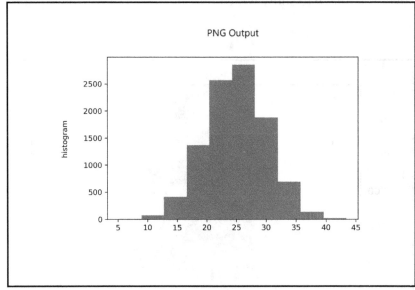

There's more...

In the `plt.savefig()` call, you can use `facecolor` and `edgecolor` and many other options to modify the figure before saving it to the chosen format. We will explore some of those in the following recipes.

By default, Matplotlib looks at the file extension specified in the file name to decide in which format the figure needs to be saved. You can also use the `format` argument to specify the output format, in which case it will ignore the file extension specified and save the figure in the format specified in the `format` argument. However, your file reader may get confused with the mis-match in the file extension and the actual format in which it is saved when you try to open it.

Avoiding truncation while saving the figure

When you save the figure with all the default options, sometimes it may get truncated. In this recipe, we will learn how to avoid such issues.

Getting ready

Import the required libraries:

```
import matplotlib.pyplot as plt
import numpy as np
```

How to do it...

The following code block plots a histogram and saves it with the default parameters, using the `bbox_inches='tight'` parameter, followed by the addition of `pad_inches=1`:

1. Set the seed for repeatability and define the `figure` with `figsize`:

```
np.random.seed(19681211)
plt.figure(figsize=(6,4))
```

2. Define the data for a histogram, plot the histogram, and set `ylabel`:

```
nd = np.random.normal(25, 5, 10000)
plt.hist(nd)
plt.ylabel('histogram', labelpad=20)
```

3. Create a list of all the supported file formats:

```
file_ext = ['png', 'pdf', 'svg', 'svgz','eps','ps']
```

4. For each file extension, save the figure in default mode, with the `bbox_inches='tight'` argument, and with the addition of the `pad_inches=1` argument:

```
for extension in file_ext:
    print('saving Histogram_truncated.%s ' % (extension))
    plt.savefig('Histogram_truncated.%s' % (extension), dpi=300)

    print('saving Histogram_tight.%s ' % (extension))
    plt.savefig('Histogram_tight.%s' % (extension), dpi=300,
                bbox_inches='tight')

    print('saving Histogram_tight_padded.%s ' % (extension))
    plt.savefig('Histogram_tight_padded.%s' % (extension), dpi=300,
                bbox_inches='tight', pad_inches=1)

plt.show()
```

How it works...

Here is the explanation of the code:

- `plt.ylabel('histogram', labelpad=20)` plots `ylable` as `'histogram'` and places it away by 20 units from the *y* axis spine.
- This is required when `yticklabels` are long so that `ylabel` does not overlap with `yticklabels`.
- However, this may lead to truncation when the figure is saved, as can be seen in the following images, again extracted from the respective output files generated by this code.

The preceding code generates the following output:

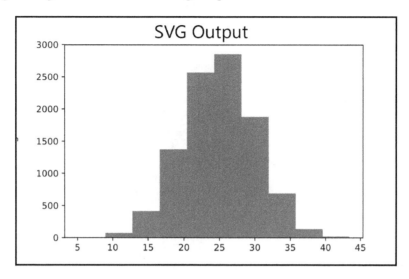

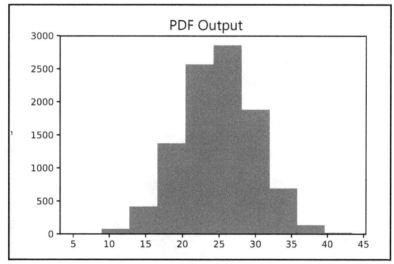

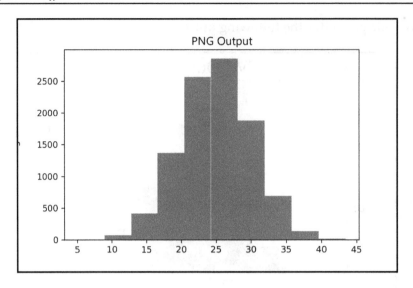

Please note that `ylabel` is missing in all the output formats!

Now let's look at the output generated when we use the `bbox_inches='tight'` parameter on the `plt.savefig()` method. This essentially tries to fit the entire figure including the labels text in the output. Now you can see the histogram label on the y axis:

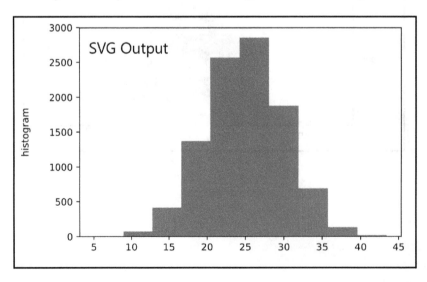

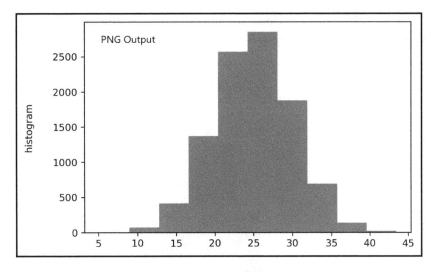

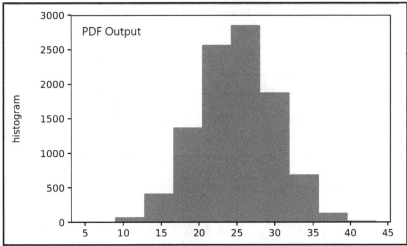

However, if `ylabel` goes too far away from the *y* axis spine, even this parameter may not be able to avoid truncation. You can try changing `labelpad=30`, instead of 20, and then try to save the figure.

As you can see from the diagram, the preceding figure is too closely fitted into the output, without much space along the borders outside. That is why we had to put the title inside the box; unlike earlier, we could place the title above the box!

So, to create some additional space along the borders, we use the `pad_inches=1` parameter. Let's look at how the output figures look with this option added:

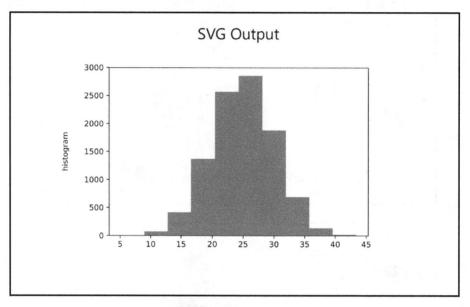

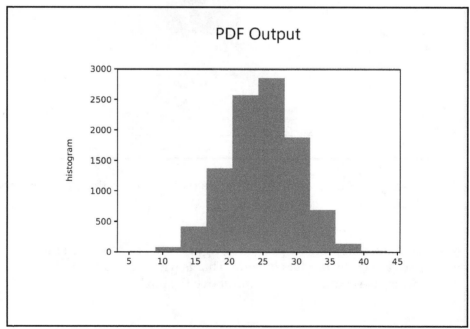

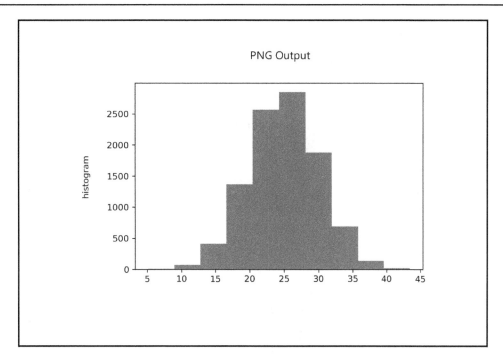

Now you can see additional space outside the box on all sides.

Saving partial figures

Sometimes, we may want to save only portions of the figure, especially when the figure has multiple grids. In this recipe, we will learn how to do that.

Getting ready

Import the required libraries:

```
import numpy as np
import matplotlib.pyplot as plt
from matplotlib.transforms import Bbox
```

How to do it...

The following code block plots a polar plot and histogram on two axes within the same figure. It then saves each plot separately to demonstrate saving part of the figure, instead of the full figure:

1. Set the seed for repeatability and define the figure:

```
np.random.seed(19681211)
plt.figure(figsize=(8, 6))
```

2. Prepare data for plotting a polar plot:

```
N = 250
r = 10 * np.random.rand(N)
theta = 2 * np.pi * np.random.rand(N)
area = r**2
colors = theta
```

3. Plot the polar chart on the first axis:

```
ax1 = plt.subplot(121, projection='polar')
ax1.scatter(theta, r, c=colors, s=area, cmap='plasma', alpha=0.6)
ax1.set_title('Polar Plot', color='m', size=15, weight='bold')
```

4. Plot a histogram on the second axis:

```
ax2 = plt.subplot(122)
nd = np.random.normal(25, 5, 10000)
ax2.hist(nd, color='c', alpha=0.6)
ax2.set_title('Histogram', color='b', size=15, weight='bold')
```

5. Adjust the space in between the plots so that there is no overlap:

```
plt.tight_layout(pad=5, w_pad=2)
```

6. Mark the boundaries of the area to be saved and save that area in PNG and PDF formats:

```
bounds = np.array([[0.0,0.0], [4.1, 6.0]])
plt.savefig('polar.png', bbox_inches=Bbox(bounds))
plt.savefig('polar.pdf', bbox_inches=Bbox(bounds))
```

7. Mark the boundaries of the remaining area of the figure to be saved separately:

```
bounds = np.array([[3.9,0.0], [8.0, 6.0]])
plt.savefig('hist.png', bbox_inches=Bbox(bounds))
plt.savefig('hist.pdf', bbox_inches=Bbox(bounds))
```

8. Display the figure on the screen and clear the canvas area:

```
plt.show()
plt.close()
```

How it works...

Here is the explanation for the code:

- `ax1.scatter()` draws the polar plot.
- `ax2.hist()` plots the histogram, both in one figure.

You should see the figure as follows:

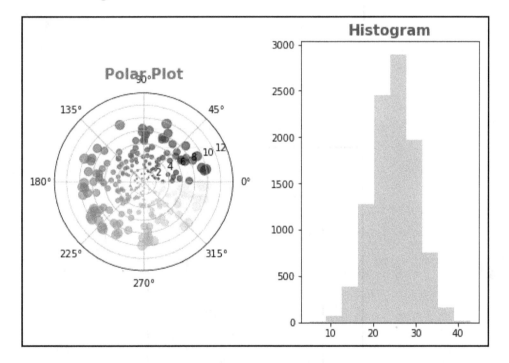

- `bounds = np.array([[0.0,0.0], [4.1, 6.0]])` specifies the boundaries of the figure to be saved. They represent the bottom-left and top-right corners of the area to be saved, and they are in the figure coordinate system.
- We have specified `figsize=(8,6)`, `[[0.0,0.0], [4.1, 6.0]]` and it represents the left side of the figure, and `[3.9,0.0], [8.0, 6.0]]` represents the right half of the figure.

First, let's look at PDF versions of polar and histogram outputs:

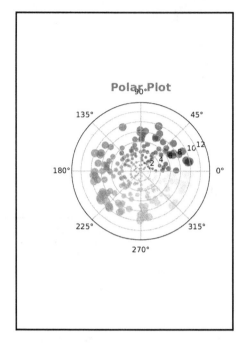

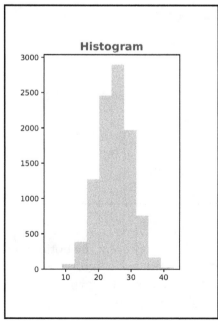

Now, let's look at PNG versions of the polar and the histogram. Here, the polar plot is a bit distorted going, from a circle to an ellipse:

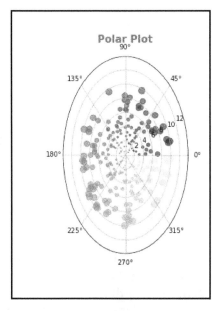

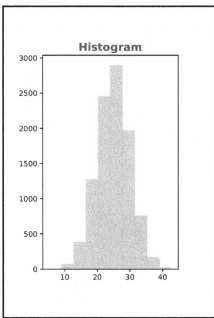

Managing image resolution

When the graphs in the output files need to be printed on paper, the quality of the printout is important. A detailed explanation of photo shopping is beyond the scope of this book, but here we will cover enough to understand the parameters available while saving the figure that influences the quality of the printout.

The quality of the printout depends on the number of pixels in the image (of the figure saved), the size of the page of the paper on which it is to be printed, and the printer resolution.

The number of pixels in the image, in general, is dependent on the resolution of the camera, such as 5 MP, 7 MP, 10 MP, and so on. The size of the paper is controlled with a setting called **Pixels Per Inch (PPI)**. A pixel is the smallest measurable element of the image, and is a tiny small square shape. If we have a 600 x 400 pixel image, and use 100 PPI, then the paper size would be 6 x 4 inches. This is how an image is created with a given number of pixels, PPI, and a size in inches.

When the image is to be printed, printers have another resolution that affects the quality of the printout, which is called **Dots Per Inch (DPI)**. It specifies the number of dots of ink the printer needs to spray in an inch of the length (same for width). The higher the DPI,the larger the amount of ink in an inch of the length, so the better the quality of the printout.

Hence, PPI is the input side of the resolution that is used while the image is being created; DPI is the output side of resolution that is used while printing the image. For a given device, PPI and DPI are predetermined by the manufacturer; for example, computer monitors have a fixed PPI, and printers have a fixed DPI.

The `plt.savefig()` method has a `dpi` parameter, which in conjunction with the figure size determines the size of the image (figure) in terms of the number of pixels. Here, DPI is a misnomer; it should ideally be PPI.

Getting ready

Import the required libraries:

```
import matplotlib.pyplot as plt
import numpy as np
```

How to do it...

The following code block plots a histogram and saves two different `dpi` parameters for comparison:

1. Set the seed and prepare the data for plotting the histogram:

```
np.random.seed(19681211)
nd = np.random.normal(25, 5, 10000)
```

2. Define the figure with the size and plot the histogram on it:

```
plt.figure(figsize=(6,4))
plt.hist(nd)
```

3. Plot grid lines on the plot:

```
plt.grid()
```

4. Save the figure in PNG format with 300 DPI, and also display it on the screen:

```
plt.savefig('histogram_300.png', dpi=300)
plt.show()
```

5. Define another figure with a larger size, plot the histogram, and save it in PNG format with 100 DPI:

```
plt.figure(figsize=(18,12))
plt.hist(nd)
plt.grid()
plt.savefig('histogram_100.png', dpi=100)
plt.show()
```

How it works...

Here is the explanation of the code:

- `plt.figure(figsize=(6,4))` sets the figure size to 6 x 4.
- `plt.hist(nd)` plots the histogram.
- Since we are using `dpi=300`, it will create the image of the figure with 1,800 x 1,200 pixels (6*300 x 4*300).

The figure saved in `histogram_300.png` looks as follows:

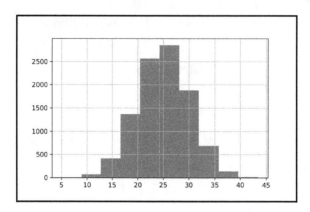

If this same figure of 1800 x 1200 pixels has to be printed at 100 DPI, we need the figure size of 18 x 12. We again save the figure with the 18 x 12 size and `dpi=100`. This is how the saved output looks:

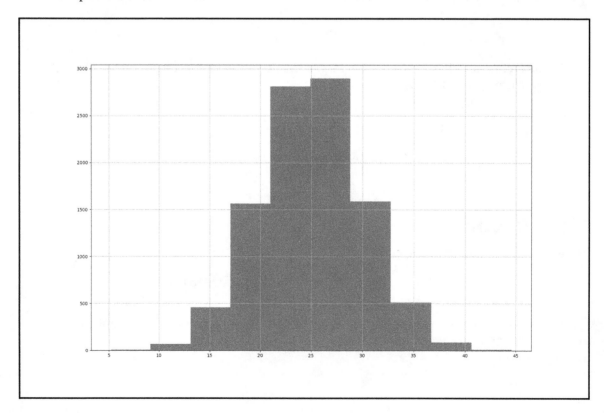

It should be noted that ticklabels and grid lines have become much smaller compared to the previous figure that we saved with `dpi=300, figsize=(6, 4)`. When you are spreading the same number of pixels (width and height) on a smaller area, then the density of the pixels will be high, and so will be the quality. So, when you are creating and saving the figure, choose the figure size and the DPI settings to create as many pixels for the width and the height of the plot, as required for the quality of the printout you need. The higher the number of pixels for the width and the height, the better the quality of your printout will be.

Managing transparency for web applications

Normally, Matplotlib plots and figures have a white background by default, which can be changed to any color we want using the `facecolor` argument. If we have to embed these figures in any to any other application, this background color will carry forward. However, the Matplotlib `savefig()` method gives an option to save figures without this background color, using a transparent argument. In this recipe, we will learn how to use this option.

Getting ready

We will plot four graphs, save them with the normal mode and the transparent option, and embed them in to HTML pages to see how different they look.

Import the required libraries:

```
import matplotlib.pyplot as plt
import numpy as np
import pandas as pd
```

How to do it...

The following code block plots four graphs and saves them in a `.png` format:

1. Set the seed for reproducible results:

```
np.random.seed(19681211)
```

2. Prepare data for a polar plot:

```
N = 250
r = np.random.rand(N)
theta = 2 * np.pi * np.random.rand(N)
area = 500 * r**2
colors = theta
```

3. Define the figure with `size` and plot a polar chart:

```
plt.figure(figsize=(6,4))
ax = plt.subplot(111, projection='polar')
c = ax.scatter(theta, r, c=colors, s=area, cmap='plasma',
alpha=0.6)
plt.title('Polar Plot', color='m', size=15, weight='bold')
```

4. Save the figure in a PNG format with `transparent` set to `True`, and display the same on the screen:

```
plt.savefig('polar_transparent.png', dpi=300, transparent=True)
plt.show()
```

5. Define another figure with `size`, prepare data for the histogram, and plot it:

```
plt.figure(figsize=(6,4))
nd = np.random.normal(25, 5, 10000)
plt.hist(nd, color='c', alpha=0.6)
plt.title('Histogram', color='b', size=15, weight='bold')
```

6. Save the figure in a PNG format with set `transparent` to `True`:

```
plt.savefig('Histogram_Transparent.png', dpi=300, transparent=True)
```

7. Define another figure with `size`, prepare data for a pie chart, and plot it:

```
plt.figure(figsize=(6,4))
labels = ['grocery', 'transportation', 'apparel', 'education',
          'capital', 'savings', 'others']
percentage = [15, 5, 19, 8, 30, 13, 10]
explode = [0, 0, 0, 0, 0.1, 0, 0]
plt.pie(percentage, labels=labels, explode=explode,
        autopct='%.1f%%', shadow=True)
plt.title('Pie Chart', color='r', size=15, weight='bold')
```

8. Save the figure in a PNG format and set `transparent` to `True`:

```
plt.savefig('Pie_Transparent.png', dpi=300, transparent=True)
plt.show()
```

9. Define one more figure with `size`, read the `Iris` dataset, and plot `Iris` clusters:

```
plt.figure(figsize=(6,4))
iris = pd.read_csv('iris_dataset.csv', delimiter=',')
x,y = iris['petal_length'], iris['petal_width']
classes = sorted(set(iris['species']))
for name in classes:
    index = iris['species'] == name
    plt.scatter(x[index], y[index], s=20*x[index]*y[index],
marker='o', label=name, alpha=0.6)
plt.legend()
plt.title('Iris Classification', color='g', size=15, weight='bold')
```

10. Save the figure in a PNG format with `transparent` set to `True`:

```
plt.savefig('iris_Transparent.png', dpi=300, transparent=True)
plt.show()
```

How it works...

All these graphs are already familiar to us, so there is no need to explain the code that plots them. However, the following is the explanation for the code that saves the plots:

- `plt.savefig('polar_transparent.png', dpi=300, transparent=True)` saves the figure.
- `transparent=True` enables you to print the plot without any background color.
- The default value for this parameter is `False`.
- When you want to embed these figures in to any application with a desired background, save the figures with the `transparent=True` option.
- We have also saved these figures without the `transparent=True` option and named them with _opaque, instead of _transparent.
- We have then embedded them in to two html pages. We used light blue as the background color for HTML pages.

The following is the image of the HTML page where we have used the figures saved *without* the `transparent=True` option:

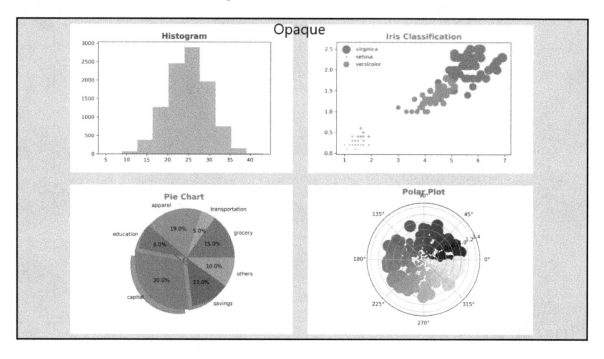

The following is the image of the HTML page where we have used the figures saved *with* the `transparent=True` option:

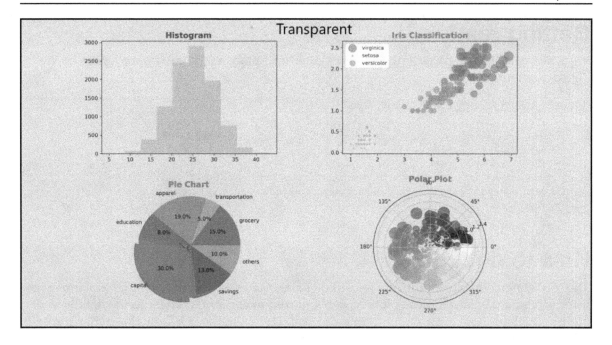

As can be seen from the HTML pages, the white background carried forward in the first HTML page and the HTML background color is visible outside the boundaries of the plots, within the boundaries of the figure.

In the second HTML page, plots did not carry any background color, so the HTML background color is visible within each of the plots.

Creating multi-page PDF reports

In this recipe, we will learn how to create a PDF document with multiple pages containing a number of figures. This will be handy if you have to create a bunch of reports for a specific user or department and ship it as one single document.

Getting ready

We will create three figures with two plots each, and place each figure in one page of the PDF document.

Let's import the required libraries:

```
import datetime
import numpy as np
import pandas as pd
from matplotlib.backends.backend_pdf import PdfPages
import matplotlib.pyplot as plt
import calendar
```

How to do it...

The following code block plots the required charts and saves them into a PDF document as three separate pages. All these plots have been used in earlier chapters, so the details of plotting each of them are already familiar to you. Here, the focus is how these charts are arranged to save in various pages of the PDF document:

1. Set the seed for repeatability:

    ```
    np.random.seed(19681211)
    ```

2. Define a function to draw a polar plot:

    ```
    def Plot_Polar():
        plt.figure(figsize=(6, 4))
        N = 250
        r = 10 * np.random.rand(N)
        theta = 2 * np.pi * np.random.rand(N)
        area = r**2
        colors = theta
        ax1 = plt.subplot(121, projection='polar')
        ax1.scatter(theta, r, c=colors, s=area, cmap='plasma',
                    alpha=0.6)
        ax1.set_title('Polar Plot', color='m', size=15, weight='bold')
    ```

3. Define a function to draw a histogram:

    ```
    def Plot_Histogram():
        ax2 = plt.subplot(122)
        nd = np.random.normal(25, 5, 10000)
        n, bins, patches = ax2.hist(nd, color='c', alpha=0.6)
        n, bins, patches = ax2.hist(nd, color='c', alpha=0.6,
    ```

```
    density=1)
    mu, sigma = 25, 5
    y = ((1 / (np.sqrt(2 * np.pi) * sigma)) * np.exp(-0.5 * (1 /
        sigma * (bins - mu))**2))
    ax2.plot(bins, y, '--')
    ax2.set_title('Histogram', color='b', size=15, weight='bold')
```

4. Define a function to draw a pie plot:

```
def Plot_Pie():
    plt.figure(figsize=(8, 6))
    ax1 = plt.subplot(121)
    labels = ['grocery', 'transportation', 'apparel', 'education',
            'capital', 'savings', 'others']
    percentage = [15, 5, 19, 8, 30, 13, 10]
    explode = [0, 0, 0, 0, 0.1, 0, 0]
    ax1.pie(percentage, labels=labels, explode=explode,
            autopct='%.1f%%', shadow=True)
    ax1.set_title('Expenses Pie Chart', color='r', size=15,
                weight='bold')
```

5. Define a function to draw an `Iris` cluster plot:

```
def Plot_iris():
    ax2 = plt.subplot(122)
    iris = pd.read_csv('iris_dataset.csv', delimiter=',')
    x,y = iris['petal_length'], iris['petal_width']
    classes = sorted(set(iris['species']))
    for name in classes:
        index = iris['species'] == name
        ax2.scatter(x[index], y[index], s=20*x[index]*y[index],
                    marker='o', label=name, alpha=0.6)
    ax2.legend()
    ax2.set_title('Iris Classification', color='g', size=15,
                weight='bold')
```

6. Define a function to draw a bar plot:

```
def Plot_Bar():
    fig = plt.figure(figsize=(10, 8))
    ax1 = plt.subplot(121)
    month_num = [1, 2, 3, 4, 5, 6, 7, 8, 9, 10, 11, 12]
    units_sold = [500, 600, 750, 900, 1100, 1050, 1000, 950, 800,
                700, 550, 450]
    plot = ax1.bar(month_num, units_sold)
    plt.xticks(np.arange(12)+1, calendar.month_name[1:13],
            rotation=75)
    for rect in plot:
```

```
        height = rect.get_height()
        ax1.text(rect.get_x() + rect.get_width()/2.,
                 1.002*height,'%d' % int(height),
                 ha='center', va='bottom')
    ax1.set_title('Batteries Sold', color='y', size=15,
                  weight='bold')
    return fig
```

7. Define a function to draw a steam plot:

```
def Plot_Steamplot(fig):
    ax2 = plt.subplot(122)
    x, y = np.linspace(-3,3,100), np.linspace(-2,4,50)
    X, Y = np.meshgrid(x, y)
    U = 1 - X**2
    V = 1 + Y**2
    speed = np.sqrt(U*U + V*V)
    # Varying line width along a streamline
    lw = 5*speed / speed.max()
    strm = ax2.streamplot(X, Y, U, V, density=[0.5, 1], color=V,
                          linewidth=lw)
    fig.colorbar(strm.lines, plt.axes([0.95, 0.125, 0.03, 0.75]))
    ax2.set_title('Varying Density, Color and Line Width')
```

8. Define a function to update the document properties:

```
def Set_Doc_Properties():
    doc_prop = pdf.infodict()
    doc_prop['Title'] = 'Multipage PDF Reports'
    doc_prop['Author'] = 'P Srinivasa Rao'
    doc_prop['Subject'] = 'saving matplotlib plots in a pdf
                          document'
    doc_prop['Keywords'] = 'PdfPages multipage author title
subject'
    doc_prop['CreationDate'] = datetime.datetime(2018, 7, 24)
    doc_prop['ModDate'] = datetime.datetime.today()
```

9. Define the main program for creating a multi-page PDF report:

```
with PdfPages('pdf_reports.pdf') as pdf:
    # Page1
    Plot_Polar()
    Plot_Histogram()
    plt.suptitle('Page One', color='C5', size=20, weight='bold')
    plt.tight_layout(pad=5, w_pad=2)
    pdf.attach_note("polar & histogram")
    pdf.savefig(dpi=300)
    plt.show()
```

```
plt.close()
# Page2
Plot_Pie()
Plot_iris()
plt.suptitle('Page Two', color='C8', size=20, weight='bold')
pdf.attach_note("pie and scatter")
plt.tight_layout(pad=5, w_pad=10)
pdf.savefig(dpi=300)
plt.show()
plt.close()

# Page3
fig = Plot_Bar()
Plot_Steamplot(fig)
plt.suptitle('Page Three', color='C9', size=20, weight='bold')
pdf.attach_note("bar & stream")
pdf.savefig(dpi=300)
plt.show()
plt.close()

# Set document properties
Set_Doc_Properties()
```

How it works...

Here is the explanation of the code:

- `PdfPages()` is the package that helps create the PDF document.
- `with PdfPages('pdf_reports.pdf') as pdf` is a Python context, which takes care of file opening and closing as we save multiple figures into this PDF document. The `pdf_reports.pdf` file is the file into which figures will be saved.
- `plt.figure(figsize=(6, 4))` defines the first figure with a (6, 4) size:
    - `ax1.scatter(theta, r, c=colors, s=area, cmap='plasma', alpha=0.6)` plots a polar plot on axis one.
    - `ax2.hist(nd, color='c', alpha=0.6, density=1)` plots a histogram on axis two.
    - `ax2.plot(bins, y, '--')` plots best fit probability density function for the histogram on the same axis two.

- `plt.suptitle('Page One', color='C5', size=20, weight='bold')` plots the title for the figure (Page One) with defined attributes.
- `pdf.attach_note("polar & histogram")` writes the note for this page as given in the argument, which will be visible when we open the PDF document page as a note.
- `pdf.savefig(dpi=300)` saves the current figure with `dpi=300` into the PDF document specified in *with context*.
- `plt.show()` displays the figure on the screen output.
- `plt.close()` closes the figure and cleans the plotting area so that the next figure can start.
- `plt.figure(figsize=(8, 6))` defines the second figure with an (8, 6) size:
    - `ax1.pie(percentage, labels=labels, explode=explode, autopct='%.1f%%', shadow=True)` plots a pie chart of expenses on axis one.
    - `ax2.scatter(x[index], y[index], s=20*x[index]*y[index], marker='o', label=name, alpha=0.6)` plots a scatter plot of iris flowers on axis two.
    - `plt.suptitle('Page Two', color='C8', size=20, weight='bold')` plots the title for the figure (Page Two).
    - `pdf.savefig(dpi=300)` saves the figure to the same PDF document on the next page.
    - `plt.show()` displays the figure on to the screen.
    - `plt.close()` closes the figure and clears the plotting area for the next figure.
- `fig = plt.figure(figsize=(10, 8))` defines the next figure with a (10,8) size:
    - `plot = ax1.bar(month_num, units_sold)` plots a bar chart on axes one.
    - `ax1.text()` writes the number of units on each of the bars.
    - `ax2.streamplot(X, Y, U, V, density=[0.5, 1], color=V, linewidth=lw)` plots a stream plot on axes two.

- `fig.colorbar(strm.lines, plt.axes([0.95, 0.125, 0.03, 0.75]))` plots the color bar for the stream plot.
- `plt.suptitle('Page Three', color='C9', size=20, weight='bold')` sets the title for the figure (`Page Three`):
  - `pdf.attach_note("bar & stream")` writes a note on `Page Three` with the `"bar & stream"` text, which can be read when we open the page in the PDF document.

- `doc_prop = pdf.infodict()` instantiates the dictionary that holds document properties, which we can see in the properties when we open the PDF document. We save *Title, Author, Subject, Keywords, CreationDate*, and *ModifiedDate* into this dictionary, which will be passed on to the document properties.
- After this code is run, you should see a PDF document named `pdf_reports.pdf` in your working directory. If you open the document, you should see the following three figures as three pages. Each of them is of a different size as we defined in the code:

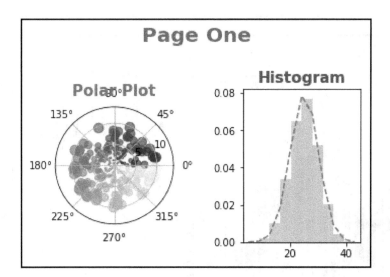

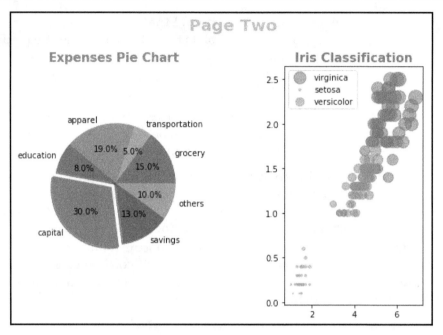

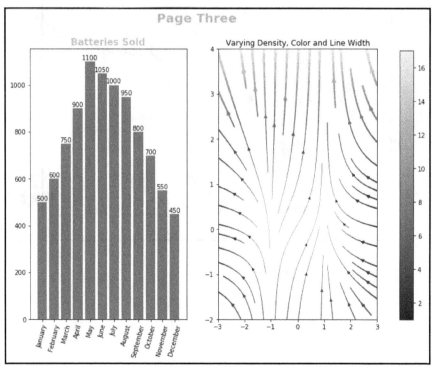

9
Developing Interactive Plots

Interactive plotting is a very large subject; there are multiple books that cover various aspects of it. In this chapter, we will cover three distinct areas, with key recipes in each of them, as follows:

- Events and callbacks:
    - Exception handling
    - Key press and release events for making the legend visible/invisible with hold time
    - Button press event for zooming
    - Motion notification and button press events for tracking coordinates
    - Pick event for making an artist active upon picking its legend label
    - Figure and axes enter and leave events for changing face colors and making artists visible/invisible
    - Using twin axes for plotting four temperature scales
- Widgets:
    - Cursor
    - Button
    - Check buttons
    - Radio buttons
    - Textbox
- Animation:
    - Animated sigmoid
    - Saving an animation to an MP4 file
    - Exponentially decaying the tan function
    - Animated bubble plot
    - Animation of multiple line plots
    - Animation of images

Introduction

For interactive plotting, the usual `%matplotlib inline` does not work as it outputs a static figure to the screen. We need to use one of the backends supported by Matplotlib. You may recall that the backend is the lowermost layer of Matplotlib architecture where the output figure created by Matplotlib is sent for display. There are two types of backends: one allows users to interact with the output and is used in interactive plotting, and the other is used to save figures for printing or embedding into other applications.

All the recipes in this chapter are tested with the following backends:

- `nbAgg`
- `Qt5Agg`
- `TkAgg`
- `WXAgg`

We have observed that a few features do not work with some of these backends.

Use one of the following options to activate any of these backends:

```
import matplotlib
matplotlib.use('nbAgg')
```

Or use this:

```
import matplotlib.pyplot as plt
plt.switch_backend('nbAgg')
```

If you chose the first option, this code has to be executed before importing the `matplotlib.pyplot` module, because the `pyplot` module loads all the elements required for the chosen backend. By default, `pyplot` loads the backend as defined in the `rcParams` file, which could come into conflict with this backend, if these statements are executed after importing the `pyplot` module.

If you choose the second option, `pyplot` will replace the current backend with a new backend by loading the relevant modules of the new backend. For this to work properly, there should have been some backend set up prior to switching to the new backend.

`nbAgg` is the standard backend used by Jupyter Notebook, and it is displayed within the Notebook's output cell, whereas other backends open another pop-up window for the output.

All these interactive backends provide standard interactive navigation features, though the look and feel are slightly different. A detailed description of the navigation and keyboard mapping for various features has been provided in the Matplotlib documentation at `https://matplotlib.org/users/navigation_toolbar.html`.

Events and callbacks

Events are the actions users take while interacting with plots, such as mouse actions, keyboard clicks, or just entering and exiting figures and axes on the visualization. Callbacks are the responses to events as they get triggered. Exceptions raised while the program is running are also events; however, most of them don't involve user intervention, except `KeyboardInterrupt`.

While we try to cover as many events as possible here, for a complete list of supported events, please refer to the Matplotlib documentation at `https://matplotlib.org/users/event_handling.html`.

Exception handling

During the course of running a program, many different exceptions are raised. If an appropriate action is not programmed, then the program crashes and an emergency intervention is required to fix the issue and restart the program. In this recipe, we will learn how to handle two exceptions, `KeyboardInterrupt` and `DivideByZero`, with their corresponding callback actions.

Getting ready

To simulate exceptions, we will start a loop that runs until an exception happens, capture the exception, trigger the appropriate callback response function, and finally close the program.

For the `KeyboardInterrupt` exception, once the program starts, you will see * in the Input cell of your notebook, click on **Kernel** tab on the top of your notebook and press the interrupt option in the drop-down box.

If there is no `KeyboardInterruption` for 30 seconds, then it will execute the code, which results in a `DivideByZero` exception.

Import the required libraries:

```
import time
```

How to do it...

We will write a class with the appropriate methods to simulate the loop, and capture the exceptions and callback functions. For explanation purposes, we provide a step by step description of various methods in the class; for execution, you will have to take the entire class at once to run the code. Please refer to the code file provided for this chapter:

1. Define the class:

```
class EventLoop:
```

2. Define the init method to initialize the status variable and define the event_handlers dictionary that maps the events to the corresponding callback function:

```
def __init__(self):
    self.status = None
    self.event_handlers = {"interrupt": self.handle_interrupt,
                           "DivideByZero":
    self.handle_DivideByZero}
```

3. Define the start() method to run the loop, capture the exceptions, and call the corresponding callback function for each of the exceptions:

```
def start(self):
    try:
        self.loop()
    except KeyboardInterrupt:
        self.handle_event("interrupt")
    except ZeroDivisionError:
        self.handle_event("DivideByZero")
    finally:
        print('Ending the program')
```

4. Define the method to create and run the event loop:

```
def loop(self):
    self.status = "loop"
    strt_time = time.time()
    while self.status == "loop":
        elapsed_time = time.time() - strt_time
        if elapsed_time > 30:
            5 / 0
```

5. Define the method to handle the event/exception:

```
def handle_event(self, event: str):
    self.event_handlers[event]()
```

6. Define the method for the callback action for the `KeyBoardInterrupt` exception:

```
def handle_interrupt(self):
    print("Stopping event loop Due to KeyboardInterrupt...")
```

7. Define the method for the callback action for the `DivideByZero` exception:

```
def handle_DivideByZero(self):
    print("Stopping event loop due to DivideByZero Error...")
```

8. Instantiate the class object and call the `start` method:

```
el = EventLoop()
el.start()
```

How it works...

Here is the explanation of how it works:

- `class EventLoop`: defines the class function for the event loop.
- `__init__(self)` is the initialization function for the `EventLoop` class object. It initializes the `status` variable and defines the `event_handlers` dictionary with two interrupts with corresponding callback functions.

- `start(self)` is the method to start the `EventLoop`, capture the exceptions, and route to the respective callback functions:
  - `try: self.loop()` runs the `loop` method.
  - `exceptKeyboardInterrupt: self.handle_event("interrupt")` captures the `KeyBoardInterrupt`, and calls the `handle_event` method with the `interrupt` argument.
  - `exceptZeroDivisionError: self.handle_event("DivideBy Zero")` captures the `DivideByZero` exception and calls the `handle_event` method with the `DivideByZero` argument.
  - `finally: print('Ending the program')` prints `Ending the program` at the end of the loop. This gets executed, even when the exception happens, in which case, it first executes the corresponding callback function and then executes the code under the `finally` clause.
- `loop(self)` is the method that runs the event loop until one of the exceptions happens. When any of the specified exceptions happens, control comes out of the loop and moves to the exception-handling method as specified under `except` in the `start(self)` method:
  - `self.status` sets the variable status equal to loop.
  - *start_time* is the starting time of the loop.
  - `while self.status == "loop":` initiates the loop and runs as long as the status remains *loop* or an exception happens.
  - `elapsed_time` is the time from starting the loop.
  - When there is no `KeyboardInterrupt` for more than 30 seconds, then the program goes inside the `if loop` and tries to divide five by zero, resulting in a `DivideByZero` exception.
- `def handle_event(self, event: str): self.event_handlers[event]()` is the method that takes the exception/event and looks it up in the `event_handlers` dictionary to pick the corresponding `callback` method and make a call to it.
- `def handle_interrupt(self): print("Stopping event loop Due to KeyboardInterrupt...")` is the `callback` method for the `KeyboardInterrupt` exception. It just prints the message that the event loop is stopping due to a `KeyboardInterrupt` exception.

- `def handle_DivideByZero(self): print("Stopping event loop due to DivideByZero Error...")` is the `callback` method for the `DivideByZero` exception. It just prints the message that the event loop is stopping due to a `DivideByZero` error.
- `el = EventLoop()` instantiates the `EventLoop` object, and `el.start()` calls the `start` method of the `EventLoop` class.

When you run the program and interrupt the program from the kernel, you should see the following text in the output cell:

```
Stopping event loop Due to KeyboardInterrupt...
Ending the program
```

When you run the program and simply wait by doing nothing, after 30 seconds, you should see the following text in the output cell:

```
Stopping event loop due to DivideByZero Error...
Ending the program
```

There's more...

There are many such exceptions in the Python programming environment. Since they don't involve any user interaction, they are not relevant for interactive plotting. If you are interested, you can find exhaustive literature on them here: `https://docs.python.org/3/library/exceptions.html#bltin-exceptions`.

Key press and release events

In this recipe, we will learn how to capture keyboard `press` and `release` events, and use them to toggle the display of the legend to **visible/invisible**, and also display the amount of time the key is pressed (time difference between the key press event and the key release event).

When the *X* key is pressed, held for some time, and then released, it reverses the status of the legend from visible to invisible, or the reverse, and also displays the time (in seconds) in the output figure, for how long the key was held before releasing.

If any other key is pressed, held, and released, then it will not change anything in the figure, but the program prints the name of the key pressed and the hold time to `sysout`.

We don't need to create an event loop explicitly when we use Matplotlib, because the `pyplot` module takes care of that functionality automatically. It is required only when we use Python code, as we did in the preceding recipe.

Getting ready

Import the required libraries and set the backend:

```
import numpy as np
import matplotlib.pyplot as plt
plt.switch_backend('Qt5Agg')
from time import time
```

How to do it...

Here is the code for plotting the `sin` and `cos` functions with a legend and title, and capturing keyboard events and associated callback functions to respond to the keyboard events:

1. Define a callback function that responds to `key_press_event`:

```
def press(event):
    global prst
    prst = time()
    print('press', event.key)
```

2. Define a callback function that responds to `key_release_event`:

```
def release(event):
    relt = time()
    ht = relt - prst
    print('hold time:',round(ht,2))
    if event.key == 'x':
        visible = lg.get_visible()
        lg.set_visible(not visible)
        tm = 'hold time: ' + str(round(ht, 2))
        t = plt.text(np.random.randint(1,4),
                    np.random.randint(-3,4), tm)
        plt.setp(t, color='r', size=15, weight='bold')
        ax.add_artist(t)
        fig.canvas.draw()
```

3. Prepare the data for the curves to be plotted:

```
x = np.arange(1, 2.6, 0.1)
y = 3*np.sin(2 * np.pi * x)
y1 = 3*np.cos(2 * np.pi * x)
```

4. Instantiate the figure and axes objects:

```
fig, ax = plt.subplots()
```

5. Plot the curves on the axes:

```
ax.plot(x ,y, 'go-', label='sin')
ax.plot(x, y1, 'bd-', label='cos')
```

6. Set the legend and title:

```
lg = ax.legend(loc='upper center', fontsize=15)
ax.set_title('Press a key', size=25)
```

7. Capture the events and map callback function for each:

```
fig.canvas.mpl_connect('key_press_event', press)
fig.canvas.mpl_connect('key_release_event', release)
```

8. Display the figure on the set backend:

```
plt.show()
```

How it works...

Here is the explanation of how it works:

- `fig, ax = plt.subplots()` defines and instantiates the figure and axis objects.
- `ax.plot(x ,y, 'go-', label='sin')` and `ax.plot(x, y1, 'bd-', label='cos')` plot the sine and cosine functions.
- `lg = ax.legend(loc='upper center', fontsize=15)` and `ax.set_title('Press a key', size=25)` set the legend and title for the plot. Here, we capture the legend in a variable, `lg`, which will be used in the callback function later.

- `fig.canvas.mpl_connect()` is the method that captures the events from the `backend` and connects them to the corresponding callback functions to respond to the events. This is equivalent to the `handle_event()` function we defined in the previous recipe.
- `fig.canvas.mpl_connect('key_press_event', press)` captures when any key is pressed, and calls the `"press"` callback function.
- `fig.canvas.mpl_connect('key_release_event', release)` captures when the key is released, and calls the `"release"` callback function.
- `press` is the `callback` function that responds to any key press event:
    - Callback functions take `event` as the argument, which is the keyword used by Matplotlib to pass pre-defined events that can capture specific details of the event, which in this case is the name of the key.
    - `global prst` defines a global variable, `prst`, for capturing the time when the key was pressed. It is defined as a global variable, since it is required in the `release` function.
    - `prst = time()` captures the current time in the `prst` variable, signifying the time when the key was pressed.
    - `print('press', event.key)` prints the name of the key that was pressed, into `sysout`, which you can see in the output cell of your notebook, and since we have declared `prst` with a global scope, we don't need to return it to pass on to the `release` function.
- `release` is another callback function that responds to any key release event:
    - It also takes the `event` as the first argument.
    - `relt` captures the current time to represent the key release time.
    - `ht` is the hold time that elapsed between the time when the key was pressed and when it was released.
    - `print('hold time:', round(ht,2))` prints the hold time to `sysout`, rounding the time to two decimal places.
    - `if event.key == 'x':` checks whether the key pressed was x; if it was, then it executes a set of instructions as follows. Otherwise, it does nothing:
        - `lg.get_visible()` gets the current status of the `lg` legend object in terms of true or false to indicate whether the legend is currently visible or invisible, and assigns that status to the `visible` variable.

- `lg.set_visible(not visible)` reverses the current status, which means if it was visible, it is now invisible, and if it was invisible, it will now be visible.
- `tm = 'hold time: ' + str(round(ht, 2))` prepares the text string for hold time to be placed on the figure.
- `t = plt.text(np.random.randint(1,4), np.random.randint(-3,4), tm)` creates the text artist to be placed at a random location on the figure.
- `plt.setp(t, color='r', size=15, weight='bold')` sets the color, size, and weight properties to the text artist defined earlier.
- `ax.add_artist(t)` adds the text artist to the axes.
- `fig.canvas.draw()` finally displays the output figure on the chosen backend.

When you run the program, you should see the plot on the left side. When you press, hold, and release the *X* key, you should see the legend toggling and the hold time appearing on the plot. When you press the *G* key, you should see the grid lines on the plot. Then, you should see the plot shown on the right side here:

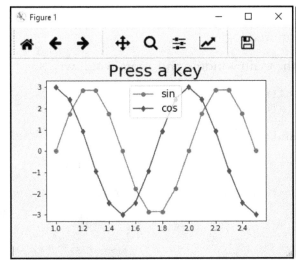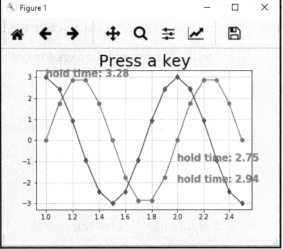

Please note that backend navigation has mapping for a few keys with special functions, such as h for home, g for major grid, l for logarithmic scale on the *y* axis, and a few others for pan, zoom, backward, forward, full screen, and so on. When any of these keys is pressed, you will see its defined function on the plot, so do not get confused with your user-defined functions. You may want to avoid defining your own functions for these keys so that there is no conflict.

Mouse button press event

In this recipe, we will learn how to capture a mouse button press event and use the co-ordinates to zoom the plot around the point where the mouse button was pressed on the main window, and display it in the zoom window separately.

Getting ready

Import the required libraries:

```
import matplotlib.pyplot as plt
import numpy as np
```

How to do it...

The following steps explain how to code the required logic:

1. Define the figure and axes for both the main window and zoom window:

```
figmain, axmain = plt.subplots()
figzoom, axzoom = plt.subplots()
```

2. Set the attributes for both the main and zoom axes:

```
axmain.set(xlim=(-5, 5), ylim=(-75, 175), autoscale_on=False,
title='Click to zoom')
axzoom.set(xlim=(-2, 2), ylim=(-8, 8), autoscale_on=False,
title='Zoom window')
```

3. Prepare the data for the plots:

```
x = np.arange(-5, 5, 0.1)
y = x ** 3
```

4. Plot the same curve on both the main and zoom axes:

```
axmain.plot(x, y, 'g-d')
axzoom.plot(x, y, 'b-.o')
```

5. Define the callback function that responds to the mouse button press event:

```
def onbuttonpress(event):
    if event.button == 1:              # left = 1, scroll=2, right=3
        x, y = event.xdata, event.ydata
        axzoom.set_xlim(x - 1, x + 1)
        axzoom.set_ylim(y - 10, y + 10)
        figzoom.canvas.draw()
```

6. Connect the button press event to the callback function:

```
figmain.canvas.mpl_connect('button_press_event', onbuttonpress)
```

7. Display the figures on the specified backend:

```
plt.show()
```

How it works...

The following is the explanation of the preceding code:

- `figmain, axmain = plt.subplots()` defines the figure and axes for the main window, and `figzoom, axzoom = plt.subplots()` defines the figure and axes for the zoom window.
- `axmain.set(xlim=(-5, 5), ylim=(-75, 175), autoscale_on=False, title='Click to zoom')` sets properties such as the x and y axis limits, whether autoscale is on or off, and the title for the main axes, and `axzoom.set(xlim=(-2, 2), ylim=(-8, 8), autoscale_on=False, title='Zoom window')` defines the same properties for the zoom axis.
- `x = np.arange(-5, 5, 0.1)` and `y = x ** 3` are the data for plotting a non-linear curve.
- `axmain.plot(x, y, 'g-d')` plots the non-linear curve on the main axis, and `axzoom.plot(x, y, 'b-.o')` plots the same on the zoom axes.

- `onbuttonpress(event)` is the callback function that responds to the button press event. As usual, `event` is the argument the function receives:
  - `if event.button == 1`: checks whether the button pressed was the left button (scroll button code is 2, and right button code is 3). If it is a left button press, then it performs the subsequent steps as follows. Otherwise, it completes the function without doing anything.
  - `x, y = event.xdata, event.ydata` captures the coordinates of the point on the plot where the mouse button was pressed, in the data coordinate system. It should be noted that `event.x` and `event.y` carry the same coordinates in the display coordinate system.
  - `axzoom.set_xlim(x - 1, x + 1)` sets the zoom axes' *x* axis limits to +/- 1 from the point where the mouse button was pressed (mouse click). So, only the points on the curve within these limits will appear on the zoom window.
  - `axzoom.set_ylim(y - 10, y + 10)` sets the zoom axes' *y* axis limits to +/- 10 from the point where the mouse button was pressed. So, only the points on the curve within these limits will appear on the zoom window.
  - `figzoom.canvas.draw()` draws the figures with new limits.
- `figmain.canvas.mpl_connect('button_press_event', onbuttonpress)` captures the button press event and invokes the callback function to respond to the event.
- `plt.show()` sends the output to the specified backend.

When you run the code, you should see two plots in separate windows, as shown here. When they both come up, they might be overlapping each other, so you will have to drag **Figure 2** to move it away from **Figure 1**:

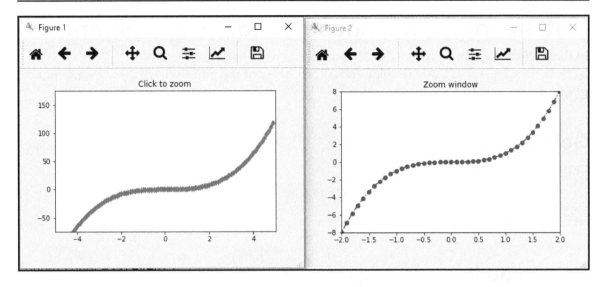

When you click the plot in **Figure 1** at the point (2, 11.5), then the plot in **Figure 2** should change, as shown here. It is the zoom version of the plot in **Figure 1** around the point (2, 11.5), so it contains the X range of 1 to 3, and the Y range of 0 to 20 approximately:

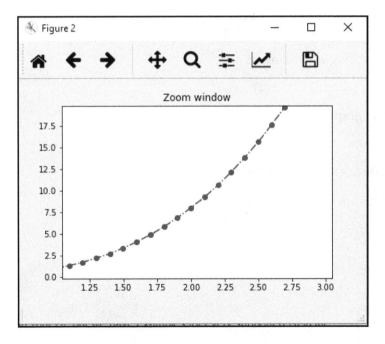

Motion notify and mouse button press events

In this recipe, we will learn how to capture motion_notify_event and
button_press_event, and display the co-ordinates of the point where these events took
place.

Getting ready

Import the required libraries:

```
import matplotlib.pyplot as plt
import numpy as np
from time import time
```

How to do it...

The following steps explain how to code the required logic:

1. Set up the data for the plot to be drawn:

```
t = np.arange(0.0, 1.0, 0.01)
s = np.sin(2 * np.pi * t)
```

2. Define the figure and axes:

```
fig, ax = plt.subplots()
```

3. Plot the graph:

```
ax.plot(t, s)
```

4. Capture the starting time in the str_time variable:

```
str_time = time()
```

5. Define the callback function that responds to the mouse move event:

```
def on_move(event):
    if event.inaxes:
        print('onmove data coords %.2f %.2f' % (event.xdata,
              event.ydata))
    elapsed_time = time() - str_time
    print('elapsed time', elapsed_time)
    if elapsed_time > 10:
        print('Closing onmove event after 10 sec')
        plt.disconnect(binding_id)
```

6. Define the callback function that responds to the mouse button press event:

```
def on_click(event):
    if event.inaxes is not None:
        if event.button == 1:
            print('left click data coords %.2f %.2f' %
(event.xdata, event.ydata))
            ax.text(event.xdata, event.ydata, 'left click here',
                    weight='bold', color='m')
        elif event.button == 2:
            print('scroll click data coords %.2f %.2f' %
(event.xdata, event.ydata))
            ax.text(event.xdata, event.ydata, 'scroll click
here',
                      weight='bold', color='m')
        elif event.button == 3:
            print('right click data coords %.2f %.2f' %
(event.xdata, event.ydata))
            ax.text(event.xdata, event.ydata, 'right click here',
weight='bold', color='m')
          fig.canvas.draw()
```

7. Connect the events to the corresponding callback function:

```
binding_id = plt.connect('motion_notify_event', on_move)
plt.connect('button_press_event', on_click)
```

8. Display the figure on the specified backend:

```
plt.show()
```

How it works...

The following is the explanation for the preceding code:

- `on_move(event)` is the callback function in response to the mouse move event:
    - `if event.inaxes` checks whether the mouse move event happened within the axes or outside of them. If it was within the axes, then it executes the next set of instructions; otherwise, it does not.
    - `print()` prints the coordinates, in the data coordinate system, of the point on the axes where the mouse was moving to `sysout`. You can see it in the output cell of your notebook.
    - `elapsed_time` is the elapsed time from the beginning of the program till now. This is used to deactivate the `move_event` callback function, since the mouse move event generates a lot of `sysout` through print statements.
    - `if elapsed_time > 10` checks whether the elapsed time is more than 10 seconds; if it is, it prints `closing onmove event after 10 sec` to `sysout`, and `plt.disconnect(binding_id)` disconnects the `on_move` event. `binding_id` is the identification captured when the connection between the event and the callback is defined.
    - `on_click(event)` is the callback function in response to the mouse click (button press) event. There are three buttons on the mouse: left is 1, scroll is 2, and right is 3. It prints the corresponding message on the plot itself, every time a button is clicked:
        - `if event.button == 1:` checks whether the button pressed was the left button, then it prints the coordinates to `sysout` and `ax.text(event.xdata, event.ydata, 'left click here', weight='bold', color='m')` creates a text artist to be displayed on the plot, which will be visible when the `draw()` function is called.
        - The same functionality is repeated for buttons 2 (scroll) and 3 (right).

- `binding_id = plt.connect('motion_notify_event', on_move)` connects the motion notify event with the corresponding callback function, `on_move()`, and its identity is saved in `binding_id`, which is required if we want to disconnect this event at a later point.
- `plt.connect('button_press_event', on_click)` connects the button press event with the corresponding callback function, `on_click()`.
- Please note that we have used the `plt.connect()` method to connect the event with the corresponding callback function in this recipe, whereas earlier we used the `mpl_connect()` method of the canvas class. The difference is `plt.connect()` is part of `pyplot` *API*, whereas `mpl_connect()` is part of the object-oriented API that we learned about in `Chapter 5`, *Plotting with Object-Oriented API*.

When you run the program, you should see the following plot, and when you hover the mouse over the plot, within 10 seconds in the output cell you should see the text message `elapsed time 0.6132094860076904, onmove data coords 0.14 -1.04` in the `sysout`. The actual elapsed time and coordinates will be different for you, depending on when and where on the plot you hover the mouse:

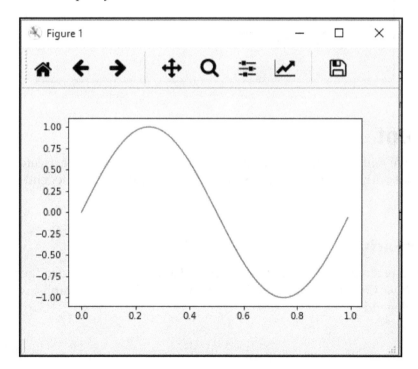

After 10 seconds, if you press the left (1), scroll (2), or right (3) button of the mouse, you will see the respective message on the plot as well as in the output cell. The plot should look like this:

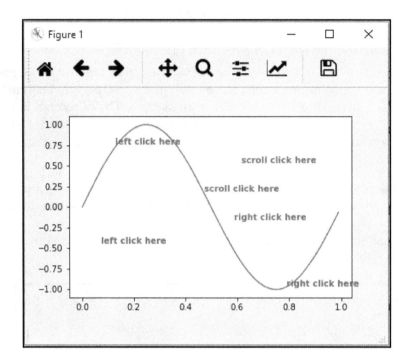

Pick event

In this recipe, we will learn how to capture a pick event and use it to activate/deactivate a specific line plot within a set of line plots on a given axis. We use the legend to pick a specific line plot.

Getting ready

We will use the **receiver operating characteristic** (**ROC**) curve data introduced in Chapter 3, *Plotting Multiple Charts, Subplots, and Figures*, to plot various line graphs, with the associated legend.

Import the required libraries and set the backend:

```
import matplotlib.pyplot as plt
plt.switch_backend('nbAgg')
import pandas as pd
```

How to do it...

The following steps code the logic to demonstrate pick event usage:

1. Read the `fpr` and `tpr` data from Excel files for various algorithms:

```
fpr_logreg = pd.read_excel('ROC_Curves.xlsx', 'fpr_logreg')
tpr_logreg = pd.read_excel('ROC_Curves.xlsx', 'tpr_logreg')
fpr_KNN = pd.read_excel('ROC_Curves.xlsx', 'fpr_KNN')
tpr_KNN = pd.read_excel('ROC_Curves.xlsx', 'tpr_KNN')
fpr_MLP = pd.read_excel('ROC_Curves.xlsx', 'fpr_MLP')
tpr_MLP = pd.read_excel('ROC_Curves.xlsx', 'tpr_MLP')
fpr_SGD = pd.read_excel('ROC_Curves.xlsx', 'fpr_SGD')
tpr_SGD = pd.read_excel('ROC_Curves.xlsx', 'tpr_SGD')
fpr_GNB = pd.read_excel('ROC_Curves.xlsx', 'fpr_GNB')
tpr_GNB = pd.read_excel('ROC_Curves.xlsx', 'tpr_GNB')
fpr_svc = pd.read_excel('ROC_Curves.xlsx', 'fpr_svc')
tpr_svc = pd.read_excel('ROC_Curves.xlsx', 'tpr_svc')
fpr_RF = pd.read_excel('ROC_Curves.xlsx', 'fpr_RF')
tpr_RF = pd.read_excel('ROC_Curves.xlsx', 'tpr_RF')
fpr_DT = pd.read_excel('ROC_Curves.xlsx', 'fpr_DT')
tpr_DT = pd.read_excel('ROC_Curves.xlsx', 'tpr_DT')
```

2. Define and instantiate the figure:

```
fig = plt.figure(figsize=(10,8))
```

3. Plot all the line graphs:

```
plt.plot([0, 1], [0, 1], 'k--')
l1, = plt.plot(fpr_logreg, tpr_logreg,
label='LogReg',color='purple')
l2, = plt.plot(fpr_KNN, tpr_KNN, label='KNN',color='green')
l3, = plt.plot(fpr_DT, tpr_DT, label='DecisionTree',
color='orange')
l4, = plt.plot(fpr_RF, tpr_RF, label='Random
Forest',color='yellow')
l5, = plt.plot(fpr_MLP, tpr_MLP, label='MLP',color='red')
l6, = plt.plot(fpr_svc, tpr_svc, label='SVC',color='violet')
l7, = plt.plot(fpr_GNB, tpr_GNB, label='GNB',color='grey')
l8, = plt.plot(fpr_SGD, tpr_SGD, label='SGD', color='pink')
```

4. Set the labels, title, and legend with alpha (transparency) set to 0.4:

```
plt.xlabel('False Positive Rate')
plt.ylabel('True Positive Rate')
plt.title('ROC curve')
lgd = plt.legend(loc='lower right', fancybox=True, shadow=True)
```

5. Create a dictionary to map plot lines with the corresponding legend label:

```
pltlines = [l1, l2, l3, l4, l5, l6, l7, l8]
leg_ln_map = dict()
for leg_line, plot_line in zip(lgd.get_lines(), pltlines):
    leg_line.set_picker(10)
    leg_ln_map[leg_line] = plot_line
```

6. Define the callback function that responds to the on_pick event:

```
def onpick(event):
 # on the pick event, find the plot line corresponding to the
legend line, and toggle the visibility
    leg_line = event.artist
    plot_line = leg_ln_map[leg_line]
    vis = not plot_line.get_visible()
    plot_line.set_visible(vis)
 # Change the alpha on the line in the legend so we can see what
lines have been toggled
    if vis:
        leg_line.set_alpha(1.0)
    else:
        leg_line.set_alpha(0.2)
    fig.canvas.draw()
```

7. Connect the event with the corresponding callback function:

```
fig.canvas.mpl_connect('pick_event', onpick)
```

8. Send the output figure to the chosen backend:

```
plt.show()
```

How it works...

The following is the explanation for the preceding code:

- The first three steps of reading the data, defining the figure, and plotting various line graphs are already familiar to us.

- `lgd = plt.legend(loc='lower right', fancybox=True, shadow=True)` sets the legend, `fancybox=True` specifies to draw a bounding box around the legend items, and `shadow=True` specifies that the bounding box to have a shadow.
- `pltlines = [l1, l2, l3, l4, l5, l6, l7, l8]` is the list of all plot lines in the figure.
- `leg_ln_map = dict()` is the dictionary mapping plot lines to the corresponding legend labels.
- `for` loop sets the picker for each of the legend labels and maps them to the corresponding line plots.
- `leg_line.set_picker(5)` sets the picker for the legend label line. The number 10 represents the number of points within which the mouse click is captured to fire the corresponding pick event. One point is 1/72 of an inch. If this number is too large, then a click can become close enough to multiple legend items and all of them could get fired at the same time! So, set this small enough to avoid overlaps between the legend lines for a given mouse click.
- There are other options for this argument of the picker, `None` means disable the picker, and **Boolean True** means the event gets triggered when the click happens on the legend line; it could also be a user-defined function.
- `onpick(event)` is the callback function for `pick_event`:
    - `leg_line = event.artist` captures the specific legend line on which the mouse click happened.
    - `plot_line = leg_ln_map[leg_line]` gets the plot line corresponding to the legend line.
    - `vis = not plot_line.get_visible()` get the current state of visibility of the plot line and sets the opposite to `vis`.
    - `plot_line.set_visible(vis)` sets the new visibility status of the plot line.
    - `if` and `else` statements set the same status to the corresponding legend line using alpha; 1 means fully visible, 0.2 means partial visibility.
    - `fig.canvas.draw()` draws the figure on the output device.
- `fig.canvas.mpl_connect('pick_event', onpick)` connects the `pick` event with the corresponding callback function, `onpick`.

You should see the following plot when you run the program and click on the **LogReg, Random Forest**, and **SVC** labels in the legend to deactivate them, so you don't see those curves in the figure:

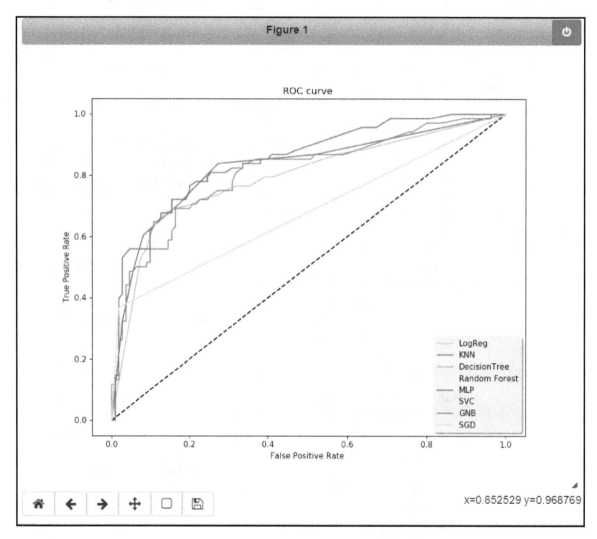

Please note the difference in the header and navigation tool bars in this figure compared to the figures shown in previous recipes. In this case, the nbAgg backend has been used, whereas earlier Qt5Agg was used. While the look and feel is different, all the backends offer the same functions in the toolbar.

Figure and axes, enter and leave events

In this recipe, we will learn how to capture figure enter and leave events, and axes enter and leave events, and use them to change the properties of figures and axes, and make the line plot on the axes visible/invisible.

Getting ready

Import the required libraries:

```
import matplotlib.pyplot as plt
import numpy as np
```

How to do it...

The following are the steps to code the required logic:

1. Define the figure, ax1, and ax2, and set the title for the figure:

```
fig = plt.figure()
fig.suptitle('mouse hover over figure or axes to trigger events')
ax1 = fig.add_subplot(211)
ax2 = fig.add_subplot(212)
```

2. Prepare the data for plotting the sine and cosine functions:

```
x = np.arange(1, 2.0, 0.1)
y = np.sin(2 * np.pi * x)
y1 = np.cos(2 * np.pi * x)
```

3. Plot the sine function on ax1 and the cosine function on ax2:

```
ax1.plot(x,y, color='g')
ax2.plot(x, y1, color='b')
```

4. Define the callback function for figure_enter_event:

```
def figure_enter(event):
    print('figure_enter', event.canvas.figure)
    event.canvas.figure.patch.set_facecolor('grey')
    event.canvas.draw()
```

5. Define the callback function for `figure_leave_event`:

```
def figure_exit(event):
    print('figure_exit', event.canvas.figure)
    event.canvas.figure.patch.set_facecolor('red')
    event.canvas.draw()
```

6. Define the callback function for `axes_enter_event`:

```
def axes_enter(event):
    print('axes_enter', event.inaxes)
    event.inaxes.patch.set_facecolor('white')
    event.inaxes.get_lines()[0].set_visible(True)
    event.canvas.draw()
```

7. Define the callback function for `axes_leave_event`:

```
def axes_exit(event):
    print('axes_exit', event.inaxes)
    event.inaxes.patch.set_facecolor('orange')
    event.inaxes.get_lines()[0].set_visible(False)
    event.canvas.draw()
```

8. Connect the events with the corresponding callback functions:

```
fig.canvas.mpl_connect('figure_enter_event', figure_enter)
fig.canvas.mpl_connect('figure_leave_event', figure_exit)
fig.canvas.mpl_connect('axes_enter_event', axes_enter)
fig.canvas.mpl_connect('axes_leave_event', axes_exit)
```

How it works...

The following is the explanation of the preceding code steps:

- The first three steps are defining the figure and its layout, preparing the data, and plotting the charts.
- `figure_enter(event)` is the callback function that responds to `figure_enter_event`.
  - `print('figure_enter', event.canvas.figure)` prints the text *figure enter* followed by the figure object, to `sysout`.

- event.canvas.figure.patch.set_facecolor('grey') sets the face color of the figure to *grey.*
- event.canvas.draw() plots the updated figure on the output device.
- figure_exit(event) is the callback function that responds to figure_leave_event. This function also prints the text to sysout, sets the face color of the figure to *red,* and plots the updated figure.
- axes_enter(event) is the callback function that responds to axes_enter_event.
  - print('axes_enter', event.inaxes) prints the text *axes_enter* followed by the access object to sysout.
  - event.inaxes.patch.set_facecolor('white') sets the *facecolor* of the axes to *white.*
  - event.inaxes.get_lines()[0].set_visible(True) sets the line plot on the axes to *visible* state; the get_lines() method fetches all line objects from the axes, so it is a list of objects, and we need to use index [0] to fetch the first object from the list.
  - event.canvas.draw() plots the updated figure on the output device
- axes_exit(event) is the callback function that responds to axes_leave_event. It also prints the text and axes object to sysout, sets the axes face color to *orange,* and sets the line plot to the *invisible* state.
- fig.canvas.mpl_connect('figure_enter_event', figure_enter) connects figure_enter_event to the corresponding callback function, figure_enter. Similarly, the other three events are also connected to their respective callback functions.

When you run the program, you should see the first figure shown as follows; when the mouse is on the upper plot you should see the second figure; and when the mouse is outside the boundaries of the figure you should see the third figure:

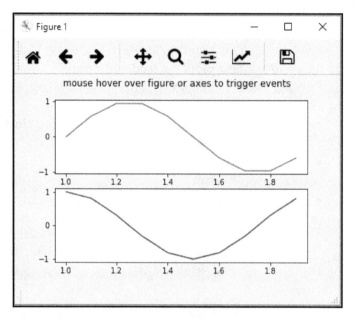

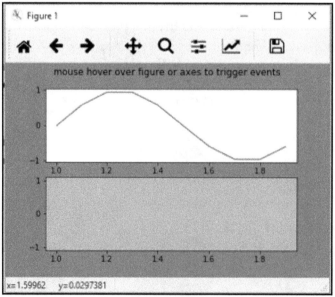

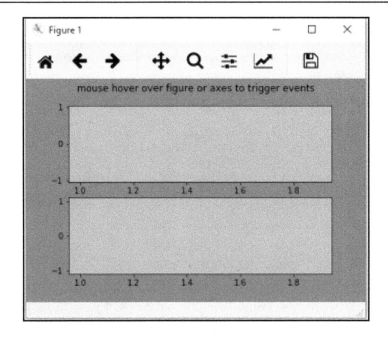

Using twin axes for plotting four temperature scales

In Chapter 4, *Developing Visualizations for Publishing Quality*, *Twin axes* recipe, we learned how to plot two different scales on the left and right axes for two independent variables. When we use this in interactive mode also, the zoom and pan functions work fine, since two variables are independent. However, when the two variables are dependent on each other, as in the case of units of measure, for example, radians and degrees; kilograms and pounds; or the temperature in Fahrenheit, Celsius, Kelvin, and Rankine, then both variables have to be synchronized.

In this recipe, we will learn how to do this using a temperature example. We will use the Celsius unit of measure on the main axis and Fahrenheit, kelvin, and Rankine on the parasite axes.

Getting ready

Set the backend for interactive analysis, import required libraries, and set the seed for random number generation:

```
import matplotlib
matplotlib.use('tkagg')

import matplotlib.pyplot as plt
import numpy as np

np.random.seed(19681211)
```

How to do it...

The following are the steps to plot the required figure:

1. Define the functions to convert Celsius to the other three units of measurement:

```
def c2f(temp):
    return (9. / 5.) * temp + 32
def c2k(temp):
    return temp + 273.15
def c2r(temp):
    return (9. / 5.) * temp + 427.9
```

2. Define the function to update all scales based on the current limits of the Celsius scale on the main axis:

```
def refresh_scales(ax_c):
    y1, y2 = ax_c.get_ylim()
    ax_f.set_ylim(c2f(y1), c2f(y2))
    ax_f.figure.canvas.draw()
    ax_k.set_ylim(c2k(y1), c2k(y2))
    ax_k.figure.canvas.draw()
    ax_r.set_ylim(c2r(y1), c2r(y2))
    ax_r.figure.canvas.draw()
```

3. Define the figure, main axis, and three parasite axes, one each for the three other units of measurement:

```
fig, ax_c = plt.subplots()
ax_f = ax_c.twinx()
ax_r = ax_c.twinx()
ax_k = ax_c.twinx()
```

4. Define two parasite axes on the right side of the plot, away from the default right axis of the plot:

```
ax_k.spines["right"].set_position(("axes", 1.18))
ax_r.spines["right"].set_position(("axes", 1.35))
```

5. Connect the `ylim_changed` event to the corresponding callback function:

```
ax_c.callbacks.connect("ylim_changed", refresh_scales)
```

6. Plot 30 days of random temperatures in degrees Celsius on the main axes:

```
ax_c.plot(np.random.uniform(low=-40., high=40., size=(30,)))
ax_c.set_xlim(0, 30)
```

7. Plot the title for the figure and y axis label for all four scales:

```
ax_c.set_title('Temperature on Four different Scales')
ax_c.set_ylabel('Celsius', color='g')
ax_f.set_ylabel('Fahrenheit')
ax_k.set_ylabel('Kelvin')
ax_r.set_ylabel('Rankine')
```

8. Set the color for the y axis labels for all axes:

```
ax_f.yaxis.label.set_color('b')
ax_k.yaxis.label.set_color('r')
ax_r.yaxis.label.set_color('m')
```

9. Set the color for the ticks and ticklabels of all y axes:

```
ax_c.tick_params(axis='y', colors='g')
ax_f.tick_params(axis='y', colors='b')
ax_k.tick_params(axis='y', colors='r')
ax_r.tick_params(axis='y', colors='m')
```

10. Set the color for all y axes lines:

```
ax_c.spines["left"].set_edgecolor('g')
ax_f.spines["right"].set_edgecolor('b')
ax_k.spines["right"].set_edgecolor('r')
ax_r.spines["right"].set_edgecolor('m')
```

11. Fit all parasite axes in one screen and Display the figure on the screen:

```
plt.tight_layout()
plt.show()
```

How it works...

Here is the explanation of the preceding code:

- `def c2f(temp):` is the function to convert Celsius to Fahrenheit.
- `def c2k(temp):` is the function to convert Celsius to kelvin.
- `def c2r(temp):` is the function to convert Celsius to Rankine.
- `def refresh_scales(ax_c):` is the function to refresh all scales on the parasite axes based on current Celsius limits:
    - `y1, y2 = ax_c.get_ylim()` gets lower and upper limits of the current Celsius scale on the main axes.
    - `ax_f.set_ylim(c2f(y1), c2f(y2))` sets new limits for the Fahrenheit scale for the given Celsius limits.
    - `ax_f.set_ylim(c2k(y1), c2f(y2))` sets new limits for the kelvin scale for the given Celsius limits.
    - `ax_f.set_ylim(c2r(y1), c2f(y2))` sets new limits for the Rankine scale for the given Celsius limits.
- `fig, ax_c = plt.subplots()` defines the figure and main axes for the Celsius scale.
- `ax_f = ax_c.twinx()` defines the parasite axes for the Fahrenheit scale over the main axes.
- `ax_k = ax_c.twinx()` defines the parasite axes for the kelvin scale over the main axes.
- `ax_r = ax_c.twinx()` defines the parasite axes for the Rankine scale over the main axes.
- `ax_k.spines["right"].set_position(("axes", 1.18))` moves the parasite axes towards the right side by 15% of the main axis width.
- `ax_r.spines["right"].set_position(("axes", 1.35))` moves the parasite axes towards the right side by 30% of the main axis width, so that none of the axes ticks, ticklabels, or axis labels overlap with one another.
- `ax_c.callbacks.connect("ylim_changed", refresh_scales)` connects the `"ylim_changed"` event to the corresponding callback function, `refresh_scales`.
- `ax_c.plot(np.random.uniform(low=-40., high=40., size=(30,)))` plots 30 random numbers between -40 and 40 on the Celsius scale.

- `ax_c.set_xlim(0, 30)` sets the lower and upper limits for the X axis to zero and 30 days, respectively.
- `ax_c.set_title('Temparature on Four different Scales')` plots the title for the plot.
- `ax_c.set_ylabel('Celsius', color='g')` sets the y axis label and color for Celsius.
- `ax_f.set_ylabel('Fahrenheit')` sets the y axis label for Fahrenheit.
- `ax_k.set_ylabel('Kelvin')` sets the y axis label for kelvin.
- `ax_r.set_ylabel('Rankine')` sets the y axis label for Rankine.
- `ax_f.yaxis.label.set_color('b')` sets the color for the y axis label of the Fahrenheit scale; the usual `set_ylabel(color='b')` does not work for parasite axes.
- `ax_k.yaxis.label.set_color('r')` sets the color for the y axis label of the kelvin scale.
- `ax_r.yaxis.label.set_color('m')` sets the color for the y axis label of the Rankine scale.
- `ax_c.tick_params(axis='y', colors='g')` sets the color for the ticks and ticklabels of the Celsius scale.
- `ax_f.tick_params(axis='y', colors='b')` sets the color for the ticks and ticklabels of the Fahrenheit scale.
- `ax_k.tick_params(axis='y', colors='r')` sets the color for the ticks and ticklabels of the Kelvin scale.
- `ax_r.tick_params(axis='y', colors='m')` sets the color for the ticks and ticklabels of the Rankine scale.
- `ax_c.spines["left"].set_edgecolor('g')` sets the color for the Celsius scale axis.
- `ax_f.spines["right"].set_edgecolor('b')` sets the color for the Fahrenheit scale axis.
- `ax_k.spines["right"].set_edgecolor('r')` sets the color for the kelvin scale axis.
- `ax_r.spines["right"].set_edgecolor('m')` sets the color for the Rankine scale axis.

Upon running the preceding code, you should see the following figure on your screen:

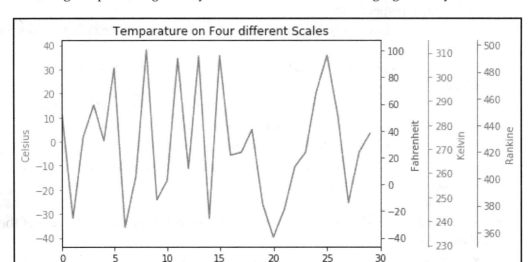

Widgets

In the preceding section, we learned how to capture events at a granular level and perform certain basic tasks using those events. This can be extended to develop rich **Graphical User Interface (GUI)** applications involving features such as buttons, checkboxes, radio buttons, sliders, and span controllers. However, this requires quite a bit of programming effort. Hence, Matplotlib has predefined many of these features, called **widgets**, which we can readily use to develop the GUI applications we need.

In this section, we will learn how to use some of these widgets.

Cursor

The Cursor widget highlights a specific point in the figure with a cross as you hover the mouse on the figure/axes. This is similar to what we did in the *Motion notify and mouse button press events* recipe, where we wrote code, but here we will use a readily available widget.

Getting ready

Import the required libraries:

```
import numpy as np
import matplotlib.pyplot as plt
from matplotlib.widgets import Cursor
```

How to do it...

The following are the steps to implement the logic:

1. Prepare the data for the plots:

```
x = np.arange(-5, 5, 0.1)
y = x ** 2
```

2. Set the figure, its layout, and axes:

```
fig = plt.figure(figsize=(8, 6))
ax = fig.add_subplot(111, facecolor='skyblue')
```

3. Plot the graph:

```
ax.plot(x, y, 'o')
```

4. Instantiate the cursor widget:

```
cursor = Cursor(ax, color='red', linewidth=5)
```

5. Send the output to the specified backend:

```
plt.show()
```

How it works...

The following is the explanation for the preceding code steps:

- The first three steps define the data and figure layout, and plot the chart.
- `cursor = Cursor(ax, color='red', linewidth=5)` defines and activates the cursor widget.

You should see the widget, as shown here. Please note we have used the TkAgg backend for this figure:

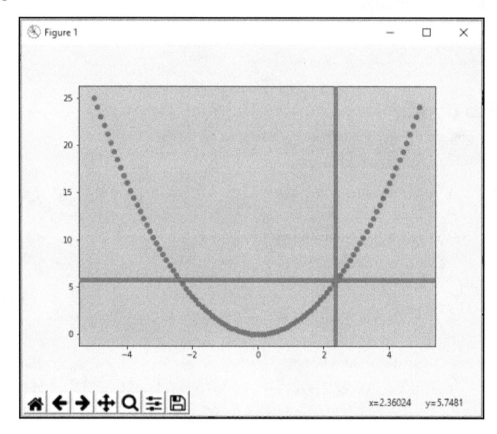

Buttons

Buttons are used to enable a certain functionality when they are clicked. Typically, they are used to scroll data back and forth using prev and next buttons. We will learn how to use this functionality.

Getting ready

We will use the familiar Iris dataset, which has three distinct clusters of data. We will implement the prev and next buttons to scroll these clusters of data back and forth.

Import the required libraries:

```
import matplotlib.pyplot as plt
import pandas as pd
from matplotlib.widgets import Button
```

How to do it...

The following steps of code implement the logic we need:

1. Define the class with the prev and next methods to represent the cluster to be displayed:

```
class Cluster(object):
    ind = 0      # index to move back and forth as we click prev and
                    next buttons

    # Method for next button click
    def next(self, event):
        self.ind += 1
        i = self.ind % len(species)
        index = iris['species'] == species[i]
        axs.clear()
        axs.scatter(x[index], y[index], s=50, marker='o')
        axs.set_title(species[i], size=25, color='r')
        plt.draw()

    # Method for prev button click
    def prev(self, event):
        self.ind -= 1
        i = self.ind % len(species)
        index = iris['species'] == species[i]
        axs.clear()
        axs.scatter(x[index], y[index], s=50, marker='o')
        axs.set_title(species[i], size=25, color='r')
        plt.draw()
```

2. Instantiate the cluster object:

```
cluster = Cluster()
```

3. Read the Iris data and set up the attributes for plotting the three clusters:

```
iris = pd.read_csv('iris_dataset.csv', delimiter=',')
species = ['setosa', 'versicolor', 'virginica']
x,y = iris['petal_length'], iris['petal_width']
index = iris['species'] == species[cluster.ind]
```

4. Define the figure and axes:

```
fig, axs = plt.subplots()
```

5. Plot the first cluster:

```
axs.scatter(x[index], y[index], s=50, marker='o')
axs.set_title(species[cluster.ind], size=25, color='r')
```

6. Define the axes for the prev and next buttons:

```
axprev = plt.axes([0.7, 0.005, 0.1, 0.05])
axnext = plt.axes([0.81, 0.005, 0.1, 0.05])
```

7. Instantiate the buttons for prev and next:

```
bnext = Button(axnext, 'Next')
bprev = Button(axprev, 'Previous')
```

8. Map the callback functions for the `on_clicked` event for both `prev` and `next`:

```
bnext.on_clicked(cluster.next)
bprev.on_clicked(cluster.prev)
```

9. Display the figure on the specified backend:

```
plt.show()
```

How it works...

The following is the explanation of the preceding code:

- `class Cluster(object)`: Defines a class named `Cluster`.
- `ind = 0` initializes the index, which moves back and forth as the `prev` and `next` buttons are pressed.
- `def next(self, event)`: defines the `next` method as a `callback` function for the `next` button:
  - `self.ind += 1` increments the index by 1.
  - `i = self.ind % len(species)` converts the running index to zero, 1, or 2 for the number of clusters in the species.
  - `index = iris['species'] == species[i]` picks up the indices of the data corresponding to the `next` cluster.

- `axs.clear()` clears previous data on the axes. If we don't do this, all the clusters will be visible on the axis, and only the color of cluster being refreshed will keep changing as per the default color set in the property cycle.
- `axs.scatter(x[index], y[index], s=50, marker='o')` plots the new cluster data using the index computed before.
- `axs.set_title(species[i], size=25, color='r')` sets the title of the axis to the current cluster name.
- `plt.draw()` refreshes the figure.

- `def prev(self, event):` defines the `prev` method as a callback function for the `prev` button:
  - `self.ind -= 1` decreases the index by 1.
  - `i = self.ind % len(species)` converts the running index to 0, 1 or 2 for number of clusters in species.
  - `index = iris['species'] == species[i]` picks up the indices of data corresponding to the prev cluster.
  - `axs.clear()` clears the previous data from the axes.
  - `axs.scatter(x[index], y[index], s=50, marker='o')` plots the new cluster data using the index computed.
  - `axs.set_title(species[i], size=25, color='r')` sets the title of the axis to the current cluster name.
  - `plt.draw()` refreshes the figure.

- `cluster = Cluster()` instantiates the `Cluster` object.
- `iris = pd.read_csv('iris_dataset.csv', delimiter=',')` reads the `iris` data.
- `species = ['setosa', 'versicolor', 'virginica']` lists unique cluster names.
- `x,y = iris['petal_length'], iris['petal_width']` picks up the required attributes from the iris dataset into *x* and *y* coordinates.
- `index = iris['species'] == species[cluster.ind]` gets the indices of the data corresponding to the first cluster. Please note `cluster.ind` has been initialized to zero.
- `fig, axs = plt.subplots()` instantiates the figure and axes.

- `axs.scatter(x[index], y[index], s=50, marker='o')` plots the scatter plot for the first cluster and `axs.set_title(species[cluster.ind], size=25, color='r')` sets the current cluster name as the title for the figure.

- `axprev = plt.axes([0.7, 0.005, 0.1, 0.05])` defines the axes for the `prev` button in the figure and `axnext = plt.axes([0.81, 0.005, 0.1, 0.05])` defines the axes for the `next` button in the figure. As explained in Chapter 6, *Plotting with Advanced Features, Taking control of axes position* recipe, the axis definition is from left, bottom, width, and height and they are in the axes coordinate system.

- `bnext = Button(axnext, 'Next')` instantiates the `next` button with the Next label and the `bnext` connection ID, and `bprev = Button(axprev, 'Previous')` instantiates the prev button with the `prev` label and the `bprev` connection ID.

- `bnext.on_clicked(cluster.next)` maps the callback function to the event for the `next` button, and `bprev.on_clicked(cluster.prev)` maps the `callback` function to the event for the `prev` button.

- `plt.show()` sends the output to the specified backend.

When you run the program and click **Next** and **Next**, you will see the following three figures, representing each of the clusters, as shown in the header of each figure:

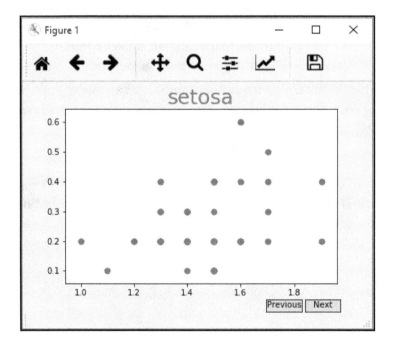

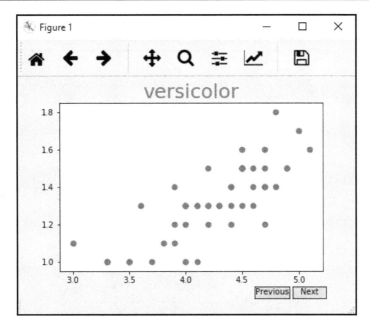

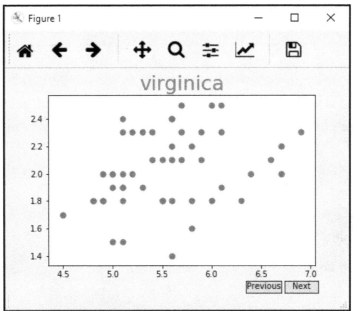

If you comment out the `axs.clear()` statement, then the figure will look as follows:

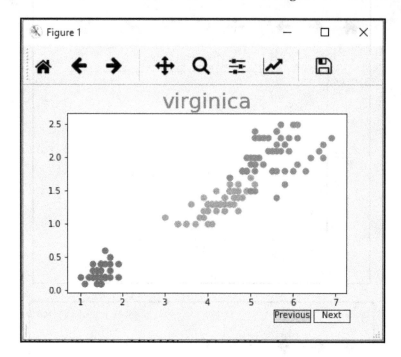

Check buttons

Checkboxes are used to select or deselect a set of attributes for visualizing the data. In this recipe, we will learn how to use the `CheckButtons` widget for implementing the checkbox feature.

Getting ready

We will use ROC plots for implementing `CheckButtons`.

Import the required libraries:

```
import matplotlib.pyplot as plt
import pandas as pd
from matplotlib.widgets import CheckButtons
```

How to do it...

The following are the steps to implement the logic:

1. Read the data from the same Excel files we used in *Pick Event* recipe earlier in this chapter:

```
fpr_logreg = pd.read_excel('ROC_Curves.xlsx', 'fpr_logreg')
tpr_logreg = pd.read_excel('ROC_Curves.xlsx', 'tpr_logreg')
fpr_KNN = pd.read_excel('ROC_Curves.xlsx', 'fpr_KNN')
tpr_KNN = pd.read_excel('ROC_Curves.xlsx', 'tpr_KNN')
fpr_MLP = pd.read_excel('ROC_Curves.xlsx', 'fpr_MLP')
tpr_MLP = pd.read_excel('ROC_Curves.xlsx', 'tpr_MLP')
fpr_SGD = pd.read_excel('ROC_Curves.xlsx', 'fpr_SGD')
tpr_SGD = pd.read_excel('ROC_Curves.xlsx', 'tpr_SGD')
fpr_GNB = pd.read_excel('ROC_Curves.xlsx', 'fpr_GNB')
tpr_GNB = pd.read_excel('ROC_Curves.xlsx', 'tpr_GNB')
fpr_svc = pd.read_excel('ROC_Curves.xlsx', 'fpr_svc')
tpr_svc = pd.read_excel('ROC_Curves.xlsx', 'tpr_svc')
fpr_RF = pd.read_excel('ROC_Curves.xlsx', 'fpr_RF')
tpr_RF = pd.read_excel('ROC_Curves.xlsx', 'tpr_RF')
fpr_DT = pd.read_excel('ROC_Curves.xlsx', 'fpr_DT')
tpr_DT = pd.read_excel('ROC_Curves.xlsx', 'tpr_DT')
```

2. Define and instantiate the figure:

```
fig = plt.figure(figsize=(10,8))
```

3. Plot all the ROC curves:

```
plt.plot([0, 1], [0, 1], 'k--')
l1, = plt.plot(fpr_logreg, tpr_logreg,
               label='LogReg',color='purple')
l2, = plt.plot(fpr_KNN, tpr_KNN, label='KNN',color='green')
l3, = plt.plot(fpr_DT, tpr_DT, label='DecisionTree',
color='orange')
l4, = plt.plot(fpr_RF, tpr_RF, label='Random
Forest',color='yellow')
l5, = plt.plot(fpr_MLP, tpr_MLP, label='MLP',color='red')
l6, = plt.plot(fpr_svc, tpr_svc, label='SVC',color='violet')
l7, = plt.plot(fpr_GNB, tpr_GNB, label='GNB',color='grey')
l8, = plt.plot(fpr_SGD, tpr_SGD, label='SGD', color='pink')
```

4. Set the attributes for the figure and adjust the space on the left to accommodate the checkboxes:

```
plt.xlabel('False Positive Rate', size=20, color='m')
plt.ylabel('True Positive Rate', size=20, color='m')
plt.title('ROC curve', size=25, color='b')
plt.subplots_adjust(left=0.35)
plt.legend()
```

5. Prepare the data axes, labels, and visibility status of each of the curves required for CheckButtons:

```
lines = [l1, l2, l3, l4, l5, l6, l7, l8]
cax = plt.axes([0.05, 0.27, 0.15, 0.5])
labels = [str(line.get_label()) for line in lines]
visibility = [line.get_visible() for line in lines]
```

6. Instantiate the CheckButtons object with the required attributes, as prepared earlier:

```
check = CheckButtons(cax, labels, visibility)
```

7. Define the callback function that responds to checkbox clicks:

```
def onclick(label):
    index = labels.index(label)
    lines[index].set_visible(not lines[index].get_visible())
    plt.draw()
```

8. Map the event to the callback function on the CheckButtons object.

How it works...

Here is the explanation of the preceding code blocks.

The first four steps are already familiar, so we will explain from step 5:

- `lines = [l1, l2, l3, l4, l5, l6, l7, l8]` is the list of all the ROC line plots.
- `cax = plt.axes([0.05, 0.27, 0.15, 0.5])` defines the axes where the CheckButtons box is plotted.

- `labels = [str(line.get_label()) for line in lines]` defines the list of labels for each of the ROC plots. This is the same as the labels we gave when we plotted these curves. Instead of hardcoding again here, we are using the system function `line.get_label()` to get them.
- `visibility = [line.get_visible() for line in lines]` is a list of visibility status (visible or invisible) for all the ROC curves.
- `check = CheckButtons(cax, labels, visibility)` instantiates the `CheckButtons` object.
- `def onclick(label):` is the callback function that gets activated when a check button is clicked. `label` is the system variable, such as `event`, that contains the label of the clicked check button:
  - `index = labels.index(label)` obtains the index of the clicked label from the list of all labels, which will be used to get access to the ROC plot for that label.
  - `lines[index].set_visible(not lines[index].get_visible())` toggles the visibility status of the clicked label.
  - `plt.draw()` refreshes the plot.
- `check.on_clicked(onclick)` connects the click event with the corresponding callback function.
- `plt.show()` send the output to the specified backend.

When you run the program, you should get the first figure, and after you uncheck **k-nearest neighbor (KNN)**, **decision tree (DT)**, and **multi-layer perceptron (MLP)** curves, then you should see the second figure:

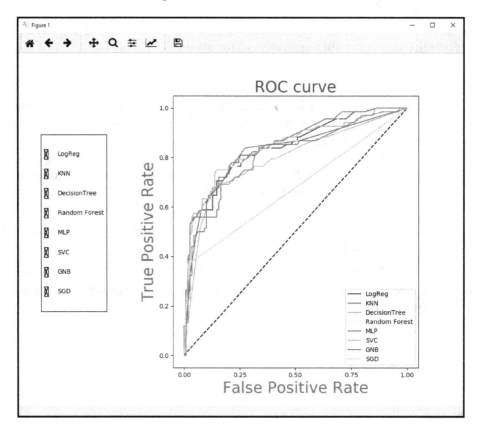

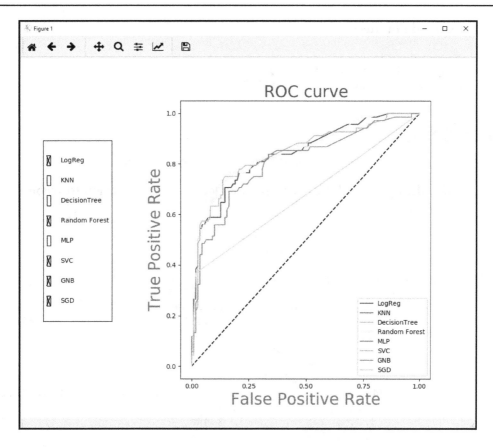

Radio buttons

`RadioButtons` is similar to `CheckButtons`, except that only one of its attributes will be active at any time. In this recipe, we will learn how to use the `RadioButtons` widget.

Getting ready

We will define GDP data for USA, China, and the UK for this recipe as Python lists and use the same for this recipe.

Import the required libraries:

```
import numpy as np
import matplotlib.pyplot as plt
from matplotlib.widgets import RadioButtons
```

How to do it...

The following are the steps to implement the RadioButtons logic:

1. Define the figure and the axes, and adjust the space on the left to accommodate RadioButtons:

```
fig, axs = plt.subplots(figsize=(14,6))
plt.subplots_adjust(left=0.18)
```

2. Prepare the data to be plotted on the axes:

```
# Data taken from https://data.worldbank.org/country
Year = ['2007', '2008', '2009', '2010', '2011', '2012', '2013',
        '2014', '2015', '2016']
China_GDP = [3.552, 4.598, 5.11, 6.101, 7.573, 8.561, 9.607,
10.482,
             11.065, 11.191]
US_GDP = [14.478, 14.719, 14.419, 14.964, 15.518, 16.155, 16.692,
          17.428, 18.121, 18.624]
UK_GDP = [3.074, 2.891, 2.383, 2.441, 2.62, 2.662, 2.74, 3.023,
          2.886, 2.651]
```

3. Plot the figure and set the label, title, and axis limits:

```
line, = axs.plot(Year, US_GDP, lw=5, color='g', ls='-.')
axs.set_ylim(1,20)
axs.set_title('GDP(in trillion $)')
axs.set_xlabel('Year')
```

4. Define the axes where the radio buttons will be plotted, and instantiate the object:

```
rax = plt.axes([0.05, 0.5, 0.15, 0.25], facecolor='skyblue')
radio = RadioButtons(rax, ('USA', 'China', 'UK'))
```

5. Define the callback function that gets executed when one of the `RadioButtons` is clicked:

```
countrydict = {'USA': [US_GDP, 'g', '-.'], 'China': [China_GDP,
'b',
                '--'], 'UK': [UK_GDP, 'm', '-']}
def country(label):
    ydata, color, ls = countrydict[label]
    line.set_ydata(ydata)
    line.set_color(color)
    line.set_linestyle(ls)
    plt.draw()
```

6. Connect the click event to the corresponding callback function defined earlier:

```
radio.on_clicked(country)
```

7. Send the output to the specified backend:

```
plt.show()
```

How it works...

Here is the explanation for the preceding code blocks:

- `Year` is the list of years for which GDP data is to be plotted.
- `China_GDP` is the list of GDP in trillion dollars ($) for the years specified in the Year list, and similarly for `US_GDP` and `UK_GDP`.
- `rax = plt.axes([0.05, 0.5, 0.08, 0.25], facecolor='skyblue')` defines the axes where `RadioButtons` will be plotted, with the facecolor set to skyblue.
- `radio = RadioButtons(rax, ('USA', 'China', 'UK'))` instantiates the `RadioButtons` object on the given axes and with the given labels.
- `countrydict()` is the dictionary containing the `country` as key with associated *GDP* and the plot attributes `color` and `linestyle` as values.

- `def GDP(label):` defines the callback function that gets activated in response to a click on `RadioButtons`. `label` is a system variable containing the label of the `RadioButton` clicked:
  - `ydata, color, ls = countrydict[label]` fetches GDP, color, and line style from the dictionary corresponding to the label clicked.
  - `line.set_ydata(ydata)` sets the data for the y axis.
  - `line.set_color(color)` sets the color of the plot.
  - `line.set_linestyle(ls)` sets the line style.
  - `plt.draw()` refreshes the plot.
- `radio.on_clicked(GDP)` connects the click event with the corresponding callback function, `country`.
- `plt.show()` sends the output to the specified backend.

When you run the program and start checking different radio buttons, you should see the following figures:

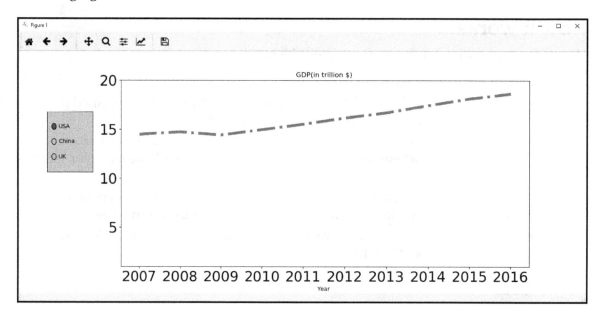

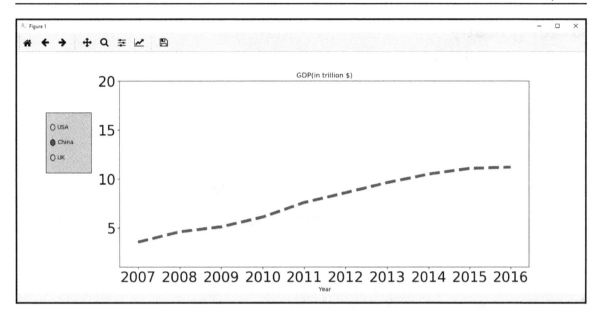

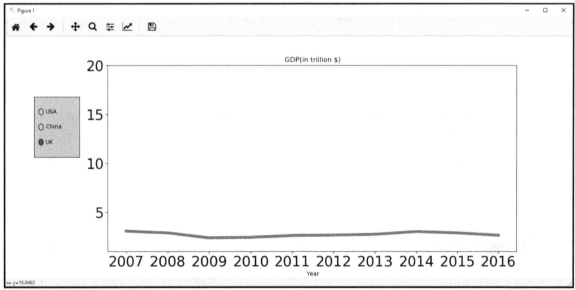

Textbox

The `TextBox` widget is a free-form implementation of evaluating any expression. It will be handy if you want to examine various different mathematical expressions/functions.

Getting ready

Import the required libraries:

```
import numpy as np
import matplotlib.pyplot as plt
from matplotlib.widgets import TextBox
```

How to do it...

The following are the steps to implement the TextBox widget:

1. Define the figure and axes, and adjust the space at the bottom to accommodate TextBox:

   ```
   fig, ax = plt.subplots()
   plt.subplots_adjust(bottom=0.2)
   ```

2. Prepare the data to be plotted initially:

   ```
   x = np.arange(-5.0, 5.0, 0.01)
   y = x ** 5
   ```

3. Plot the data:

   ```
   l, = plt.plot(x, y, lw=2)
   ```

4. Define the callback function to be executed when the new expression in TextBox is submitted:

   ```
   def submit(text):
       ydata = eval(text)
       l.set_ydata(ydata)
       ax.set_ylim(np.min(ydata), np.max(ydata))
       plt.draw()
   ```

5. Define the axes and initial_text required for TextBox implementation:

   ```
   axbox = plt.axes([0.1, 0.05, 0.8, 0.075])
   initial_text = "x ** 5"
   ```

6. Instantiate the `TextBox` object:

```
text_box = TextBox(axbox, 'Evaluate', initial=initial_text)
```

7. Connect the submit event with the corresponding callback function defined previously:

```
text_box.on_submit(submit)
```

8. Send the output to the specified `backend`:

```
plt.show()
```

How it works...

Here is the explanation of the preceding code blocks:

- The first three steps are familiar, so we will start with the fourth step.
- `def submit(text):` defines the submit callback function. `text` is the system variable containing the expression entered in the textbox before submitting it:
  - `eval()` is a Python function that computes the expression supplied as the argument.
  - `eval(text)` is the result of executing the expression entered in the `TextBox` and assigned to the `ydata` variable.
  - `l.set_ydata(ydata)` sets the new `ydata` to the y axis of the line object.
  - `ax.set_ylim(np.min(ydata), np.max(ydata))` sets the limits for the x and y axis scales with the current data.
  - `plt.draw()` refreshes the plot.
- `axbox = plt.axes([0.1, 0.05, 0.8, 0.075])` defines the axes where the `TextBox` will be placed.
- `initial_text = "x ** 5"` is the expression that comes up in `TextBox` when the plot comes up for the first time.
- `text_box = TextBox(axbox, 'Evaluate', initial=initial_text)` defines the `TextBox` object and instantiates it.
- `text_box.on_submit(submit)` connects the `submit` event with the corresponding callback function, `submit`.
- `plt.show()` sends the output to the specified `backend`.

When you run the program, you should see the first figure. When you change the text to different expressions, then you will see the second and third figure:

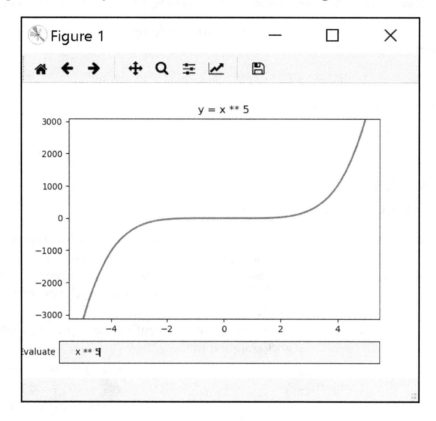

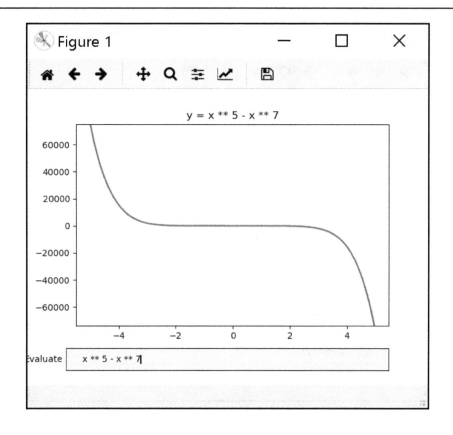

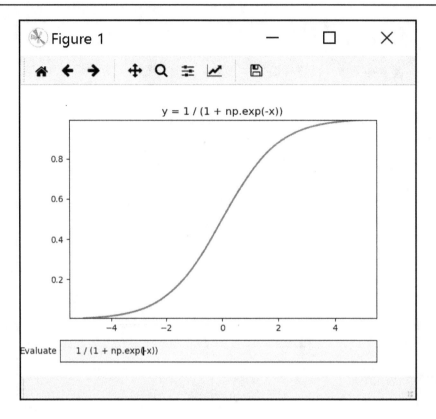

Animation

In this section, we will cover the animation of plots. Animation is a power tool used to create a story line from raw data. It is a series of frames of visual charts connected together to create a video. Animated plots in Matplotlib can be saved as .mp4 files that can be played back using a media player, just like any other video.

Matplotlib provides the following two classes to implement animated plots:

- `FuncAnimation`
- `ArtistAnimation`

We will learn how to use both of them in this section.

Animated sigmoid curve

In this recipe, we will learn how to use the `FuncAnimation` class to animate a sigmoid curve.

Getting ready

Import the required libraries:

```
import numpy as np
import matplotlib.pyplot as plt
from matplotlib.animation import FuncAnimation
```

How to do it...

The following are the steps to implement the required logic:

1. Define the figure and axes:

   ```
   fig, ax = plt.subplots()
   ```

2. Prepare the data for the graph to be plotted, sigmoid in this case, and plot it:

   ```
   x = np.arange(-10, 10, 0.01)
   y = 1 / (1 + np.exp(-x))
   line, = ax.plot(x, y)
   ```

3. Define the initialization function, `init()`:

   ```
   def init():
       line.set_ydata([np.nan] * len(x))
       return line
   ```

4. Define the animation function, `animate()`:

```
def animate(i):
    line.set_ydata(1 / (1 + np.exp(-(x+i/100)))) # keep refreshing
frame by frame
    return line,
```

5. Activate the animation:

```
ani = FuncAnimation(fig, animate, 1000, init_func=init, blit=True,
                    interval=2, save_count=50,
                    repeat=False, repeat_delay=1000)
```

6. Send the output to the specified backend:

```
plt.show()
```

How it works...

Here is the explanation for the preceding code blocks:

- `ani = FuncAnimation(fig, animate, 1000, init_func=init, blit=True, interval=2, save_count=50, repeat=False, repeat_delay=1000)` activates the animation. Since we need to maintain the state of the object, we must assign it to a variable, as we have done here: `ani`. This also helps in saving the animation to an `.mp4` file, which we will learn how to do in the next recipe:
    - `fig` is the figure that is being animated.
    - `animate` is the function that directs the way the animation is applied to the plot:
        - `i` is the system variable, containing the frame number of the current frame being processed.
        - We are keeping the *x* axis data constant, but changing the *y* axis data as a function of the frame number.
    - `1000` is the number of frames to complete the animation. This can be any number, based on how long you want the animation to run for. This can also be another function supplying data for the `animate` function. We will learn this in subsequent recipes.

- `init_func=init` specifies the initialization function to be applied at the beginning, once. This is an optional function, which can be omitted as well. It helps only when `blit=True` to start afresh. In this case, we are simply setting the data to `nan` (not a number).
- `blit=True` specifies to refresh only the parts of the figure that have changed from the previous frame to the current frame. This improves the processing speed.
- `interval=2` specifies that the time delay between consecutive frames is two milliseconds.
- `save_count=50` specifies the number of frames to be saved in the cache, again for performance improvement.
- `repeat=False` specifies to stop the animation after completing all 1,000 frames. If we say *yes*, then it will repeat the cycle of 1,000 frames again and again for ever, or until we close the session.
- `repeat_delay=1000` specifies to start next cycle 1,000 milliseconds after completing the previous cycle.

You should see the following figure at the end of the animation:

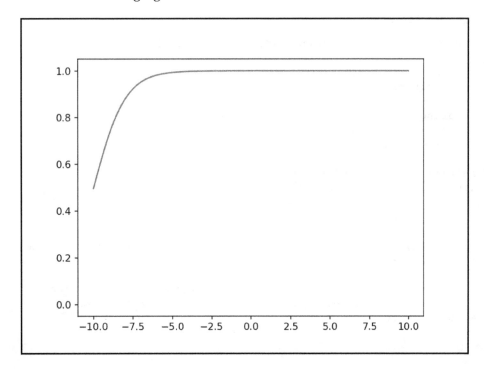

Saving the animation to an mp4 file

In this recipe, we will learn how to save an animation that can be played by a media player. We will recreate the animation we learned in the previous recipe and save it.

You need to install the ffmpeg package on your computer to be able to save the animation in the .mp4 file format. For Windows installation, you can get the instructions here: https://www.youtube.com/watch?v=n7-rLDq8uSE. For more details on this package and its applications, you can see the documentation here: https://www.ffmpeg.org/documentation.html.

Getting ready

Import the required libraries:

```
import numpy as np
import matplotlib.pyplot as plt
from matplotlib.animation import FuncAnimation
```

How to do it...

You can run all the steps of the previous recipe at once, as shown here, to create the animation:

```
fig, ax = plt.subplots()

x = np.arange(-10, 10, 0.01)
y = 1 / (1 + np.exp(-x))
line, = ax.plot(x, y)

def init(): # only required for blitting to give a clean slate.
    line.set_ydata([np.nan] * len(x))
    return line

def animate(i):
    line.set_ydata(1 / (1 + np.exp(-(x+i/100)))) # update the data.
    return line

ani = FuncAnimation(fig, animate, 1000, init_func=init, blit=True,
                    interval=2, save_count=50, repeat=False,
repeat_delay=1000)
```

There are two ways you can save the figure:

```
ani.save("sigmoid.mp4")
```

You can also save it like this:

```
from matplotlib.animation import FFMpegWriter
writer = FFMpegWriter(fps=25,
metadata=dict(title='expdecay',artist='line'),
                        bitrate=1800)
ani.save("sigmoid.mp4", writer=writer)
```

How it works...

`ani.save("sigmoid.mp4")` saves the `ani` animation in the working directory with the name `sigmoid.mp4`.

The second option also does the same thing, but gives more flexibility in the way you want to save the file by passing various arguments. You can refer to the documentation for detailed explanation of these arguments, as well as other writer functions that are supported by Matplotlib; see `https://matplotlib.org/api/animation_api.html` for details.

You can see the `sigmoid.mp4` file in the code library. You can run it and see how the animation works.

Exponentially decaying tan function

In this recipe, we will see one more example of `FuncAnimation` using an exponentially decaying function plot.

Getting ready

Import the required libraries:

```
import numpy as np
import matplotlib.pyplot as plt
from matplotlib.animation import FuncAnimation
```

How to do it...

The following are the steps to implement the required logic:

1. Define the figure and axes:

```
fig, ax = plt.subplots()
```

2. Plot a blank line:

```
xdata, ydata = [], []
line, = ax.plot(xdata, ydata)
```

3. Set the limits and grid to `True`:

```
ax.set_xlim(0, 10)
ax.set_ylim(-3.0, 3.0)
ax.grid()
```

4. Define the function to generate data, which will be used in place of the number of frames:

```
def frame_gen(x=0):
    while x < 50:
        x += 0.1
        yield x, np.tan(2*np.pi*x) * np.exp(-x/5.)
```

5. Define the function to direct the animation:

```
def animate(data):
    x, y = data
    xdata.append(x)
    ydata.append(y)
    xmin, xmax = ax.get_xlim()
    if x >= xmax:
        ax.set_xlim(xmin, 2*xmax)
        ax.figure.canvas.draw()
    line.set_data(xdata, ydata)
    return line
```

6. Activate the animation:

```
ani = FuncAnimation(fig, animate, frame_gen, blit=True, interval=2,
repeat=False)
```

7. Send the output to the specified backend:

```
plt.show()
```

How it works...

Here is the explanation of the preceding code blocks. It works similar to the way the previous sigmoid animation worked.

However, we are not using `init_func` here, but rather initializing in the main function itself. Instead of using a fixed number of frames, we are using a function to generate data for every frame, until the value of x reaches 50. When x reaches 50, one cycle gets completed, and if `repeat=yes` is set, then the full cycle will keep repeating itself. Otherwise, it will stop after one cycle:

- `ax.set_xlim(0, 10)` sets the *x* axis limits from 0 to 10 to start with, and `ax.set_ylim(-3.0, 3.0)` sets the *y* axis limits from -3.0 to +3.0.
- `def frame_gen(x=0):` is the function that generates the frames one by one, in 0.1 increments of x. The `while` loop terminates when x reaches the value of 50. It returns x and y = `np.tan(2*np.pi*x) * np.exp(-x/5.)`
- `def animate(data):` is the function that directs the way the animation has to function:
    - It receives the frame returned by the `frame_gen()` function into the `data` variable.
    - `data` variable is split it into *x* and *y* coordinates.
    - *x* and *y* coordinates of the current frame are appended to the list containing all the previous frames.
    - `xmin, xmax = ax.get_xlim()` gets the current limits of the *x* axis in `xmin` and `xmax` variables.
    - `if x >= xmax:` checks whether the *x* coordinate of the current frame is greater than `xmax`, if yes, then `ax.set_xlim(xmin, 2*xmax)` sets new limits to the *x* axis by retaining the lower limit and doubling the upper limit.
    - `ax.figure.canvas.draw()` refreshes the figure to get the new limits.
    - `line.set_data(xdata, ydata)` plots the graph with the new frame, including all the previous frames.
- Calls to `frame_gen()` and `animate()` happen within `FuncAnimation`, so we don't need to worry about passing the data between the functions.

You should see the following figure at the end of the animation. You can also find `Exp_decay.mp4` in the code library, which you can run and see:

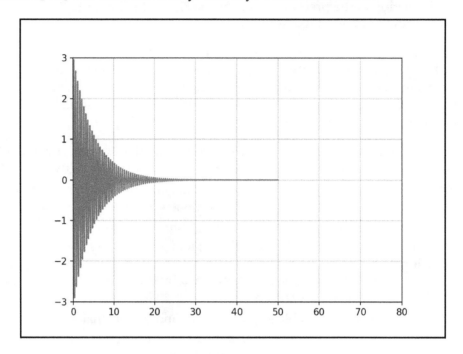

Animated bubble plot

This example has been adopted from Matplotlib `https://matplotlib.org/examples/animation/rain.html`. The original example simulates rain drops, but here we have added a different color combination to make it a bubble plot with animation.

Getting ready

Import the required libraries:

```
import numpy as np
import matplotlib.pyplot as plt
from matplotlib.animation import FuncAnimation
```

How to do it...

The following are the steps to implement the required logic:

1. Define and instantiate the figure and axes:

```
fig = plt.figure(figsize=(5, 5))
ax = fig.add_axes([0, 0, 1, 1], frameon=False)
```

2. Define the bubbles data structure:

```
n_bubbles = 50
bubbles = np.zeros(n_bubbles, dtype=[('position', float, 2),
('size', float, 1),
                                     ('growth', float, 1),
('color', float, 4)])
```

3. Initialize the starting positions randomly:

```
bubbles['position'] = np.random.uniform(0, 1, (n_bubbles, 2))
```

4. Plot the scatter plot:

```
scat = ax.scatter(bubbles['position'][:, 0], bubbles['position'][:,
1],
                  s=bubbles['size'], lw=0.5,
facecolors=bubbles['color'])
```

5. Define the animate function that directs the animation:

```
def animate(frame_number):
    # Get the index of the bubble to update in this frame, repeat
the cycle after all
    # bubbles are covered
    current_index = frame_number % n_bubbles
    # Make all colors more transparent as time progresses.
    bubbles['color'][:, 3] -= 1.0/len(bubbles)
    bubbles['color'][:, 3] = np.clip(bubbles['color'][:, 3], 0, 1)

    # Increase the bubble size by growth factor
    bubbles['size'] += bubbles['growth']

    # reset position, size, color and growth factor for the current
bubble
    bubbles['position'][current_index] = np.random.uniform(0, 1, 2)
    bubbles['size'][current_index] = 5
    bubbles['color'][current_index] = (0.5, 0.2, 0.8, 0.8)
    bubbles['growth'][current_index] = np.random.uniform(50, 250)
```

```
    # Update the scatter collection, with the new colors, sizes and
positions.
    scat.set_facecolors(bubbles['color'])
    scat.set_sizes(bubbles['size'])
    scat.set_offsets(bubbles['position'])
```

6. Activate the animation:

```
animation = FuncAnimation(fig, animate, interval=20)
```

7. Send the output to the specified backend:

```
plt.show()
```

How it works...

Here is the explanation of the preceding code blocks:

- `ax = fig.add_axes([0, 0, 1, 1], frameon=False)` sets the axes,and `frameon=False` specifies not to plot the spines.
- `n_bubbles = 50` sets the number of bubbles to 50.
- `bubbles` defines the data structure with position, size, growth factor, and color and initializes all of them with zeros. The position is the x and y coordinates, size and growth are one attribute each, and color is RGBA, hence four attributes.
- `bubbles['position'] = np.random.uniform(0, 1, (n_bubbles, 2))` sets the initial position for all bubbles randomly with all coordinates between zero and 1.
- `ax.scatter()` plots the scatter plot with position coordinates, size, and color arguments.
- `def animate(frame_number):` defines the animate function that directs how the animation should behave:
    - `frame_number` specifies the current frame being processed, it is automatically managed by `FuncAnimation`.
    - `current_index = frame_number % n_bubbles` derives the index of the current bubble within 0 to `n_bubbles`. In each frame, one bubble gets updated.
    - `bubbles['color'][:, 3] -= 1.0/len(bubbles)` decreases the transparency (alpha) attribute for all bubbles so that they get more transparent as time progresses.

- `bubbles['color'][:, 3] = np.clip(bubbles['color'][:, 3], 0, 1)` clips the value of the transparency attribute to zero if it goes below zero, and to 1 if it goes above 1.
- `bubbles['size'] += bubbles['growth']` increase the size of all bubbles by their corresponding growth rate. Since growth is initialized to zeros, the first time it will only add zeros for all bubbles.
- `bubbles['position'][current_index] = np.random.uniform(0, 1, 2)` resets the position of the current bubble, with two coordinates falling between zero and 1.
- `bubbles['size'][current_index] = 5` resets the size to five points for the current bubble.
- `bubbles['color'][current_index] = (0.5, 0.2, 0.8, 0.8)` resets the color in RGBA format for the current bubble.
- `bubbles['growth'][current_index] = np.random.uniform(50, 250)` resets the growth factor for the current bubble.
- `scat.set_facecolors(bubbles['color'])` resets the facecolor of bubbles, `scat.set_sizes(bubbles['size'])` resets the size, and `scat.set_offsets(bubbles['position'])` resets the position on the scatter plot.
- `animation = FuncAnimation(fig, animate, interval=20)` activates the animation.
- `plt.show()` sends the output to the specified backend.

At the end of the animation, the `figure` should look like the one shown here. You can also see `bubbles.mp4` in the code library:

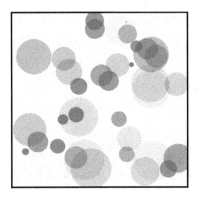

Animating multiple line plots

In this recipe, we will learn how to use `ArtistAnimation` for animating a number of line plots in a sequence. We will use same ROC curves data that we have already used twice in this chapter, for this example too.

Getting ready

Import the required libraries:

```
import matplotlib.pyplot as plt
import pandas as pd
from matplotlib.animation import ArtistAnimation
```

How to do it...

The following are the steps to implement the required logic:

1. Read the `tpr` and `fpr` data for all ROC plots from the corresponding Excel files:

```
fpr_logreg = pd.read_excel('ROC_Curves.xlsx', 'fpr_logreg')
tpr_logreg = pd.read_excel('ROC_Curves.xlsx', 'tpr_logreg')
fpr_KNN = pd.read_excel('ROC_Curves.xlsx', 'fpr_KNN')
tpr_KNN = pd.read_excel('ROC_Curves.xlsx', 'tpr_KNN')
fpr_MLP = pd.read_excel('ROC_Curves.xlsx', 'fpr_MLP')
tpr_MLP = pd.read_excel('ROC_Curves.xlsx', 'tpr_MLP')
fpr_SGD = pd.read_excel('ROC_Curves.xlsx', 'fpr_SGD')
tpr_SGD = pd.read_excel('ROC_Curves.xlsx', 'tpr_SGD')
fpr_GNB = pd.read_excel('ROC_Curves.xlsx', 'fpr_GNB')
tpr_GNB = pd.read_excel('ROC_Curves.xlsx', 'tpr_GNB')
fpr_svc = pd.read_excel('ROC_Curves.xlsx', 'fpr_svc')
tpr_svc = pd.read_excel('ROC_Curves.xlsx', 'tpr_svc')
fpr_RF = pd.read_excel('ROC_Curves.xlsx', 'fpr_RF')
tpr_RF = pd.read_excel('ROC_Curves.xlsx', 'tpr_RF')
fpr_DT = pd.read_excel('ROC_Curves.xlsx', 'fpr_DT')
tpr_DT = pd.read_excel('ROC_Curves.xlsx', 'tpr_DT')
```

2. Define the figure and plot all the ROC curves:

```
fig = plt.figure()
l0 = plt.plot([0, 1], [0, 1], 'k--')
l1 = plt.plot(fpr_logreg, tpr_logreg, label='LogReg',
color='purple', animated=True)
l2 = plt.plot(fpr_KNN, tpr_KNN, label='KNN', color='green',
animated=True)
```

```
13 = plt.plot(fpr_DT, tpr_DT, label='DecisionTree', color='orange',
animated=True)
14 = plt.plot(fpr_RF, tpr_RF, label='Random Forest',
color='yellow', animated=True)
15 = plt.plot(fpr_MLP, tpr_MLP, label='MLP', color='red',
animated=True)
16 = plt.plot(fpr_svc, tpr_svc, label='SVC', color='violet',
animated=True)
17 = plt.plot(fpr_GNB, tpr_GNB, label='GNB', color='grey',
animated=True)
18 = plt.plot(fpr_SGD, tpr_SGD, label='SGD', color='pink',
animated=True)
```

3. Set labels, title, and legend for the plot:

```
plt.xlabel('False Positive Rate', size=15, color='m')
plt.ylabel('True Positive Rate', size=15, color='m')
plt.title('ROC curve', size=25, color='b')
plt.legend(loc='lower right', fancybox=True, shadow=True)
```

4. Define a list for the lines of all ROC curves:

```
lines = [11, 12, 13, 14, 15, 16, 17, 18]
```

5. Activate the animation:

```
ani = ArtistAnimation(fig, lines, blit=True, interval=1000,
repeat=True, repeat_delay=2500)
```

6. Send the output to the specified backend:

```
plt.show()
```

How it works...

Here is the explanation of the preceding code blocks.

The first three steps are familiar to you, except that in each of the plot statements we add an extra argument, animated=True, to indicate that the artist is going to be part of the animation.

lines = [11, 12, 13, 14, 15, 16, 17, 18] is the list of all the artists, defined in *step 2*, to be part of the animation, which is passed to ArtistAnimation as an argument.

```
ani = ArtistAnimation(fig, lines, blit=True, interval=1000,
repeat=True, repeat_delay=2500)
```
activates the animation by displaying one artist at a time, with a time interval of 1,000 milliseconds, and repeats the cycle with a time delay of 2,500 milliseconds.

Here is how the output looks. You can also see `ROC_Curves.mp4` in the code library:

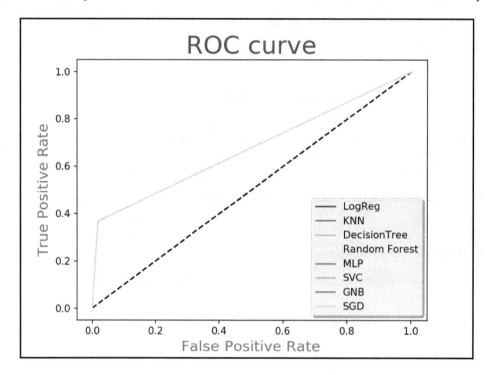

Animation of images

In this recipe, we will learn how to animate images using the same `ArtistAnimation` class.

Getting ready

Import the required libraries:

```
import matplotlib.pyplot as plt
from matplotlib.pyplot import imshow, imread
from matplotlib.animation import ArtistAnimation
```

How to do it...

The following are the steps to implement the required logic:

1. Define the figure and the axes:

```
fig = plt.figure(figsize=(5,5), dpi=50)
ax = fig.add_axes([0, 0, 1, 1], frameon=False)
```

2. Read the required images and create a list of all those images:

```
images = []
image1 = imshow(imread("monet.png"), animated=True)
images.append([image1])

image2 = imshow(imread("louvre_small.png"), animated=True)
images.append([image2])

image3 = imshow(imread("vangogh.png"), animated=True)
images.append([image3])

image4 = imshow(imread("persepalis.png"), animated=True)
images.append([image4])
```

3. Activate the animation:

```
ani = ArtistAnimation(fig, images, interval=1000, blit=False,
                      repeat=True, repeat_delay=2500)
```

4. Send the output to the specified `backend`:

```
plt.show()
```

How it works...

Four images are read and saved into a list that is passed on to `ArtistAnimation`. When we save the image, we use the `animated=True` argument, similar to what we did in the previous recipe. The animation will display one image at a time. So, here we are not showing any of the four images, but you can see the `images.mp4` file in the code library for the animated plot.

10
Embedding Plots in a Graphical User Interface

In this chapter, we will cover the following recipes:

- Using the slider and button widgets of Matplotlib
- Using the slider and button widgets of a Tkinter GUI embedded in a Matplotlib application
- Embedding Matplotlib in a Tkinter GUI application
- Using the Slider and Button widgets of a wxPython GUI embedded in a Matplotlib application
- Embedding Matplotlib in a wxPython GUI application
- Using the Slider and Button widgets of a Qt GUI embedded in a Matplotlib application
- Embedding Matplotlib in a Qt GUI application

Introduction

GUI in itself is a very large subject, and each GUI framework/tool kit requires a separate book to cover it holistically. So, a detailed discussion of each of the GUI framework's features is beyond the scope of this book. The objective here is to demonstrate how certain GUI frameworks can leverage Matplotlib's visualization capabilities.

In the previous chapter, we learned how to use events, widgets, and animation using three **Graphical User Interface** (**GUI**) frameworks Tkinter, wxPython, and Qt as backends. There, we used these backend GUI only for display purposes, so the same code of Matplotlib could be used across all GUI frameworks, by just switching the backend.

In this chapter, we will learn one more feature of interactive plotting, embedding Matplotlib in GUI, using the same three GUI frameworks. First, we will learn how to leverage a few features of the GUI toolkit in Matplotlib figures, in place of Matplotlib's native features. This means that we will still be running a Matplotlib application for controlling the flow, including opening and closing the application. This is essentially embedding GUI features into Matplotlib's figure. Since each GUI framework has its own architecture and syntax, the same code can't be used for all GUI frameworks as we did in the last chapter. This has to be repeated for each of the three GUI frameworks.

Then, we will learn how to run the application with a GUI framework, but leverage Matplotlib's features for plotting. This will come in handy when your main application is written in any of these GUI frameworks, but you want to leverage Matplotlib's rich visualization features in those applications.

There are many GUI frameworks that Matplotlib supports. We have chosen Tkinter, wxPython and Qt based on their popularity and the fact that they come with standard distributions such as Anaconda, so there is no further installation and configuration required, unlike other GUI frameworks. However, Matplotlib interface is similar to all GUI frameworks, so learning from these three GUI frameworks can be easily extended to other GUI frameworks also.

Interface between the Matplotlib and GUI applications

Before we proceed with specific recipes, it is important to understand the internal workings of how the interface between Matplotlib and the backend GUI toolkit works. This makes it easier to understand the differences between three modes of operation:

1. A Matplotlib application using the GUI backend for display only
2. A Matplotlib application using a few GUI features/widgets (embedding GUI features in the Matplotlib application)
3. A GUI application using Matplotlib plots (embedding Matplotlib in the GUI application)

The following three objects from Matplotlib are involved in this interface:

- Figure
- Canvas
- Manager

Although the internal workings and relationships between these objects are a bit complicated, it is enough to understand here that the figure is the root artist of all the artists that go into the overall plot (including subplots, grids, and so on), the canvas is the playground on which the figure is plotted, and the manager controls the interface with the specified backend.

The job of the manager is to handle three GUI elements: window, canvas, and navigation toolbar. window is the main GUI application, Navigation Toolbar is specific to the GUI application that enables interactive analysis of the figure, canvas. Each GUI subclasses its canvas from `FigureCanvasBase`. Hence, the interface between the GUI and Matplotlib is the canvas, and interactions between GUI framework and Matplotlib objects are managed by the manager.

In the first mode of operation, where the backend is used only for display, `plt.figure()` invokes the `Figure`, `FigureCanvas`, and `FigureManager` appropriate for the specified backend; `FigureManager` in turn will result in the creation of the GUI's main window and navigation toolbar objects, and packs `FigureCanvas` and navigation toolbar into the window.

In the second mode of operation, where some of the GUI features are used in a Matplotlib application, we will still use `plt.figure()` to perform the functions as in the first mode; in addition, the Matplotlib application connects the GUI widgets and events on those widgets with the canvas through the main window completing the event loop.

In the third mode of operation, we will completely eliminate the use of `pyplot`, and thereby `FigureManager`, for two reasons. First, `pyplot` by default assumes opening and closing of the application, whereas in this mode we need the GUI to control the application flow. Second, all the functions of `FigureManager` are now to be controlled by the GUI application. Hence, in this mode GUI toolkit features control the opening, closing of the application as well controlling the interactions between GUI toolkit and Matplotlib. These features vary from one GUI toolkit to other, so there is no common syntax or code.

Using the Slider and Button Widgets of Matplotlib

We learned about the `Button` widget of Matplotlib in the previous chapter, but Slider is a new widget that we will learn here. However, the objective of this recipe is to demonstrate how a Matplotlib widget application can be used across GUI frameworks without any code changes, by just changing the backend. We will also use the same polar plot across all the GUI frameworks, so that we can see the difference in the way they work, rather than getting lost in the details of the plot itself!

We will use the `Slider` to determine the number of leaves to be plotted in the polar plot. Each time the `Slider` is dragged, the value of the `Slider` is taken to plot that many leaves in the plot.

We will use the `Quit` Button to exit the application by closing the figure and window objects.

Getting ready

Let's set up the `backend` to be used. This is the only code to be changed for different GUI frameworks to run this plot across the three chosen GUI frameworks:

```
import matplotlib
matplotlib.use('tkagg')
```

Let's import the required libraries:

```
import numpy as np
import matplotlib.pyplot as plt
from matplotlib.widgets import Button, Slider
```

How to do it...

Here are the steps required to code the required logic:

1. Prepare the data for the polar plot:

    ```
    theta = np.arange(0., 2., 1./180.)*np.pi
    ```

2. Define and instantiate the figure:

```
fig = plt.figure(figsize=(6, 5), dpi=100)
```

3. Define the axes and instantiate it on the figure:

```
ax = fig.add_subplot(111, projection='polar')
```

4. Plot the polar graph:

```
initial_n = 4
ax.plot(theta, 5*np.cos(initial_n*theta))
```

5. Define and instantiate the Slider widget:

```
ax_s = plt.axes([0.15, 0.05, 0.25, 0.05])
slider_n = Slider(ax_s, '#of leaves', 3, 10, valinit=initial_n,
                  valstep=1.0)
```

6. Define the callback function for the Slider widget:

```
def onchanged(s_value):
    ax.clear()
    ax.plot(theta, 5*np.cos(int(s_value)*theta))
```

7. Map the on_changed event with the corresponding callback function, onchanged, for the Slider widget:

```
slider_n.on_changed(onchanged)
```

8. Define and instantiate the Button Widget:

```
ebx = plt.axes([0.5, 0.005, 0.1, 0.05])
exit = Button(ebx, 'Quit')
```

9. Define the callback function for the Button:

```
def close(event):
    plt.close('all')
```

10. Map the on_clicked event with the corresponding callback function close:

```
exit.on_clicked(close)
```

11. Display the plot on the specified backend:

```
plt.show()
```

How it works...

Here is the explanation of the code:

- The first four steps are already familiar to you.
- `ax_s = plt.axes([0.15, 0.05, 0.25, 0.05])` defines the axes on which the `Slider` widget is to be placed.
- `slider_n = Slider(ax_s, '#of leaves', 3, 10, valinit=initial_n, valstep=1.0)` defines the slider:
    - The first argument is the axes reference, the second one is the label to be displayed on the slider in the figure.
    - *Three* is the minimum value, that is, the starting point, and 10 is the maximum value of the slider bar. So, by dragging the slider with the mouse, the value changes from 3 to 10.
    - `valinit` specifies the starting point on the slider, when the figure gets displayed the first time. Here, we have specified it as 4.
    - `valstep` specifies in what steps the value increases as we drag the mouse over the slider. Here, we have specified it as 1.0, since it represents the number of leaves.
- `def onchanged(s_value):` is the callback function for the slider. It receives the current value of the slider, clears the previous plot on the axis, and plots the graph with the new value.
- `slider_n.on_changed(onchanged)` captures the `on_changed` event on the slider, then calls the callback function, `onchanged`.
- `ebx = plt.axes([0.5, 0.005, 0.1, 0.05])` defines the axes on which the **Quit** button is to be placed and `exit = Button(ebx, 'Quit')` defines the button.
- ebx is the axes reference; **Quit** is the label to be placed on the button widget in the figure
- `def close(event):` is the callback function for the `Button` widget. It simply closes all figure windows.
- `exit.on_clicked(close)` captures the `on_clicked` event on the Button and calls the callback function, `close`
- `plt.show()` displays the plot on the **tkagg** backend.

When you run the preceding code, you should get the following output plots. The first plot is what you see the first time when you get the plot; it will have four leaves as we have initialized the slider with 4. When you drag the slider to 8.00, then you will see the second plot:

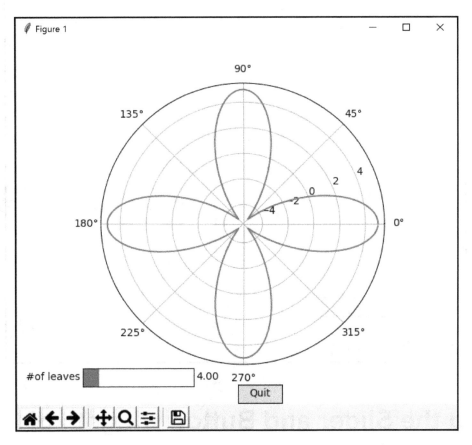

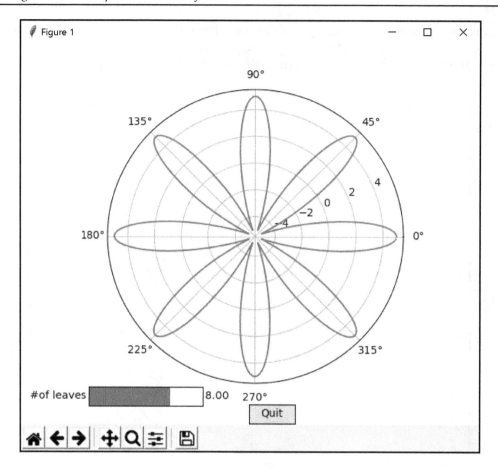

Using the Slider and Button widgets of Tkinter GUI

In this recipe, we will learn how to use the Slider and Button widgets of Tkinter GUI in place of Matplotlib widgets. The functionality of the plot is exactly the same as the previous recipe. The program control flow is still with Matplotlib, and we will still use `plt.figure()` for invoking the backend and associated widgets. In addition, we will invoke `Tkinter's tk.Scale` scaler and `tk.Button` button widgets with associated callback functions, replacing Matplotlib's slider and button widgets, which we used in the previous recipe.

Getting ready

Set up the `backend`:

```
import matplotlib
matplotlib.use('tkagg')
```

Import the required libraries:

```
import tkinter as tk
import numpy as np
import matplotlib.pyplot as plt
```

How to do it...

The following are the steps required to implement the logic:

1. Prepare the data for the polar plot:

   ```
   theta = np.arange(0., 2., 1./180.)*np.pi
   ```

2. Define and instantiate the figure:

   ```
   fig = plt.figure(figsize=(6, 5), dpi=100)
   ```

3. Define and instantiate the axes on the figure:

   ```
   ax = fig.add_subplot(111,projection='polar')
   ```

4. Plot the polar graph:

   ```
   ax.plot(theta, 5*np.cos(3*theta))
   ```

5. Define the window into which the Tkinter widgets will be placed:

   ```
   window = fig.canvas.manager.window
   ```

6. Define the callback function for the Slider widget:

   ```
   def update():
       n=n_slider.get()
       ax.clear()
       ax.plot(theta, 5*np.cos(n*theta))
       fig.canvas.draw()
   ```

7. Define and instantiate the slider:

```
n_slider = tk.Scale(master=window,variable=tk.IntVar(), from_=3,
                    to=10, label='#of leaves',
orient=tk.HORIZONTAL,length=int(fig.bbox.width),
      width=int(fig.bbox.height * 0.05), command = lambda i :
                update())
```

8. Pack the slider into the window:

```
n_slider.set(4)
n_slider.pack(after=fig.canvas.get_tk_widget())
```

9. Define the callback function for the **Quit** Button:

```
def close():
    plt.close('all')
    window.quit()
```

10. Define and instantiate the Button:

```
button = tk.Button(master=window, text="Quit", command=close)
```

11. Pack the Button into the window:

```
button.pack(side=tk.BOTTOM)
```

12. Display the plot on the Tkinter backend:

```
plt.show()
```

How it works...

Here is the explanation for the preceding code:

- The first four steps are already familiar to you.
- `window = fig.canvas.manager.window` gets access to Tkinter's application through its window.
- `def update():` is the callback function for the `tk.Scale` widget:
    - `n=n_slider.get()` gets the current value of the slider, when the mouse was dragged and released, which in this case is 7.
    - `ax.clear()` erases the previous plot on the axes.

- `ax.plot(theta, 5*np.cos(n*theta))` plots the new graph with a current value of `n`.
- `fig.canvas.draw()` refreshes the figure.

- `n_slider = tk.Scale()` defines the slider widget with the following arguments:

  - `master=window` specifies that the slider widget should be created as a child of the main window.
  - `variable=tk.IntVar()` specifies that the slider variable is an integer; since it represents the number of leaves on the plot, it makes sense to define it as an integer.
  - `from_=3` and `to=10` represent the starting value and ending value for the slider, so the user can drag the slider between 3 and 10.
  - `label='#of leaves'` specifies the label for the slider to be displayed on the left of the slider.
  - `orient=tk.HORIZONTAL` specifies that the scaler is plotted horizontally, not vertically.
  - `length=int(fig.bbox.width)` specifies the length of the widget in pixels. `fig.bbox.width` returns the width of the figure in a floating point number, and `int` converts it to an integer. Hence, the scaler spreads the complete figure horizontally.
  - `width=int(fig.bbox.height * 0.05)` specifies the height of the scaler in pixels. We are taking 5% of the total figure height for the scaler, by multiplying by 0.05.
  - `command = lambda i : update()` specifies the callback function for the slider as `update()`, so when we drag the mouse on the slider and release, it invokes the update function.

- `n_slider.set(4)` sets the initial value for the slider, which will be displayed the first time the plot is displayed. So, when the plot is displayed for the first time, we should see it with four leaves.

- `n_slider.pack(after=fig.canvas.get_tk_widget())` specifies to plot the slider widget below (after) the canvas. Tkinter does not have a subclass for the canvas, but the canvas is accessible through the `get_tk_widget()` method. `pack()` is the Tkinter method to pack widgets into the window.

- `def close():` is the callback function for the Button widget:

  - `plt.close('all')` closes all the figures
  - `window.quit()` exits the window application

- `button = tk.Button()` defines the button widget of Tkinter:
  - `master=window` specifies that the button widget should be created as a child of the main window.
  - `text="Quit"` specifies the label for the button, which will be displayed on the button.
  - `command=close` specifies the callback function to be `close()`.
- `button.pack(side=tk.BOTTOM)` specifies that the button should be packed into the window at the bottom.
- `plt.show()` displays the figure on the Tkinter backend.

When you run the preceding code, you should get the first plot for the first time. When you drag the slider to 7, you should see the second plot. You can exit by clicking the **Quit** button:

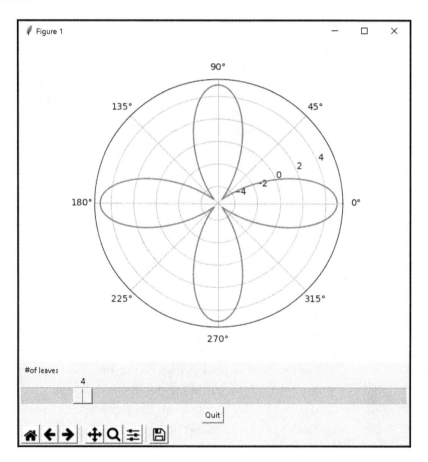

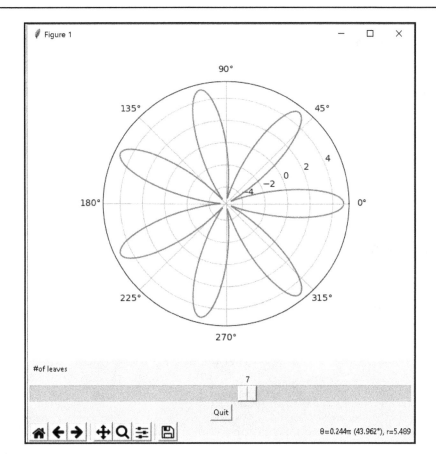

Embedding Matplotlib in a Tkinter GUI application

In this recipe, we will learn how to embed Matplotlib in a Tkinter GUI application. Here, the control of the application flow will be with Tkinter. Here, we will not use the pyplot module and associated `plt.figure()` method. Instead, we invoke the Tkinter application and embed Matplotlib's canvas as a widget.

Getting ready

Here, we will not set up the backend, as the application itself is to be started from the GUI.

Import the required libraries:

```
import tkinter as tk
import numpy as np
from tkinter.font import Font
from matplotlib.figure import Figure
from matplotlib.backends.backend_tkagg import (FigureCanvasTkAgg,
NavigationToolbar2Tk)
```

How to do it...

The following are the steps to be followed to implement the logic:

1. Define and instantiate the figure:

    ```
    fig = Figure(figsize=(6, 5), dpi=100)
    ```

2. Define the Tkinter window and set the title for the window:

    ```
    window=tk.Tk()
    window.wm_title("Embedding in Tk")
    ```

3. Define the canvas and navigation toolbar, and pack them into the Tkinter window:

    ```
    canvas = FigureCanvasTkAgg(fig, master=window)
    toolbar = NavigationToolbar2Tk(canvas, window)
    canvas._tkcanvas.pack(side=tk.TOP, fill=tk.BOTH, expand=1)
    ```

4. Define the font to be used for the text on various widgets:

    ```
    myfont = Font(family='Helvetica', size=12, weight='bold')
    ```

5. Define the axes on the figure, prepare the data, and plot the polar graph:

    ```
    ax = fig.add_subplot(111,projection='polar')
    theta = np.arange(0., 2., 1./180.)*np.pi
    ax.plot(theta, 5*np.cos(3*theta))
    ```

6. Define the callback function for the `Slider` widget:

```
def update():
    n=n_slider.get()
    ax.clear()
    ax.plot(theta, 5*np.cos(n*theta))
    fig.canvas.draw()
```

7. Define and instantiate the `Slider` widget and pack it into the `window`:

```
n_slider = tk.Scale(master=window,variable=tk.IntVar(), from_=3,
                    to=10, label='#of leaves',
                    orient=tk.HORIZONTAL,length=int(fig.bbox.width),
                    width=int(fig.bbox.height * 0.05), command =
                    lambda i : update(),font=myfont)
n_slider.set(4)
n_slider.pack(after=fig.canvas.get_tk_widget())
```

8. Define the `callback` function for the **Quit** Button widget:

```
def exit():
    window.quit()
    window.destroy()
```

9. Define and instantiate `Quit` **Button** and pack it into the `window`:

```
button = tk.Button(master=window, text="Quit", command=exit,
                   font=myfont)
button.pack(side=tk.BOTTOM)
```

10. Initiate the `mainloop` to capture events triggered by the user:

```
tk.mainloop()
```

How it works...

Here is the explanation for the preceding code:

- `fig = Figure(figsize=(6, 5), dpi=100)` defines and instantiates the figure object. `Figure()` is imported from the `matplotlib.figure` class. In the two previous recipes, we used `plt.figure()` for this purpose!
- `window=tk.Tk()` invokes the Tkinter GUI application through its main window widget.
- `window.wm_title("Embedding in Tk")` sets the title for the window, which will appear on the top of the window.

- `canvas = FigureCanvasTkAgg(fig, master=window)` defines the canvas (the playground for the figure, such as the paper on which a graph is plotted), and attaches the figure to this canvas:
  - `master=window` specifies that the canvas is a child of the Tkinter window object.
  - `toolbar = NavigationToolbar2Tk(canvas, window)` specifies the navigation toolbar, again as a child to Tkinter window, and attaches it to the canvas.
- `canvas._tkcanvas.pack(side=tk.TOP, fill=tk.BOTH, expand=1)` packs the canvas and navigation toolbar into Tkinter's main window:
  - `side=tk.TOP` specifies that the canvas to be placed at the top of the `window`, and the toolbar below it.
  - `fill=tk.BOTH` specifies that the canvas should fill the `window` in both *X* (horizontally) and *Y* (vertically) directions
  - `expand=1` specifies to adjust equally any additional space in the main `window`, after accommodating all the widgets, to widgets that have `expand=1`.
  - `myfont = Font(family='Helvetica', size=12, weight='bold')` defines the font dictionary to be used for the text on the widgets so that all of them look similar in the figure.
- *Step 5* defines the axes, data for the polar plot, and plots it on the axes.
- `def update():` is the callback function for the slider widget, as explained in the preceding recipe.
- `n_slider = tk.Scale()` defines the slider widget, then initializes it to 4, followed by packing it into the window, as explained in the preceding recipe.
- `def exit():` is the callback function for the **Quit** button used to exit from the application. This is different than the `close()` function used in the preceding recipes:
  - `window.quit()` exits from the `mainloop`.
  - `window.destroy()` destroys the application to avoid an error in Windows OS specifically.
  - `button = tk.Button()` and `button.pack(side=tk.BOTTOM)` are the same as explained in the preceding recipe.
- `tk.mainloop()` invokes Tkinter's main application loop to capture the events and invoke the appropriate callback functions.

When you run the preceding code, you should see the first plot for the first time, and when you drag the slider to 9, you should see the second plot. You can exit the application by clicking on the **Quit** button:

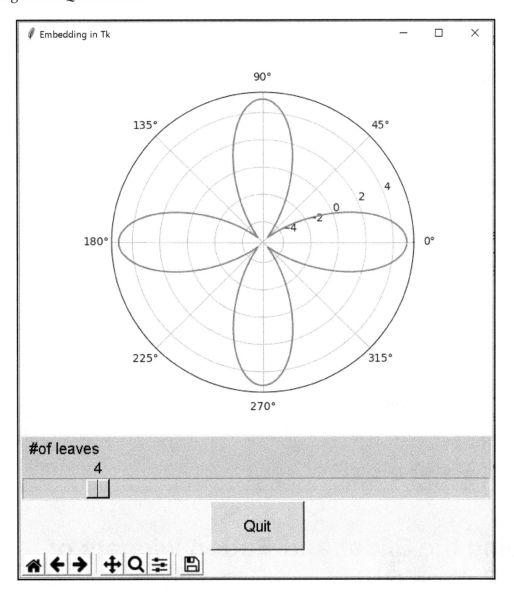

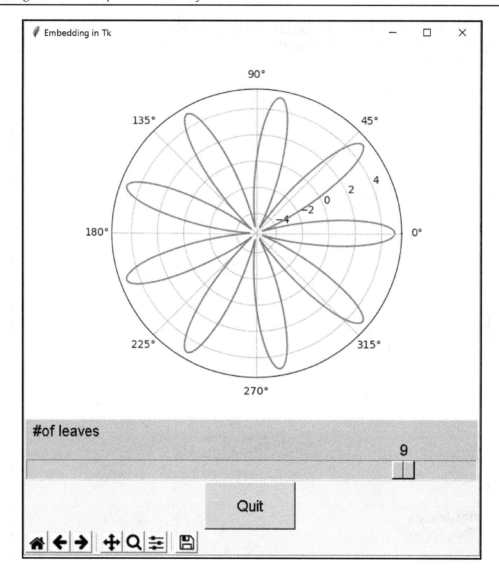

Using the Slider and Button widgets of WxPython GUI

In this recipe, we will learn how to use wxPython's Slider and Button widgets in place of Matplotlib widgets, just the way we did with Tkinter widgets.

wxPython is a wrapper around the wxWidgets module. It also comes packaged with standard Python distributions such as Anaconda.

Getting ready

Set the backend as wxAgg:

```
import matplotlib
matplotlib.use('wxagg')
```

Import the required libraries:

```
import wx
import numpy as np
import matplotlib.pyplot as plt
```

How to do it...

The following are the steps to implement the required logic:

1. Define and instantiate the figure:

   ```
   fig = plt.figure(figsize=(6, 5), dpi=100)
   ```

2. Define the axes, define the data for the polar plot, and plot the polar graph:

   ```
   ax = fig.add_subplot(111,projection='polar')
   theta = np.arange(0., 2., 1./180.)*np.pi
   ax.plot(theta, 5*np.cos(4*theta))
   ```

3. Define the window through which we connect wx widgets with Matplotlib:

   ```
   window = fig.canvas.manager.window
   ```

4. Define the callback function for the Slider widget:

   ```
   def update(event):
       n=n_slider.GetValue()
       ax.clear()
       ax.plot(theta, 5*np.cos(n*theta))
       fig.canvas.draw()
   ```

5. Define and instantiate the Slider widget of `wxPython` and bind it with the callback function:

```
n_slider = wx.Slider(window, wx.ID_ANY, 4, 3, 10, size=(250,10),
                     style=(wx.SL_AUTOTICKS | wx.SL_HORIZONTAL |
                            wx.SL_LABELS))
n_slider.Bind(wx.EVT_SCROLL, update)
```

6. Define the callback function for the **Quit** Button widget:

```
def close(event):
    plt.close('all')
```

7. Define and instantiate the `Quit` Button widget and bind it with the callback function:

```
button = wx.Button(window, wx.ID_ANY, "Quit")
button.Bind(wx.EVT_BUTTON, close)
```

8. Define the `sizer` with the current `window` size:

```
sizer = window.GetSizer()
```

9. Insert the Button widget into the `window`:

```
sizer.Insert(0, button, 0, wx.ALIGN_CENTER)
```

10. Insert the Slider widget into the `window`:

```
sizer.Insert(2, n_slider, 0, wx.ALIGN_RIGHT)
```

11. Display the figure on the `wxPython` backend:

```
plt.show()
```

How it works...

Here is the explanation for the preceding code:

- The first two steps define the figure using `plt.figure()`, axes, and data, and plots the polar graph on the figure.
- `window = fig.canvas.manager.window` gets access to the `wxPython` application through its window.

- `def update(event):` is the callback function for the `wx.Slider()` widget. Here, we have to pass the *event* argument to the function:
  - `n=n_slider.GetValue()` gets the current value of the slider. Please note the difference in syntax compared to what we had for Tkinter.
  - The remaining three steps of this function are exactly the same as with Tkinter.
- `n_slider = wx.Slider(window, wx.ID_ANY, 3, 3, 10, size=(250,10), style=(wx.SL_AUTOTICKS | wx.SL_HORIZONTAL | wx.SL_LABELS))` defines the Slider widget:
  - `window` specifies that the slider is the child object of the main window.
  - `wx.ID_ANY` specifies to use the system generated identification number for this widget.
  - 3 is the initial value for the slider, when it comes up for the first time.
  - 3 and 10 are the starting and ending values for the slider.
  - `size=(250,10)` specifies the length and height of the slider widget in pixels.
  - `style()` specifies various parameters for the slider:
    - `wx.SL_AUTOTICKS` specifies that the slider should display tick marks.
    - `wx.SL_HORIZONTAL` specifies that the slider should be placed horizontally.
    - `wx.SL_LABELS` specifies the print labels for starting, current value, and ending value for the slider.
- `n_slider.Bind(wx.EVT_SCROLL, update)` connects the scroll event of the slider with the corresponding callback function, `update()`.
- `def close(event):` is the callback function for the **Quit** button. It essentially closes all the figures.

- `button = wx.Button(window, wx.ID_ANY, "Quit")` defines WxPython's Button widget:
    - `window` specifies that button is the child object of the main window
    - `wx.ID_ANY` specifies to use the system generated identification number for this widget
    - `"Quit"` is the label to be printed on the button widget
- `button.Bind(wx.EVT_BUTTON, close)` connects the click event of the button to the corresponding callback function `close()`.
- `sizer = window.GetSizer()` gets the current window dimensions. `sizer` is the way WxPython creates the layout of various widgets that get plotted on the figure.
- `sizer.Insert(0, button, 0, wx.ALIGN_CENTER)` plots the button widget in the main window:
    - `0` specifies the order in which this widget is to be placed in the window. 0 means it is placed at index 0, which means the button will be placed at the top of the window.
    - `button`, the widget being placed on the figure.
    - `0` specifies that no relative sizing of the widget is to be done.
    - `wx.ALIGN_CENTER` specifies that the widget should be aligned centrally.
- `sizer.Insert(2, n_slider, 0, wx.ALIGN_RIGHT)` plots the slider widget at the second index. At index 1, the canvas will be placed automatically, pushing the slider to the bottom of the window:
    - `wx.ALIGN_RIGHT` specifies that the slider widget should be right-aligned in the window
- `plt.show()` displays the figure in `wxPython's` backend.

When you run the preceding code, you should see the first plot for the first time, and the second plot when you drag the slider to 10. You can exit the application by clicking on the **Quit** button:

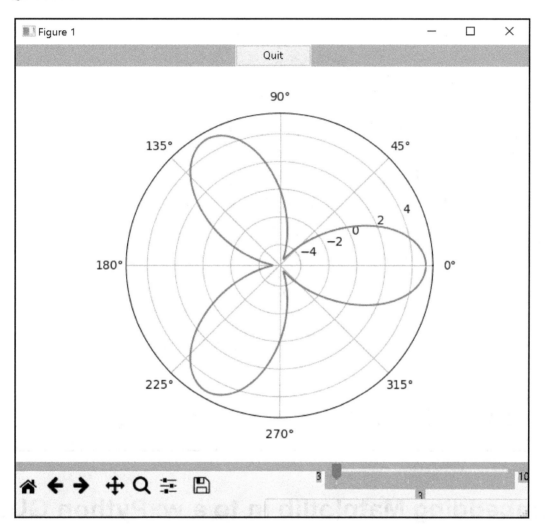

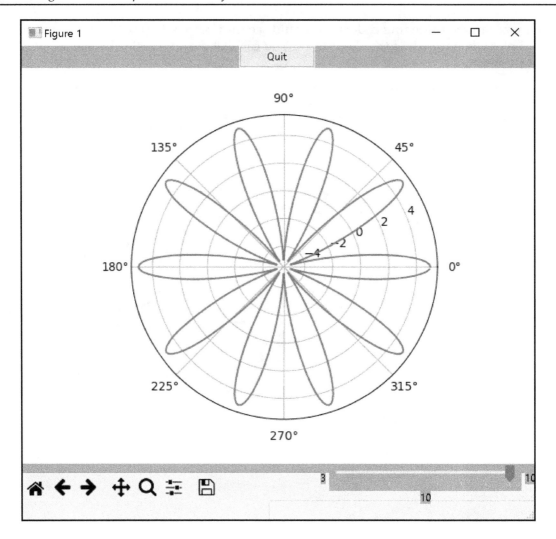

Embedding Matplotlib in to a wxPython GUI application

In this recipe, we will learn how to embed Matplotlib plots in a wxPython GUI application. We will use the same data and plot that we have been using in this chapter.

Getting ready

Import the required libraries:

```
import wx
import numpy as np
from matplotlib.figure import Figure
from matplotlib.backends.backend_wxagg import FigureCanvasWxAgg as
FigureCanvas
from matplotlib.backends.backend_wxagg import NavigationToolbar2WxAgg
```

How to do it...

The following are the steps needed to implement the logic:

1. Define the wxPython application:

   ```
   app = wx.App()
   ```

2. Define the window where the plot and widgets are displayed:

   ```
   window = wx.Frame(None, -1, "Embedding with wxPython")
   ```

3. Define and instantiate the figure, canvas, and toolbar:

   ```
   fig = Figure(figsize=(6, 5), dpi=100)
   canvas = FigureCanvas(window, -1, fig)
   toolbar = NavigationToolbar2WxAgg(canvas)
   ```

4. Define the axes and data for the polar plot, and plot the polar graph:

   ```
   ax = fig.add_subplot(111,projection='polar')
   theta = np.arange(0., 2., 1./180.)*np.pi
   ax.plot(theta, 5*np.cos(3*theta))
   ```

5. Define the callback function for the Slider widget:

   ```
   def update(event):
       n=n_slider.GetValue()
       ax.clear()
       ax.plot(theta, 5*np.cos(n*theta))
       fig.canvas.draw()
   ```

6. Define the `Slider` widget and bind it with the `callback` function:

```
n_slider = wx.Slider(window, wx.ID_ANY, 3, 3, 10, size=(250,20),
                     style=(wx.SL_AUTOTICKS | wx.SL_HORIZONTAL |
                            wx.SL_LABELS))
n_slider.Bind(wx.EVT_SCROLL, update)
```

7. Define the font to be applied to text on the widgets:

```
myfont = wx.Font(12, wx.ROMAN, wx.ITALIC, wx.BOLD)
```

8. Set the font for the Slider widget:

```
n_slider.SetFont(myfont)
```

9. Define the `callback` function for the `Quit` Button widget:

```
def close(event):
    window.Close()
```

10. Define the `Quit` Button widget and bind it with the `callback` function:

```
button = wx.Button(window, wx.ID_ANY, "Quit", size=
                   (int(fig.bbox.width),int(fig.bbox.height)*0.1))
button.Bind(wx.EVT_BUTTON, close)
```

11. Set the font of the `Quit` button widget:

```
button.SetFont(myfont)
```

12. Set the initial size of the `window` to that of the `figure`:

```
window.SetInitialSize(wx.Size(int(fig.bbox.width),
                      int(fig.bbox.height)))
```

13. Define the `sizer` and insert the `canvas`, `toolbar`, `slider`, and `button` widgets into the `window`:

```
sizer = wx.BoxSizer(wx.VERTICAL)
sizer.Insert(0, canvas, 1, wx.EXPAND | wx.ALL)
sizer.Insert(1, button, 0, wx.EXPAND)
sizer.Insert(2, n_slider, 0, wx.ALIGN_RIGHT)
sizer.Insert(3, toolbar, 0, wx.ALIGN_LEFT)
```

14. Set the `window` to fit all the widgets properly:

```
window.SetSizer(sizer)
window.Fit()
window.Show()
```

15. Initiate the mainloop to capture events triggered by the user:

```
app.MainLoop()
```

How it works...

Here is the explanation for the preceding code:

- `app = wx.App()` initiates the `wxPython` GUI application.
- `window = wx.Frame(None, -1, "Embedding with wxPython")` defines and instantiates the `window` object in which the `figure` will be displayed:
    - `None` specifies that the `window` is the parent object
    - `-1` specifies the `window` identification number
    - `"Embedding with wxPython"` specifies the label for the window that will appear on top of the `window`
- `fig = Figure(figsize=(6, 5), dpi=100)` defines and instantiates the figure
- `canvas = FigureCanvas(window, -1, fig)` defines the canvas connecting the figure and packing it into the `window`
- `toolbar = NavigationToolbar2WxAgg(canvas)` defines the `toolbar` and packs it into the `canvas`
- *Step 4* defines the axes and data for the polar plot, and plots it on the axes
- `def update(event):` is the same `callback` function for the `Slider` widget as the preceding recipe
- `n_slider = wx.Slider()` and `n_slider.Bind()` are exactly the same as the preceding recipe
- `myfont = wx.Font(12, wx.ROMAN, wx.ITALIC, wx.BOLD)` defines the font dictionary to be applied to the text on the widgets, with a font size of 12, Roman font, italic style, and bold weight

- `n_slider.SetFont(myfont)` applies the font dictionary to the text on the slider widget
- `def close(event):` is the callback function for the `Quit` button:
- `window.Close()` closes the `window` and the GUI application
- `button = wx.Button()` and `button.Bind()` are the same as the preceding recipe, except that we specify a specific width and height for the button widget here, whereas we used the default size in the preceding recipe
- `button.SetFont(myfont)` applies the font dictionary to the text on the button.
- `window.SetInitialSize(wx.Size(int(fig.bbox.width), int(fig.bbox.height)))` sets the window size equal to the figure size
- `sizer = wx.BoxSizer(wx.VERTICAL)` defines the sizer object for the layout of the figure with a vertical layout. That means all the widgets added on to this slider will be arranged vertically, one below the other:
- `sizer.Insert(0, canvas, 1, wx.EXPAND | wx.ALL)` adds the canvas to the sizer at index 0 (top); `wx.EXPAND | wx.ALL` ensures that the size of the figure and canvas go together
- `sizer.Insert(1, button, 0, wx.EXPAND)` adds a button to the sizer; `wx.EXPAND` specifies to spread the button the full length of the figure
  - `sizer.Insert(2, n_slider, 0, wx.ALIGN_RIGHT)` adds the Slider to the `sizer` with a right alignment
  - `sizer.Insert(3, toolbar, 0, wx.ALIGN_LEFT)` adds the toolbar to the sizer with a left alignment
- `window.SetSizer(sizer)` adds the `sizer` layout to the main `window`
- `window.Fit()` adjusts the space in such a way that all the widgets fit into the figure properly
- `window.Show()` displays the `figure` in the `window`
- `app.MainLoop()` initiates the GUI application loop to capture events and fire the respective callback functions.

When you run the preceding code, you should see the first plot for the first time, when it comes up with three leaves, and the second plot after dragging the slider to the end of the slider with a value of 10:

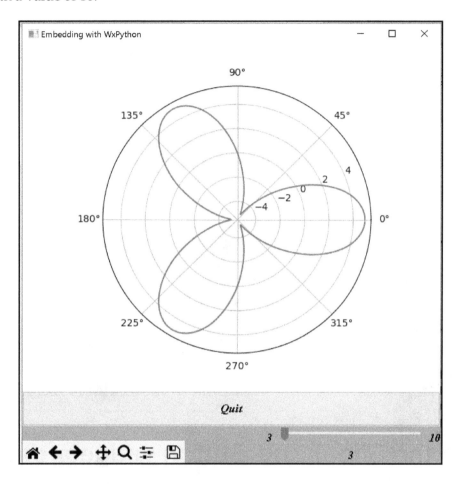

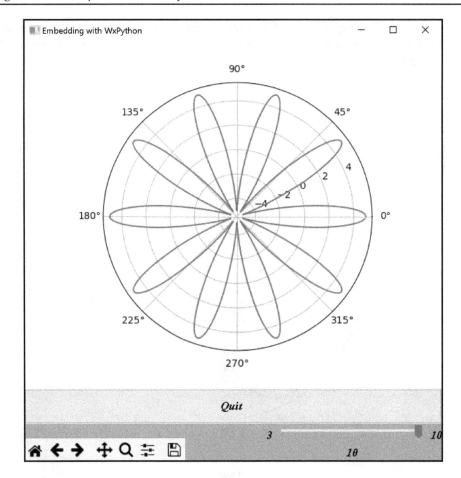

Using the Slider and Button widgets of Qt's GUI

In this recipe, we will learn how to leverage the Qt GUI Slider and Button widgets in place of Matplotlib widgets. Code in this and the next recipe should work for both the Qt4 as well as Qt5 GUI versions.

The Qt GUI is very similar to the `wxPython` GUI. In place of the `sizer`, we will have `QHBoxLayout` and `QVBoxLayout`; in place of `fig.canvas.manager.window`, we will have `fig.canvas.setLayout`; and in place of `Bind`, we will have `connect`.

Getting ready

1. Set up the backend to `Qt5`:

    ```
    import matplotlib
    matplotlib.use('Qt5Agg')
    ```

2. Import the required libraries:

    ```
    import numpy as np
    import matplotlib.pyplot as plt
    from matplotlib.backends.qt_compat import QtCore, QtWidgets,
    is_pyqt5, QtGui
    if is_pyqt5():
        from matplotlib.backends.backend_qt5agg import FigureCanvas
    else:
        from matplotlib.backends.backend_qt4agg import FigureCanvas
    ```

How to do it...

The following are the steps to implement the logic:

1. Define and instantiate the `figure`:

    ```
    fig = plt.figure(figsize=(8, 6), dpi=100)
    ```

2. Define the axes and data for the polar plot, and plot the polar graph:

    ```
    ax = fig.add_subplot(111,projection='polar')
    theta = np.arange(0., 2., 1./180.)*np.pi
    ax.plot(theta, 5*np.cos(4*theta))
    ```

3. Define the callback function for the Slider widget:

    ```
    def update():
        n=n_slider.value()
        ax.clear()
        ax.plot(theta, 5*np.cos(n*theta))
        fig.canvas.draw()
    ```

4. Define the Slider widget:

```
n_slider = QtWidgets.QSlider(QtCore.Qt.Horizontal)
n_slider.setRange(3, 10)
n_slider.setSingleStep(1)
n_slider.setValue(4)
n_slider.setTickPosition(QtWidgets.QSlider.TicksBelow)
n_slider.setTickInterval(1)
n_slider.setFont(QtGui.QFont("Arial",30))
```

5. Connect the Slider widget with the corresponding `callback` function:

```
n_slider.sliderReleased.connect(update)
```

6. Define the `callback` function for the Quit button:

```
def close():
    plt.close('all')
```

7. Define the Quit button widget:

```
button = QtWidgets.QPushButton("Quit")
button.setGeometry(QtCore.QRect(250, 0, 75, 25))
```

8. Connect the Quit button with the corresponding `callback` function:

```
button.clicked.connect(close)
```

9. Define the horizontal box, and add the Slider and Button widgets to it:

```
hbox = QtWidgets.QHBoxLayout()
hbox.addWidget(n_slider)
hbox.addWidget(button)
```

10. Define the vertical box and add the spacer object and the `hbox` horizontal layout box:

```
vbox = QtWidgets.QVBoxLayout()
vspace = QtWidgets.QSpacerItem(0, 0,
QtWidgets.QSizePolicy.Expanding, QtWidgets.QSizePolicy.Expanding)
vbox.addItem(vspace)
vbox.addSpacing(20)
vbox.addLayout(hbox)
```

11. Connect the `vbox` vertical layout box to the figure's canvas:

```
fig.canvas.setLayout(vbox)
```

12. Display the figure on Qt backend:

```
plt.show()
```

How it works...

Here is the explanation for the preceding code:

- The first two steps are already familiar to the ones you have seen in preceding recipes.
- `def update():` is the callback function for the slider widget. `n=n_slider.value()` gets the current value of the slider. Please note the difference in syntax from the other two GUIs in the preceding sections. The remaining three statements of this function are exactly the same as in the preceding recipes
- `n_slider = QtWidgets.QSlider(QtCore.Qt.Horizontal)` defines the slider widget of `Qt` and specifies that it should be plotted horizontally:
    - `n_slider.setRange(3, 10)` specifies the minimum and maximum values for the slider
    - `n_slider.setSingleStep(1)` specifies the size of each step when you drag the mouse on the slider. Here, we have specified it to be 1
    - `n_slider.setValue(4)` specifies the initial value for the slider when it comes up for the first time
    - `n_slider.setTickPosition(QtWidgets.QSlider.TicksBelow)` specifies that the slider should have ticks plotted and they should be below the slider
    - `n_slider.setTickInterval(1)` specifies the gap between the ticks. Here, we have specified it to be 1
    - `n_slider.setFont(QtGui.QFont("Arial",30))` sets the font to be *Arial* and the font size to be 30.
- `n_slider.sliderReleased.connect(update)` connects the slider event `"sliderReleased"` with the corresponding callback function, `update()`

- `def close():` is the callback function for the `Quit` button, which is exactly the same as earlier GUIs
- `button = QtWidgets.QPushButton("Quit")` specifies the button widget with the label `Quit`
- `button.setGeometry(QtCore.QRect(250, 0, 75, 25))` defines where the button should be placed and the length and height. `(250, 0, 75, 25)` specifies 250 pixels from the left of the figure, 0 pixels from the bottom, 75 pixels in length, and 25 pixels in height
- `button.clicked.connect(close)` connects the button event `clicked` with the corresponding callback function, `close()`
- `hbox = QtWidgets.QHBoxLayout()` defines the horizontal layout box:
  - `hbox.addWidget(n_slider)` adds the slider to the horizontal box
  - `hbox.addWidget(button)` adds the button widget to the horizontal box
  - The slider and button widgets will be placed next to each other horizontally in one row
- `vbox = QtWidgets.QVBoxLayout()` defines the vertical layout box:
  - `vspace = QtWidgets.QSpacerItem(0, 0, QtWidgets.QSizePolicy.Expanding, QtWidgets.QSizePolicy.Expanding)` creates a space object to be included in the vertical layout box so that the Slider and Button widgets are plotted at the bottom of the figure
  - `vbox.addItem(vspace)` adds vertical space to the vertical layout box
  - `vbox.addSpacing(20)` adds additional space to pixels in the vertical layout box
  - `vbox.addLayout(hbox)` adds a horizontal layout box into the vertical layout box
  - `fig.canvas.setLayout(vbox)` connects the vertical layout box to the figure's canvas.
- `plt.show()` displays the figure on the `Qt5` backend.

After running the preceding code, you should see the first plot for the first time, and after dragging the slider to 5, you should see the second plot:

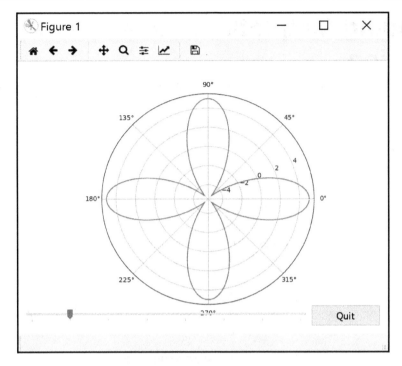

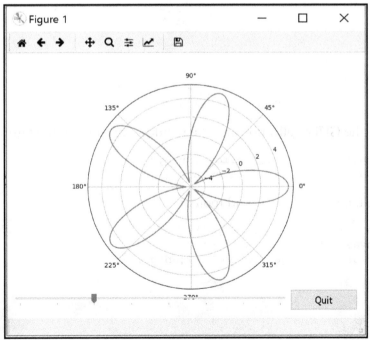

Embedding Matplotlib in to a Qt GUI application

In this recipe, we will learn how to embed a Matplotlib canvas in a Qt GUI application.

Getting ready

Import the required libraries:

```
import sys
import numpy as np
from matplotlib.figure import Figure
from matplotlib.backends.qt_compat import QtCore, QtWidgets, is_pyqt5,
    QtGui

if is_pyqt5():
    from matplotlib.backends.backend_qt5agg import (
                                FigureCanvas, NavigationToolbar2QT
                                as  NavigationToolbar)
else:
    from matplotlib.backends.backend_qt4agg import (
                                FigureCanvas, NavigationToolbar2QT
                                as NavigationToolbar)
```

How to do it...

The following are the steps to implement the logic:

1. Define the GUI application and the window for plotting the figure:

   ```
   qApp = QtWidgets.QApplication(sys.argv)
   window = QtWidgets.QMainWindow()
   ```

2. Define the figure, canvas and toolbar:

   ```
   fig = Figure(figsize=(8, 6), dpi=100)
   canvas = FigureCanvas(fig)
   toolbar = NavigationToolbar(canvas, window)
   ```

3. Define the axes and data, and plot the polar graph:

```
ax = fig.add_subplot(111,projection='polar')
theta = np.arange(0., 2., 1./180.)*np.pi
ax.plot(theta, 5*np.cos(4*theta))
```

4. Define the callback function for the Slider:

```
def update():
    n=n_slider.value()
    ax.clear()
    ax.plot(theta, 5*np.cos(n*theta))
    fig.canvas.draw()
```

5. Define the Slider widget and connect it with the corresponding callback function:

```
n_slider = QtWidgets.QSlider(QtCore.Qt.Horizontal)
n_slider.setRange(3, 10)
n_slider.setSingleStep(1)
n_slider.setValue(4)
n_slider.setTickPosition(QtWidgets.QSlider.TicksBelow)
n_slider.setTickInterval(1)
n_slider.setFont(QtGui.QFont("Arial",20))
n_slider.sliderReleased.connect(update)
```

6. Define the callback function for the **Quit** button:

```
def close():
    window.close()
```

7. Define the **Quit** button widget and connect it to the corresponding callback function:

```
button = QtWidgets.QPushButton("Quit")
button.setFont(QtGui.QFont("Arial",30))
button.clicked.connect(close)
```

8. Define the horizontal box and place the slider and its label items in it:

```
hbox = QtWidgets.QHBoxLayout()
minn = QtWidgets.QLabel('3')
minn.setFont(QtGui.QFont("Arial",20))
maxn = QtWidgets.QLabel('10')
maxn.setFont(QtGui.QFont("Arial",20))
hbox.addWidget(minn)
hbox.addWidget(n_slider)
hbox.addWidget(maxn)
```

9. Define the vertical box and place the toolbar, spacer, button widget, and horizontal box in it:

```
vbox = QtWidgets.QVBoxLayout()
vbox.addWidget(toolbar)
vspace = QtWidgets.QSpacerItem(0, 750)
vbox.addItem(vspace)
vbox.addSpacing(20)
vbox.addLayout(hbox)
vbox.addWidget(button)
```

10. Attach the vertical box to the figure canvas:

```
fig.canvas.setLayout(vbox)
```

11. Set the title for the window and display it:

```
window.setWindowTitle("Embedding with Qt")
window.setCentralWidget(canvas)
window.show()
```

12. Initiate the application loop to capture user actions:

```
qApp.exec_()
```

How it works...

Here is the explanation of the preceding code:

- `qApp = QtWidgets.QApplication(sys.argv)` invokes the `Qt` GUI application. It expects `sys.argv` as arguments, even if it is empty
- `window = QtWidgets.QMainWindow()` defines the main window in which the figure is displayed
- `fig = Figure(figsize=(8, 6), dpi=100)` defines the figure
- `canvas = FigureCanvas(fig)` defines the canvas and attaches the figure to it
- `toolbar = NavigationToolbar(canvas, window)` defines the toolbar for the GUI and attaches it to the main `window` and `canvas`
- Step 3 defines the axes and data for the polar plot, and plots the polar graph
- `def update():` is the callback function for the slider and exactly the same as in the preceding recipe
- `n_slider = QtWidgets.QSlider(QtCore.Qt.Horizontal)` defines the slider and all the parameters are exactly the same as in the preceding recipe

- `n_slider.sliderReleased.connect(update)` connects the `"sliderReleased"` event to the corresponding callback function, `update()`
- `def close():` is the callback function for the `Quit` button and it simply closes the window and the application
- `button = QtWidgets.QPushButton("Quit")` defines the button widget of `Qt`. Unlike the preceding recipe, there is no need to set `button.setGeometry(QtCore.QRect(250, -10, 75, 25))` here, as we are going to place the button vertically in a row by itself
- `button.setFont(QtGui.QFont("Arial",30))` sets the font to be *Arial* and the font size to be 30
- `button.clicked.connect(close)` connects the `"clicked"` event of the button to the corresponding callback function, `close()`
- `hbox = QtWidgets.QHBoxLayout()` defines the horizontal layout box:
    - `minn = QtWidgets.QLabel('3')` defines the label object for the minimum value of the slider to be displayed
    - `minn.setFont(QtGui.QFont("Arial",20))` sets the font and font size for the minimum value
    - `maxn = QtWidgets.QLabel('10')` defines the label object for the maximum value of the slider to be displayed
    - `maxn.setFont(QtGui.QFont("Arial",20))` sets the font and font size for the maximum value
    - `hbox.addWidget(minn)` adds the `minn` label to `hbox`
    - `hbox.addWidget(n_slider)` adds the slider to `hbox`
    - `hbox.addWidget(maxn)` adds the `maxn` label to the `hox`
- `vbox = QtWidgets.QVBoxLayout()` defines the vertical layout box
    - `vbox.addWidget(toolbar)` adds the toolbar at the top of the figure
    - `vspace = QtWidgets.QSpacerItem(0, 750)` defines the space object
    - `vbox.addItem(vspace)` adds the space object where the canvas/figure will appear
    - `vbox.addSpacing(20)` adds additional space of 20 pixels below the canvas
    - `vbox.addLayout(hbox)` adds the `hbox` containing the slider and associated minimum and maximum labels
    - `vbox.addWidget(button)` adds the button widget to `vox`

- `fig.canvas.setLayout(vbox)` adds a `vbox` layout to the figure canvas
- `window.setWindowTitle("Embedding with Qt")` sets the title for the main window
- `window.setCentralWidget(canvas)` sets the canvas as the central widget so that the main polar figure appears at the center
- `window.show()` displays the figure window
- `qApp.exec_()` invokes the main loop to capture events and fire the corresponding callback functions

When you run the preceding code, you should see the plot on the left the first time, and the plot on the right when you drag the slider to 8. You can exit the application by clicking on the Quit button:

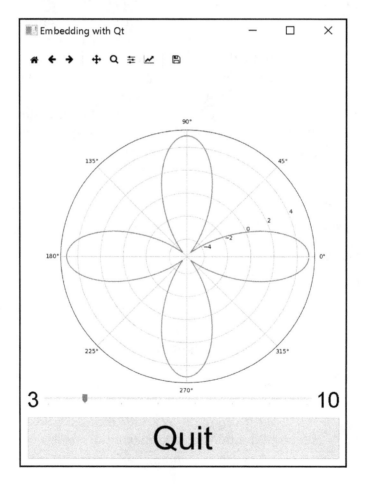

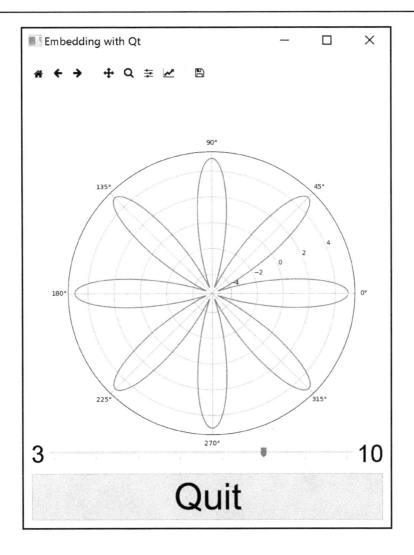

11
Plotting 3D Graphs Using the mplot3d Toolkit

In this chapter, we will cover the recipes for plotting the following graphs:

- Line plot
- Scatter plot
- Bar plot
- Polygon plot
- Contour plot
- Surface plot
- Wireframe plot
- Triangular surface plot
- Plotting 2D data in 3D
- 3D visualization of linearly non-separable data in 2D
- Plotting word embeddings

Introduction

Early versions of Matplotlib were limited to 2D plotting, and 3D features were added later as an add-on toolkit: `mplot3d`. Although it has limited 3D functionality, it covers most of the common business requirements of 3D plotting.

Plotting commands are similar to their 2D counterparts. It is just that we register with Matplotlib that we will be using 3D plots, by importing **Axes3D** from the `mplot3d` toolkit, and in the axes definition, we specify `projection='3d'`.

You can also rotate the 3D picture to get different views, if you are using any of the interactive backends, by dragging the figure in any direction you want. You can also create an animation by rotating the figure with a small pause in between the frames. We will learn how to use these features in some of the plots, although they can be applied to all plots.

Line plot

In this recipe, we will learn how to create a 3D line plot. It is similar to a 2D equivalent line plot, and many of the attributes of a 2D line plot are carried forward to 3D.

We will draw concave and convex curves in the same axes and view them from different angles, such as parallel view, top view, and rotation around the *z* axis.

Getting ready

Import the required libraries:

```
import numpy as np
import matplotlib.pyplot as plt
from mpl_toolkits.mplot3d import Axes3D
```

How to do it...

Here are the steps to plot 3D line graphs:

1. Prepare the data for the *x*, *y*, and *z* axis coordinates:

```
x = np.linspace(-5, 5, 25)
y = np.linspace(-5, 5, 25)
z = x**2 + y**2
z1 = 1 - (x**2 + y**2)
```

2. Define a function to plot the graph and set its attributes:

```
def plot_graph(axes, xlabel, ylabel, zlabel, title, elevation,
rotation):
    axes.plot3D(x, y, z, label='concave')
    axes.plot(x, y, z1, label='convex')
    axes.view_init(elev=elevation, azim=rotation)
    axes.set_xlabel(xlabel)
    axes.set_ylabel(ylabel)
    axes.set_zlabel(zlabel)
```

```
axes.set_title(title)
axes.legend(loc='best')
```

3. Define the figure and axes, `ax1`, for 3D plotting:

```
fig = plt.figure(figsize=(15,9))
ax1 = fig.add_subplot(231, projection='3d')
```

4. Plot the curves on `ax1` with the default elevation and rotation:

```
plot_graph(ax1, 'X', 'Y', 'Z', 'default view', None, None)
```

5. Define a second axes, `ax2`, and plot it with an elevation angle of 0 degrees and the default `azimuth` angle:

```
ax2 = fig.add_subplot(232, projection='3d')
plot_graph(ax2, 'X', 'Y', 'Z', 'elevation angle = 0,\n azimuth
angle=None', 0, None)
```

6. Define a third axes, `ax3`, and plot it with an elevation angle of 90 degrees and the default `azimuth` angle:

```
ax3 = fig.add_subplot(233, projection='3d')
plot_graph(ax3, 'X', 'Y', ' ', 'elevation angle = 90,\n azimuth
angle=None', 90, None)
ax3.set_zticks([])
```

7. Define the fourth axes, `ax4`, and plot it with the default elevation angle, and an azimuth angle of −30 degrees:

```
ax4 = fig.add_subplot(234, projection='3d')
plot_graph(ax4, 'X', 'Y', 'Z', 'elevation angle = None,\n azimuth
angle=-30', None, -30)
```

8. Define the fifth axes, `ax5`, and plot it with the default elevation angle, and an azimuth angle of 30 degrees:

```
ax5 = fig.add_subplot(235, projection='3d')
plot_graph(ax5, 'X', 'Y', 'Z', 'elevation angle = None,\n azimuth
            angle=30', None, 30)
```

9. Display it on the screen:

```
plt.show()
```

How it works...

Here is the explanation of the preceding code block:

- `x = np.linspace(-5, 5, 25)` creates an array with 25 points spaced equally between –5 and +5, and *z* and *z1* are defined as a function of *x* and *y*
- `def plot_graph(axes, xlabel, ylabel, zlabel, title, elevation, rotation):` is the function to plot the graphs with the given attributes:
  - Axes specifies the axes on which the graphs are to be plotted.
  - `xlabel`, `ylabel`, and `zlabel` specify labels for the *x*, *y*, and *z* axis respectively.
  - Title specifies the title for the plot.
  - Elevation specifies the view angle with respect to the *xy* plane: 0 means parallel to the *xy* plane, 90 means top view.
  - Rotation specifies the view of the plot rotated on the *z* axis.
  - Both elevation and rotation are specified in degrees.
  - `axes.plot3D(x, y, z, label='concave')` is similar to a 2D line plot syntax, except that we also include the *z* axis. You can also use `axes.plot()`, instead of `axes.plot3D()`, as we have done for the *convex* curve. This is true for most other plots also, but not for all.
  - `axes.view_init(elev=elevation, azim=rotation)` specifies the view of the plot when it comes up.
  - The rest of the statements in the function are already familiar to us.
- `ax1 = fig.add_subplot(231, projection='3d')` adds an axes to the figure, whose layout is specified as a 2 x 3 grid:
  - `projection='3d'` specifies that it is a 3D axes and graphs on it are to be plotted with three dimensions. This is the main difference between 2D and 3D plot syntax.
- On `ax1`, we plot the graphs with the default elevation and rotation angles
- On `ax2` to `ax4`, we plot the same graphs with a different elevation and rotation angles to see the differences in their views.

On executing the preceding code, you should see the following figure and plots on your screen:

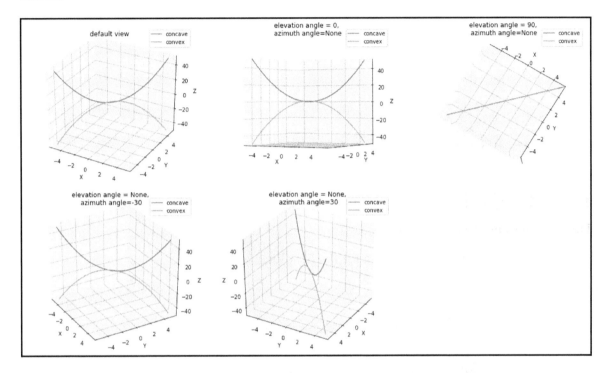

Scatter plot

In this recipe, we will learn how to plot a scatter plot in 3D. We will use the `Iris` dataset, which has three distinct clusters, for this example. We have seen it in 2D several times in previous chapters, so let's see how it looks in 3D.

We will also learn how to create an animated 3D plot using the `init_view` method that we learned in the preceding recipe. For this, we need to use any of the backends, since animation does not work with the inline display `%matplotlib inline`.

Getting ready

Set the desired backend:

```
import matplotlib
matplotlib.use('tkAgg')
```

Import the required libraries:

```
import pandas as pd
import numpy as np
import matplotlib.pyplot as plt
from mpl_toolkits.mplot3d import Axes3D
```

How to do it...

Here are the steps to implement the logic:

1. Load and prepare the data for the 3D plot:

```
iris = pd.read_csv('iris_dataset.csv', delimiter=',')
iris['species'] = iris['species'].map({"setosa" : 0, "versicolor" :
1, "virginica" : 2})
x, y, z = iris['petal_length'], iris['petal_width'],
iris['species']
```

2. Define and instantiate the figure and axes for 3D plotting:

```
fig = plt.figure(figsize=(8,6))
ax = fig.add_subplot(111, projection='3d')
```

3. Draw the scatter plot using a for loop to plot each of the clusters with a different color and marker:

```
for name, c, marker in zip((0, 1, 2), ('r', 'b', 'g'), ('o', '^',
'*')):
    index = iris['species'] == name
    ax.scatter(x[index], y[index], z[index],
s=25*x[index]*y[index],
            c=c, marker=marker)
```

4. Set the labels for the figure:

```
ax.set_xlabel('petal length')
ax.set_ylabel('petal width')
ax.set_zlabel('species')
ax.set_zticks([0, 1, 2])
```

5. Define a loop to create the animated 3D plot:

```
for angle in range(0, 360):
    ax.view_init(30, angle)
    plt.pause(.001)
```

6. Show the animated figure on the **Tkinter** backend:

```
plt.show();
```

How it works...

Here is the explanation of the preceding code:

- `matplotlib.use('tkAgg')` sets the backend to Tkinter.
- `x, y, z = iris['petal_length'], iris['petal_width'], iris['species']` prepares the data for the *x*, *y*, and *z* coordinates. We are plotting `petal_length` and `petal_width` on the *x* and *y* axes, then *species* (cluster number) on the *z* axis.
- `ax.scatter(x[index], y[index], z[index], s=25*x[index]*y[index], c=c, marker=marker)` is similar to a 2D scatter plot syntax, except that we also include the *z* axis.
- To create an animation, we use a for loop and keep changing the view rotation angle from 0 to 360 degrees:
    - `ax.view_init(30, angle)` keeps the elevation angle fixed at 30 degrees and varies the rotation angle by one degree in each iteration
    - `plt.pause(.001)` pauses between the iterations by 0.001 seconds

Upon execution of the preceding code, you should see an animated plot in a new window opened with the Tkinter backend. The static version of that plot should look like the one shown here:

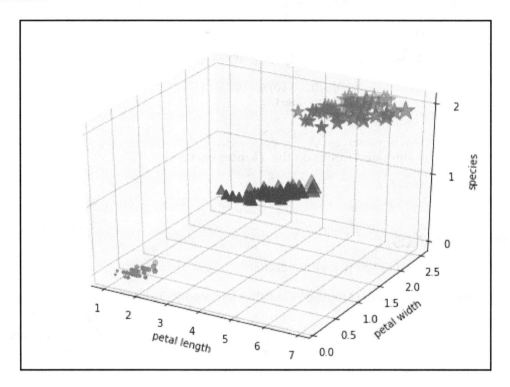

Bar plot

In this recipe, we will learn how to plot a bar graph in 3D. We will use the battery sales data that we used for table plotting in Chapter 2, *Getting Started with Basic Plots*. Here, we will only plot a bar chart, not the table chart, below the bar graph.

Getting ready

Import the required libraries:

```
import numpy as np
import matplotlib.pyplot as plt
from mpl_toolkits.mplot3d import Axes3D
```

How to do it...

The following are the steps to implement the logic:

1. Define the figure and axes for 3D plotting:

```
fig = plt.figure(figsize=(10,6))
ax = fig.add_subplot(111, projection='3d')
```

2. Prepare the data for the *x, y,* and *z* axis:

```
# Years for which we have battery sales data
x = [2011, 2012, 2013, 2014, 2015]

# Repeat X, 5 times to represent each of the 5 battery ratings
X = x * 5

# List of Battery ratings
battery_ratings = ['7Ah', '35Ah', '40Ah', '135Ah', '150Ah']

# Number of units sold each year, each rating. e.g. 75 units of
7Ah(0) batteries, 144 units of 35Ah(1) #batteries sold in 2011
Y = np.array([[75, 144, 114, 102, 108],
              [90, 126, 102, 84, 126],
              [96, 114, 75, 105, 135],
              [105, 90, 175, 90, 75],
              [90, 75, 135, 75, 90]])

# Represent battery rating in numeric codes
yticks = [0, 1, 2, 3, 4]

# Use different color for each of the battery ratings
colors = ['r', 'g', 'b', 'y', 'm']
```

3. Plot the bar graph:

```
i=0
for c, k in zip(colors, yticks):
    cs = [c] * len(X)
    ax.bar(X[i:i+5], Y[:,int(i/5)], zs=k, zdir='y', color=cs,
        alpha=0.8)
    i += 5
```

4. Set the labels for the graph:

```
ax.set_yticks(yticks)
ax.set_yticklabels(battery_ratings)
ax.set_xlabel('Year')
ax.set_ylabel('Battery Type')
ax.set_zlabel('Units Sold')
```

5. Display the figure on the screen:

```
plt.show()
```

How it works...

Here is the explanation of the preceding code:

- *x* and *y* are lists of length 25, representing years and the number of units sold respectively.
- `yticks` represent battery ratings in numeric format, which are to be plotted on the *y* axis.
- `colors` is the list of five colors to be used for each of the battery ratings in a row.
- `for` loop plots one item of battery rating data in a row in each iteration.
- `cs = [c] * len(X)` creates a list of same color c with a length of X.
- `ax.bar(X[i:i+5], Y[:,int(i/5)], zs=k, zdir='y', color=cs, alpha=0.8)` plots the bar graph:
  - Extracts five elements (representing five years) from the X and Y arrays for each of the battery types to plot a row of bars.
  - `zs=k` specifies to map numeric battery ratings to the z axis.

- zdir='y' specifies to swap the z and y axes so that Z data is plotted on the y axis, and y data is plotted on the z axis.
- alpha=0.8 specifies the level of transparency required for the graphs

- *Step 4* and *step 5* are very familiar to you.

After executing the code, you should see the graph shown here:

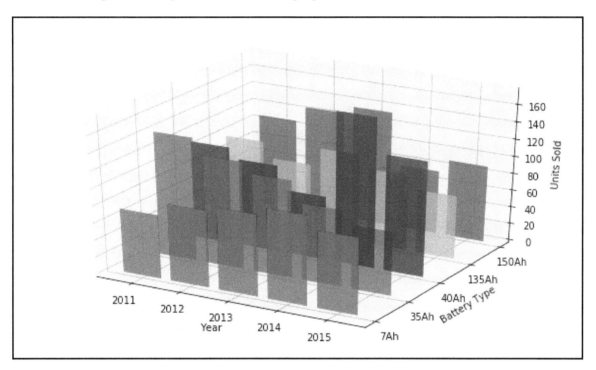

Polygon plot

In this recipe, we will learn how to plot a polygon plot. It is similar to a line plot, but filled under the line. We will use the same battery sales data for this example also.

Getting ready

Import the required libraries:

```
import numpy as np
import matplotlib.pyplot as plt
from mpl_toolkits.mplot3d import Axes3D
from matplotlib.collections import PolyCollection
from matplotlib.ticker import MultipleLocator
```

How to do it...

Here are the steps to code the logic:

1. Define the figure and axes for 3D plotting:

```
fig = plt.figure(figsize=(10,6))
ax = fig.add_subplot(111, projection='3d')
```

2. Prepare the data for the *x, y,* and *z* axis:

```
# Years for which we have battery sales data
x = [2011, 2012, 2013, 2014, 2015]

# Repeat X, 5 times to represent each of the 5 battery ratings
X = x * 5

# List of Battery ratings
battery_ratings = ['7Ah', '35Ah', '40Ah', '135Ah', '150Ah']

# Number of units sold each year, each rating. e.g. 75 units of
7Ah(0) batteries,
# 144 units of 35Ah(1) batteries sold in 2011
Y = np.array([[75, 144, 114, 102, 108],
              [90, 126, 102, 84, 126],
              [96, 114, 75, 105, 135],
              [105, 90, 175, 90, 75],
              [90, 75, 135, 75, 90]])

# Represent battery rating in numeric codes
yticks = [0, 1, 2, 3, 4]

# Use different color for each of the battery ratings
colors = ['r', 'g', 'b', 'y', 'm']
```

3. Prepare the vertices of the polygons to be plotted:

```
vertices = []
for i in np.arange(0, 25, 5):
    vertices.append([(xs[i], 0.)] + list(zip(xs[i:i+5],
Y[:,int(i/5)])) + [(xs[i+4], 0.)])
```

4. Plot the bar graph:

```
poly = PolyCollection(vertices, facecolors=['r', 'g', 'b', 'y',
'm'], alpha=0.6)
ax.add_collection3d(poly, zs=yticks, zdir='y')
```

5. Set the major ticks for the *x* axis as increments of 1:

```
majorLocator = MultipleLocator(1)
ax.xaxis.set_major_locator(majorLocator)
```

6. Set the limits for the *x*, *y*, and *z* axes:

```
ax.set_xlim(2011, 2015)
ax.set_ylim(-1,4)
ax.set_zlim(0,175)
```

7. Set the ticks for the *y* axis, and labels for the *x*, *y*, and *z* axes:

```
ax.set_yticks(yticks)
ax.set_yticklabels(battery_ratings)
ax.set_xlabel('Year')
ax.set_ylabel('Battery Type')
ax.set_zlabel('Units Sold')
```

8. Display the figure on the screen:

```
plt.show()
```

How it works...

Here is the explanation of the code:

- The first two steps are exactly the same as the preceding recipe
- `vertices.append([(xs[i], 0.)] + list(zip(xs[i:i+5], Y[:,int(i/5)]))) + [(xs[i+4], 0.)])` creates vertices for a given battery rating. The for loop creates such vertices for all battery ratings. `(xs[i], 0)` and `(xs[i+4],0.)` are the end points that terminate on the *x* axis, where the *y* coordinate is zero, and the *x* coordinate is the first and last point in the series. These two points are added to complete the loop around the *x* axis so that the filled polygon can be plotted.
- `poly = PolyCollection(vertices, facecolors=['r', 'g', 'b', 'y', 'm'], alpha=0.6)` defines a collection of polygons with the given vertices:
    - `facecolors=['r', 'g', 'b', 'y', 'm']` defines the color to fill the polygon for each of the battery ratings.
    - `alpha=0.6` defines the level of transparency for each of the filled polygons.
- `ax.add_collection3d(poly, zs=yticks, zdir='y')` adds the collection to the axes, which essentially plots the graph of the collection:
    - `zs=yticks` sets `yticks` to the z axis
    - `zdir='y'` exchanges the z and y axis data so that the y data is used for the z axis and the z data is used for the y axis, as we did in the preceding recipe.
- `majorLocator = MultipleLocator(1)` defines the `majorLocator` with a step of 1, and `ax.xaxis.set_major_locator(majorLocator)` applies it to the *x* axis so that it does not plot the floating-point numbers for years.
- `ax.set_xlim(2011, 2015)`, `ax.set_ylim(-1,4)`, and `ax.set_zlim(0,175)` apply the lower and upper limits for *x*, *y*, and *z* axes. These are required here to display the figure, since polygons, and patches here are floating objects, `pyplot` would not know what default limits to use, unlike in all other cases where it determines the limits based on the data points in the source data.
- The last two steps are already familiar to you.

On running the preceding code, you should see the following graph on your screen:

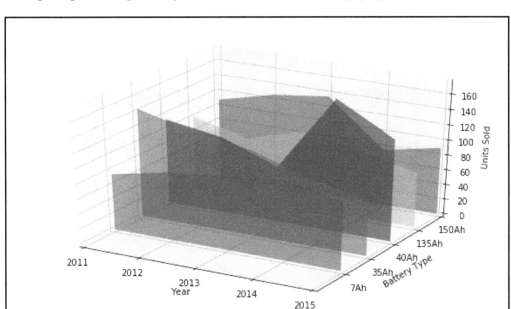

There's more...

For the preceding example, we used `PolyCollection`. There are two other options available in Matplotlib, `LineCollection` and `PatchCollection`.

Contour plot

We learned how to draw a 2D contour plot in `Chapter 2`, *Getting Started with Basic Plots*. Here, we will learn how to draw it in 3D. We will use the same data that we used earlier, so that we can see the difference between 2D and 3D visualization.

Getting ready

Import the required libraries:

```
from mpl_toolkits.mplot3d import axes3d
import matplotlib.pyplot as plt
import pandas as pd
from matplotlib import cm
```

How to do it...

Here are the steps to create the desired plot:

1. Define the figure and axes for 3D plotting:

   ```
   fig = plt.figure(figsize=(10,8))
   ax = fig.gca(projection='3d')
   ```

2. Load data for the `Loss`, `theta1`, and `theta2` variables:

   ```
   # Read Loss, theta0 and theta1 values
   Loss = pd.read_excel('Loss.xlsx')
   theta0_vals = pd.read_excel('theta0.xlsx')
   theta1_vals = pd.read_excel('theta1.xlsx')
   ```

3. Prepare `X` and `Y` coordinates using `np.meshgrid`:

   ```
   X, Y = np.meshgrid(theta0_vals, theta1_vals)
   ```

4. Draw the `contour` plot:

   ```
   # Plot contour curves
   cset = ax.contour(X, Y, Loss, np.logspace(-2,3,100),
   cmap=cm.coolwarm)
   ```

5. Draw the colorbar:

   ```
   fig.colorbar(cset, shrink=0.5, aspect=5)
   ```

6. Set the labels:

   ```
   ax.set_xlabel('theta0')
   ax.set_ylabel('theta1')
   ax.set_zlabel('Loss')
   ```

7. Display the figure on the screen:

```
plt.show()
```

How it works...

Here is the explanation of the preceding code:

- The first two steps are self-explanatory.
- X, Y = np.meshgrid(theta0_vals, theta1_vals) creates *x* and *y* coordinates for the theta0 and theta1 variables. Please refer to Chapter 2, *Getting Started with Basic Plots*, for a detailed explanation of meshgrid.
- cset = ax.contour(X, Y, Loss, np.logspace(-2,3,100), cmap=cm.coolwarm) plots the contour graph. It plots the contour of the Loss variable for various values of X and Y. Each contour has a fixed value of Loss (*z* axis), so that contours are placed vertically along the *z* axis, and the lowest-valued contour is at the bottom:
  - np.logspace(-2,3,100) specifies the range of loss values for which contours are to be plotted. They range in logarithmic space from -2 (0.01 in linear) to +3 (1000 in linear), and take 100 samples equally spaced in this range.
  - cmap=cm.coolwarm specifies to use a coolwarm colormap for the visualization of contours.
- We had also plotted actual value of the loss for each of the contours in 2D, but the same is not implemented for 3D.
- fig.colorbar(cset, shrink=0.5, aspect=5) sets the colorbar for the visualization of contours in different colors from the specified colormap:
  - shrink=0.5 specifies the amount of shrinkage of the size of the colorbar from the default size.
  - aspect=5 specifies the ratio of the larger dimension to the smaller dimension of the data on the colorbar.
- The last two steps are self-explanatory.

Upon running the preceding code, you should see the following figure on your screen:

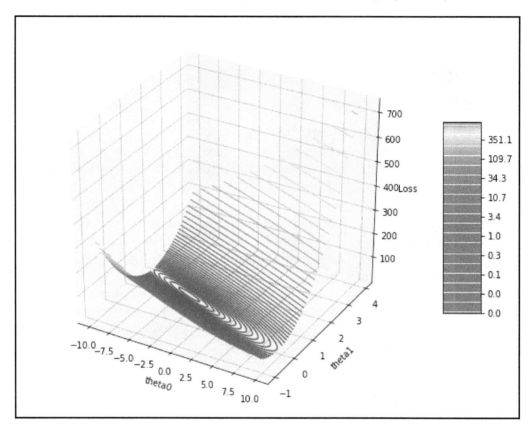

There's more...

There is another option for a filled contour plot, where the entire contour is filled with the specified color. You just have to replace contour with `contourf` in the plot statement.

Surface plot

In this recipe, we will learn how to draw a surface plot. This is typically used to visualize the loss (error) surface in machine-learning problems. It helps to see whether the algorithm is stuck in any **local minima**, when the error surface has **multiple minima**. We will use the same data that we used in the preceding contour plot.

Getting ready

Import the required libraries:

```
from mpl_toolkits.mplot3d import axes3d
import matplotlib.pyplot as plt
import pandas as pd
import numpy as np
```

How to do it...

The following are the steps to draw a surface plot:

1. Define the figure and axes for 3D plotting:

   ```
   fig = plt.figure(figsize=(10,8))
   ax = fig.gca(projection='3d')
   ```

2. Read the data for the surface plot:

   ```
   # Read Loss, theta0 and theta1 values
   Loss = pd.read_excel('Loss.xlsx')
   theta0_vals = pd.read_excel('theta0.xlsx')
   theta1_vals = pd.read_excel('theta1.xlsx')
   ```

3. Create a `meshgrid` for the X and Y coordinates for a range of values of `theta0` and `theta1`:

   ```
   X, Y = np.meshgrid(theta0_vals, theta1_vals)
   ```

4. Plot the surface graph:

   ```
   # Plot surface graph
   surf = ax.plot_surface(X, Y, Loss, cmap='plasma')
   ```

5. Add the colorbar to the figure:

   ```
   fig.colorbar(surf, shrink=0.5, aspect=5)
   ```

6. Set the labels for the figure:

   ```
   ax.set_xlabel('theta0')
   ax.set_ylabel('theta1')
   ax.set_zlabel('Loss')
   ```

7. Display the figure on the screen:

```
plt.show()
```

How it works...

All the steps are exactly the same as the preceding contour plot, except *step 4*, where we replace `ax.contour()` with `ax.plot_surface()`. We have also replaced the `coolwarm` colormap with the `plasma` color map. Everything else is the same as the contour plot.

Upon executing the code, you should see the following figure on your screen:

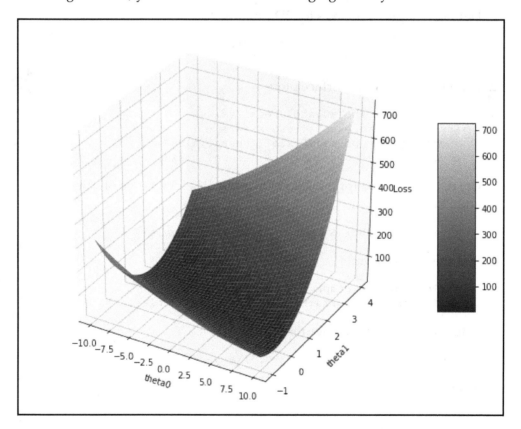

Wireframe plot

In this recipe, we will learn how to draw a wireframe plot. It is similar to a surface plot, with the option of sampling a number of points in each of the directions to connect on the surface. Here, we will implement an animated wireframe plot.

Getting ready

Set the desired backend for the interactive output:

```
import matplotlib
matplotlib.use('Qt5Agg')
```

Import the required libraries:

```
import numpy as np
import matplotlib.pyplot as plt
from mpl_toolkits.mplot3d import Axes3D
```

How to do it...

Here are the steps involved in drawing a wireframe plot:

1. Define the figure and axes for 3D plotting:

   ```
   fig = plt.figure(figsize=(8,6))
   ax = fig.add_subplot(111, projection='3d')
   ```

2. Prepare the data for the x and y coordinates:

   ```
   x = np.linspace(-2, 2, 25)
   y = np.linspace(-5, 5, 25)
   X, Y = np.meshgrid(x, y)
   ```

3. Set labels for the x, y, and z axes:

   ```
   ax.set_xlabel('X')
   ax.set_ylabel('Y')
   ax.set_zlabel('Z')
   ```

4. Set limits for the z axis so that the axis ticks don't keep changing while the animation is active:

```
ax.set_zlim(-4, 4)
```

5. Plot the animated wireframe by making the z axis data a function of X, Y and using a variable, phi, that varies from 0 to 90 degrees:

```
wframe = None
for phi in np.linspace(0, 90, 100):
    if wframe:
        ax.collections.remove(wframe)
    Z = np.cos(2 * np.pi * X + phi) * (1 - np.sqrt(X**2 + Y**2))
    wframe = ax.plot_wireframe(X, Y, Z, rstride=2, cstride=2)
    plt.pause(0.1)
```

6. Display the figure on the **Qt5** backend:

```
plt.show()
```

How it works...

Here is the explanation for the code:

- *x* is a list of 25 numbers varying from -2 to +2 with equal spacing between them; similarly, *y* is a list of 25 numbers varying from -5 to +5, and *x* and *y* are the meshgrid between *x* and *y*.
- `ax.set_zlim(-4, 4)` sets the z axis limits to -4 to +4. Since z is a function of a variable, phi, these data limits keep varying on the z axis. To avoid changing limits on the plot, set the limits with a maximum boundary of -4 to +4.
- `wframe = None` initializes the wframe variable.
- `for phi in np.linspace(0, 90, 100):` is the for loop and starts with 0, then goes all the way to 90 degrees in 100 equal steps.
- `if wframe:` checks whether the wireframe is already there. It will only not be there the first time, since we initialized it with none. Subsequently, it will always be true, so it will be deleted using `ax.collections.remove(wframe)` before plotting a new wireframe.
- `Z = np.cos(2 * np.pi * X + phi) * (1 - np.sqrt(X**2 + Y**2))` computes Z as a function of *x*, *y*, and *phi*.

- `wframe = ax.plot_wireframe(X, Y, Z, rstride=2, cstride=2)` draws the wireframe plot:
    - `rstride` is the number of points to skip along the row before connecting the points.
    - `cstride` is the number of points to skip along the column before connecting the points.
- `plt.pause(0.1)` pauses for 0.1 seconds before plotting the next wireframe. This is what creates the animation effect.
- Here, we don't need to use `plt.draw()` or any other equivalent function to refresh the figure. `plot_wireframe` takes care of it.

Upon running the code, you should see the following figure after the completion of the animation:

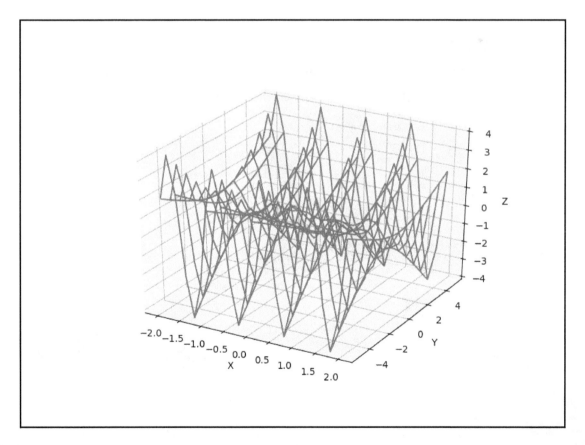

Triangular surface plot

In this recipe, we will learn how to draw a triangular surface plot. It is similar to surface plot, but the surface will have triangular connections. We will draw three such plots with different data, and with and without the axes being shown.

Getting ready

Import the required libraries:

```
from mpl_toolkits.mplot3d import Axes3D
import matplotlib.pyplot as plt
import numpy as np
```

How to do it...

The following are the steps to draw triangular surface plots:

1. Prepare data for three different plots:

```
# Make radii and angles arrays.
radii = np.linspace(0., 1.0, 16)
angles = np.linspace(0, 2*np.pi, 32)

# Repeat all angles for each radius.
angles = np.repeat(angles[..., np.newaxis], n_radii, axis=1)

# Convert polar (radii, angles) coords to cartesian (x, y) coords.
x = (radii*np.cos(angles)).flatten()
y = (radii*np.sin(angles)).flatten()

# Compute z to make the triangle surface.
z = np.tan(x**2 + y**2)
z1 = np.cos(x**2 + y**2)
z2 = np.cos(x**3 + y**3)
```

2. Define the figure:

```
fig = plt.figure(figsize=(12,6))
```

3. Draw the first triangular surface plot:

```
ax1 = fig.add_subplot(131, projection='3d')
ax1.plot_trisurf(x, y, z, linewidth=0.5, cmap='viridis')
```

4. Draw the second triangular surface plot:

```
ax2 = fig.add_subplot(132, projection='3d')
ax2.plot_trisurf(x, y, z1, linewidth=0.5, cmap='cool')
plt.axis('off')
```

5. Draw the third triangular surface plot:

```
ax3 = fig.add_subplot(133, projection='3d')
ax3.plot_trisurf(x, y, z2, linewidth=0.5, color='c')
plt.axis('off')
```

6. Display the figure on the screen:

```
plt.show()
```

How it works...

Here is the explanation for the code:

- `np.linspace(0., 1.0, 16)` divides the 0 to 1 range into 16 equal parts, as radii define the number of radii equally spread between 0 and 1, and similarly angles define the number of angles equally spread between 0 and 2*pi (360 degrees).
- `np.repeat(angles[..., np.newaxis], n_radii, axis=1)`, repeats the angles array for each of the radii, creating a 32 x 16 matrix:
  - `np.newaxis` creates an additional dimension for each of the radii.
  - `axis=1` specifies that each new dimension should be added as a column.
- `x = (radii*np.cos(angles)).flatten()` creates *x* coordinates in Cartesian coordinate system using polar coordinates.
- `y = (radii*np.sin(angles)).flatten()` creates *x* coordinates in the Cartesian coordinate system using polar coordinates.

- `z = np.tan(x**2 + y**2)` computes the z coordinates for `plot1`.
- `z1 = np.cos(x**2 + y**2)` computes the z coordinates for `plot2`.
- `z2 = np.cos(x**3 + y**3)` computes the z coordinates for `plot3`.
- `fig = plt.figure(figsize=(12,6))` defines and instantiates the figure.
- `ax1 = fig.add_subplot(131, projection='3d')` defines the first axes and `ax1.plot_trisurf(x, y, z, linewidth=0.5, cmap='viridis')` plots the first graph. The colormap specified is `'viridis'`.
- `ax2 = fig.add_subplot(132, projection='3d')` defines the second axes and `ax2.plot_trisurf(x, y, z1, linewidth=0.5, cmap='cool')` plots the second graph. The colormap specified is `cool`.
- `plt.axis('off')` specifies to not show the axes on the plot.
- `ax3 = fig.add_subplot(133, projection='3d')` defines the third axes. and `ax3.plot_trisurf(x, y, z2, linewidth=0.5, color='c')` plots the third graph. Instead of a colormap, we use a single color for this graph and again the axes are turned off.

Upon executing the code, you should see this figure on your screen with three plots:

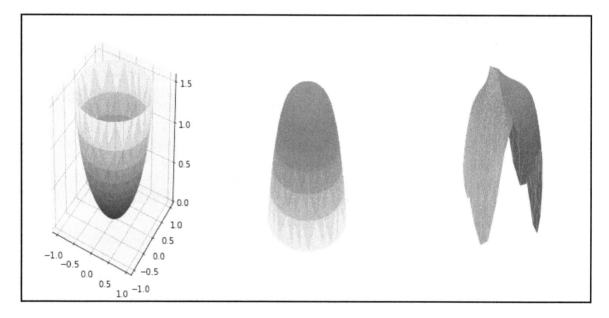

Plotting 2D data in 3D

In this recipe, we will learn how we can plot 2D data in 3D. We will plot product defects by reason code as a bar plot, and cumulative defects as a line plot. We will have defect reason codes on the *x* axis, the number of defects on the *z* axis, and cumulative defect percentage on the *y* axis. There are kind of two *y* axes in 2D space, where one of them will have the scale for the bar graph and the other will have the scale for the line graph.

Getting ready

Import the required libraries:

```
import matplotlib.pyplot as plt
from mpl_toolkits.mplot3d import Axes3D
```

How to do it...

Here are the steps to plot the required 3D plot:

1. Define the figure and axes for 3D plotting:

```
fig = plt.figure(figsize=(10,6))
ax = fig.add_subplot(111, projection='3d')
```

2. Define the data for the bar graph and plot it:

```
x = [0, 1, 2, 3, 4, 5]
y = [19, 12, 6, 4, 3, 2]
ax.bar(x, y, zs=0, zdir='y', label='Number of Defects in (X,Z)')
```

3. Define the data for the cumulative defects graph and plot it:

```
x = [0, 1, 2, 3, 4, 5]
y = [41, 67, 80, 89, 96, 100]
ax.plot(x, y, zs=0, zdir='z', color='g', lw=5, label='Cumulative
Defects in (X,Y)')
```

4. Set the limits for the *y* and *z* axes:

```
ax.set_ylim(0,100)
ax.set_zlim(0,20)
```

5. Set the labels for the *x*, *y*, and *z* axes, and the legend:

```
ax.set_xlabel('Defect Reason Code')
ax.set_ylabel('Cumulative %of defects')
ax.set_zlabel('Number of Defects')
ax.legend(loc='best')
```

6. Display the plot on the screen:

```
plt.show()
```

How it works...

Here is the explanation for the code:

- x = [0, 1, 2, 3, 4, 5] is the list of product defect reason codes.
- y = [19, 12, 6, 4, 3, 2] is the list of defect counts by reason code.
- ax.bar(x, y, zs=0, zdir='y', label='Number of Defects in (X,Z)') draws the bar plot:
    - The defect reason codes go on the *x* axis and the count of defects on the *z* axis.
    - zdir='y' swaps the *y* and *z* axes so that *y* data is plotted on the *z* axis and *z* data is plotted on the *y* axis, which in this case are zeros.
    - The label specified gets displayed in the legend.
- y = [41, 67, 80, 89, 96, 100] is the list of cumulative defects as a percentage of the total.
- ax.plot(x, y, zs=0, zdir='z', color='g', lw=5, label='Cumulative Defects in (X,Y)') draws the line plot:
    - The defect reason codes go on the *x* axis and the cumulative defects on the *y* axis.
    - zdir='z' specifies to plot *z* data on the *z* axis, which in this case consists of zeros, as specified by zs=0.
    - color='g' specifies that the line plot should be in green.
    - lw=5 specifies that the line width of the plot should be five units.
    - The label gets displayed on the legend.
- ax.set_ylim(0,100) sets the lower and upper limits for the *y* axis and ax.set_zlim(0,20) sets the same for the *z* axis.
- ax.set_xlabel('Defect Reason Code') sets the label for the *x* axis.

- `ax.set_ylabel('Cumulative %of defects')` sets the label for the y axis.
- `ax.set_zlabel('Number of Defects')` sets the label for the z axis.
- `ax.legend(loc='best')` specifies that the best location is chosen for the legend automatically.

Upon running the code, you should see the following figure on your screen:

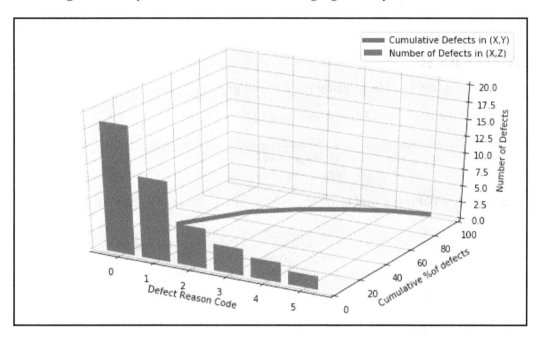

3D visualization of linearly non-separable data in 2D

In this recipe, we will learn how we can visualize 2D data that is linearly non-separable in 3D. This is typically used to explain the internal workings of the Support Vector Machines algorithm, which takes lower dimensional data to higher dimensional space so that it can find a plane that separates the data into various clusters neatly.

We will plot both 2D and 3D plots with the same data to visualize it better.

Getting ready

Import the required libraries:

```
import pandas as pd
import numpy as np
import matplotlib.pyplot as plt
from mpl_toolkits.mplot3d import Axes3D
```

How to do it...

Here are the steps involved in plotting the desired graphs:

1. Read the data from Excel files into a list:

```
# Read the Data, two product test scores, and result 1 means
accepted and 0 means rejected
scores_data = pd.read_csv('test_scores_results.txt',header=None)
```

2. Create a pandas DataFrame to easily split the data into different categories:

```
# Add columns labels to the data
columns = ['Test1_Score', 'Test2_Score', 'Accepted']
scores_data = np.array(scores_data)
df = pd.DataFrame(data=scores_data, columns=columns)
```

3. Separate the data into `accepted` and `rejected` categories:

```
df_accepted = df[(df['Accepted'] == 1.0)]
df_rejected = df[(df['Accepted'] == 0.0)]
```

4. Split the data into *x* and *y* coordinates for both `accepted` and `rejected` categories:

```
accepted_score1 = np.array(df_accepted)[:,0]
accepted_score2 = np.array(df_accepted)[:,1]

rejected_score1 = np.array(df_rejected)[:,0]
rejected_score2 = np.array(df_rejected)[:,1]
```

5. Define and instantiate the figure:

```
fig = plt.figure(figsize=(12,8))
```

6. Define axes for 2D plotting and plot the `accepted` and `rejected` data points:

```
ax = fig.add_subplot(121)
ax.plot(accepted_score1, accepted_score2, 'gD', label='Accepted')
ax.plot(rejected_score1, rejected_score2, 'ro', label='rejected')
```

7. Plot the labels and legend for the 2D plot:

```
plt.xlabel('Test1 Score')
plt.ylabel('Test2 Score')
plt.legend(loc='best')
```

8. Define the axes for 3D plotting:

```
ax = fig.add_subplot(122, projection='3d')
```

9. Plot the accepted and rejected data points as scatter plots:

```
ax.scatter(accepted_score1, accepted_score2, zs=-0.75, zdir='z',
s=50, color='g',
        marker='D',    label='Accepted')
ax.scatter(rejected_score1, rejected_score2, zs=0.75, zdir='y',
s=50, color='r',
        marker='o', label='rejected')
```

10. Set labels, limits, and legend for the 3D plot:

```
ax.set_xlabel('Test1 Score')
ax.set_ylabel('Test2 Score')
ax.set_zlabel('Test2 Score')
ax.set_zlim(-1, 1)
ax.legend(loc='best')
```

11. Display the figure on the screen:

```
plt.show()
```

How it works...

Here is the explanation of the preceding code:

- `scores_data = pd.read_csv('test_scores_results.txt',header=None)` reads the data from the Excel file, which does not have a header. It has *test1* and *test2* scores and the status 0 for `rejected` and 1 for `accepted`.

- `scores_data = np.array(scores_data)` converts `scores_data` to a NumPy array.

- `df = pd.DataFrame(data=scores_data, columns=columns)` creates a `pandas` DataFrame, `df`, using the `scores_data` array and the column names list.

- `df_accepted = df[(df['Accepted'] == 1.0)]` creates the `df_accepted` DataFrame for `accepted` data with `test1` and `test2` scores.

- `df_rejected = df[(df['Accepted'] == 0.0)]` creates the `df_rejected` DataFrame for `rejected` data with `test1` and `test2` scores.

- `accepted_score1 = np.array(df_accepted)[:,0]` and `accepted_score2 = np.array(df_accepted)[:,1]` are the *x* and *y* coordinates for the `accepted` category.

- `rejected_score1 = np.array(df_rejected)[:,0]` and `rejected_score2 = np.array(df_rejected)[:,1]` are the *x* and *y* coordinates for the `rejected` category.

- `ax.plot(accepted_score1, accepted_score2, 'gD', label='Accepted')` draws a 2D plot with the `accepted` category points as a scatter plot in green and with a diamond-shaped marker. Since no line style parameter was provided, it takes it to be a scatter plot.

- `ax.plot(rejected_score1, rejected_score2, 'ro', label='rejected')` plots the `rejected` category points as a scatter plot in red and with a circle-shaped marker. Since no line style parameter was provided, it takes it to be a scatter plot.

- `ax.scatter(accepted_score1, accepted_score2, zs=-0.75, zdir='z', s=50, color='g', marker='D', label='Accepted')` draws a 3D scatter plot on the *xy* plane, where z=-0.75 for the `accepted` category.

- `ax.scatter(rejected_score1, rejected_score2, zs=0.75, zdir='y', s=50, color='r', marker='o', label='rejected')` draws a 3D scatter plot on the *xy* plane, where z=0.75 for the `rejected` category.

- The rest of the statements are self-explanatory.

Upon running the code, you should see the following figure on your screen:

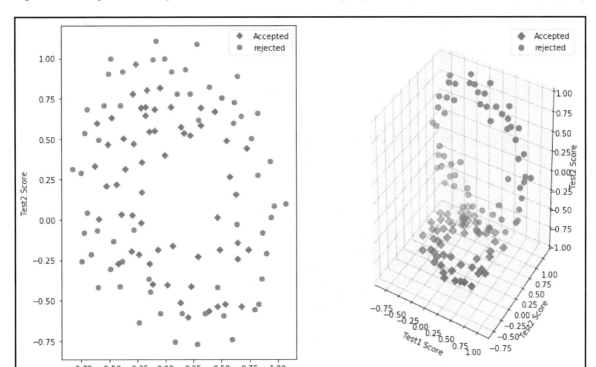

Word embeddings

In Chapter 7, *Embedding Text and Expressions*, we learned how to plot word embeddings in 2D space. Here, we will learn how to plot the same word embeddings in 3D space. To create the required data, we will have to run t-SNE algorithm with three components to generate x, y, and z coordinates. We will use this output to plot the graph.

Getting ready

Import the required libraries:

```
from mpl_toolkits.mplot3d import Axes3D
import matplotlib.pyplot as plt
import pickle
```

How to do it...

Here are the steps involved in plotting a word embeddings graph:

1. Load the required data using `pickle`:

```
threed_embeddings = pickle.load(open('threed_embeddings','rb'))
reverse_dictionary = pickle.load(open('word_reverse_dictionary',
                                       'rb'))
```

2. Create the figure and axes for 3D plotting:

```
fig = plt.figure(figsize=(20,20))
ax = fig.gca(projection='3d')
```

3. Draw the scatter plot with text annotation for each of the top 400 words:

```
num_points = 400
words = [reverse_dictionary[i] for i in range(1, num_points+1)]
for i, label in enumerate(words):
    x, y, z = threed_embeddings[i,:]
    ax.scatter(x, y, z)
    ax.text(x, y, z, label, ha='right', va='bottom')
```

4. Set the limits and labels for the *x, y,* and *z* axes:

```
ax.set_xlim(-800,400)
ax.set_ylim(-200,800)
ax.set_zlim(-800,400)
ax.set_xlabel('x')
ax.set_ylabel('y')
ax.set_zlabel('z')
```

5. Display the figure on the screen:

```
plt.show()
```

How it works...

It works similar to its 2D equivalent explained in Chapter 7, *Embedding Text and Expressions*, with the exception that the input file has three components, which are mapped to the three dimensions *x, y,* and *z*.

Upon running the code, you should see the following figure on your screen:

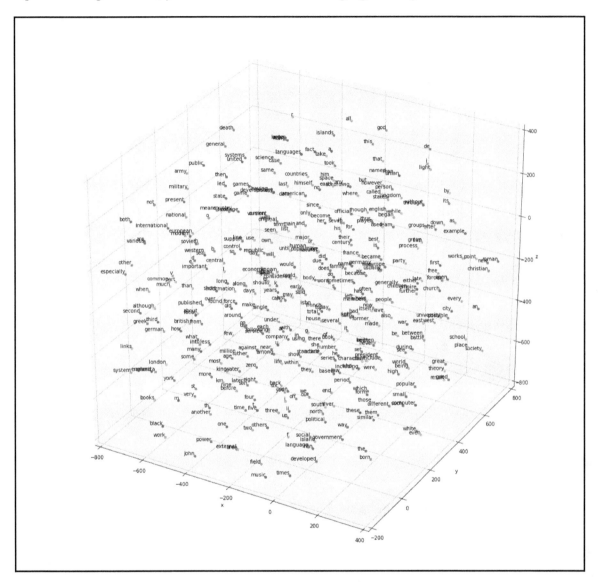

Here, similar words look little far compared to 2D equivalent. For example, numbers one, two, three, four, five, and so on, look little further, whereas in 2D they look like a nice cluster. However, they are still together relatively.

Using the axisartist Toolkit

12

In this chapter, we will learn how to use various features of the `axisartist` toolkit through the following recipes:

- Understanding attributes in axisartist
- Defining curvilinear grids in rectangular boxes
- Defining polar axes in rectangular boxes
- Using floating axes for a rectangular plot
- Creating polar axes using floating axes
- Plotting planetary system data on floating polar axes

Introduction

The primary motivation for developing the `axisartist` toolkit is to support curvilinear grids, such as those used for plotting planetary systems in astronomy. It helps in plotting graphs with curved axes on both rectangular and polar axes, and can also assist in plotting graphs with floating axes.

`axisartist` uses a custom `Axes` class derived from the main `Axes` class of Matplotlib, where each axis (left, bottom, top, and right) is managed by a separate artist. They are accessed by `ax.axis["left"]`, `ax.axis["bottom"]`, `ax.axis["top"]`, and `ax.axis["right"]`, since `ax.axis` acts like a dictionary. We can also define additional axes as required.

Understanding attributes in axisartist

In this recipe, we will learn how to use the basic attributes and properties of `AxisArtist`, such as fixed axis, floating axis, labels, and ticks. We will not be plotting any graphs using these properties in this recipe.

Getting ready

You'll need to import the required libraries using the following commands:

```
import matplotlib.pyplot as plt
import mpl_toolkits.axisartist as AxisArtist
```

How to do it...

Here are the steps involved in plotting the required graph:

1. Define the figure and `AxisArtist` parameters, and then add the latter to the figure, as follows:

```
fig = plt.figure()
ax = AxisArtist.Axes(fig, [0.1, 0.1, 0.8, 0.8])
fig.add_axes(ax)
```

2. Set the top and right axes as invisible, and then set up the labels for the axes, using the following commands:

```
ax.axis["right", "top"].set_visible(False)
ax.set_xlabel("X Axis")
ax.axis["bottom"].label.set_rotation(30)
ax.set_ylabel("Y Axis")
```

3. Create a floating axis at y=1 as follows:

```
ax.axis["y=1"] = ax.new_floating_axis(nth_coord=0, value=1.0)
ax.axis["y=1"].label.set_text("floating X axis on top")
```

4. Create another floating axis at x=0.5 as follows:

```
ax.axis["x=0.5"] = ax.new_floating_axis(nth_coord=1, value=0.5)
ax.axis["x=0.5"].set_axis_direction("top")
ax.axis["x=0.5"].label.set_text("floating Y axis in the middle")
```

5. Create a fixed axis on the right using these commands:

```
ax.axis["right"] = ax.new_fixed_axis(loc="right", offset=(20, 20))
ax.axis["right"].set_axis_direction("bottom")
ax.axis["right"].label.set_text("fixed Y axis on right")
```

6. Allocate color properties to the ticks, tick labels, and label attributes of all axes, as shown here:

```
ax.axis["left", "bottom"].major_ticks.set_color("darkblue")
ax.axis["left", "bottom"].major_ticklabels.set_color("darkblue")
ax.axis["left", "bottom"].label.set_color("darkblue")

ax.axis["right", "y=1"].major_ticks.set_color("green")
ax.axis["right", "y=1"].major_ticklabels.set_color("green")
ax.axis["right", "y=1"].label.set_color("green")
```

7. Set tick alignment, padding, and *x* and *y* axis limits as follows:

```
ax.axis[:].major_ticks.set_tick_out(True)
ax.axis[:].label.set_pad(10)
ax.set_xlim(0,2)
ax.set_ylim(-1,2)
```

8. Set attributes for the axis `y=1` with the following commands:

```
ax.axis["x=0.5"].toggle(all=False, label=True)
ax.axis["x=0.5"].label.set_color("red")
```

9. Set the title for the figure (here, we've used `AxisArtist Demo`) and finally, display the figure on the screen, as shown here:

```
ax.set_title('AxisArtist Demo', pad=50, loc='right')
plt.show()
```

How it works...

Here is the explanation for the preceding code:

- `fig = plt.figure()` defines the figure object.
- `ax = AxisArtist.Axes(fig, [0.1, 0.1, 0.8, 0.8])` defines the axes of the `AxisArtist` class at given coordinates, starting from the left, through to the bottom, width, and height, respectively.
- `fig.add_axes(ax)` adds an axes object to the figure.
- `ax.axis["right", "top"].set_visible(False)` sets top and right axes (spines) as invisible. You can set this for each of the axes separately also.
- `ax.set_xlabel("X Axis")` sets the label of the *x* axis as "X Axis".

- `ax.axis["bottom"].label.set_rotation(30)` rotates the *x* axis label by 30 degrees counterclockwise.
- `ax.set_ylabel("Y Axis")` sets the label of the *y* axis label as `"Y Axis"`.
- `ax.axis["y=1"] = ax.new_floating_axis(nth_coord=0, value=1.0)` defines a new axis as follows:
  - `floating axis` is the one whose position changes with the limits set for the *x* or *y* axis, since it is created at a fixed value of an axis in the data coordinate system.
  - `nth_coord` specifies whether the new axis is aligned with the *x* or *y* axis. When set to 0, it is parallel to the *x* axis; if it is 1, then the new axis will be parallel to the *y* axis.
  - The `value` parameter specifies a value on the axis; this new axis is to be created. In this case, it is created at `y=1`, due to the `value=1.0` parameter.
  - `"y=1"` is the name given to this new axis and with which it is saved in the `ax.axis` dictionary.
- `ax.axis["y=1"].label.set_text("floating X axis on top")` sets the label for the new floating axis.
- `ax.axis["x=0.5"] = ax.new_floating_axis(nth_coord=1, value=0.5)` creates one more floating axis as follows:
  - `nth_coord=1` specifies that this new axis should be parallel to the *Y* axis.
  - `value=0.5` specifies that new floating axis should be created at `x=0.5`.
  - `"x=0.5"` is the name given to this new axis .
- `ax.axis["x=0.5"].set_axis_direction("top")` specifies on which side of the axis ticks, ticklabels, and axis labels should be displayed. Top means they all should be on the top or left-hand sides of the axis, depending on whether it is parallel to the *x* or *y* axes.
- `ax.axis["x=0.5"].label.set_text("floating Y axis in the middle")` sets the label for the new axis.
- `ax.axis["right"] = ax.new_fixed_axis(loc="right", offset=(20, 20))` creates a fixed axis as follows:
  - A fixed axis is the one whose location is fixed, since it is created with a specified offset with respect to a given axis/spine.

- loc="right" specifies that the new axis should be created on the right-hand side of the plot.
    - offset=(20, 20) specifies the offset in points (1 point=1/72 inch) from the default right axis, which, in this case, is made invisible. It is 20 points above the *x* (bottom) axis, and 20 points to the right of the default right axis.
- ax.axis["right"].set_axis_direction("bottom") specifies that ticks, ticklabels, and axis labels should be plotted on the right side (or bottom when the axis is parallel to the *x* axis) of the new axis.
- ax.axis["right"].label.set_text("fixed Y axis on right") sets the label for the new axis.
- ax.axis["left", "bottom"].major_ticks.set_color("darkblue") sets a dark blue color for major ticks of the left (*y*) and bottom (*x*) axes.
- ax.axis["left", "bottom"].major_ticklabels.set_color("darkblue") sets dark blue as the color for ticklabels.
- ax.axis["left", "bottom"].label.set_color("darkblue") sets dark blue as the color for axis labels.
- ax.axis["right", "y=1"].major_ticks.set_color("green") sets a green color for major ticks of the "right" and "y=1" axes.
- ax.axis["right", "y=1"].major_ticklabels.set_color("green") sets a green color for ticklabels.
- ax.axis["right", "y=1"].label.set_color("green") sets a green color for axis labels.
- ax.axis[:].major_ticks.set_tick_out(True) sets ticks on the same side of tick labels. By default in the axisartist class, ticks and ticklabels are on opposite sides of the axis. It should be noted that in the main, Matplotlib axes, classes, ticks, and ticklabels are plotted on the same side of the axis by default. axis[:] includes all the elements of the dictionary, which means all the axes—by default, four axes, and three newly added axes. Of course, the "top" and "right" default axes are set to an "invisible" state, so you can't see their ticks and ticklabels! So, this function is applied to all visible axes only.
- ax.axis[:].label.set_pad(10) adds padding between an axis and its label (so that there is no overlap), again for all visible axes.
- ax.set_xlim(0,2) sets minimum and maximum limits for the *x* axis.

- `ax.set_ylim(-1,2)` sets minimum and maximum limits for the *y* axis.
- `ax.axis["x=0.5"].toggle(all=False, label=True)` makes ticks and ticklabels invisible and the axis label visible for axis x=0.5:
  - `all=False` makes ticks, tick labels, and axis labels all invisible. You can also change the setting for ticks, tick labels, and labels individually, instead of all at once.
  - `label=True` makes the axis label visible.
  - We use the default option for `set_axis_direction` parameter, which is *bottom* (right for the axis parallel to the *y* axis).
- `ax.axis["x=0.5"].label.set_color("red")` sets a red color for the axis label for axis x=0.5.
- `plt.show()` displays the graph on screen.

Upon executing the preceding code, you should see the following diagram on your screen:

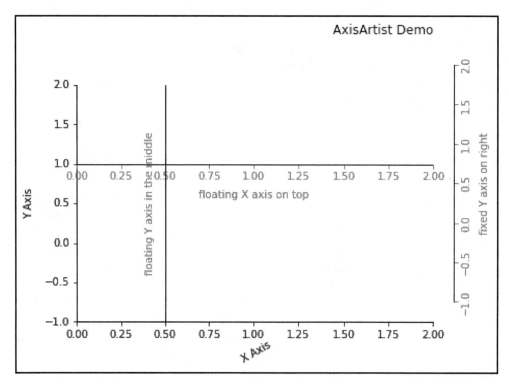

New floating axes and fixed axes use the same scale as the corresponding main x or y axis scale. Matplotlib currently does not support different scales for each of these new axes. Version 3.0 of Matplotlib is expected to remove this limitation.

Defining curvilinear grids in rectangular boxes

In this recipe, we will learn how to create a curvilinear grid with its own coordinate system, within a rectangular axis that uses the Cartesian coordinate system. We will plot a simple line graph between two points represented by curvilinear coordinates.

This is essentially a custom-developed curvilinear coordinate system, for which we have to define the functions that map from curvilinear coordinates to Cartesian coordinates and in reverse direction. In subsequent recipes, we will learn about the predefined transformations provided by the axistartist class.

Getting ready

You'll need to import the required libraries using the following commands:

```
import numpy as np
import matplotlib.pyplot as plt
from mpl_toolkits.axisartist import Subplot
from mpl_toolkits.axisartist.grid_helper_curvelinear import
GridHelperCurveLinear
```

How to do it...

Here are the steps involved in plotting the required graph:

1. First, define the figure as follows:

```
fig = plt.figure(1, figsize=(7, 4))
```

2. Next, define the transformation function to convert curvilinear coordinates to rectilinear coordinates:

```
# Transformation Function to convert curvilinear coordinates to
rectilinear coordinates
def curv2rect_tr(x, y):
    x, y = np.asarray(x), np.asarray(y)
    return x, y - x
```

3. Define the transformation function to convert rectilinear coordinates to curvilinear coordinates:

```
# Transformation Function to convert rectilinear coordinates to
curvilinear coordinates
def rect2curv_tr(x, y):
    x, y = np.asarray(x), np.asarray(y)
    return x, y + x
```

4. Define the `grid_helper` function, which is responsible for plotting grid lines with curvilinear coordinates on a rectangular axis with rectilinear coordinates. It takes transformation functions as input and uses these to draw grid lines:

```
grid_helper = GridHelperCurveLinear((curv2rect_tr, rect2curv_tr))
```

5. Define the axes that use the grid helper function, defined in the previous step:

```
ax = Subplot(fig, 1, 1, 1, grid_helper=grid_helper)
```

6. Add the axes that you just defined to the figure:

```
fig.add_subplot(ax)
```

7. Define two points in curvilinear coordinates and convert them to equivalent rectilinear coordinates:

```
x, y = curv2rect_tr([2.0, 8.0], [4.0, 16.0])
```

8. Plot a line graph using rectilinear coordinates, as shown here:

```
ax.plot(x, y, linewidth=2.0, color='g')
```

9. Set values for the aspect ratio and x and y axis limits:

```
ax.set_aspect(1.)
ax.set_xlim(0, 15.)
ax.set_ylim(0, 15.)
```

10. Create *x* and *y* axes in curvilinear co-ordinates using the floating axis method, as follows:

```
ax.axis["y"] = ax.new_floating_axis(nth_coord=0, value=4.0)
ax.axis["y"].set_ticklabel_direction('+')
ax.axis["x"] = ax.new_floating_axis(1, 9.0)
ax.axis["x"].set_ticklabel_direction('-')
```

11. Turn the background grid on:

```
ax.grid(True, zorder=0)
```

12. Print points A, B, C, and D to represent the *x* and *y* axes, and the points in curvilinear co-ordinates that are plotted as a line graph:

```
ax.text(-1.5, 8.5, 'A', size=25, weight=50, color='b')
ax.text(8.5, -1.5, 'B', size=25, weight=50, color='b')
ax.text(3.5, -1.5, 'C', size=25, weight=50, color='b')
ax.text(3.5, 15, 'D', size=25, weight=50, color='b')
ax.text(2.0, 1.5, '(2.0, 4.0)', weight='bold', color='b')
ax.text(7.5, 8.5, '(8.0, 16.0)', weight='bold', color='b')
```

13. Finally, display the figure on screen with the following command:

```
plt.show()
```

How it works...

Here is the explanation for the preceding code:

- def curv2rect_tr(x, y) defines the function that converts curvilinear coordinates into rectilinear co-ordinates. It retains *x* in the new coordinates, but *y* in rectilinear coordinates is defined as *y* - *x*:
  - x, y = np.asarray(x), np.asarray(y) redefines input parameters *x* and *y* to NumPy arrays.
  - Maps curvilinear coordinates to rectilinear coordinates, *x* = *x* (same value in both systems), and *y* in rectilinear *system* = *y* - *x* of the curvilinear system.
- def rect2curv_tr(x, y) defines the function that converts rectilinear coordinates to curvilinear coordinates. It is the inverse of the curv2rect function.

- `grid_helper = GridHelperCurveLinear((curv2rect_tr, rect2curv_tr))` defines a helper function that draws grid lines in two directions, using the transformation functions provided as arguments. Accordingly, their axes will be set up along these grid lines, using new floating axes.
- `ax = Subplot(fig, 1, 1, 1, grid_helper=grid_helper)` defines the axes as a subplot, as follows:
  - `fig` is the figure object defined at the beginning.
  - `1,1,1` is similar to the `plt.subplot()` notation, and specifies that it is the first axis within a 1 x 1 grid.
  - Takes `grid_helper`, defined earlier, as an argument.
- `fig.add_subplot(ax)` adds the axes to the figure.
- `x, y = curv2rect_tr([2.0, 8.0], [4.0, 16.0])` takes points (2.0, 4.0) and (8.0, 16,0) in curvilinear coordinates and transforms them to equivalent rectilinear coordinates, which will be *(2.0, 2.0),* and *(8.0, 8.0)*.
- `ax.plot(x, y, linewidth=2.0, color='g')` plots a green line graph with a line width of 2.0 points.
- `ax.set_aspect(1.)` sets the aspect ratio to 1, which means that both the *x* and *y* axis data scales are equal.
- `ax.set_xlim(0, 15.)` sets minimum and maximum limits for the *x* axis, and `ax.set_ylim(0, 15.)` sets the limits for the *y* axis.
- `ax.axis["0"] = ax.new_floating_axis(nth_coord=0, value=4.0)` defines a floating axis in curvilinear coordinates for the first coordinate that cuts the grid line at the value of 4.0. It is named the `"0"` axis in the axis dictionary. This line is represented by points C and D highlighted in blue in the figure.
- `ax.axis["0"].set_ticklabel_direction('+')` specifies that tick labels should be placed to the right of the axis in the direction of increasing values along the axis. If it is `'-'`, then they will be placed on the left of the axis. However, ticks are placed in the opposite direction of the tick labels by default.
- `ax.axis["1"] = ax.new_floating_axis(1, 9.0)` defines a second floating axis that goes through a value of 9.0 on the X axis. It is named as `"1"` in the axis dictionary. This line is represented in the figure by points A and B highlighted in blue.
- `ax.axis["1"].set_ticklabel_direction('-')` specifies that ticklabels should be placed to the left of the axes in increasing order. In this case, the axis increases downward (from 0 to 8), so the left of that direction is above the line! Hence, ticklabels are placed above the line, while ticks are placed below it.

- `ax.grid(True)` displays the grid lines.
- `ax.text(-1.5, 8.5, 'A', size=25, weight=50, color='b')` plots the point "A", in blue, with a size of 25, and a weight of 50. Similarly, the B, C, and D points, and the (2.0, 4.0), and (8.0, 16.) coordinates, are plotted with these specified attributes.
- `plt.show()` displays the graph on the screen.

Upon execution of the preceding code, you should see the following diagram on your screen:

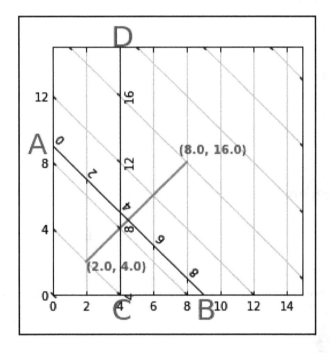

Defining polar axes in rectangular boxes

In the preceding recipe, we learned to define custom transformation and used it to draw curved grid lines in curvilinear coordinates. However, they both use the Cartesian coordinate system of *x*, *y* co-ordinates. In this recipe, we will learn how to use polar coordinates (angle and radius coordinates) in a rectangular box. In this recipe, as well as in all upcoming ones, we will use pre-built transformations provided by Matplotlib.

Getting ready

You'll need to import the requisite libraries using the following commands:

```
import matplotlib.pyplot as plt
import numpy as np
from mpl_toolkits.axisartist.grid_helper_curvelinear import
GridHelperCurveLinear
import mpl_toolkits.axisartist.angle_helper as angle_helper
from matplotlib.projections import PolarAxes
from matplotlib.transforms import Affine2D
from mpl_toolkits.axisartist import SubplotHost, ParasiteAxesAuxTrans
import matplotlib.cbook as cbook
```

How to do it...

The following are the steps required to plot the graph:

1. Define the figure as follows:

```
fig = plt.figure(1, figsize=(7, 4))
```

2. Define the transformation function as shown here:

```
# PolarAxes.PolarTransform needs angle units as radian. However, we
# plot the coordinate system in degrees for easier visualization
curv2rect_tr = Affine2D().scale(np.pi/180., 1.) +
                          PolarAxes.PolarTransform()
```

3. Compute boundary values for both the angle and radius, in order to draw the grid lines:

```
#(25, 25) is the number of steps it takes from minimum limit to
  maximum limit for x and y
# number of grid lines(circular for radius, diagonal for angle)
will
  be influenced by these steps
extreme_finder = angle_helper.ExtremeFinderCycle(25, 25,
                                        lon_cycle=360,
                                        lat_cycle=None,
                                        lon_minmax=None,
                                        lat_minmax=(0, 50))
```

4. Define the grid locator for the angle:

```
# Determine grid values appropriate for the coordinate (degree,
   minute, second).
grid_locator1 = angle_helper.LocatorDMS(18)
```

5. Define the tick formatter for the angle:

```
# Use an appropriate formatter to show angle values in degree,
   minute and second format.
tick_formatter1 = angle_helper.FormatterDMS()
```

6. Define the grid locator for the radius:

```
grid_locator2 = MaxNLocator(12)
```

7. Define the grid helper that plots the grids:

```
grid_helper = GridHelperCurveLinear(curv2rect_tr,
                                    extreme_finder=extreme_finder,
                                    grid_locator1=grid_locator1,
                                    tick_formatter1=tick_formatter1,
                                    grid_locator2=grid_locator2)
```

8. Define the main axes using the figure and grid helper defined earlier:

```
ax = SubplotHost(fig, 1, 1, 1, grid_helper=grid_helper)
```

9. Make the ticklabels of the right and top axes visible using this command:

```
ax.axis["right", "top"].major_ticklabels.set_visible(True)
```

10. Map the angle ticks to the right axis, and the radius ticks to the bottom axis, as follows:

```
ax.axis["right"].get_helper().nth_coord_ticks = 0
ax.axis["bottom"].get_helper().nth_coord_ticks = 1
```

11. Add the main axes to the figure with this command:

```
fig.add_subplot(ax)
```

12. Define a parasite axes and append it to the main axes:

```
axp = ParasiteAxesAuxTrans(ax, curv2rect_tr, "equal")
ax.parasites.append(axp)
```

13. Plot a line graph on the parasite axes:

```
intp = cbook.simple_linear_interpolation
axp.plot(intp(np.array([0, 75, 180, 300]), 100), intp(np.array([9.,
                    12., 16, 21]), 100),
                    linewidth=2.0, color='g')
```

14. Annotate the starting and endpoints on the line graph:

```
axp.text(0,7.5, '.', color='r', size=50)
axp.text(3,9.5, 'A(0,9)', color='b', weight='bold')
axp.text(295, 20.5, '.', color='r', size=50)
axp.text(300,21, 'B(300,21)', color='b', weight='bold')
```

15. Set the aspect ratio and x and y limits for the main axes:

```
ax.set_aspect(1.0)
ax.set_xlim(-20, 22)
ax.set_ylim(-25, 20)
```

16. Set the grid option to `True` to display the grid:

```
ax.grid(True)
```

17. Lastly, display the graph on the screen with this command:

```
plt.show()
```

How it works...

The following is the explanation for the preceding code:

- `curv2rect_tr = Affine2D().scale(np.pi/180., 1.) + PolarAxes.PolarTransform()` defines the transformation between the main and parasite axes:
  - `PolarAxes.PolarTransform()` needs the angle in radians; hence, we add `scale(np.pi/180., 1.)` to facilitate the transformation between degrees and radians.
  - `Affine2D` is the linear transformation between two axes.
- `extreme_finder = angle_helper.ExtremeFinderCycle()` computes boundary values for the angle and radius for given X, Y limits, and other parameters set in this function:
  - `(25, 25)` is the number of steps it takes from the minimum and maximum limits set for x and y.

- The number of grid lines (circular for radius, diagonal for angle) will be influenced by these steps.
- `lon_cycle=360` sets a one-cycle limit for the angle. Since we want polar axes, we set this to 360 degrees.
- `lat_minmax=(0, 50)` sets the minimum and maximum values for the radius.

- `grid_locator1 = angle_helper.LocatorDMS(30)` determines grid values appropriate for the angle coordinate (degree, minute, second):
  - The digit 30 in the argument specifies that it should plot 30 grid lines for the angle coordinate, which translates to 12 degrees each (360/30). However, you see the grid lines plotted every 10 degrees.
  - Grid lines depend on three sets of parameters, and will decide optimal placement of grid lines balancing all three sets of parameters:
    - Given x and y limits.
    - Various arguments given to the `extreme_finder` function.
    - The argument specified in `grid_locator`.

- `tick_formatter1 = angle_helper.FormatterDMS()` formats angle tick labels to show degrees.
- `grid_locator2 = MaxNLocator(12)` determines grid values for the radius. The digit *12* specifies the number of circular grids to be plotted on the plot. In this case, we see 12 grid lines on the plot. However, this could also be slightly different based on other parameters set.
- `grid_helper = GridHelperCurveLinear()` plots grid lines for a given transformation function, grid locators, and formatters.
- `ax = SubplotHost(fig, 1, 1, 1, grid_helper=grid_helper)` defines the main axes using the figure and grid helper objects created earlier.
- `ax.axis["right", "top"].major_ticklabels.set_visible(True)` makes right and top axis ticklabels visible, where these are not visible by default.
- `ax.axis["right"].get_helper().nth_coord_ticks = 0` maps the right axis to an angle coordinate. In polar coordinates, the first (0) coordinate is an angle, and the second one (1) is the radius.
- `fig.add_subplot(ax)` adds main axes to the figure.
- `axp = ParasiteAxesAuxTrans(ax, curv2rect_tr)` defines the parasite axes for polar coordinates on the main axes with a defined transformation function.

- `ax.parasites.append(axp)` adds parasite axes to the main axes.
- `intp = cbook.simple_linear_interpolation` means that linear interpolation will be applied to the data to be plotted on the parasite axes.
- `axp.plot()` plots four points on parasite axes as a line graph in green and with a line width of 2.0. The argument `100` specifies the number of increments to be taken while moving from the start point to the endpoint, so that there is a smooth transition along the trajectory.
- `axp.text()` plots red dots and annotates them with coordinates for the start and endpoints of the line plot.
- `ax.set_aspect(1.0)` sets the aspect ratio between the *x* and *y* coordinates.
- `ax.set_xlim(-20, 22)` and `ax.set_ylim(-25, 20)` specifies the lower and upper limits for the *x* and *y* coordinates for which the figure and graph are plotted.
- `ax.grid(True, zorder=0)` sets the grid lines on, and `zorder=0` specifies that grid lines should be drawn before drawing any other artists. If we don't set this, then you will see grid lines overlapping the green line plot, as the line plot is drawn first, and then the grid lines! To avoid this overlap, we set `zorder=0` for the grid lines' draw function.

Upon executing the preceding code, you should see the following diagram on your screen:

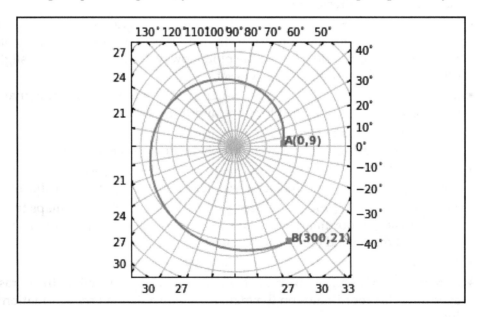

Using floating axes for a rectangular plot

In this recipe, we will learn how to plot floating axes. These are useful when we have to design a complex dashboard application, where we may have to place individual graphs or plots in various orientations other than the standard horizontal or vertical orientations.

We will plot three different graphs to demonstrate various features of floating axes.

Getting ready

You'll need to import the requisite libraries using the following commands:

```
import pandas as pd
import numpy as np
import matplotlib.pyplot as plt
from matplotlib.transforms import Affine2D
import mpl_toolkits.axisartist.floating_axes as floating_axes
```

How to do it...

The following are the steps required to plot all three graphs:

1. Define the figure as follows:

   ```
   fig = plt.figure(1, figsize=(14, 6))
   ```

2. Prepare the data as follows:

   ```
   month_num = [1, 2, 3, 4, 5, 6, 7, 8, 9, 10, 11, 12]
   units_sold = [500, 600, 750, 900, 1100, 1050, 1000, 950, 800, 700,
                 550, 450]
   ```

3. Define the transformation function, as shown here:

   ```
   curv2rect_tr1 = Affine2D().scale(200, 1).rotate_deg(30)
   ```

4. Define the grid helper function as follows:

   ```
   grid_helper1 = floating_axes.GridHelperCurveLinear(curv2rect_tr1,
                                     extremes=(0, 13, 0, 1400))
   ```

5. Define main and parasite axes using the following commands:

```
ax1 = floating_axes.FloatingSubplot(fig, 131,
                                    grid_helper=grid_helper1)
fig.add_subplot(ax1)
axp1 = ax1.get_aux_axes(curv2rect_tr1)
```

6. Plot a bar graph with the following parameters:

```
bars = axp1.bar(month_num, units_sold)
for bar in bars:
    height = bar.get_height()
    axp1.text(bar.get_x() + bar.get_width()/2., 1.002*height,'%d' %
              int(height),
              ha='center', va='bottom', rotation=30)
```

7. Set the ticks to be in proper alignment with the grid lines, and stipulate the title as follows:

```
grid_helper1.grid_finder.grid_locator1._nbins = 14 # X axis ticks
grid_helper1.grid_finder.grid_locator2._nbins = 5 # Y axis ticks
axp1.text(5, 1900, 'bar plot', rotation=30, size=15, weight='bold',
          color='b')
```

8. Repeat all of the preceding steps for the box plot, as shown here:

```
# Read data
wine_quality = pd.read_csv('winequality.csv', delimiter=';')
data = [wine_quality['alcohol'], wine_quality['fixed acidity'],
wine_quality['quality']]

# Define transformation function
curv2rect_tr2 = Affine2D().scale(4, 1).rotate_deg(-30)

# Define grid helper function
grid_helper2 = floating_axes.GridHelperCurveLinear(curv2rect_tr2,
extremes=(0, 4, 0, 20))

# Define main axes
ax2 = floating_axes.FloatingSubplot(fig, 132,
grid_helper=grid_helper2)
fig.add_subplot(ax2)

# Define parasite axes
axp2 = ax2.get_aux_axes(curv2rect_tr2)

# Plot boxplot
axp2.boxplot(data)
```

```
# Set the tick and grid lines
grid_helper2.grid_finder.grid_locator1._nbins = 4
grid_helper2.grid_finder.grid_locator2._nbins = 5

# Set title and labels
axp2.text(1, 21, 'box plot', rotation=-30, size=15, weight='bold',
color='b')
ax2.axis["bottom"].label.set_text('X axis')
ax2.axis["bottom"].label.set_color('blue')
ax2.axis["left"].label.set_text('Y axis')
ax2.axis["left"].label.set_color('red')
```

9. Likewise, repeat the same for plotting the sine/cosine function, as shown in the
   following code block:

```
# Prepare data, define transformation and grid helper functions,
  main axes
x = np.linspace(0, 10, 100)
curv2rect_tr3 = Affine2D().scale(1, 1).rotate_deg(10)
grid_helper3 = floating_axes.GridHelperCurveLinear(curv2rect_tr3,
extremes=(0, 10, -5, 5))
ax3 = floating_axes.FloatingSubplot(fig, 133,
grid_helper=grid_helper3)
fig.add_subplot(ax3)

# Define parasite axes, plot sine and cosine graphs, set title,
  legend and grid
axp3 = ax3.get_aux_axes(curv2rect_tr3)
axp3.plot(x, 5*np.sin(x), label='sine')
axp3.plot(x, 5*np.cos(x), label='cosine')
ax3.legend(bbox_to_anchor=(0.35, 0., 1.05, 1.0), borderaxespad=0)
ax3.set_title('Sine/Cosine waves')
ax3.grid()
grid_helper3.grid_finder.grid_locator1._nbins = 5
grid_helper3.grid_finder.grid_locator2._nbins = 5

# Set labels, ticks and ticklabel attributes
ax3.axis["bottom"].label.set_text('X axis')
ax3.axis["bottom"].label.set_color('green')
ax3.axis["bottom"].major_ticks.set_color("green")
ax3.axis["bottom"].major_ticklabels.set_color("green")
ax3.axis["left"].label.set_text('Y axis')
ax3.axis["left"].label.set_color('red')
ax3.axis["left"].major_ticks.set_color("red")
ax3.axis["left"].major_ticklabels.set_color("red")
ax3.axis["bottom", "left"].major_ticks.set_tick_out(True)
ax3.axis["top", "right"].major_ticks.set_visible(False)
```

10. Set the title for the figure, and adjust the space between the plots, using the following commands:

```
plt.suptitle('Floating Axes Demo',size=20, weight='bold',
color='g')
plt.show()
```

How it works...

Here is the explanation for the preceding code:

- `curv2rect_tr1 = Affine2D().scale(200, 1).rotate_deg(30)` is the transformation function, which works as follows:
    - `Affine2D` is the linear transformation.
    - `scale(200,1)` specifies the data scale between the x and y axes. This needs to be set based on the data range to be plotted on the x and y axes.
    - `rotate_deg(30)` specifies that the plot be rotated by 30 degrees counter clockwise.
- `grid_helper1 = floating_axes.GridHelperCurveLinear(curv2rect_tr1, extremes=(0, 13, 0, 1400))` defines the grid lines as follows:
    - `curv2rect_tr1` is the transformation function defined earlier.
    - `extremes=(0,13,0,1400)` defines the lower and upper limits for the x and y axes. Here, the x axis ranges from 0 to 13, and the y axis from 0 to 1,400. Notice the gap between the two ranges! That is why we had set (200,1) for the scale in the transformation function.
- `ax1 = floating_axes.FloatingSubplot(fig, 131, grid_helper=grid_helper1)` defines the main axes as follows:
    - `131` indicates that it is the first plot in a 1 x 3 grid of three plots.
- `fig.add_subplot(ax1)` adds main axes to the figure.
- `axp1 = ax1.get_aux_axes(curv2rect_tr1)` defines parasite axes for the bar plot.
- `bars = axp1.bar(month_num, units_sold)` plots the bar graph on the parasite axes.

- `for bar in bars` prints text with the numbers of units on each of the bars. This is the same as what we learned earlier, with the addition of `rotation=30`, to orient the text along the same angle as the floating axes.
- `grid_helper1.grid_finder.grid_locator1._nbins = 14` defines the number of ticks for the x axis.
- `grid_helper1.grid_finder.grid_locator2._nbins = 5` defines the number of ticks for the y axis.
- `axp1.text(5, 1900, 'bar plot', rotation=30, size=15, weight='bold', color='b')` plots the title for the bar plot. The usual `set_title()` method does not work here, so we use the `text` option!
- `curv2rect_tr2 = Affine2D().scale(4, 1).rotate_deg(-30)` defines the transformation function for the box plot to be plotted on different axes, as follows:
  - Here, we use `scale(4,1)` based on the data we have for the x and y axes for this plot.
  - We use `rotate_deg(-30)` to stipulate clockwise rotation of the plot by 30 degrees.
- `grid_helper2 = floating_axes.GridHelperCurveLinear(curv2rect_tr2, extremes=(0, 4, 0, 20))` defines the grid helper function for the box plot:
  - `extremes=(0, 4, 0, 20)` specifies the lower and upper limits for the x and y axes.
- `ax2 = floating_axes.FloatingSubplot(fig, 132, grid_helper=grid_helper2)` defines second axes to be used for plotting the box plot:
  - `132` specifies that it is the second plot on a 1 x 3 grid of plots.
  - `grid_helper=grid_helper2` specifies the grid helper function to be used for this plot.
- `axp2 = ax2.get_aux_axes(curv2rect_tr2)` defines the parasite axes to be used for the box plot.
- `axp2.boxplot(data)` plots a box plot on the parasite axes.
- `grid_helper2.grid_finder.grid_locator1._nbins = 4` sets the number of ticks for the x axis.
- `grid_helper2.grid_finder.grid_locator2._nbins = 5` sets the number of ticks for the y axis.

- `axp2.text(1, 21, 'box plot', rotation=-30, size=15, weight='bold', color='b')` prints the title for the box plot aligned with the axes' orientation of 30 degrees.
- `x = np.linspace(0, 10, 100)` is the data for plotting sine and cosine waves as the third plot in the figure.
- `curv2rect_tr3 = Affine2D().scale(1, 1).rotate_deg(10)` defines the transformation function with a scale of 1:1 and an orientation of 10 degrees for the third plot.
- `grid_helper3 = floating_axes.GridHelperCurveLinear(curv2rect_tr3, extremes=(0, 10, -5, 5))` defines the grid function for the third plot, with x limits of 0 to 10, and y limits of -5 to +5.
- `ax3 = floating_axes.FloatingSubplot(fig, 133, grid_helper=grid_helper3)` defines the third main axis for the third plot, where "133" specifies that it is the third plot on a 1 x 3 grid of plots in the figure.
- `axp3 = ax3.get_aux_axes(curv2rect_tr3)` defines the parasite axes for the third plot.
- `axp3.plot(x, 5*np.sin(x), label='sine')` plots a sine wave on the parasite axes.
- `axp3.plot(x, 5*np.cos(x), label='cosine')` plots a cosine wave on the same parasite axes.
- `ax3.legend(bbox_to_anchor=(0.35, 0., 1.05, 1.0), borderaxespad=0)` sets the legend, but that is not aligned with the axes' orientation.
- `ax3.set_title('Sine/Cosine waves')` prints the title again, but won't be properly aligned, so it's better to use the text method, as we did for first two plots.
- `ax3.grid()` plots grid lines. These will be properly aligned with the axes' orientation, as these are controlled by grid helper function parameters and have `nbins` parameters specified.
- `grid_helper3.grid_finder.grid_locator1._nbins = 5` specifies the number of ticks/grid lines on the x axis.
- `grid_helper3.grid_finder.grid_locator2._nbins = 5` specifies the number of ticks/grid lines on the y axis.
- `plt.suptitle('Floating Axes Demo', size=20, weight='bold', color='g')` prints the title for the overall figure.

Upon executing the preceding code, you should see the following diagram on your screen:

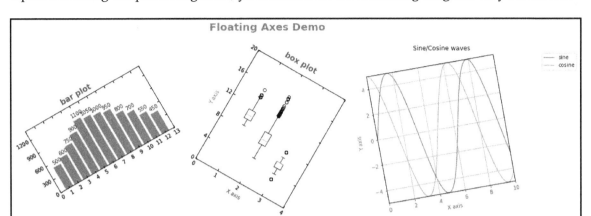

Creating polar axes using floating axes

In Chapter 2, *Getting Started with Basic Plots*, we learned how to draw polar plots using pyplot's projection='polar' option while defining the axes. In this recipe, we will learn how to draw a polar plot using floating axes.

Getting ready

You'll need to import the requisite libraries using the following commands:

```
import numpy as np
import matplotlib.pyplot as plt
from matplotlib.transforms import Affine2D
import mpl_toolkits.axisartist.floating_axes as floating_axes
from matplotlib.projections import PolarAxes
from mpl_toolkits.axisartist.grid_finder import (FixedLocator, MaxNLocator,
DictFormatter)
```

How to do it...

The following are the steps required to draw our plot:

1. Define the figure as follows:

```
fig = plt.figure(1, figsize=(8, 4))
```

2. Define the transformation function, as shown here:

```
curv2rect_tr = PolarAxes.PolarTransform()
```

3. Define the custom ticks dictionary for angle coordinates as follows:

```
pi = np.pi
angle_ticks = [(0, r"$0$"), (.25*pi, r"$\frac{1}{4}\pi$"),
               (.5*pi, r"$\frac{1}{2}\pi$"), (.75*pi, r"$\frac{3}
               {4}\pi$"),
               ( pi, r"$\pi$"), (1.25*pi, r"$1.25\pi$"),
               (1.5*pi, r"$1.5\pi$"), (1.75*pi, r"$1.75\pi$")]
```

4. Define the grid locators and formatters for the following angle and radius coordinates:

```
grid_locator1 = FixedLocator([value for value, string in
                              angle_ticks])
tick_formatter1 = DictFormatter(dict(angle_ticks))
grid_locator2 = MaxNLocator(5)
```

5. Define the grid helper function as shown here:

```
grid_helper = floating_axes.GridHelperCurveLinear(curv2rect_tr,
                         extremes=(2*pi, 0, 5, 0),
                         grid_locator1=grid_locator1,
                         grid_locator2=grid_locator2,
                         tick_formatter1=tick_formatter1,
                         tick_formatter2=None)
```

6. Define the main and parasite axes:

```
main_axes = floating_axes.FloatingSubplot(fig, 111,
                              grid_helper=grid_helper)
fig.add_subplot(main_axes)
parasite_ax = main_axes.get_aux_axes(curv2rect_tr)
```

7. Next, plot the polar graph on the parasite axes:

```
theta = np.arange(0., 2., 1./180.)*np.pi
parasite_ax.fill(theta, 5*np.cos(8*theta), color=(0.8,0.0,0.9),
hatch='//', alpha=0.5)
```

8. Set the grid on what, the title for the plot, and display the figure on screen:

```
main_axes.grid(True, zorder=0)
main_axes.set_title('Polar Plot using Floating Axes',
weight='bold', color='b', pad=50)
plt.show()
```

How it works...

The following is an explanation for the preceding code:

- `curv2rect_tr = PolarAxes.PolarTransform()` defines the polar transformation function.
- `angle_ticks` is a dictionary of ticks for angle coordinates, containing the value of the angle and its corresponding text representation.
- `grid_locator1 = FixedLocator([value for value, string in angle_ticks])` defines the grid locator for the angle coordinate. `FixedLocator()` defines tick/grid locations at fixed positions, as specified by the dictionary.
- `tick_formatter1 = DictFormatter(dict(angle_ticks))` formats angle coordinate values to be displayed.
- `grid_locator2 = MaxNLocator(5)` specifies the grid locator for the radius coordinate. The digit "5" specifies that we should have 5 grid lines on the plot for the radius.
- `grid_helper = floating_axes.GridHelperCurveLinear()` defines the grid helper function. It uses extremes in reverse order, that is, the upper limit, followed by the lower limit, for both coordinates. We have used (2*pi, 0, 5, 0), which means the upper limit for the angle is 2*pi, and the lower limit is zero. Similarly, the upper limit for the radius is 5 and the lower limit is zero.
- `main_axes = floating_axes.FloatingSubplot(fig, 111, grid_helper=grid_helper)` defines the main axes.
- `parasite_ax = main_axes.get_aux_axes(curv2rect_tr)` defines the parasite axes.

- `parasite_ax.fill(theta, 5*np.cos(8*theta), color=(0.8,0.0,0.9), hatch='//', alpha=0.5)` plots a polar graph using the fill method and hatch. `color=(0.8,0.0,0.9)` is a custom color using a combination of RGB channels.
- `main_axes.grid(True, zorder=0)` sets the grid lines to be visible. Grid lines will be plotted before the main graph, so they are in the background of the main graph.

Upon executing the preceding code, you should see the following diagram on your screen:

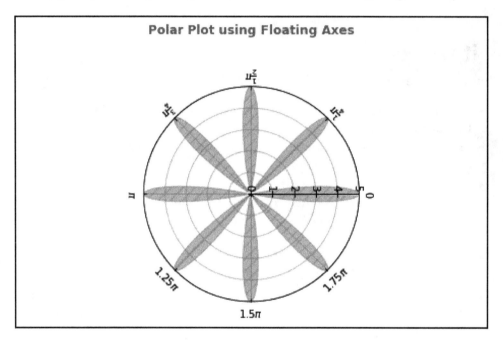

Plotting planetary system data on floating polar axes

In this recipe, we will learn about plotting planetary system data in polar coordinates using floating axes. We will plot two charts with different limits and attributes to demonstrate multiple possibilities. We are not learning any new features or code, just applying, in practical applications, the features that we learned in preceding recipes.

Getting ready

You'll need to import the requisite libraries using the following commands:

```
import numpy as np
import matplotlib.pyplot as plt
from matplotlib.transforms import Affine2D
import mpl_toolkits.axisartist.floating_axes as floating_axes
from matplotlib.projections import PolarAxes
import mpl_toolkits.axisartist.angle_helper as angle_helper
from mpl_toolkits.axisartist.grid_finder import MaxNLocator
```

How to do it...

The following are the steps required to plot our two graphs:

1. Fix the seed to ensure the repeatability of the data:

   ```
   np.random.seed(19681211)
   ```

2. Define the figure as follows:

   ```
   fig = plt.figure(1, figsize=(12, 6))
   ```

3. Define the transformation function, grid locators, and formatters,as shown here:

   ```
   curv2rect_tr1 = Affine2D().translate(-85, 5).scale(np.pi/180., 1.)
   + PolarAxes.PolarTransform()
   grid_locator1 = angle_helper.LocatorDMS(10)
   tick_formatter1 = angle_helper.FormatterDMS()
   grid_locator2 = MaxNLocator(4)
   ```

4. Set the limits for the angle and radius coordinates as follows:

   ```
   # Specify angle coordinate limits in degrees
   langle, uangle = 120., 225.
   # Specify radial coordinate limits in '1000 km
   lradius, uradius = 8, 16
   ```

5. Define the grid helper function:

```
grid_helper1 = floating_axes.GridHelperCurveLinear(curv2rect_tr1,
                    extremes=(langle, uangle, lradius, uradius),
                    grid_locator1=grid_locator1,
                    grid_locator2=grid_locator2,
                    tick_formatter1=tick_formatter1,
                    tick_formatter2=None)
```

6. Define the main axes and add them to the figure as follows:

```
main_axes1 = floating_axes.FloatingSubplot(fig, 121,
grid_helper=grid_helper1)
fig.add_subplot(main_axes1)
```

7. Define a function to set various attributes for the axes, as shown here:

```
def set_axis_attr(axes, leftlabel, toplabel):
    axes.axis["bottom"].toggle(all=False) # by default all are
visible, this makes them all invisible
    axes.axis["right"].toggle(all=False) # by default ticks are
visible, so this will make them invisible
    axes.axis["left"].set_axis_direction("bottom")
    axes.axis["left"].label.set(text=leftlabel, color='blue')
    # by default label and ticklabels are invisible, this will make
them visible
    axes.axis["top"].toggle(all=True)
    axes.axis["top"].set_axis_direction("bottom")
    axes.axis["top"].major_ticklabels.set_axis_direction("top")
    axes.axis["top"].label.set_axis_direction("top")
    axes.axis["top"].label.set(text=toplabel, color='blue')

    axes.axis[:].major_ticks.set_tick_out(True)
```

8. Call the function defined in the previous step:

```
set_axis_attr(main_axes1, "left axis", "top axis")
```

9. Next, define the parasite axes as follows:

```
parasite_axes1 = main_axes1.get_aux_axes(curv2rect_tr1)
```

10. Plot the scatter and line plots on the parasite axes:

```
theta = np.random.randint(langle, uangle, 25) # in degrees
radius = np.random.randint(lradius, uradius, 25)
parasite_axes1.scatter(theta, radius)
parasite_axes1.plot([135, 165, 195, 225], [8, 10, 12, 16],
                    color='r')
```

11. Set grid lines to show using the following command:

```
main_axes1.grid(True, zorder=0)
```

12. Repeat steps 2 through 10 for the second plot, giving you something along the lines of the following:

```
curv2rect_tr2 = Affine2D().scale(np.pi/180., 1.) +
PolarAxes.PolarTransform()
grid_locator3 = angle_helper.LocatorHMS(10)
tick_formatter3 = angle_helper.FormatterHMS()
grid_locator4 = MaxNLocator(5)

langle, uangle = 0., 135.
lradius, uradius = 0, 25
grid_helper2 = floating_axes.GridHelperCurveLinear(curv2rect_tr2,
                    extremes=(langle, uangle, lradius, uradius),
                    grid_locator1=grid_locator3,
                    grid_locator2=grid_locator4,
                    tick_formatter1=tick_formatter3,
                    tick_formatter2=None)

main_axes2 = floating_axes.FloatingSubplot(fig, 122,
grid_helper=grid_helper2)
fig.add_subplot(main_axes2)

set_axis_attr(main_axes2, "Radius('1000KM)", "Angle(HMS)")

parasite_axes2 = main_axes2.get_aux_axes(curv2rect_tr2)

theta = np.random.randint(langle, uangle, 25) # in degrees
radius = np.random.randint(lradius, uradius, 25)
parasite_axes2.scatter(theta, radius)
parasite_axes2.plot([0, 45, 90, 135], [5, 15, 20, 25], color='r')
main_axes2.grid(True, zorder=0)
```

13. Lastly, set the title for the figure and display the figure on the screen using the following command:

```
plt.suptitle('Planetary System Plots',size=20, weight='bold',
             color='g')
plt.show()
```

How it works...

Since there are no new features or syntax introduced in this recipe, we will not repeat the explanation for the code here again. All these statements and functions have been explained already in earlier recipes of this chapter.

The only minor difference here is that we are using a different grid locator and formatter for the second plot, compared to that used for the first plot. The first one follows a degree, minute, and second (DMS) format, while the second one follows an hour, minute, and second (HMS) format. The same can be noticed in the top axis tick labels for both plots.

Upon running the preceding code, you should see the following diagram on your screen:

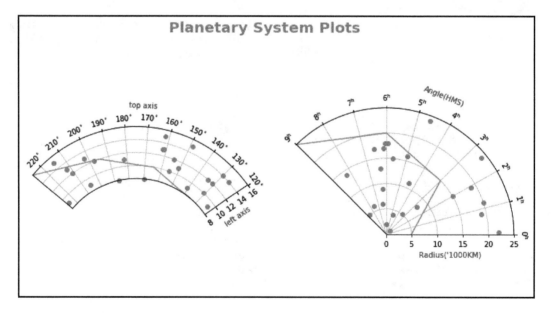

Using the axes_grid1 Toolkit

13

In this chapter, we will learn about features of the `axes_grid1` toolkit. We will cover the following recipes:

- Plotting twin axes using the `axisartst` and `axesgrid1` toolkits
- Using AxesDivider to plot a scatter plot and associated histograms
- Using AxesDivider to plot a colorbar
- Using `ImageGrid` to plot images with a colorbar in a grid
- Using `inset_locator` to zoom in on an image
- Using `inset_locator` to plot inset axes

Introduction

The `axes_grid1` toolkit has been designed to provide a collection of helper classes to plot images with colorbars in a grid, with the proper alignment of colorbars with the image size. It can be used to zoom in on a portion of the image, plot inset axes (similar to picture in picture), and plot a two-dimensional graph and an associated histogram of each of the two variables, parasite axes, and anchored artists.

Plotting twin axes using the axisartist and axesgrid1 toolkits

In Chapter 4, *Developing Visualizations for Publishing Quality*, we learned how to plot two different scales on the left and right axes of a plot using twin axes methods. In Chapter 9, *Developing Interactive Plots*, we learned how to plot different units of measurements on multiple y axes, again using the `twinx` method for interactive analysis. In this recipe, we will learn how to plot multiple scales on various y axes using the main Matplotlib `twinx` method, as well as using the `axisartist` and `axes_grid1` toolkits.

Getting ready

We will first plot our graph using the Matplotlib `twinx()` method. Then, in the *There's more...* section of this recipe, we will plot our graph again using the `axisartist` and `axes_grid1` toolkits.

You'll need to import the required libraries using the following commands:

```
import matplotlib.pyplot as plt
from matplotlib.ticker import MultipleLocator
```

How to do it...

The following are the steps required to plot our twin axes graph:

1. Define the figure and the main axes (`ax1`, a *y* axis on the left) as follows:

    ```
    fig, ax1 = plt.subplots(1,1)
    ```

2. Define the twin axes (`ax2`, a *y* axis on the right, and `ax3`, another *y* axis on the right):

    ```
    ax2 = ax1.twinx()
    ax3 = ax1.twinx()
    ```

3. Position `ax3` so that it does not overlap with `ax2`, the right axis:

    ```
    ax3.spines["right"].set_position(("axes", 1.15))
    ```

4. Prepare the data and plot a product defects bar graph on the main axis, `ax1`:

    ```
    x = [0, 1, 2, 3, 4, 5]
    y = [19, 12, 6, 4, 3, 2]
    b = ax1.bar(x, y, label='Number of Defects')
    ```

5. Prepare data and plot cumulative defects as a percentage, on a line graph on the right axis, `ax2`:

    ```
    y = [41, 67, 80, 89, 96, 100]
    l, = ax2.plot(x, y, color='g', lw=5, label='Cumulative Defects as
    %')
    ```

6. Prepare data and plot a cumulative defects-count line graph on the second right axis, `ax3`:

```
y = [19, 31, 37, 41, 44, 46]
l1, = ax3.plot(x, y, color='m', lw=5, label='Cumulative Defects
               Count')
```

7. Define the major locator with a step size of 2, and apply this to the *y* axis of the main axes, `ax1`:

```
majorLocator = MultipleLocator(2)
ax1.yaxis.set_major_locator(majorLocator)
```

8. Set the *x* and *y* labels and the limits for all axes using the following code:

```
ax1.set(xlabel='Defect Reason Codes', ylabel='Number of Defects')
ax2.set(ylabel='Cumulative Defects as %')
ax3.set_ylim(15,50)
ax3.set_ylabel('Cumulative Defects Count', labelpad=10)
```

9. Set the legend and the title for the main axes as follows:

```
graphs = [b, l, l1]
ax1.legend(graphs, [g.get_label() for g in graphs], loc=5)
ax1.set_title('Product Defects - August 2018')
```

10. Set the color for your labels:

```
ax1.yaxis.label.set_color(b.patches[0].get_facecolor())
ax2.yaxis.label.set_color(l.get_color())
ax3.yaxis.label.set_color(l1.get_color())
```

11. Set the color for both right axes, as shown here:

```
ax2.spines["right"].set_edgecolor(l.get_color())
ax3.spines["right"].set_edgecolor(l1.get_color())
```

12. Set the color for ticks and ticklabels as follows:

```
ax1.tick_params(axis='y', colors=b.patches[0].get_facecolor())
ax2.tick_params(axis='y', colors=l.get_color())
ax3.tick_params(axis='y', colors=l1.get_color())
```

13. Lastly, display the graph on the screen with the following command:

```
plt.show()
```

How it works...

Here is the explanation of the preceding code:

- `ax2 = ax1.twinx()` and `ax3 = ax1.twinx()` create logical axes called `ax2` and `ax3`, which share the *x* axis of the main axes (`ax1`), but have a different *y* axis on the right.
- `ax3.spines["right"].set_position(("axes", 1.15))` moves the second *y* axis to the right by 15% of the main axes' width. If we don't do this, both the `ax2` and `ax3` *y* axes will overlap each other, and display both of their ticks and ticklabels on the same axis.
- `x = [0, 1, 2, 3, 4, 5]` is the list of product defect codes and `y = [19, 12, 6, 4, 3, 2]` is the list of defects by reason codes.
- `b = ax1.bar(x, y, label='Number of Defects')` plots the bar graph of the number of product defects.
- `y1 = [41, 67, 80, 89, 96, 100]` is the list of cumulative defects as a percentage of the total.
- `l, = ax2.plot(x, y1, color='g', lw=5, label='Cumulative Defects as %')` plots this as a line graph.
- `y2 = [19, 31, 37, 41, 44, 46]` is the list of the cumulative defects count.
- `l1, = ax3.plot(x, y2, color='m', lw=5, label='Cumulative Defects Count')` plots this as a line graph.
- `majorLocator = MultipleLocator(2)` defines the locator with a step size of 2, and `ax1.yaxis.set_major_locator(majorLocator)` applies the locator to the *y* axis of the main axis, `ax1`.
- `ax3.set_ylabel('Cumulative Defects Count', labelpad=10)` sets the *y* axis label for the rightmost axis, while `labelpad=10` specifies the gap between the axis and its label, so that label does not overlap the ticklabels of the axis.
- `ax1.legend(graphs, [g.get_label() for g in graphs], loc=5)` plots the legend as follows:
    - `[g.get_label() for g in graphs]` gets the list of labels for each of the graphs as it was set at the time of plotting the graphs.
    - `loc=5` specifies that the legend is to be plotted on the right-hand side of the axes. Please refer to `Chapter 4`, *Developing Visualizations for Publishing Quality*, for more options to place the legend.

- `ax1.yaxis.label.set_color(b.patches[0].get_facecolor())` sets the color for the *y* axis label of the main axes as follows:
    - `b.patches[0].get_facecolor()` gets the `facecolor` value of first bar in the bar plot, and `b.patches[]` is a container of bars saved as patches.
    - With this command, instead of setting the color explicitly, we take the color used for plotting the graph and use it for the *y* axis label. This that the same colors are used throughout.
- `ax2.yaxis.label.set_color(l.get_color())` and `ax3.yaxis.label.set_color(l1.get_color())` gets the color of line plots `l` and `l1`, and applies them to their respective labels.
- `ax2.spines["right"].set_edgecolor(l.get_color())` sets the color for the right axis, used to plot line graph `l`.
- `ax3.spines["right"].set_edgecolor(l1.get_color())` sets the color for the second right axis, used to plot line graph `l1`.
- `ax1.tick_params(axis='y', colors=b.patches[0].get_facecolor())` sets the color for ticks and ticklabels.

Upon execution of the preceding code, you should see the following graph on your screen:

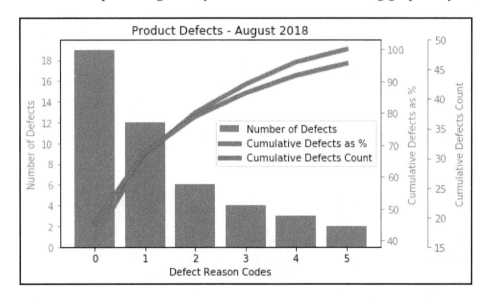

There's more...

We will now plot the same figure using the `axisartist` and `axes_grid1` toolkits. The steps to be followed are the same, so we will not describe each step here, but rather list the entire code in one block. We will explain the key differences between the two methods thereafter.

Here is the full code block for plotting the graph using the `axisartist` and `axes_grid1` toolkits:

```
from mpl_toolkits.axes_grid1 import host_subplot
import mpl_toolkits.axisartist as AA
import matplotlib.pyplot as plt

plt.figure()
ax1 = host_subplot(111, axes_class=AA.Axes)

ax1.axis["top"].toggle(all=False) # switch off ticks and ticklabels for
                                  the top axis
ax2 = ax1.twinx()
ax3 = ax1.twinx()

new_fixed_axis = ax3.get_grid_helper().new_fixed_axis
ax3.axis["right"] = new_fixed_axis(loc="right", axes=ax3, offset=(60,
                                                                  0))

ax2.axis["right"].toggle(all=True)
ax3.axis["right"].toggle(all=True)

ax1.set_xlabel('Defect Reason Codes')
ax1.set_ylabel('Number of Defects')
ax2.set_ylabel('Cumulative Defects as %')
ax3.set_ylabel('Cumulative Defects Count')

x = [0, 1, 2, 3, 4, 5]
y = [19, 12, 6, 4, 3, 2]
y1 = [41, 67, 80, 89, 96, 100]
y2 = [19, 31, 37, 41, 44, 46]

b = ax1.bar(x, y, label='Number of Defects')
l, = ax2.plot(x, y1, lw=5, label='Cumulative Defects as %', color='b')
l1, = ax3.plot(x, y2, lw=5, label='Cumulative Defects Count',
               color='g')

ax3.set_ylim(15, 50)
ax1.legend(loc=5)
ax1.set_title('Product Defects - August 2018')
```

```
ax1.axis["left"].label.set_color(b.patches[0].get_facecolor())
ax2.axis["right"].label.set_color(l.get_color())
ax3.axis["right"].label.set_color(l1.get_color())

ax1.axis["left"].major_ticks.set_color(b.patches[0].get_facecolor())
ax2.axis["right"].major_ticks.set_color(l.get_color())
ax3.axis["right"].major_ticks.set_color(l1.get_color())

ax1.axis["left"].major_ticklabels.set_color(b.patches[0].get_facecolor())
ax2.axis["right"].major_ticklabels.set_color(l.get_color())
ax3.axis["right"].major_ticklabels.set_color(l1.get_color())

# setting the color for axis itself is not working in AA
ax2.spines["right"].set_color(l.get_color())
ax3.spines["right"].set_color(l1.get_color())

ax1.axis[:].major_ticks.set_tick_out(True)
ax2.axis[:].major_ticks.set_tick_out(True)
ax3.axis[:].major_ticks.set_tick_out(True)

plt.show()
```

Here is an explanation of the key differences between the two methods:

- Instead of using `plt.subplots()`, here we are using `ax1 = host_subplot(111, axes_class=AA.Axes)`, which is a helper function of the `axes_grid1` toolkit that takes `axisartist` as an argument. This means that the `ax1` axis gets the properties of both `host_subplot()` and `axisartist`.
- `ax2=ax1.twinx()` automatically maps the right spine of `ax1` for its *y* axis.
- However, for `ax3`, we will have to create another right axis manually using the following commands:
    - `new_fixed_axis = ax3.get_grid_helper().new_fixed_axis`.
    - `ax3.axis["right"] = new_fixed_axis(loc="right", axes=ax3, offset=(60, 0))`.
    - `offset=(60,0)` pushes the axis to the right by 60 points, and 0 points toward the top.
- `ax2.axis["right"].toggle(all=True)` sets as visible the axis label, ticks, and ticklabels for right spine of `ax1`.
- `ax3.axis["right"].toggle(all=True)` sets as visible the axis label, ticks, and ticklabels for the newly created right axis.

- The way we set various attributes for labels, ticks, and ticklabels is same as what we learned in `Chapter 12`, *Using the axisartist Toolkit*.

- However, some of the attributes don't work as expected with the original axes class, as `axisartist` does not inherit all the properties of the original axes class.

- When you open this plot with an interactive backend and zoom in on some part of the graph, only the main *y* axis limits change, whereas the data of the other two *y* axes on the right (parasite axes) remain the same as their initial settings. This is not the case with the figure plotted previously, without using `axes_grid1` and `axisartist`, where all *y* axis limits change to reflect the current portion of the graph.

Upon executing the preceding code block, you should see the following graph:

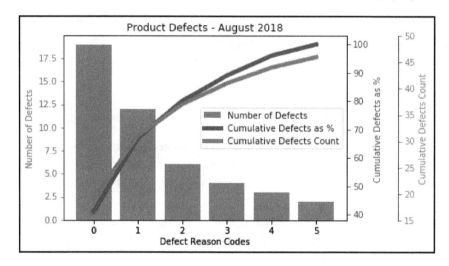

Using AxesDivider to plot a scatter plot and associated histograms

In this recipe, we will learn how to use the AxesDivider class of `axes_grdi1` to draw a bivariate plot on the main axes, and two univariate plots, on any two sides of the main axes. This helps in visualizing the relationship between two variables, and the distribution of the same two variables individually all in one figure (though three different axes/plots).

Technically, variables plotted on the main axes and univariate plots on the two sides of the main axes can be different. And you can choose any two sides out of the four sides of the main axes for univariate plots. However, the usual practice is to plot on the top and the right side of the main axes.

In this recipe, we will plot a scatter graph on the main axes with two variables, and at the top and right-hand side of the main axes, we will plot a histogram for each of the two variables used for the scatter graph.

Getting ready

Let's import the required libraries. It should be noted that we are not importing `AxesDiveder` directly; rather, we're using a helper function of this class, `make_axes_locatable`. You'll need to import the libraries using the following commands:

```
import numpy as np
import matplotlib.pyplot as plt
from mpl_toolkits.axes_grid1 import make_axes_locatable
import pandas as pd
```

How to do it...

The following are the steps involved in plotting our graph:

1. Load the `Iris` dataset, which we have already used earlier, with the following commands:

```
iris = pd.read_csv('iris_dataset.csv', delimiter=',')
iris['species'] = iris['species'].map({"setosa" : 0, "versicolor" :
                                        1, "virginica" : 2})
x, y = iris['sepal_length'], iris['sepal_width']
```

2. Define the figure and the main axes as follows:

```
fig, axmain = plt.subplots(figsize=(8, 6))
```

3. Plot a scatter graph on the main axes using an aspect ratio of 1:

```
axmain.scatter(x, y)
axmain.set_aspect(1.)
```

4. Define the axes divider so that we have one axis on top of the main axes, and another axis to the right of the main axes, as follows:

```
divider = make_axes_locatable(axmain)
axtop = divider.append_axes("top", size=1.5, pad="15%",
                            sharex=axmain)
axright = divider.append_axes("right", "100%", 0.1, sharey=axmain)
```

5. Make ticklabels invisible for the *x* axis of the top axes, and the *y* axis of the right axes, so that they don't overlap with the labels of the main axes:

```
axtop.xaxis.set_tick_params(labelbottom=False)
axright.yaxis.set_tick_params(labelleft=False)
```

6. Plot histograms on the top and right axes:

```
axtop.hist(x, bins=15)
axright.hist(y, bins=10, orientation='horizontal')
```

7. Set `yticks` for the top axes and `xticks` for the right axes:

```
axtop.set_yticks([0, 5, 10, 15, 20])
axright.set_xticks([0, 10, 20, 30, 40])
```

8. Set labels and titles for all axes as follows:

```
axmain.set(xlabel='sepal length', ylabel='sepal width', title='iris
           scatter plot')
axtop.set_title('sepal length', size=10)
axright.set_title('sepal width', size=10)
```

9. Finally, display the graph on the screen with the following command:

```
plt.show()
```

How it works...

Here is the explanation of the preceding code:

- The first three steps are familiar to you already from previous examples.
- `divider = make_axes_locatable(axmain)` defines the axes divider. It essentially locates the boundaries of the given axes.

- `axtop = divider.append_axes("top", size=1.5, pad="15%", sharex=axmain)` defines a new axis on top of the main axes, as follows:
  - `"top"` specifies that the new axis to be plotted on top of the current axes.
  - `size=1.5` specifies that the height of this new axis is 1.5 inches, with a width the same as the main access width.
  - `pad=15%` specifies that the gap between the main axes and this new axis on top is 15% of the height of main axes.
  - `sharex=axmain` specifies that this new axis should share the *x* axis properties, such as the axis label, ticks, and ticklabels, with those of main axes

- `axright = divider.append_axes("right", "100%", 0.1, sharey=axmain)` defines a new axis on the right-hand side of the main axes, as follows:
  - `"right"` specifies that the new axis should be plotted on the right-hand side of the main axes.
  - `100%` specifies that the width of the new axes is the same as the width of the main axes. The height of the new axis is also the same as that of the main axes, since they both share the *y* axis.
  - `0.1` is the padding, in points, between the main axes and this new axis.
  - `sharey=axmain` specifies that this new axis should share the *y* axis properties, such as axis label, ticks, and ticklabels, with that of the main axes.

- `axtop.xaxis.set_tick_params(labelbottom=False)` makes the *x* axis label invisible for the top axis.

- `axright.yaxis.set_tick_params(labelleft=False)` makes the *y* axis label invisible for the right axis.

- `axtop.hist(x, bins=15)` plots a histogram on the top axis with 15 bins.

- `axright.hist(y, bins=10, orientation='horizontal')` plots the histogram on the right axis with 10 bins, using horizontal bars instead of the default vertical bars.

- The remaining statements set the ticks, labels, and titles for all three axes.

Upon running the code, you should see the following graph on your screen:

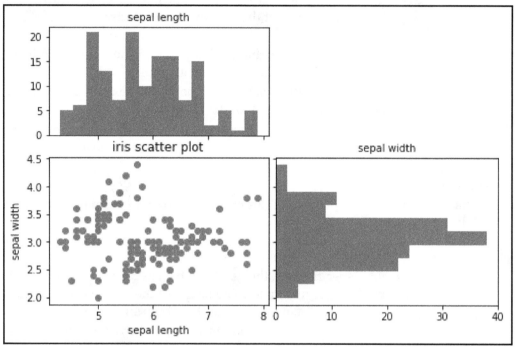

Using AxesDivider to plot a colorbar

In this recipe, we will learn how to use AxesDivider to plot the colorbar for an image, ensuring that it is properly aligned with the image. We have used `pyplot.colorbar()` many times, but at times, colorbar goes beyond the image boundaries. With AxesDivider and `ImageGrid`, we will not see this problem, as shall be shown in this recipe.

We will plot the image on three axes—one using a regular `pyplot.colorbar()` without AxesDivider; the second using AxesDivider and a vertical colorbar on the right-hand side; and the third again using AxesDivider, but this time with a horizontal colorbar on top of the image.

Getting ready

You'll need to import the required libraries using the following commands:

```
import matplotlib.pyplot as plt
from matplotlib.pyplot import imshow
from mpl_toolkits.axes_grid1 import make_axes_locatable
import numpy as np
import pandas as pd
```

How to do it...

The following are the steps involved in plotting the image with a colorbar:

1. Load the dataset on `winequality.csv`, as follows:

```
wine_quality = pd.read_csv('winequality.csv', delimiter=';')
corr_wine = wine_quality.corr()
```

2. Define the figure with the following command:

```
fig = plt.figure(1, (16., 6.))
```

3. Define the first subplot, plot the image and the colorbar, and set the *x* and *y* ticks using this code:

```
plt.subplot(131)
plt.imshow(corr_wine, cmap='plasma')
plt.colorbar()
plt.xticks(range(len(corr_wine)),corr_wine.columns, rotation=75)
plt.yticks(range(len(corr_wine)),corr_wine.columns)
```

4. Using the following code, define the second subplot, plot the image, define AxesDivider, plot the colorbar on the right, and set the *x* and *y* ticks:

```
ax2 = plt.subplot(132)
im1 = ax2.imshow(corr_wine, cmap='Blues')
ax2_divider = make_axes_locatable(ax2)
cax1 = ax2_divider.append_axes("right", size="7%", pad=0.03)
plt.colorbar(im1, cax=cax1)
ax2.set_xticks(range(len(corr_wine)))
ax2.set_xticklabels(corr_wine.columns, rotation=75)
ax2.set(yticks=range(len(corr_wine)),
yticklabels=corr_wine.columns)
```

5. Define the third subplot, plot the image, define AxesDivider, plot the horizontal colorbar on top, and set the *x* and *y* ticks as follows:

```
ax3 = plt.subplot(133)
im2 = ax3.imshow(corr_wine)
ax3_divider = make_axes_locatable(ax3)
cax2 = ax3_divider.append_axes("top", size="7%", pad="2%")
cb2 = plt.colorbar(im2, cax=cax2, orientation="horizontal")
cax2.xaxis.set_ticks_position("top")
ax3.set_xticks(range(len(corr_wine)))
ax3.set_xticklabels(corr_wine.columns, rotation=75)
ax3.set(yticks=range(len(corr_wine)),
yticklabels=corr_wine.columns)
```

6. Adjust the space between the plots using this command:

```
plt.tight_layout(w_pad=-1)
```

7. Lastly, display the graph on the screen with this command:

```
plt.show()
```

How it works...

Here is an explanation of the preceding code:

- `fig = plt.figure(1, (16., 6.))` defines figure 1 with a size of 16 x 6 inches.
- `plt.subplot(131)` defines the first axes on a 1 x 3 grid.
- `plt.imshow(corr_wine, cmap='plasma')` plots a correlation map using the `'plasma'` colormap.
- `plt.colorbar()` plots the colorbar for the image on its right side.
- `plt.xticks(range(len(corr_wine)),corr_wine.columns, rotation=75)` plots *x* axis ticks and ticklabels with attribute names on an inclination of 75 degrees.
- `plt.yticks(range(len(corr_wine)),corr_wine.columns)` plots *y* axis ticks and ticklabels without any rotation.
- `ax2 = plt.subplot(132)` defines second axes on a grid of 1 x 3.

- `im1 = ax2.imshow(corr_wine, cmap='Blues')` plots a correlation map using the `'Blues'` colormap.
- `ax2_divider = make_axes_locatable(ax2)` defines the AxesDivider function for the second axis.
- `cax1 = ax2_divider.append_axes("right", size="7%", pad=0.03)` defines a new axis for the colorbar using AxesDivider.
- `"right"` specifies that new axes are to be placed on the right-hand side of `ax2`.
- `size="7"` specifies that the width of new axes should be 7% of the width of `ax2`.
- `pad=0.03` specifies that the gap between the `ax2` axes and colorbar axes should be 3% of the width of `ax2`.
- `plt.colorbar(im1, cax=cax1)` plots the colorbar on the right-hand side of `ax2`, with the given image and colorbar axes.
- `ax2.set_xticks(range(len(corr_wine)))` sets the x axis ticks to as many as the number of attributes we have in the input data.
- `ax2.set_xticklabels(corr_wine.columns, rotation=75)` sets the ticklabels with attribute names and a `75` degree inclination.
- `ax2.set(yticks=range(len(corr_wine)), yticklabels=corr_wine.columns)` sets the y axis ticks and ticklabels without any rotation.
- `ax3 = plt.subplot(133)` defines the third axis on a grid of 1 x 3.
- The remaining steps are exactly the same as the second plot covered previously, except that the colorbar is plotted on top of the image with a horizontal orientation, rather than the default vertical orientation.
- `plt.tight_layout(w_pad=-1)` adjusts the space in between the plots so that there are no overlaps. A negative `w_pad` value is used to reduce the default gap used by `tight_layout()`.

Upon running the preceding code, you should see the following graph on your screen. It should be noted that in the first plot, the colorbar extends beyond the height of the image, whereas in the second and third plots, it exactly matches with the height or width of the image—this is the advantage of using AxesDivider:

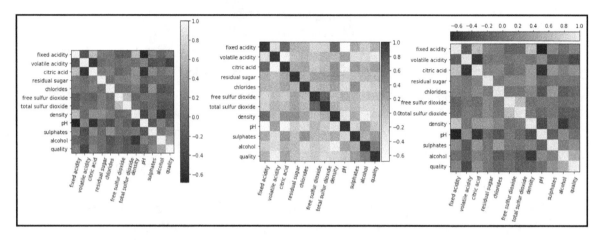

Using ImageGrid to plot images with a colorbar in a grid

In Chapters 3, *Plotting Multiple Graphs, Subplots and Figures* and Chapter 6, *Plotting with Advanced Features*, we had learned how to draw multiple plots on a grid with various grid options. When you try to plot images with a colorbar on a grid with those options, the colorbar alignment may not be the way we want it. The ImageGrid helper function of the axes_grid1 toolkit enables the plotting of images with a colorbar in a grid with proper alignment. We will learn how to use these functions in this recipe.

We will plot the same correlation map in three different plots in a row, but use different features of the grid to demonstrate most, if not all, of the available features.

Getting ready

You'll need to import the required libraries using the following commands:

```
import matplotlib.pyplot as plt
from matplotlib.pyplot import imread, imshow
from mpl_toolkits.axes_grid1 import ImageGrid
import pandas as pd
```

How to do it...

The following are the steps involved in plotting the desired figure:

1. Load data and create a list of four images with the same correlation matrix, as follows:

```
wine_quality = pd.read_csv('winequality.csv', delimiter=';')
corr_wine = wine_quality.corr()

images = []
images.append(corr_wine)
images.append(corr_wine)
images.append(corr_wine)
images.append(corr_wine)
```

2. Define the figure with a size of 12 x 8 inches:

```
fig = plt.figure(1, (12, 8.))
```

3. Define a 2 x 2 grid to be plotted on the first axes:

```
grid1 = ImageGrid(fig, 131, nrows_ncols=(2, 2), axes_pad=0.0,
                  label_mode="1")
```

4. Set up *x* and *y* ticks and ticklabels as follows:

```
grid1.axes_llc.set_xticks(range(len(corr_wine)))
grid1.axes_llc.set_xticklabels(corr_wine.columns, rotation=90)
grid1.axes_llc.set(yticks=range(len(corr_wine)),
                   yticklabels=corr_wine.columns)
```

5. Plot four images of the same correlation matrix, without a colorbar, on the 2 x 2 grid defined earlier:

```
for i in range(4):
    gd = grid1[i].imshow(images[i], cmap='coolwarm')
```

6. Define another 2 x 2 grid to be plotted on the second axes:

```
grid2 = ImageGrid(fig, 132, nrows_ncols=(2, 2), axes_pad=0.1,
label_mode="L", cbar_location="top",
                  cbar_mode="single")
```

7. Plot four images of the same correlation matrix on the 2 x 2 grid defined earlier:

```
for i in range(4):
    im = grid2[i].imshow(images[i])
grid2.cbar_axes[0].colorbar(im)
```

8. Define a third 2 x 2 grid to be plotted on the third axes:

```
grid3 = ImageGrid(fig, 133, nrows_ncols=(2, 2), axes_pad=(0.5,
0.3),
                      abel_mode="0",
                      cbar_location="right", cbar_mode="each",
                      cbar_size="10%", cbar_pad="3%")
```

9. Plot four images of the same correlation matrix on the 2 x 2 grid defined earlier:

```
limits = ((-1, 1), (-1, 0), (0, 1.), (-0.5, 0.5))
for i in range(4):
    im = grid3[i].imshow(images[i], interpolation="nearest",
                         vmin=limits[i][0], vmax=limits[i][1])
    grid3.cbar_axes[i].colorbar(im)
    grid3.cbar_axes[i].set_yticks((limits[i][0], limits[i][1]))
```

10. Lastly, display the figure on the screen with this command:

```
plt.show()
```

How it works...

Here is an explanation of the preceding code:

- `images = []` initializes the images list with blank.
- `images.append(corr_wine)` appends the `corr_wine` correlation matrix to the list of images. We repeat this four times to create the list of four images to be plotted on the 2 x 2 grid.

- `grid1 = ImageGrid(fig, 131, nrows_ncols=(2, 2), axes_pad=0.0, label_mode="1")` defines the image grid as follows:
    - `fig` specifies the figure on which the grid is to be plotted.
    - `131` specifies that it is a 1 x 3 grid, and this one is the first grid.
    - `nrows_ncols=(2,2)` specifies the grid format as 2 x 2.
    - `axes_pad=0.0` specifies that the space between the images is zero.
    - `label_mode="1"` specifies that ticklabels and axis labels should be printed only for the bottom left corner image of the grid.
- `grid1.axes_llc.set_xticks(range(len(corr_wine)))` sets the tick marks on the *x* axis with as many as the number of variables in the correlation matrix.
- `grid1.axes_llc.set_xticklabels(corr_wine.columns, rotation=90)` prints ticklabels with variable names on the *x* axis with a 90 degree inclination.
- `grid1.axes_llc.set(yticks=range(len(corr_wine)), yticklabels=corr_wine.columns)` prints ticks and ticklabels for the *y* axis with the same variable names, without any rotation.
- `for i in range(4):` is the `for` loop to plot images one by one in the grid of four:
    - `gd = grid1[i].imshow(images[i], cmap='coolwarm')` plots the image using the `coolwarm` colormap.
- `grid2 = ImageGrid()` defines the second image grid with the following arguments:
    - `fig` specifies the figure on which this grid is to be plotted.
    - `132` specifies that it is a second grid within another 1 x 3 grid.
    - `nrows_ncols=(2,2)` specifies the grid format as 2 x 2.
    - `axes_pad=0.1` specifies the gap between the images as 0.1 inches.
    - `label_mode="L"` specifies that are labels to be plotted for the left and bottom images, forming an `"L"` shape.
    - `cbar_location="top"` specifies the colorbar should be plotted on top of the image.
    - `cbar_mode="single"` specifies that only one colorbar should be plotted on top of the grid.
- `for i in range(4):` is the `for` loop to plot images one by one on the grid of four:
    - `im = grid2[i].imshow(images[i], cmap='ocean')` plots the image using the `'ocean'` colormap.
- `grid2.cbar_axes[0].colorbar(im)` prints the colorbar.

- `grid3 = ImageGrid()` defines the third image grid with the following arguments:
  - `fig` specifies the figure on which this grid is to be plotted.
  - `133` specifies that it is a third grid within another 1 x 3 grid.
  - `nrows_ncols=(2,2)` specifies the grid format as 2 x 2.
  - `axes_pad=(0.5,0.3)` specifies the gap between the images as `0.5` inches horizontally, and `0.3` vertically.
  - `label_mode="0"` specifies that labels are to be plotted for all the images.
  - `cbar_location="right"` specifies that the colorbar should be plotted on the right-hand side of the image.
  - `cbar_mode="each"` specifies that the colorbar should be plotted on the right-hand side of every image in the grid.
  - `cbar_size="10%"` specifies that the colorbar width should be `10%` of the image axes' width.
  - `cbar_pad="3%"` specifies that the space between colorbar and the image is 3% of the image axes' width.
  - `limits = ((-1, 1), (-1, 0), (0, 1.), (-0.5, 0.5))` specifies the lower and upper limits to be applied to the colorbar of each of the four images, instead of plotting full range of -1 to +1.
- `for i in range(4):` is the for loop to plot images one by one in the grid of four:
  - `im = grid3[i].imshow(images[i], interpolation="nearest", vmin=limits[i][0], vmax=limits[i][1], cmap='ocean')` plots the image using the `'ocean'` colormap.
  - `interpolation="nearest"` specifies that cells with values outside the specified limits will be filled with nearest cell value within those limits.
  - `vmin=limits[i][0]` specifies the lower limit for the given `i` image (the first entry of the tuple).
  - `vmax=limits[i][1]` specifies the upper limit for the given `i` image (the second entry of the tuple).
  - `grid3.cbar_axes[i].colorbar(im)` prints the colorbar.
  - `grid3.cbar_axes[i].set_yticks((limits[i][0], limits[i][1]))` sets ticks and ticklabels for the y axis with the given limits.

Upon executing the preceding code, you should see the following graph on your screen:

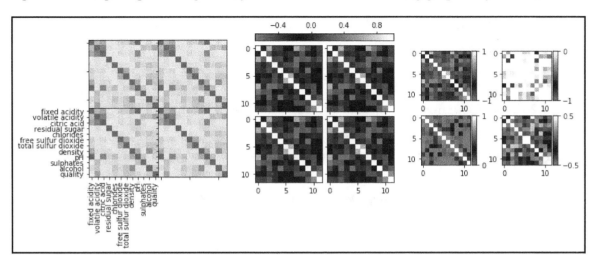

Using inset_locator to zoom in on an image

In Chapter 6, *Plotting with Advanced Features*, we learned how to plot inset axes within the main axes, using the object-oriented interface of Matplotlib. In this recipe and the next one, we will learn how to use the `inset_locator` helper functions of the `axes_grid1` toolkit to create inset axes and plot images and other graphs.

In this recipe, we will learn how to zoom in on a portion of an image and display it in the inset axes of the same main axes.

We will plot the image on two axes and zoom in on different portions of the image in each of the plots.

Getting ready

You'll need to import the required libraries using the following commands:

```
import matplotlib.pyplot as plt
import numpy as np
import pandas as pd

from mpl_toolkits.axes_grid1.inset_locator import zoomed_inset_axes
from mpl_toolkits.axes_grid1.inset_locator import mark_inset
```

How to do it...

Here are the steps necessary to plot our graphs:

1. Define the figure and the two axes as follows:

```
fig, (ax1, ax2) = plt.subplots(1, 2, figsize=[8, 4])
```

2. Load the `winequality` data and compute the correlation matrix using these commands:

```
wine_quality = pd.read_csv('winequality.csv', delimiter=';')
corr_wine = wine_quality.corr()
```

3. Create an extended image with zeros, and insert the correlation matrix into it:

```
extended_image = np.zeros([100, 100], dtype="d")
ny, nx = corr_wine.shape
extended_image[25:25 + ny, 25:25 + nx] = corr_wine
```

4. Plot the extended image with the given extent, that is, the x and y limits, as follows:

```
extent = [-2, 2, -3, 1]
ax1.imshow(extended_image, extent=extent, interpolation="nearest",
          origin="lower")
```

5. Define the inset axes as shown here:

```
axins1 = zoomed_inset_axes(ax1, 3, loc=1)
```

6. Plot the extended image on the inset axes:

```
axins1.imshow(extended_image, extent=extent,
             interpolation="nearest", origin="lower")
```

7. Set the inset axes' data limits for the x and y axes, specifying the portion of the correlation matrix to be zoomed in on:

```
axins1.set_xlim(-1.0, -0.5)
axins1.set_ylim(-2.0, -1.5)
```

8. Set the ticks with these given values:

```
axins1.xaxis.get_major_locator().set_params(nbins=8)
axins1.yaxis.get_major_locator().set_params(nbins=8)
```

9. Set the ticklabels for the inset axes as invisible on both the *x* and *y* axes:

```
plt.xticks(visible=False)
plt.yticks(visible=False)
```

10. Mark a bounding box around the portion chosen for zooming, and connect it with zoomed inset axes using lines:

```
mark_inset(ax1, axins1, loc1=2, loc2=4, fc="none", ec="b")
```

11. Repeat *step 4* to *step 8* for the second axes, which will display a more zoomed-in, smaller portion of the image:

```
ax2.imshow(extended_image, extent=extent, interpolation="nearest",
           origin="lower")

axins2 = zoomed_inset_axes(ax2, 3, loc=1) # zoom = 3
axins2.imshow(extended_image, extent=extent,
              interpolation="nearest", origin="lower")

axins2.set_xlim(-1.0, -0.75)
axins2.set_ylim(-2.0, -1.75)

axins2.yaxis.get_major_locator().set_params(nbins=8)
axins2.xaxis.get_major_locator().set_params(nbins=8)

plt.xticks(visible=False)
plt.yticks(visible=False)

mark_inset(ax2, axins2, loc1=2, loc2=4, fc="none", ec="m")
```

12. Lastly, display the plot on the screen using this command:

```
plt.show()
```

How it works...

Here is the explanation for the preceding code:

- `extended_image = np.zeros([100, 100], dtype="d")` creates an 100 x 100 NumPy array filled with zeros, and specifies the data type as a double precision floating point.
- `nx, ny = corr_wine.shape` gets the shape of the correlation matrix into `nx` and `ny`.

- `extended_image[25:25 + nx, 25:25 + ny] = corr_wine` embeds the correlation matrix within a 100 x 100 zero matrix at the (25, 25) position, replacing zeros with values of `corr_wine`.
- `extent = [-2, 2, -3, 1]` specifies the data limits on the x (-2, 3) and *y* (-3, 1) coordinates for the main axes. Please refer to the recipe in `Chapter 6`, *Plotting with Advanced Features, Origin and Extent*, for more details.
- `ax1.imshow(extended_image, extent=extent, interpolation="nearest", origin="lower")` plots the extended image on the main `ax1` axis.
- `axins1 = zoomed_inset_axes(ax1, 3, loc=1)` defines the inset axes as follows:
  - `ax1` is the axes on which the inset axes to be created.
  - 3 specifies that the inset axes data scale is three times that of the main axes, so one unit on the main axes is zoomed to three units on the inset axes for both the *x* and *y* axes.
  - `loc=1` specifies that the inset axes should be placed at the top-right corner of the main axes.
- `axins1.imshow(extended_image, extent=extent, interpolation="nearest", origin="lower")` plots the same extended image on the inset axes, with the same arguments that we used for the main axes.
- `axins1.set_xlim(-1.0, -0.5)` and `axins1.set_ylim(-2.0, -1.5)` specify the portion of the image on the main axes to be zoomed in on.
- `axins1.xaxis.get_major_locator().set_params(nbins=8)` and `axins1.yaxis.get_major_locator().set_params(nbins=8)` define the number of ticks on the *x* and *y* axes of the inset axes.
- `plt.xticks(visible=False)` and `plt.yticks(visible=False)` make ticklabels invisible for both the *x* and *y* axes of the inset axes.
- `mark_inset(ax1, axins1, loc1=2, loc2=4, fc="none", ec="b")` draws boundaries around the image being zoomed, and the zoomed image itself, and then connects them to lines, as follows:
  - `ax1` refers to the main axes.
  - `axins1` refers to the inset axes.
  - `loc1` and `loc2` specify which corners of the images are to be connected; 2 refers to the top-left corner, and 4 is the bottom-right corner.

- fc="none" specifies not to fill the area in between the lines connecting both the images.
- ec="b" specifies that lines connecting the images should be colored blue.
  - Our second plot is exactly the same as the first one, except that the portion of the image being zoomed in on is smaller than the first one.
  - axins2.set_xlim(-1.0, -0.75) and axins2.set_ylim(-2.0, -1.75) specify the area of the main image to be zoomed in on for the second plot.

Upon executing the preceding code, you should see the following graph on your screen:

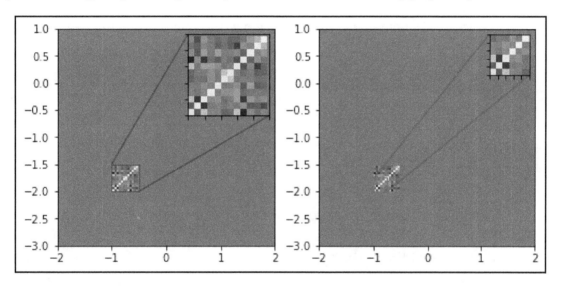

Using inset_locator to plot inset axes

In this recipe, we will learn to plot a scatter graph on the main axes and create a histogram of each of the two variables on the two inset axes. We will use the familiar Iris dataset to do this.

Getting ready

You'll need to import the required libraries using the following commands:

```
import matplotlib.pyplot as plt
import numpy as np
import pandas as pd
from mpl_toolkits.axes_grid1.inset_locator import inset_axes
```

How to do it...

Here is the step-by-step approach to plotting our graph:

1. Load the `Iris` dataset and map the *x* and *y* coordinates using the `sepal_length` and `sepal_width` variables:

```
iris = pd.read_csv('iris_dataset.csv', delimiter=',')
iris['species'] = iris['species'].map({"setosa" : 0, "versicolor" :
                        1, "virginica" : 2})
x, y = iris['sepal_length'], iris['sepal_width']
```

2. Define the figure and the main axes as follows:

```
plt.figure(1, (8., 6.))
ax = plt.subplot(111)
```

3. Plot the scatter graph with a colorbar on the right-hand side:

```
im = ax.scatter(x, y, c=iris.petal_length, s=100*iris.petal_width,
cmap='viridis', alpha=0.7)
plt.colorbar(im)
```

4. Define the inset axes 1 properties as follows:

```
inset_ax1 = inset_axes(ax, width="40%", height=1., loc=4)
```

5. Plot a `sepal_length` histogram on inset axes 1:

```
inset_ax1.hist(iris.sepal_length)
```

6. Set a title and labels for the inset axes as follows:

```
inset_ax1.set_title('sepal length', size=10, pad=20)
inset_ax1.axis["bottom"].toggle(all=False)
inset_ax1.axis["top"].toggle(all=True)
inset_ax1.xaxis.get_major_locator().set_params(nbins=5)
inset_ax1.yaxis.get_major_locator().set_params(nbins=10)
```

7. Define the inset axes 2 properties as follows:

```
inset_ax2 = inset_axes(ax, width=1.5, height="25%", loc=2)
```

8. Plot a `sepal_width` histogram on inset axes 2:

```
inset_ax2.hist(iris.sepal_width)
```

9. Set the title and labels for the inset axes as follows:

```
inset_ax2.set_title('sepal width', size=10)
inset_ax2.axis["left"].toggle(all=False)
inset_ax2.axis["right"].toggle(all=True)
inset_ax2.xaxis.get_major_locator().set_params(nbins=6)
inset_ax2.yaxis.get_major_locator().set_params(nbins=10)
```

10. Set the title and labels for the main axes as shown here:

```
ax.set(xlabel='sepal length', ylabel='sepal width')
ax.set_title('iris plot', size=20, color='g')
```

11. Lastly, display the plot on the screen using this command:

```
plt.show()
```

How it works...

Here is the explanation of the preceding code:

- `im = ax.scatter(x, y, c=iris.petal_length, s=100*iris.petal_width, cmap='viridis', alpha=0.7)` plots the scatter graph on the main axes, as follows:
  - x and y are the `sepal_length` and `sepal_width` variables to be plotted.

- `c=iris.petal_length` specifies that the color of points should be according to their `petal_length` value.
- `s=100*iris.petal_width` specifies that the size of the points on the scatter graph should be according to their `petal_width` value, multiplied by `100`.
- `cmap='viridis'` specifies the colormap to be used.
- `alpha=0.7` specifies the transparency level of the points on the plot.
- `plt.colorbar(im)` plots the colorbar on the right-hand side of the main axes.
- `inset_ax1 = inset_axes(ax, width="40%", height=1., loc=4)` defines the inset axes 1 properties as follows:
    - `ax` is the main axes on which the inset axes is to be placed.
    - `width="40%"` specifies that the width of the inset axes should be `40%` of that of the main axes.
    - `height=1.` specifies that the height of the inset axes should be one inch.
    - `loc=4` specifies that the inset axes should be placed at the bottom-right corner of the main axes.
- `inset_ax1.hist(iris.sepal_length)` plots the histogram of the `sepal_length` variable.
- `inset_ax1.set_title('sepal legth', size=10, pad=20)` prints the title for the inset axes with a size of `10` points, and locates it `20` points above the top axis, so that the ticklabels and the title don't overlap.
- `inset_ax1.axis["bottom"].toggle(all=False)` sets as invisible the axis label, ticks, and ticklabels for the bottom axis.
- `inset_ax1.axis["top"].toggle(all=True)` sets as visible the axis label, ticks, and ticklabels for the top axis.
- `inset_ax1.xaxis.get_major_locator().set_params(nbins=5)` specifies the number of ticks on the *x* axis.

- `inset_ax1.yaxis.get_major_locator().set_params(nbins=10)` specifies the number of ticks on the *y* axis.
- `inset_ax2 = inset_axes(ax, width=1.5, height="25%", loc=2)` defines the second inset axes as follows:
    - `width=1.5` specifies the width of the inset axes as `1.5` inches.
    - `height="25%"` specifies that the height of the inset axes is `25%` of the height of the main axes.
    - `loc=2` specifies that inset axes should be placed at the top-left corner of the main axes.
- `ax.set(xlabel='sepal length', ylabel='sepal width')` sets the *x* and the *y* axis labels for the main axes.
- `ax.set_title('iris plot', size=20, color='g')` sets the title for the figure with a size of `20` points and a green color.

Upon execution of the preceding code, you should see the following graph on your screen:

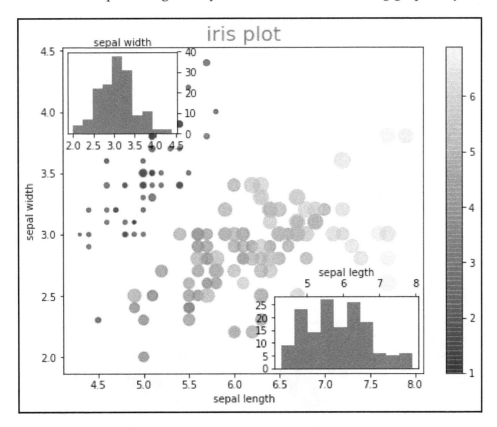

14
Plotting Geographical Maps Using Cartopy Toolkit

In this chapter, we will cover the following recipes:

- Plotting basic map features
- Plotting projections
- Using grid lines and labels
- Plotting locations on the map
- Plotting country maps with political boundaries
- Plotting country maps using GeoPandas and cartopy
- Plotting populated places of the world
- Plotting the top five and bottom five populated countries
- Plotting temperatures across the globe
- Plotting time zones
- Plotting an animated map

Introduction

Cartopy is a third-party toolkit for plotting geographical maps on top of Matplotlib. Cartopy is expected to replace *basemap* by 2020. Cartopy has a wide variety of features that allow it to cater to many different user communities. Here we will try to cover most of the features typically used in business enterprises.

Geographical maps are plotted in longitude and latitude, both measured in degrees. Longitude is plotted on x axis, and varies from 180 degrees to the west (-180) to 180 degrees to the east (180). Latitude is plotted on the y axis, and varies from 90 degrees to the south (-90) to 90 degrees to the north (90). Locations on the map are identified with their longitude and latitude values.

Plotting basic map features

In this recipe, we will learn the basic features provided by cartopy for plotting the map. This recipe will cover features such as borders of countries, coastal area borders with land, land areas, oceans, rivers, and lakes. It will also cover how to provide a background image for better visualizations.

Getting ready

You'll need to import the required libraries using the following commands:

```
import matplotlib.pyplot as plt
import cartopy.crs as ccrs
import cartopy.feature as cfeature
```

How to do it...

Here are the steps involved in plotting a basic map:

1. Define the figure and axes as follows:

```
fig = plt.figure(figsize=(12,8))
ax = fig.add_subplot(1, 1, 1, projection=ccrs.PlateCarree())
```

2. Set the extent and background image with these commands:

```
ax.set_global()
ax.stock_img()
```

3. Add desired features to be plotted in the map as follows:

```
ax.add_feature(cfeature.LAND, color='wheat')
ax.add_feature(cfeature.OCEAN, color='skyblue')
ax.add_feature(cfeature.COASTLINE, linestyle='-',lw=3)
ax.add_feature(cfeature.BORDERS, linestyle=':')
ax.add_feature(cfeature.LAKES, alpha=0.5, color='y')
ax.add_feature(cfeature.RIVERS, color='blue')
ax.tissot(facecolor='orange', alpha=0.4) # Tissot's indicatrix in
cartography
```

4. Set the title and labels as shown here:

```
ax.set_title('Cartopy Map Features - Demo', size=20, weight='bold',
color='g')

ax.text(0.5, -0.06, 'Longitude', va='bottom', ha='center', size=15,
color='r',
        rotation='horizontal', rotation_mode='anchor',
transform=ax.transAxes)
ax.text(-0.02, 0.55, 'Latitude', va='bottom', ha='center', size=15,
color='b',
        rotation='vertical', rotation_mode='anchor',
transform=ax.transAxes)
```

5. Lastly, display the map on the screen with this command:

```
plt.show()
```

How it works...

Here is the explanation for the preceding code:

- `import cartopy.crs as ccrs` imports the package responsible for setting up the reference coordinate system.
- `import cartopy.feature as cfeature` imports the package used for plotting various features, such as land, oceans, rivers, and lakes.
- `ax = fig.add_subplot(1, 1, 1, projection=ccrs.PlateCarree())` defines the axes on which the map is to be plotted, as follows:
    - `(1,1,1)` specifies that it is the first axes in a 1 x 1 grid, which essentially means that it is the only plot in the overall figure.
    - `projection=ccrs.PlateCarree()` specifies the coordinate reference system to be used for plotting the map. Many such projections (reference coordinate systems) are provided by cartopy. We will see many of them in the next recipe.
    - The projection only gives the outline for the map, so depending on what we want to plot, we can add various predefined features, and then plot the data that is of interest to us.

- `ax.set_global()` specifies that the limits for the coordinate system are formed by the entire globe, which happens to be a default setting. We can set up smaller limits to plot specific areas of interest by overriding this global setting. We will learn how to do this in subsequent recipes.
- `ax.stock_img()` plots a default image on the background that gives better visualization. It can be overwritten with our own image as well.
- `ax.add_feature(cfeature.LAND, color='wheat')` plots the areas tagged as land with the `wheat` color setting.
- `ax.add_feature(cfeature.OCEAN, color='skyblue')` plots oceans with the `skyblue` color setting.
- `ax.add_feature(cfeature.COASTLINE, linestyle='-',lw=3)` plots lines separating land and water along the coastal areas, with a line width of 3 points and a line style of dashes.
- `ax.add_feature(cfeature.BORDERS, linestyle=':')` plots country borders with a line style of colons.
- `ax.add_feature(cfeature.LAKES, alpha=0.5, color='y')` plots lakes with the `yellow` color setting.
- `ax.add_feature(cfeature.RIVERS, color='blue')` plots rivers with the color `blue`.
- `ax.tissot(facecolor='orange', alpha=0.4)` plots Tissot's indicatrix.
- `ax.set_title('Cartopy Map Features - Demo', size=20, weight='bold', color='g')` prints the title with various text-related attributes.
- `ax.text()` is used to print the *x* and *y* labels. The usual `ax.set_xlabel` and `ax.set_ylabel` commands don't work here, since axis controls are given to the `ax.gridlines()` function, which also does not have predefined methods for plotting the *x* and *y* axis labels.

Upon running the preceding code, you should see the following map on your screen:

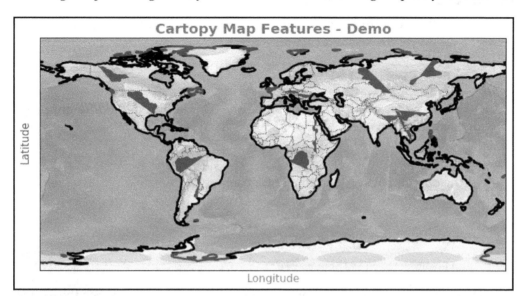

Plotting projections

As mentioned in the previous recipe, a projection is a coordinate reference system in which a map is plotted. Cartopy provides many different projections, and in this recipe, we will plot nine such projections with default arguments to demonstrate how they look. A full list of available projections can be found at `https://scitools.org.uk/cartopy/docs/latest/crs/projections.html`.

Getting ready

You'll need to import the required libraries using the following commands:

```
import cartopy.crs as ccrs
import matplotlib.pyplot as plt
```

How to do it...

The following are the steps involved in plotting our nine different projections:

1. Define the figure:

```
fig = plt.figure(figsize=(12,9))
```

2. Define axes in a 3 x 3 grid as subplots, one by one, and use a different projection for each, as shown here:

```
ax1 = fig.add_subplot(331, projection=ccrs.PlateCarree())
```

3. Set the default background image for each of the plots:

```
ax1.stock_img()
```

4. Print the title for the plot as follows:

```
ax1.set_title('PlateCarree', color='green')
```

5. Then, repeat *step 1* to *step 4* for our nine different projections. See the example here:

```
ax2 = fig.add_subplot(332, projection=ccrs.Mercator())
ax2.stock_img()
ax2.set_title('Mercator', color='green')

ax3 = fig.add_subplot(333, projection=ccrs.LambertCylindrical())
ax3.stock_img()
ax3.set_title('LambertCylindrical', color='green')

ax4 = fig.add_subplot(334, projection=ccrs.Robinson())
ax4.stock_img()
ax4.set_title('Robinson', color='green')

ax5 = fig.add_subplot(335, projection=ccrs.Mollweide())
ax5.stock_img()
ax5.set_title('Mollweide', color='green')

ax6 = fig.add_subplot(336, projection=ccrs.Orthographic())
ax6.stock_img()
ax6.set_title('Orthographic', color='green')

ax7 = fig.add_subplot(337, projection=ccrs.Sinusoidal())
ax7.stock_img()
ax7.set_title('Sinusoidal', color='green')
```

```
ax8 = fig.add_subplot(338, projection=ccrs.RotatedPole())
ax8.stock_img()
ax8.set_title('RotatedPole', color='green')

ax9 = fig.add_subplot(339,
projection=ccrs.InterruptedGoodeHomolosine())
ax9.stock_img()
ax9.set_title('InterruptedGoodeHomolosine', color='green')
```

6. Print a super title for the overall figure:

```
fig.suptitle("Cartopy Projections - Demo", size=20, weight='bold',
color='blue')
```

7. Lastly, display the overall figure on the screen with this command:

```
plt.show()
```

How it works...

Here is the explanation for the preceding code:

- `ax1 = fig.add_subplot(331, projection=ccrs.PlateCarree())` defines the first axes on a 3 x 3 grid of 9 axes (plots), and uses a `PlateCarree` projection for the axes, as shown in the following screenshot
- `ax1.stock_img()` plots the default image as the background for the map.
- The previous two steps are repeated for all nine projections
- Since this is the demonstration of sample projections available, we are not adding any predefined features or any other user defined maps

Upon executing the preceding code, you should see the following plots on your screen:

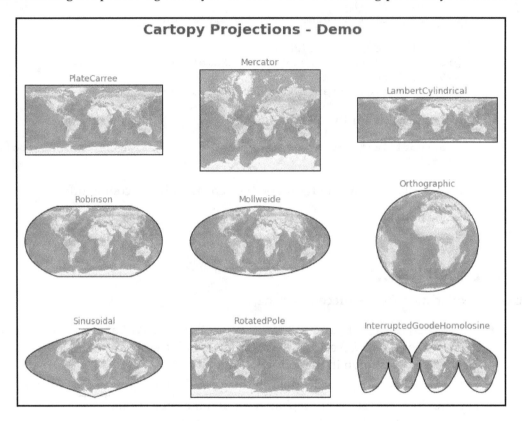

Using grid lines and labels

In this recipe, we will learn how to plot grid lines, and manage ticks and ticklabels. Cartopy has a predefined `gridlines()` function to manage these features, which has many helper functions to format the labels as desired.

We will plot four charts to demonstrate the default options, as well as the degree of customization possible when we want to plot the labels in a particular customized way.

Getting ready

You'll need to import the required libraries using the following commands:

```
import matplotlib.pyplot as plt
import matplotlib.ticker as mticker
from cartopy.mpl.ticker import LongitudeFormatter, LatitudeFormatter
import cartopy.crs as ccrs
from cartopy.mpl.gridliner import LONGITUDE_FORMATTER, LATITUDE_FORMATTER
```

How to do it...

The following are the steps involved in plotting four charts using various options for formatting ticks and labels:

1. Define the figure and axes with a `PlateCarree` projection for the first plot, as follows:

```
fig = plt.figure(figsize=(12,8))
ax1 = fig.add_subplot(221, projection=ccrs.PlateCarree())
```

2. Apply the default image for the background, and add the coastlines feature to the plot:

```
ax1.stock_img()
ax1.coastlines()
```

3. Define the `gridlines()` function as shown here:

```
gl1 = ax1.gridlines(crs=ccrs.PlateCarree(), draw_labels=True,
                    linewidth=2, color='gray', alpha=0.5,
                    linestyle='--')
```

4. Switch off the top and right axis labels:

```
gl1.xlabels_top = False
gl1.ylabels_right = False
```

5. Define the *x* and *y* axis label styles as shown here:

```
gl1.xlabel_style = {'size': 10, 'color': 'indigo', 'weight':
'bold'}
gl1.ylabel_style = {'size': 10, 'color':'darkblue','weight':
'bold'}
```

6. Print the title and *x* and *y* labels, and use default ticks and ticklabels for the first plot as follows:

```
ax1.set_title('PlateCarree - Default Ticks', color='green',
size=15)
ax1.text(0.5, -0.15, 'Longitude', va='bottom', ha='center',
        size=10, color='r', rotation='horizontal',
        rotation_mode='anchor', transform=ax1.transAxes)
ax1.text(-0.08, 0.55, 'Latitude', va='bottom', ha='center',
        size=10, color='b', rotation='vertical',
        rotation_mode='anchor', transform=ax1.transAxes)
```

7. Define the axes for the second plot using the Mercator projection. Apply the background image, and add the coastlines feature, as before:

```
ax2 = fig.add_subplot(222, projection=ccrs.Mercator())
ax2.stock_img()
ax2.coastlines()
```

8. Define the gridlines() function as follows:

```
gl2 = ax2.gridlines(crs=ccrs.PlateCarree(), draw_labels=True,
                    linewidth=2, color='gray', alpha=0.5,
                    linestyle='--')
```

9. Switch off the bottom and left axis labels:

```
gl2.xlabels_bottom = False
gl2.ylabels_left = False
```

10. Define the formatting function for the *x* and *y* axis labels:

```
gl2.xformatter = LONGITUDE_FORMATTER
gl2.yformatter = LATITUDE_FORMATTER
```

11. Define label styles, then print the title and labels for the second chart:

```
gl2.xlabel_style = {'size': 10, 'color': 'indigo', 'weight':
'bold'}
gl2.ylabel_style = {'size': 10, 'color': 'darkblue', 'weight':
            'bold'}
ax2.set_title('Mercator - Formatted Ticks', color='green', size=15,
        pad=30)
ax2.text(0.5, -0.1, 'Longitude', va='bottom', ha='center',
        size=10, color='r', rotation='horizontal',
        rotation_mode='anchor', transform=ax2.transAxes)
ax2.text(-0.05, 0.55, 'Latitude', va='bottom', ha='center',
        size=10, color='b', rotation='vertical',
        rotation_mode='anchor', transform=ax2.transAxes)
```

12. For the third plot, we will do the following:
    - Use fixed tick locations for the *x* axis
    - Switch off gridlines for the *x* axis
    - Switch off labels for the top and left axes

The rest of the features are the same as in the first two plots. See the following code block for an example:

```
ax3 = fig.add_subplot(223, projection=ccrs.Mercator())
ax3.stock_img()
ax3.coastlines()

gl3 = ax3.gridlines(crs=ccrs.PlateCarree(), draw_labels=True,
            linewidth=2, color='gray', alpha=0.5,
linestyle='--')
gl3.xlabels_top = False
gl3.ylabels_left = False
gl3.xlines = False
gl3.xlocator = mticker.FixedLocator([-180, -45, 0, 45, 180])
gl3.xformatter = LONGITUDE_FORMATTER
gl3.yformatter = LATITUDE_FORMATTER
gl3.xlabel_style = {'size': 10, 'color': 'indigo', 'weight':
'bold'}
gl3.ylabel_style = {'size': 10, 'color': 'darkblue', 'weight':
'bold'}
ax3.set_title('Mercator - Xticks at fixed locations',
color='green', size=15)
```

13. In the fourth plot, we will use completely customized labels and formatting options without using the `gridlines()` function at all, as shown here:

```
ax4 = fig.add_subplot(2, 2, 4,
projection=ccrs.PlateCarree(central_longitude=180))
ax4.set_global()
ax4.stock_img()
ax4.coastlines()

ax4.set_xticks([0, 60, 120, 180, 240, 300, 360],
crs=ccrs.PlateCarree())
ax4.set_yticks([-90, -60, -30, 0, 30, 60, 90],
crs=ccrs.PlateCarree())
lon_formatter = LongitudeFormatter(zero_direction_label=True,
                                   number_format='.1f',
degree_symbol='')
lat_formatter = LatitudeFormatter(number_format='.1f')
ax4.xaxis.set_major_formatter(lon_formatter)
ax4.yaxis.set_major_formatter(lat_formatter)

[i.set_color("indigo") for i in ax4.get_xticklabels()]
[i.set_weight("bold") for i in ax4.get_xticklabels()]
[i.set_color("darkblue") for i in ax4.get_yticklabels()]
[i.set_weight("bold") for i in ax4.get_yticklabels()]

ax4.set_title('PlateCarree - Xticks & Yticks at fixed locations',
              color='green', size=15)
```

14. Lastly, display the figure on the screen with the following command:

```
plt.show()
```

How it works...

Here is the explanation for the preceding code:

- `gl1 = ax1.gridlines(crs=ccrs.PlateCarree(), draw_labels=True, linewidth=2, color='gray', alpha=0.5, linestyle='--')` defines the format of grid lines to be plotted:
  - `ccrs.PlateCarree()` specifies the reference coordinate system (that is, the projection) to be used. In this case, we'll use the PlateCarree projection.

- draw_labels=True specifies that the ticks and tick labels aligned with the grid lines are to be plotted. By setting this parameter to False, you can switch them off.
- linewidth=2 specifies the width of the grid lines.
- color='gray' specifies the color of the grid lines.
- alpha=0.5 specifies the transparency of the grid lines.
- linestyle='--' specifies the style of the grid lines.

- gl1.xlabels_top = False switches off the top axis labels. By default, the gridlines() function plots labels for all four axes (left, bottom, top and right). You can switch any of them on or off by changing this command.
- gl1.ylabels_right = False switches off the right axis labels.
- gl1.xlabel_style = {'size': 10, 'color': 'indigo', 'weight': 'bold'} defines the dictionary of various attributes to be used for the *x* axis label.
- gl1.ylabel_style = {'size': 10, 'color': 'darkblue', 'weight': 'bold'} defines the dictionary of various attributes to be used for the *y* axis label.
- ax1.set_title('PlateCarree - Default Ticks', color='green', size=15) prints the title for the chart with various attributes.
- ax1.text(0.5, -0.15, 'Longitude', va='bottom', ha='center', size=10, color='r', rotation='horizontal', rotation_mode='anchor', transform=ax1.transAxes) plots the *x* axis label:
  - (0.5, -0.15) are the coordinates, in the axes coordinate system from left and bottom, where the *x* axis label will be printed.
  - 'Longitude' is the *x* axis label to be printed.
  - va='bottom' specifies that the label should be aligned vertically at the bottom.
  - ha='center' specifies that the label should be aligned horizontally in the center.
  - size=10 specifies the font size.
  - color='r' specifies font color.

- rotation='horizontal' specifies the angle at which the label is to be printed with respect to the axis. In this case, the angle is set to horizontal.
- rotation_mode='anchor' specifies that the label is an anchor object.
- transform=ax1.transAxes specifies that the coordinates given are in the axes coordinate system.

- ax2 = fig.add_subplot(222, projection=ccrs.Mercator()) defines the axes for the second chart, which uses the Mercator projection.
- gl2.xformatter = LONGITUDE_FORMATTER specifies the formatting options for x ticklabels.
- gl2.yformatter = LATITUDE_FORMATTER specifies the formatting options for y ticklabels.
- LONGITUDE_FORMATTER and LATITUDE_FORMATTER are predefined helper functions within the gridliner function. They both have their own formatting options, but in the second chart, we are using all default arguments for both of them. They basically set the directions of east/west for longitude, and north/south for latitude, and also display the degrees symbol. Compare the ticklabels of the first two charts to see the difference.
- gl3.xlines = False switches off grid lines landing on the x axis for the third chart. You can switch off y axis grid lines as well, by using gl.ylines.
- gl3.xlocator = mticker.FixedLocator([-180, -45, 0, 45, 180]) defines the tick locations for the x axis. Instead of leaving the choice of tick locations for gridliner, we are manually defining them here.
- ax4 = fig.add_subplot(2, 2, 4, projection=ccrs.PlateCarree(central_longitude=180)) defines the axes for the fourth chart as follows:
  - (2, 2, 4) is the same as (224), and specifies that this is the fourth chart on a 2 x 2 grid of charts
  - PlateCarree() is the projection to be used
  - central_longitude=180 specifies that the center of the longitudinal axis should be at 180 degrees, instead of the default value of 0

- `ax4.set_xticks([0, 60, 120, 180, 240, 300, 360], crs=ccrs.PlateCarree())` defines the tick locations and labels for the *x* axis. In the fourth chart, we are not using the `gridlines()` function; hence, we have to set the tick locations manually:
    - `crs=ccrs.PlateCarree()` specifies that tick locations given are in the `PlateCarree` coordinate system. This is different from a projection, which specifies the coordinate system to be used while plotting the map.
    - If a projection uses one reference coordinate system, and tick labels are provided by a different coordinate system, then by specifying which coordinate system the data is provided in, it will convert the data into the projection coordinate system before plotting the map.
- `ax4.set_yticks([-90, -60, -30, 0, 30, 60, 90], crs=ccrs.PlateCarree())` defines tick locations and labels for the *y* axis.
- `lon_formatter = LongitudeFormatter(zero_direction_label=True, number_format='.1f', degree_symbol='')` defines the formatting function for the longitudinal axis:
    - `zero_direction_label=True` specifies whether or not 0 degrees should be printed with the E symbol (for east)
    - `number_format='.1f'` specifies the number of decimal points to be used for the number labels
    - `degree_symbol=''` specifies that the degree symbol will not be printed—the default option is to print it
- `[i.set_color("indigo") for i in ax4.get_xticklabels()]` applies the `'indigo'` color to the tick labels on the *x* axis, and `[i.set_weight("bold") for i in ax4.get_xticklabels()]` prints tick labels in bold typeface:
    - `get_xticklabels()` gets the current ticklabels
    - The `set_color()` and `set_weight()` statements apply the specified color and bold font to each of the ticklabels
    - The next two statements do the same for *y* axis ticklabels, but use the `darkblue` color

Upon executing the preceding code, you should see the following plot on your screen:

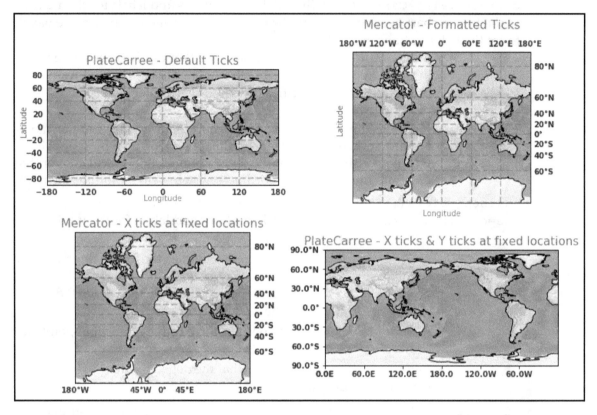

 It should be noted that ticklabels and associated formatting are defined for `PlateCarree` and `Mercator` projections only. For other projections, `gridlines()` makes plots without ticklabels, so we can't use the `(draw_labels=True)` argument on `gridlines()` for these projections.

Plotting locations on the map

In this recipe, we will learn how to plot locations with given longitude and latitude parameters on the map. This gives a visual representation of locations in terms of how they are placed relative to each other. We will also learn how to connect two locations in a straight line and a spherical direction around the globe.

Getting ready

You'll need to import the required libraries using the following commands:

```
import matplotlib.pyplot as plt
import cartopy.crs as ccrs
```

How to do it...

Here are the steps required to plot the map and various locations across the globe. You can get longitude and latitude information for various locations on the internet. Here, we will plot major cities, mostly capitals of countries:

1. Define the figure and axes on which the map is to be plotted:

```
fig = plt.figure(figsize=(10, 5))
ax = fig.add_subplot(1, 1, 1, projection=ccrs.Robinson())
```

2. Set the background image and add the coastlines feature:

```
ax.set_global()
ax.stock_img()
ax.coastlines()
```

3. Plot the location with given longitude and latitude coordinates, as shown here:

```
ax.plot(-0.08, 51.53, 'o', transform=ccrs.PlateCarree(),
markersize=7, color='r')
```

4. Label the location with a text function:

```
plt.text(-0.08, 51.53, 'London', size=10, color='indigo',
        horizontalalignment='right', transform=ccrs.Geodetic())
```

5. Now repeat *step 1* to *step 4* for all of the cities we want to plot, as shown in the following code block:

```
ax.plot(37.6173, 55.7558, 'o', transform=ccrs.PlateCarree(),
markersize=7, color='r')
plt.text(37.6173, 55.7558, 'Moscow', size=10, color='indigo',
        horizontalalignment='left', transform=ccrs.Geodetic())

ax.plot(77.1, 28.7, 'o', transform=ccrs.PlateCarree(),
markersize=7, color='r')
plt.text(77.1, 28.7, 'New Delhi', size=10, color='indigo',
        horizontalalignment='left', transform=ccrs.Geodetic())
```

```
ax.plot(-118.2437, 34.0522, 'o', transform=ccrs.PlateCarree(),
markersize=7, color='r')
plt.text(-118.2437, 34.0522, 'Los Angeles', size=10,
color='indigo',
          horizontalalignment='right', transform=ccrs.Geodetic())

ax.plot(-74, 40.7128, 'o', transform=ccrs.PlateCarree(),
markersize=7, color='r')
plt.text(-74, 40.7128, 'New York', size=10, color='indigo',
          horizontalalignment='left', transform=ccrs.Geodetic())

ax.plot(149.13, -35.2809, 'o', transform=ccrs.PlateCarree(),
markersize=7, color='r')
plt.text(149.13, -35.2809, 'Canberra', size=10, color='indigo',
          horizontalalignment='left', transform=ccrs.Geodetic())

ax.plot(116.4074, 39.9042, 'o', transform=ccrs.PlateCarree(),
markersize=7, color='r')
plt.text(116.4074, 39.9042, 'Beijing', size=10, color='indigo',
          horizontalalignment='right', transform=ccrs.Geodetic())

ax.plot(18.4241, -33.9249, 'o', transform=ccrs.PlateCarree(),
markersize=7, color='r')
plt.text(18.4241, -33.9249, 'Cape Town', size=10, color='indigo',
          horizontalalignment='left', transform=ccrs.Geodetic())

ax.plot(55.2708, 25.2048, 'o', transform=ccrs.PlateCarree(),
markersize=7, color='r')
plt.text(55.2708, 25.2048, 'Dubai', size=10, color='indigo',
          horizontalalignment='right', transform=ccrs.Geodetic())

ax.plot(139.6917, 35.6895, 'o', transform=ccrs.PlateCarree(),
markersize=7, color='r')
plt.text(139.6917, 35.6895, 'Tokyo', size=10, color='indigo',
          horizontalalignment='left', transform=ccrs.Geodetic())

ax.plot(-79.3832, 43.6532, 'o', transform=ccrs.PlateCarree(),
markersize=7, color='r')
plt.text(-79.3832, 43.6532, 'Toronto', size=10, color='indigo',
          horizontalalignment='right', transform=ccrs.Geodetic())

ax.plot(7.3986, 9.0765, 'o', transform=ccrs.PlateCarree(),
markersize=7, color='r')
plt.text(7.3986, 9.0765, 'Abuja', size=10, color='indigo', #
Capital of Nigeria
          horizontalalignment='right', transform=ccrs.Geodetic())

ax.plot(-47.9218, -15.8267, 'o', transform=ccrs.PlateCarree(),
```

```
markersize=7, color='r')
plt.text(-47.9218, -15.8267, 'Brasilia', size=10, color='indigo', #
Capital of Brazil
         horizontalalignment='right', transform=ccrs.Geodetic())

ax.plot(-99.1332, 19.4326, 'o', transform=ccrs.PlateCarree(),
        markersize=7, color='r')
plt.text(-99.1332, 19.4326, 'Mexico City', size=10, color='indigo',
# Capital of Brazil
         horizontalalignment='right', transform=ccrs.Geodetic())
```

6. Now, plot both a straight line and a spherical line between London and New
    Delhi, as follows:

```
ax.plot([-0.08, 77.1], [51.53, 28.7], color='g',
transform=ccrs.PlateCarree())
ax.plot([-0.08, 77.1], [51.53, 28.7], color='m',
transform=ccrs.Geodetic())
```

7. Lastly, display the figure on the screen with the following command:

```
plt.show()
```

How it works...

Here is the explanation for the preceding code:

- `ax = fig.add_subplot(1, 1, 1, projection=ccrs.Robinson())` defines
  the axes with the `Robinson` projection.
- `ax.plot(-0.08, 51.53, 'o', transform=ccrs.PlateCarree(),`
  `markersize=7, color='r')` plots the location as London, as follows:
  - `(-0.08, 51.53)` are the longitude and latitude coordinates for
    London.
  - `'o'` is the marker for the location to be plotted on the map.
  - `transform=ccrs.PlateCarree()` specifies the coordinate
    system in which longitude and latitude parameters are provided.
    These coordinates will be transformed internally to `Robinson`
    coordinates, since we are plotting the map with a `Robinson`
    projection.
  - `markersize=7` specifies the size of the point being plotted on the
    map, which is seven points (one point is 1/72nd of an inch).
  - `color='r'` location points are colored in red.

- plt.text(-0.08, 51.53, 'London', size=10, color='indigo', horizontalalignment='right', transform=ccrs.Geodetic()) prints the label for the location, containing its name:
    - (-0.08, 51.53) represents the longitude and latitude coordinates where the label will be printed.
    - 'London' represents the text to be printed on the label.
    - size=10 is the size of the label to be printed.
    - color='indigo' is the color of label.
    - horizontalalignment='right' specifies that the location point should be aligned to the right-hand side of the label.
    - transform=ccrs.Geodetic() specifies that coordinates are in longitude and latitude, measured in degrees. There is a Cartesian equivalent as well, which is ccrs.Geocentric, where the coordinates are in regular x, y, and z axis format, measured in regular distance metrics.
- ax.plot([-0.08, 77.1], [51.53, 28.7], color='g', transform=ccrs.PlateCarree()) plots a line graph connecting London and New Delhi, specifying their respective longitude and latitude coordinates:
    - [-0.08, 77.1] are the longitude coordinates of London and New Delhi
    - [51.53, 28.7] are the latitude coordinates of London and New Delhi
    - color='g' means that the color of the line drawn between the two cities will green
    - transform=ccrs.PlateCarree() specifies the coordinate system to be used, which in this case is Cartesian, hence a straight line will be plotted
- ax.plot([-0.08, 77.1], [51.53, 28.7], color='m', transform=ccrs.Geodetic()) plots the same line graph in spherical format along the actual globe, since we are using transform=ccrs.Geodetic(). The color of the line is magenta, thanks to the 'm' value of the color parameter.

Upon executing the code, you should see the following plot on your screen:

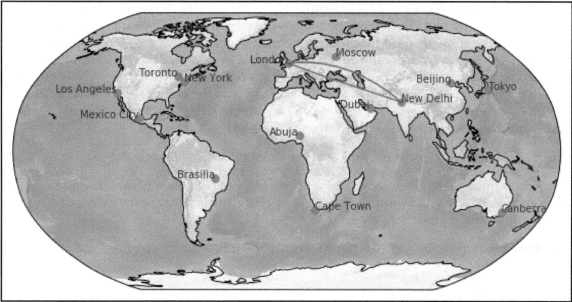

Plotting country maps with political boundaries

So far, we have worked on maps covering the entire globe, which is useful when you are plotting, for example, a company's offices globally, areas affected by an epidemic disease across continents, or an earthquake across many countries.

However, if you want to view a phenomenon specific to a region, which could be a country, state, province, or even a city within a country, then you will need to set a smaller extent for the map. In this recipe, we will learn how to do this.

Getting ready

Typically, map data is organized and distributed in the form of shapefiles. To be able to read those files and plot the data on the map, we need the `ShapeReader` package, usually provided by the software used for plotting the maps, which in this case is cartopy. Source mapping data is prepared, organized, and distributed by several different entities, both commercial and open source. Cartopy primarily supports two such sources: one is available at `https://www.naturalearthdata.com/downloads/` and the other can be found at `http://www.soest.hawaii.edu/wessel/gshhg/`. You can refer to these sites for additional information on each package.

In this chapter, we will focus only on data provided by *Natural Earth* data.

For demonstration purposes, we will plot maps for three countries: USA, UK, and India. You can plot for any other country, province, or city by just changing the extent in the longitude and latitude range.

You'll need to import the required libraries using the following commands:

```
import matplotlib.pyplot as plt
import cartopy.crs as ccrs
import cartopy.feature as cfeature
from cartopy.mpl.gridliner import LONGITUDE_FORMATTER, LATITUDE_FORMATTER
import cartopy.io.shapereader as shpreader
```

How to do it...

Here are the steps required to plot our map:

1. Define the figure:

   ```
   fig = plt.figure(figsize=(16,8))
   ```

2. Define the axes with a `PlateCarree` projection:

   ```
   ax1 = fig.add_subplot(131, projection=ccrs.PlateCarree())
   ```

3. Define the extent of longitude and latitude ranges for the USA as follows:

   ```
   ax1.set_extent([-130, -66.5, 25, 47], ccrs.Geodetic())
   ```

4. Plot the map of the USA by using the `add_feature()` function. Cartopy provides this for the USA for convenience, so we don't have to read an external shapefile:

```
ax1.add_feature(cfeature.STATES, facecolor='wheat')
```

5. Define the `gridlines()` function as follows:

```
gl1 = ax1.gridlines(crs=ccrs.PlateCarree(), draw_labels=True,
                    linewidth=2, color='gray', alpha=0.5,
                    linestyle='--')
```

6. Switch off the top and right axes' labels as follows:

```
gl1.xlabels_top = False
gl1.ylabels_right = False
```

7. Apply longitude and latitude formatter's to display the labels in degrees with the appropriate direction, as shown here:

```
gl1.xformatter = LONGITUDE_FORMATTER
gl1.yformatter = LATITUDE_FORMATTER
```

8. Define the dictionary of attributes to be applied on the *x* and *y* labels:

```
gl1.xlabel_style = {'size': 10, 'color': 'b'}
gl1.ylabel_style = {'size': 10, 'color': 'r', 'weight': 'bold'}
```

9. Print the title and the *x* and *y* labels as follows:

```
ax1.set_title('United States of America(lon/lat)\n[-130, -66.5, 25,
               47]', color='g', size=15)
ax1.text(0.5, -0.2, 'Longitude', va='bottom', ha='center', size=10,
         color='r', rotation='horizontal', rotation_mode='anchor',
         weight='bold', transform=ax1.transAxes)
ax1.text(-0.1, 0.55, 'Latitude', va='bottom', ha='center', size=10,
         color='b', rotation='vertical', rotation_mode='anchor',
         weight='bold', transform=ax1.transAxes)
```

10. Define the axes with a Mercator projection for plotting the map of India:

```
ax2 = fig.add_subplot(132, projection=ccrs.Mercator())
```

11. Set the extent of the longitude and latitude range for India as follows:

```
ax2.set_extent([68.12, 97.42, 8.07, 37.1], ccrs.Geodetic())
```

12. Read the shapefile containing country-specific data from *Natural Earth* data:

```
shapename = 'admin_1_states_provinces_lakes_shp'
states_shp = shpreader.natural_earth(resolution='10m',
                        category='cultural', name=shapename)
```

13. Plot different segments of the country on the map as follows:

```
for state in shpreader.Reader(states_shp).geometries():
    ax2.add_geometries([state], ccrs.PlateCarree(),
    facecolor='wheat', edgecolor='black')
```

14. Define the grid lines and axis labels, and print them along with the title with appropriate formatting, as done for USA and shown here:

```
gl2 = ax2.gridlines(crs=ccrs.PlateCarree(), draw_labels=True,
                    linewidth=2, color='gray', alpha=0.5,
                    linestyle='--')

gl2.xlabels_top = False
gl2.ylabels_right = False

gl2.xformatter = LONGITUDE_FORMATTER
gl2.yformatter = LATITUDE_FORMATTER

gl2.xlabel_style = {'size': 10, 'color': 'blue'}
gl2.ylabel_style = {'size': 10, 'color': 'red', 'weight': 'bold'}
ax2.set_title('India(lon/lat)\n[68.12, 97.42, 8.07, 37.1]',
            color='g', size=15)
```

15. Now, repeat the previous steps for the UK:

```
ax3 = fig.add_subplot(133, projection=ccrs.Mercator())
ax3.set_extent([-8.62, 1.77, 49.9, 60.84], ccrs.Geodetic())

for state in shpreader.Reader(states_shp).geometries():
    ax3.add_geometries([state], ccrs.PlateCarree(),
    facecolor='wheat', edgecolor='black')

gl3 = ax3.gridlines(crs=ccrs.PlateCarree(), draw_labels=True,
                    linewidth=2,
                    color='gray', alpha=0.5, linestyle='--')

gl3.xlabels_top = False
gl3.ylabels_right = False

gl3.xformatter = LONGITUDE_FORMATTER
gl3.yformatter = LATITUDE_FORMATTER
```

```
gl3.xlabel_style = {'size': 10, 'color': 'blue'}
gl3.ylabel_style = {'size': 10, 'color': 'red', 'weight': 'bold'}

ax3.set_title('United Kingdom(lon/lat)\n[-8.62, 1.77, 49.9,
60.84]',
                color='g', size=15)
```

16. Lastly, display the figure on the screen with the following command:

```
plt.show()
```

How it works...

Here is the explanation for the code:

- `ax1.set_extent([-130, -66.5, 25, 47], ccrs.Geodetic())` specifies the extent of the area to be plotted as follows:
    - `(-130, -66.5)` are the minimum and maximum longitude coordinates for the USA
    - `(25, 47)` are the minimum and maximum latitude coordinates for the USA
    - `ccrs.Geodetic()` specifies that the data coordinate format used is longitude and latitude, measured in degrees
- `ax1.add_feature(cfeature.STATES, facecolor='wheat')` plots the internal borders of the states of the USA. Cartopy provides this as a feature, similar to other physical features such as land, oceans, rivers, and lakes that we learned earlier. For other countries, we will have to get the data from shapefiles and plot it separately.
- `gridlines()` and its associated label formatting is the same as in the preceding recipe.
- `ax1.set_title('United States of America(lon/lat)\n[-130, -66.5, 25, 47]', color='g', size=15)` prints the title for the chart, including the name in the first line, and its longitude and latitude coordinates in the next line (\n, the new line character, divides the text into two separate lines).

- `ax2.set_extent([68.12, 97.42, 8.07, 37.1], ccrs.Geodetic())` specifies the extent of the area to be plotted on the second axes as follows:
    - `(68.12, 97.42)` are the minimum and maximum longitude coordinates for India.
    - `(8.07, 37.1)` are the minimum and maximum latitude coordinates for India.
    - `crs.Geodetic()` specifies that data coordinates are longitude and latitude, measured in degrees.
- `shapename = 'admin_1_states_provinces_lakes_shp'` specifies the name of the shapefile to be downloaded from the *Natural Earth* data site for plotting our maps. It is not exactly the name of the file, but the type of file among various types that are available. There are many types, such as *admin 0, admin 1, populated places, railroads, roads, airports*, and *ports*. Please refer to the *Natural Earth* data site for details, available at `https://www.naturalearthdata.com/downloads/10m-cultural-vectors/`.
- `states_shp = shpreader.natural_earth(resolution='10m', category='cultural', name=shapename)` downloads, unzips, and reads the shapefile from *Natural Earth* data:
    - `resolution='10m'` specifies the level of detail in the data. There are three levels, `10m`, `50m` and `110m`, with `10m` being the most detailed, and `110m` providing a more aggregated level of data.
    - `category='cultural'` specifies the category of the data. Again, there are three categories, `cultural`, `physical` and `raster`. `Cultural` deals with political and administrative boundaries, `physical` deals with land, oceans, rivers, and lakes, and `raster` deals with data on environmental and climate-related conditions.
    - `name=shapename` specifies the type of data to be downloaded in shapefile format.

- `for state in shpreader.Reader(states_shp).geometries():` initiates a `for` loop to read the contents of the shapefile downloaded in the previous step:
    - `shapereader` accesses the file, unzips it, and downloads the contents of shapefile
    - `Reader` accesses the contents of the shapefile
    - There are two methods under `Reader`, namely `records` and `geometries`:
        - `geometries` accesses the shapes to be plotted, and is useful when we know the metadata of the shapefile. In this case, we know that we are plotting states' boundaries within the country, so we use `geometries` directly.
        - The `records` method is used when we need additional information on the metadata of the contents of a shapefile. Once we have the metadata, we can use `records.geometries` to access the shapes to be plotted.
- `ax2.add_geometries([state], ccrs.PlateCarree(), facecolor='wheat', edgecolor='black')` plots given a `state` boundary in each iteration of the `for` loop. It uses `black` color for the boundary edges and `wheat` color for the area of the state.
- The rest of the code deals with grid lines and associated formatting, as we learned in the previous recipes.
- We repeat exactly the same process for plotting the UK. We just need to set up the appropriate extent of the area to be plotted as follows:
    - `ax3.set_extent([-8.62, 1.77, 49.9, 60.84], ccrs.Geodetic())` sets the extent for the UK
    - `(-8.62, 1.77)` are the minimum and maximum longitude coordinates for the UK
    - `(49.9, 60.84)` are the minimum and maximum latitude coordinates for the UK

Upon executing the preceding code, you should see the following maps plotted on your screen:

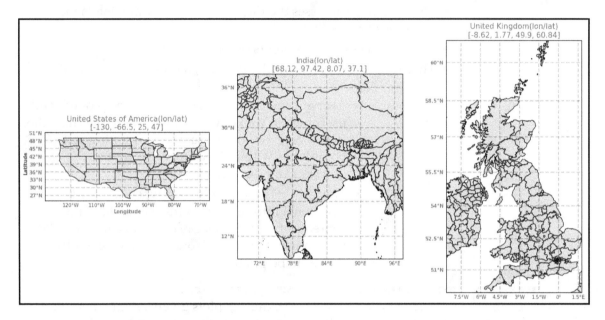

Plotting country maps using GeoPandas and cartopy

In the preceding recipe, we used `shapereader` to download the file, and `Reader` to read the contents of shapefiles and plot them. Both `shapereader` and `Reader` are provided by cartopy. In this recipe, we will continue to use `shapereader` to download the required shapefile, but use GeoPandas to read and plot the contents of the shapefile. We used GeoPandas earlier in `Chapter 6`, *Plotting with Advanced Features* to plot maps in that part of the book.

We will plot the same three country maps used in the preceding recipe. However, we will use two different types of files, *admin 0* and *admin 1*, and plot three countries for each type, giving us a total of six plots.

Getting ready

You'll need to import the required libraries using the following commands:

```
import matplotlib.pyplot as plt
import numpy as np
import geopandas
from cartopy.io import shapereader
import cartopy.crs as ccrs
```

How to do it...

The following are the steps to plot our country maps:

1. Define the figure as follows:

```
fig = plt.figure(figsize=(12, 6))
```

2. Define six axes to plot six different graphs, all with the `PlateCarree` projection. This time, we don't plot the background image, and there is no addition of `coastlines()` either:

```
ax1 = fig.add_subplot(231, projection=ccrs.PlateCarree())
ax2 = fig.add_subplot(232, projection=ccrs.PlateCarree())
ax3 = fig.add_subplot(233, projection=ccrs.PlateCarree())
ax4 = fig.add_subplot(234, projection=ccrs.PlateCarree())
ax5 = fig.add_subplot(235, projection=ccrs.PlateCarree())
ax6 = fig.add_subplot(236, projection=ccrs.PlateCarree())
```

3. Download the *admin 0* shapefile using `shapereader`:

```
shpfilename = shapereader.natural_earth(resolution='10m',
            category='cultural', name='admin_0_countries')
```

4. Read the contents of the shapefile into a pandas DataFrame:

```
df0 = geopandas.read_file(shpfilename)
```

5. Set the extent of the USA on the map projection:

```
ax1.set_extent([-130, -66.5, 25, 50], crs=ccrs.PlateCarree())
```

6. Extract the polygons (that is, the blocks forming the country) related to the USA:

```
poly = df0.loc[df0['ADMIN'] == 'United States of
America']['geometry']
```

7. Plot the polygons on the map using the `geometries` method, as follows:

```
ax1.add_geometries(poly, crs=ccrs.PlateCarree(), facecolor='none',
edgecolor='0.5')
```

8. Print the title for the plot:

```
ax1.set_title('United States of America - Admin0')
```

9. Repeat *step 4* to *step 8* for India, followed by the UK. See the following example:

```
ax2.set_extent([-8.62, 1.77, 49.9, 60.84], crs=ccrs.PlateCarree())
# United Kingdom
poly = df0.loc[df0['ADMIN'] == 'United Kingdom']['geometry']
ax2.add_geometries(poly, crs=ccrs.PlateCarree(), facecolor='none',
                    edgecolor='0.5')
ax2.set_title('United Kingdom - Admin0')

ax3.set_extent([68.12, 97.42, 8.07, 37.1], crs=ccrs.PlateCarree())
# India
poly = df0.loc[df0['ADMIN'] == 'India']['geometry']
ax3.add_geometries(poly, crs=ccrs.PlateCarree(), facecolor='none',
edgecolor='0.5')
ax3.set_title('India - Admin0')
```

10. Download the *admin 1* shapefile using `shapereader`:

```
shpfilename = shapereader.natural_earth(resolution='10m',
                            category='cultural',
name='admin_1_states_provinces_lakes_shp')
df1 = geopandas.read_file(shpfilename)
```

11. Repeat *step 4* to *step 8* for each of the countries, as shown here:

```
ax4.set_extent([-130, -66.5, 25, 50], crs=ccrs.PlateCarree()) #
United States of America
poly = df1.loc[df1['admin'] == 'United States of America']
                                ['geometry']
ax4.add_geometries(poly, crs=ccrs.PlateCarree(), facecolor='none',
                    edgecolor='0.5')
ax4.set_title('United States of America - Admin1')

ax5.set_extent([-8.62, 1.77, 49.9, 60.84], crs=ccrs.PlateCarree())
# United Kingdom
poly = df1.loc[df1['admin'] == 'United Kingdom']['geometry']
ax5.add_geometries(poly, crs=ccrs.PlateCarree(), facecolor='none',
                    edgecolor='0.5')
ax5.set_title('United Kingdom - Admin1')
```

```
ax6.set_extent([68.12, 97.42, 8.07, 37.1], crs=ccrs.PlateCarree())
# India
poly = df1.loc[df1['admin'] == 'India']['geometry']
ax6.add_geometries(poly, crs=ccrs.PlateCarree(), facecolor='none',
                   edgecolor='0.5')
ax6.set_title('India - Admin1')
```

12. Finally, display the plot on the screen as follows:

```
plt.show()
```

How it works...

Here is the explanation for the preceding code:

- `shpfilename = shapereader.natural_earth(resolution='10m', category='cultural', name='admin_0_countries')` downloads the required shapefile from the *Natural Earth* data website.
- `df0 = geopandas.read_file(shpfilename)` reads the contents of the shapefile into the `df0` pandas DataFrame object.
- `ax1.set_extent([-130, -66.5, 25, 50], crs=ccrs.PlateCarree())` sets the extent for the USA.
- `poly = df0.loc[df0['ADMIN'] == 'United States of America']['geometry']` reads specific blocks to be plotted as polygons from the pandas DataFrame:
    - The `df0` DataFrame has an `'ADMIN'` column that stores the name of the country, which is used to extract specific contents related to the USA.
    - `geometry` is another column in `df0`, which stores the information of blocks forming the specific country.
    - There is only one object for each country in this shapefile. Hence, it plots only the outline of the country as one single polygon, without any interior blocks for states or provinces.
- `ax1.add_geometries(poly, crs=ccrs.PlateCarree(), facecolor='none', edgecolor='0.5')` plots polygons on the map using the `geometries` method:
    - `facecolor='none'` specifies not to fill the blocks with any color.
    - `edgecolor = '0.5'` specifies the use of a gray color for plotting the edges.

- `ax1.set_title('United States of America - Admin0')` prints the title for the plot.
- `shpfilename = shapereader.natural_earth(resolution='10m', category='cultural', name='admin_1_states_provinces_lakes_shp')` reads the *admin 1* shapefile that we used in the previous recipe. This will have not only country borders, as in `admin0`, but also internal state and province borders.
- `df1 = geopandas.read_file(shpfilename)` reads the shapefile contents into the pandas DataFrame.
- `poly = df1.loc[df1['admin'] == 'United States of America']['geometry']` filters polygons forming the USA. In this case, the `geometry` column will have multiple objects for each country, specifying states and provinces within the country.
- The remaining steps are exactly the same as the ones for the *admin 0* file.

Upon executing the preceding code, you should see the following maps on your screen. It should be noted that we have not used the default image for the background, hence, we don't see the color images here. The first row is just the outline of the countries, whereas the plots in the second row depicts states and provinces within each country, as given in the `Admin 0` and `Admin 1` files:

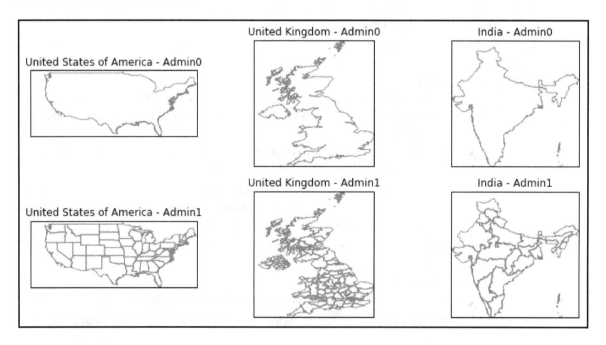

Plotting populated places of the world

In this recipe, we will plot locations inhabited by human beings across the globe. We will use the corresponding shapefile from the *Natural Earth* data website.

Getting ready

You'll need to import the required libraries using the following commands:

```
import matplotlib.pyplot as plt
import cartopy.crs as ccrs
import cartopy.io.shapereader as shpreader
```

How to do it...

The following are the steps involved in plotting our map:

1. Define the figure and axes with a `PlateCarree` projection:

    ```
    plt.figure(figsize=(12, 6))
    ax = plt.axes(projection=ccrs.PlateCarree())
    ```

2. Set the background image and coastlines as follows:

    ```
    ax.stock_img()
    ax.coastlines()
    ```

3. Download the required shapefile from the *Natural Earth* data website:

    ```
    shp_fn = shpreader.natural_earth(resolution='10m',
                        category='cultural',
    name='populated_places')
    ```

4. Get specific coordinates for each of the locations, as shown here:

    ```
    xy = [pt.coords[0] for pt in shpreader.Reader(shp_fn).geometries()]
    ```

5. Unzip the coordinates using the following command:

```
x, y = zip(*xy)
```

6. Plots these points using a scatter plot:

```
ax.scatter(x,y, transform=ccrs.Geodetic())
```

7. Plot the title for the plot as follows:

```
ax.set_title('Populated places of the world.')
```

8. Lastly, display the maps on the screen using the following command:

```
plt.show()
```

How it works...

Here is the explanation for the preceding code:

- `shp_fl = shpreader.natural_earth(resolution='10m', category='cultural', name='populated_places')` downloads the shapefile containing the information of locations that are populated by human beings
- `xy = [pt.coords[0] for pt in shpreader.Reader(shp_fl).geometries()]` extracts the coordinates of locations into the `xy` variable
- `x, y = zip(*xy)` unzips coordinates into *x* and *y* coordinates
- `ax.scatter(x,y, transform=ccrs.Geodetic())` draws a scatter plot of the locations
- `ax.set_title('Populated places of the world.')` sets the title for the plot

Upon executing the preceding code, you should see the following map on your screen. Blue dots represent locations where human beings are present:

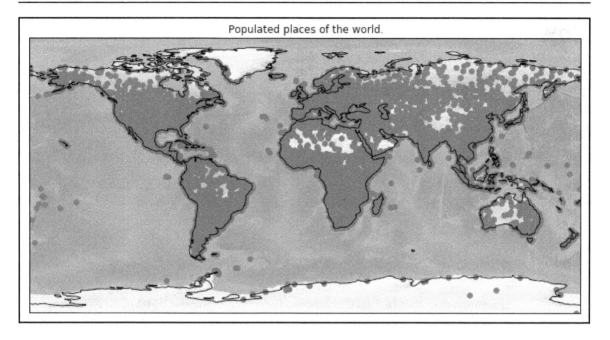

Populated places of the world.

Plotting the top five and bottom five populated countries

In this recipe, we will learn how to extract population data for each of the countries, sort it by population amounts, and plot the top five and bottom five countries, in terms of population, on the global map. We will download and use the admin 0 shapefile with a resolution of 110m.

Getting ready

You'll need to import the required libraries using the following commands:

```
import matplotlib.pyplot as plt
import cartopy.crs as ccrs
import cartopy.io.shapereader as shpreader
```

How to do it...

The following are the steps required to plot our map:

1. Download the required shapefile using the following command:

```
shpfilename = shpreader.natural_earth(resolution='110m',
category='cultural', name='admin_0_countries')
```

2. Extract and sort the data to get countries by population in ascending order, as follows:

```
reader = shpreader.Reader(shpfilename)
countries = reader.records()
country = next(countries)

population = lambda country: country.attributes['POP_EST']
sort_by_pop = sorted(countries, key=population)
```

3. Extract first five and last five entries, which represent the bottom five and top five populated countries. Get corresponding longitude and latitude coordinates from the net offline:

```
# get the first 5 entries that represent lowest population
B5_countries_by_pop = sort_by_pop[:5]
B5_Country_Names = ', '.join([country.attributes['NAME_LONG'] for
                             country in B5_countries_by_pop])

# get the last 5 entries that represent highest population
T5_countries_by_pop = sort_by_pop[-5:]
T5_Country_Names = ', '.join([country.attributes['NAME_LONG'] for
                             country in T5_countries_by_pop])

#B5_Country_Names = ['French Southern and Antarctic Lands',
  'Falkland Islands', 'Antarctica', 'Greenland', #'Northern
Cyprus']
B5_lat = [49.28, 51.796, 82.862, 71.71, 35.32]
B5_lon = [69.35, 59.523, 135, 42.60, 33.31]

#T5_Country_Names = ['Brazil', 'Indonesia', 'United States',
                    'India', 'China']
T5_lat = [-14.2350, -0.7893, 37.0902, 20.5937, 40]
T5_lon = [-51.9253, 113.9213, -95.7129, 78.9629, 116.5]
```

4. Define the figure, axes, and set defaults:

```
fig = plt.figure(figsize=(10, 5))
ax = fig.add_subplot(1, 1, 1, projection=ccrs.Robinson())

ax.set_global()
ax.stock_img()
ax.coastlines()
```

5. Plot these points on a global map as follows:

```
ax.plot(B5_lon[0], B5_lat[0], 'o', transform=ccrs.Geodetic(),
markersize=10, color='r')
ax.plot(B5_lon[1], B5_lat[1], 'o', transform=ccrs.Geodetic(),
markersize=10, color='r')
ax.plot(B5_lon[2], B5_lat[2], 'o', transform=ccrs.Geodetic(),
markersize=10, color='r')
ax.plot(B5_lon[3], B5_lat[3], 'o', transform=ccrs.Geodetic(),
markersize=10, color='r')
ax.plot(B5_lon[4], B5_lat[4], 'o', transform=ccrs.Geodetic(),
markersize=10, color='r')

ax.plot(T5_lon[0], T5_lat[0], 'o', transform=ccrs.Geodetic(),
markersize=10, color='g')
ax.plot(T5_lon[1], T5_lat[1], 'o', transform=ccrs.Geodetic(),
markersize=10, color='g')
ax.plot(T5_lon[2], T5_lat[2], 'o', transform=ccrs.Geodetic(),
markersize=10, color='g')
ax.plot(T5_lon[3], T5_lat[3], 'o', transform=ccrs.Geodetic(),
markersize=10, color='g')
ax.plot(T5_lon[4], T5_lat[4], 'o', transform=ccrs.Geodetic(),
markersize=10, color='g')
```

6. Plot labels corresponding to each of the points by using the text embedding feature:

```
plt.text(B5_lon[0], B5_lat[0], 'FSAL', size=12, color='indigo',
        horizontalalignment='left', transform=ccrs.Geodetic())
plt.text(B5_lon[1], B5_lat[1], 'FI', size=12, color='indigo',
        horizontalalignment='left', transform=ccrs.Geodetic())
plt.text(B5_lon[2], B5_lat[2], 'Antarctica', size=12,
        color='indigo', horizontalalignment='left',
transform=ccrs.Geodetic())
plt.text(B5_lon[3], B5_lat[3], 'Greenland', size=12,
color='indigo',
        horizontalalignment='right', transform=ccrs.Geodetic())
plt.text(B5_lon[4], B5_lat[4], 'NC', size=12, color='indigo',
        horizontalalignment='left', transform=ccrs.Geodetic())
```

```
plt.text(T5_lon[0], T5_lat[0], 'Brazil', size=12, color='m',
        horizontalalignment='left', transform=ccrs.Geodetic())
plt.text(T5_lon[1], T5_lat[1], 'Indonesia', size=12, color='m',
        horizontalalignment='left', transform=ccrs.Geodetic())
plt.text(T5_lon[2], T5_lat[2], 'United States', size=12, color='m',
        horizontalalignment='left', transform=ccrs.Geodetic())
plt.text(T5_lon[3], T5_lat[3], 'India', size=12, color='m',
        horizontalalignment='left', transform=ccrs.Geodetic())
plt.text(T5_lon[4], T5_lat[4], 'China', size=12, color='m',
        horizontalalignment='right', transform=ccrs.Geodetic())
```

7. Display the plot on the screen using the following command:

```
plt.show()
```

How it works...

Here is the explanation for the code:

- `shpfilename = shpreader.natural_earth(resolution='110m', category='cultural', name='admin_0_countries')` downloads the required shapefile from the *Natural Earth* data website.
- `reader = shpreader.Reader(shpfilename)` sets up the reader to extract data from shapefile.
- `countries = reader.records()` sets up a generator object to start reading the file.
- `country = next(countries)` extracts the next country record.
- `population = lambda country: country.attributes['POP_EST']` defines an anonymous function that returns the population for a given country record. `'POP_EST'` is one of the attributes of the imported country record. `lambda` is a Python construct for defining temporary, one-time use anonymous functions.
- `sort_by_pop = sorted(countries, key=population)` sorts the imported shapefile, which is mapped to `countries`, by population in ascending order.
- `B5_countries_by_pop = sort_by_pop[:5]` picks up the first five records from the sorted file. These records represent the bottom five countries by population size.
- `B5_Country_Names = ', '.join([country.attributes['NAME_LONG'] for country in B5_countries_by_pop])` picks up the long name of the country, as given in the attribute NAME_LONG for each of these five countries.

- `T5_countries_by_pop = sort_by_pop[-5:]` picks up last five entries from the sorted file. These entries represent the top five countries by population size.
- `T5_Country_Names = ', '.join([country.attributes['NAME_LONG'] for country in T5_countries_by_pop])` picks up the long name for each of these countries.
- `B5_lat = [49.28, 51.796, 82.862, 71.71, 35.32]` and `B5_lon = [69.35, 59.523, 135, 42.60, 33.31]` are the lists of longitude and latitude coordinates for the bottom five countries.
- `T5_lat = [-14.2350, -0.7893, 37.0902, 20.5937, 40]` and `T5_lon = [-51.9253, 113.9213, -95.7129, 78.9629, 116.5]` are the longitude and latitude coordinates for the top five countries.
- `fig = plt.figure(figsize=(10, 5))` defines the figure with a size of (10, 5) inches.
- `ax = fig.add_subplot(1, 1, 1, projection=ccrs.Robinson())` defines the axes for plotting the map with a `Robinson` projection.
- `ax.plot(B5_lon[], B5_lat[], 'o', transform=ccrs.PlateCarree(), markersize=10, color='r')` plots the bottom five country locations with an `'0'` marker, set to a size of 10 points and colored red.
- `ax.plot(T5_lon[], T5_lat[], 'o', transform=ccrs.PlateCarree(), markersize=10, color='g')` plots the top five country locations with an `'0'` marker, set to a size of 10 points and colored green.
- `plt.text()` statements print labels for each of these 10 locations with their respective long names. For some of the countries we have used abbreviations, since their names are too long for the map. You can see their full names in this chapter's code file.

Upon executing the preceding code, you should see the following plot on your screen:

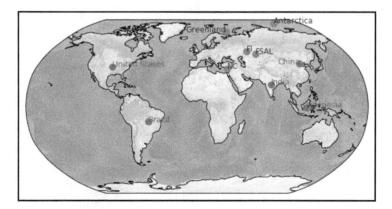

Plotting temperatures across the globe

In this recipe, we will learn how to plot given temperatures across the globe to visualize how they look relative to each other. You will need to download the temperature file required for plotting the map from `http://data.nodc.noaa.gov/thredds/fileServer/woa/WOA09/NetCDFdata/temperature_annual_1deg.nc`.

Getting ready

You'll need to import the required libraries using the following commands:

```
from netCDF4 import Dataset
import matplotlib.pylab as plt
import numpy as np
from matplotlib import cm
import cartopy.crs as ccrs
from cartopy.util import add_cyclic_point
```

How to do it...

The following are the steps required for plotting the map:

1. Load the temperature file to be used for plotting the map as follows:

   ```
   netCDF_temp = Dataset('temperature_annual_1deg.nc')
   ```

2. Extract the longitude and latitude coordinates, and the corresponding temperature in Celsius, for all the points to be plotted on the map:

   ```
   lat = netCDF_temp.variables['lat'][:]
   lon = netCDF_temp.variables['lon'][:]

   temp = netCDF_temp.variables['t_an'][0,0,:,:]
   ```

3. Add cyclic points to temperature and longitude to remove the white vertical line, which otherwise shows up on the plot:

   ```
   temp_cyc, lon_cyc = add_cyclic_point(temp, coord=lon)
   ```

4. Define the figure and axes with the `Robinson` projection:

   ```
   plt.figure(figsize=(12,6))
   ax = plt.subplot(111, projection=ccrs.Robinson())
   ```

5. Add the background image and coastlines to the map with the following commands:

```
ax.stock_img()
ax.coastlines()
```

6. Plot temperatures with the `pcolormesh` function using the `seismic` colormap:

```
temp_map = ax.pcolormesh(lon_cyc, lat, temp_cyc, vmin=-10, vmax=40,
transform=ccrs.PlateCarree(),cmap=cm.seismic)
```

7. Plot the colorbar with a `'horizontal'` orientation, as shown here:

```
plt.colorbar(temp_map, orientation='horizontal')
```

8. Display the plot on the screen with the following command:

```
plt.show()
```

How it works...

Here is the explanation for the preceding code:

- `netCDF_temp = Dataset('temperature_annual_1deg.nc')` loads the temperature data. It is a `netCDF-compliant` file, so will need the appropriate utility to read the data, which (dataset) we have already imported in the *Getting Ready* section of this recipe.
- `lon = netCDF_temp.variables['lon'][:]` and `lat = netCDF_temp.variables['lat'][:]` extract longitude and latitude coordinates of the locations for which temperature is being plotted.
- `temp = netCDF_temp.variables['t_an'][0,0,:,:]` extracts the temperature of the first layer.
- `temp_cyc, lon_cyc = add_cyclic_point(temp, coord=lon)` adds cyclical points to avoid the vertical white line at zero longitude.
- `temp_map = ax.pcolormesh(lon_cyc, lat, temp_cyc, vmin=-10, vmax=40,    transform=ccrs.PlateCarree(),cmap=cm.seismic)` plots the required temperature map as follows:
  - `lon_cyc`, `lat`, and `temp_cyc` are the longitude, latitude, and temperature data to be plotted

- vmin and vmax specify minimum and maximum temperatures to be plotted on the map
- cmap=cm.seismic specifies that the seismic colormap will be used
- plt.colorbar(temp_map, orientation='horizontal') plots the colorbar with a horizontal orientation.

Upon execution of the code, you should see the following map on the screen:

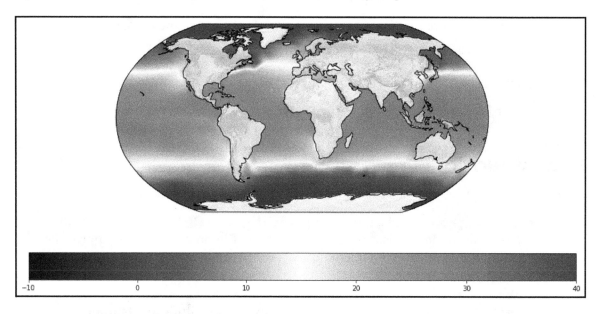

Plotting time zones

In this recipe, we will learn how to plot time zones on the map. A time zones shapefile is available at the *Natural Earth* data website, so we could use shapereader to download it, as we have been doing. However, we have downloaded the file offline and are using it here to demonstrate another feature provided by cartopy: ShapelyFeature.

Getting ready

You'll need to import the required libraries using the following commands:

```
import matplotlib.pyplot as plt
import numpy as np
import cartopy.crs as ccrs
from cartopy.io.shapereader import Reader
from cartopy.feature import ShapelyFeature
import matplotlib.ticker as mticker
```

How to do it...

The following are the steps required to plot time zones on our map:

1. Define the figure and axes with a `PlateCarree` projection:

```
plt.figure(figsize=(12, 6))
ax = plt.axes(projection=ccrs.PlateCarree())
```

2. Apply the background image and coastlines features to the map as follows:

```
ax.stock_img()
ax.coastlines(zorder=0)
```

3. Read the contents of the time zones shapefile using the `ShapelyFeature` function as a feature:

```
shape_feature =
ShapelyFeature(Reader('ne_10m_time_zones.shp').geometries(),
                  ccrs.PlateCarree(), edgecolor='black')
```

4. Plot the feature on the map as follows:

```
ax.add_feature(shape_feature, alpha=0.4, zorder=5, lw=1)
```

5. Apply the `gridlines()` function as shown here:

```
gl = ax.gridlines(crs=ccrs.PlateCarree(), draw_labels=True,
            linewidth=2, color='gray', alpha=0.5, linestyle='--
')
```

6. Switch off the left, top, and right axis labels:

```
gl.xlabels_top = False
gl.ylabels_left = False
gl.ylabels_right = False
```

7. Apply fixed tick locations for the *x* axis, overriding default ticks, like so:

```
gl.xlocator = mticker.FixedLocator(np.linspace(-180, 180, 25))
```

8. Format ticklabels on the *x* axis as follows:

```
gl.xlabel_style = {'size': 10, 'color': 'blue'}
```

9. Plot the title for the map:

```
ax.set_title('Global Time Zones', size=15, color='g')
```

10. Lastly, display the map on the screen with the following command:

```
plt.show()
```

How it works...

Here is the explanation for the preceding code:

- `ax.coastlines(zorder=0)` plots coastlines on the map as follows:
    - `zorder=0` specifies that the coastlines should be plotted first, so that they don't come into the foreground and obscure the time zone lines
- `shape_feature = ShapelyFeature(Reader('ne_10m_time_zones.shp').geometries(),ccrs.PlateCarree(), edgecolor='black')` creates a feature object that can be added to the map:
    - `Reader` extracts the contents from the shapefile as we have been doing so far
    - `ShapelyFeature` prepares the contents as a feature that can be added to the map using the `add_feature` method
- `ax.add_feature(shape_feature, alpha=0.4, zorder=5, lw=1)` adds the feature, created in the previous step, to the map:
    - `shape_feature` is the feature to be plotted
    - `alpha=0.4` specifies the transparency level

- zorder=5 specifies that time zone lines are printed later than coastlines, so that they come in the foreground, with coastlines shown in the background
- lw=1 specifies the width of the time zone lines

- There are 24 time zone lines on the map: 12 on the left-hand side of 0 degrees longitude, and 12 on the right-hand side. Zero degrees longitude itself represents **Greenwich Mean Time (GMT)**, so that longitudinal coordinates to the right of zero degrees are ahead of GMT, and coordinates to the left of zero degrees longitude are behind GMT.
- gridlines() and associated formatting is similar to what we have been doing so far in this chapter.
- gl.xlocator = mticker.FixedLocator(np.linspace(-180, 180, 25)) applies the ticks on the *x* axis, starting from -180 degrees to +180 degrees in 25 equal intervals of 15 degrees each.
- Every 15 degrees of longitude represents 1 hour of time on the time zones. So, the first time zone to the right of zero degrees longitude is 30 minutes ahead of GMT (7.5 degrees longitude). Similarly, the first time zone to the left of zero degree longitude is 30 minutes behind GMT. India is 5.5 hours ahead of GMT. These time zones represent standard time, when daylight saving time is not in use.

Upon execution of the preceding code, you should see the following plot on the screen:

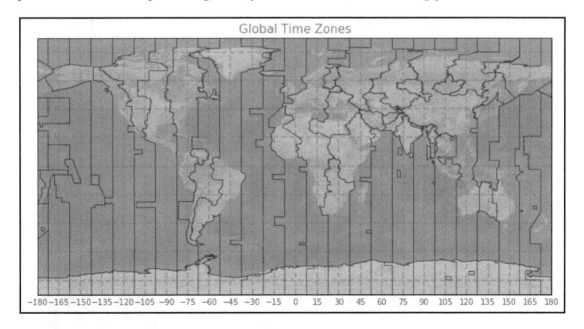

Plotting an animated map

In this recipe, we will learn how to plot an animated map for the purposes of three-dimensional visualization.

Getting ready

You'll need to import the required libraries using the following commands:

```
import cartopy.crs as ccrs
import matplotlib.animation as animation
import matplotlib.pyplot as plt
import numpy as np
```

How to do it...

The following are the steps to plot an animated map and save it as an MP4 file:

1. Set up the backend on which the map is to be animated, as follows:

```
import matplotlib
matplotlib.use('tkagg')
```

2. Define the figure:

```
fig = plt.figure(figsize=(6, 6))
```

3. Define a function to keep updating the map with new frames:

```
def animate(longitude):
    ax = plt.gca()
    ax.remove()
    ax = plt.axes([0, 0, 1, 1],
projection=ccrs.Geostationary(central_longitude=longitude))
    ax.set_global()
    ax.coastlines()
    ax.stock_img()
    ax.gridlines()
```

4. Activate the animation as follows:

```
ani = animation.FuncAnimation(fig, animate, frames=np.linspace(0,
360, 10),
                                     interval=50, repeat=True,
repeat_delay=500)
```

5. Save the animated map as an MP4 file using the following command:

```
ani.save("Geostationary.mp4")
```

6. Display the animation on the screen using the following command:

```
plt.show()
```

How it works...

Here is the explanation for the preceding code:

- `matplotlib.use('tkagg')` sets up a Tkinter backend for displaying the animation
- `fig = plt.figure(figsize=(6, 6))` defines the figure
- `def animate(longitude):` is the function to update the map with new frames as they come in:
    - `ax = plt.gca()` gets currently active axes' references.
    - `ax.remove()` deletes the plot on this axis, if it is already there.
    - `ax = plt.axes([0, 0, 1, 1], projection=ccrs.Geostationary(central_longitude=longitude))` refreshes the map on the axes with the current longitude received by this function, using a `Geostationary` projection.
    - `ax.coastlines()` adds the coastlines feature to the map.
    - `ax.stock_img()` adds the background image to the map.
    - `ax.gridlines()` adds grid lines to the image. We can't use the `draw_labels=True` argument here, since we are using a `Geostationary` projection.
- `ani = animation.FuncAnimation(fig, animate, frames=np.linspace(0, 360, 10), interval=50, repeat=True, repeat_delay=500)` activates the animation:
    - `fig` is the figure object on which the map is to be drawn.

- `animate` is the update function for the animation defined previously.
- `frames` is a list of 10 entries, where entries are separated equally by 36 degrees. This number is automatically passed on to the animate function, which receives it and maps to the current longitude. Hence, the globe rotates by 36 degrees in each iteration.
- `interval=50` specifies the time gap in milliseconds between consecutive frames.
- `repeat=True` specifies that after all the frames are displayed, the cycle should be repeated so that the animation continues forever.
- `repeat_delay=500` specifies the time delay in milliseconds before starting the next cycle.

- `ani.save("Geostationary.mp4")` saves the animation, with the filename of `Geostationary.mp4`, into the present working directory

Upon running the preceding code, you should see something like the following (here, a snapshot of the animated plot) on the screen. You can find the MP4 file in the code directory to view the actual animation:

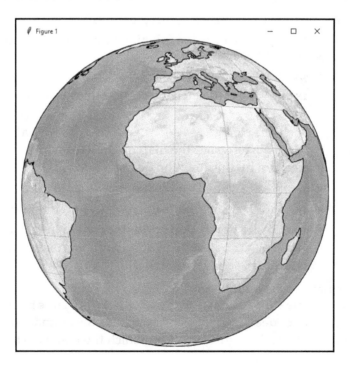

15
Exploratory Data Analysis Using the Seaborn Toolkit

In this chapter, we will learn how to use one more third-party toolkit, `seaborn`, with the recipes that plot the following types of graphs:

- Relational plots (`sns.relplot`):
  - Line plots (`sns.lineplot`)
  - Scatter plots (`sns.scatterplot`)
- Categorical plots (`sns.catplot`):
  - Strip and swarm plots (`sns.stripplot`, `sns.swarmplot`)
  - Box and boxn plots (`sns.boxplot`, `sns.boxnplot`)
  - Bar and count plots (`sns.barplot`, `sns.countplot`)
  - Violin plots (`sns.violinplot`)
  - Point plots (`sns.pointplot`)
- Distribution plots:
  - Distribution, **Kernel Density Estimate** (**KDE**), and rug plots (`sns.distplot`, `sns.kdeplot`, `sns.rugplot`)
- Regression plots:
  - Regression plots and residual plots (`sns.regplot`, `sns.residplot`)
  - Lm plots (`sns.lmplot`)
- Multi-plot grids:
  - Joint plots and joint grid plots (`sns.jointplot`, `sns.JointGrid`)
  - Pair Plots and pair grid plots (`sns.pairplot`, `sns.PairGrid`)
  - Facet grids (`sns.FacetGrid`)

- Matrix plots:
  - Heatmaps (`sns.heatmap`)
  - Cluster maps (`sns.clustermap`)

Introduction

Seaborn is a powerful visualization tool built on top of Matplotlib. It makes multi-variable exploratory data analysis easier and intuitive, and it adds a few new types of plots, and its background styles and color maps are much more pleasing. It has many built-in statistical functions, making it a preferred tool for statistical data analysis. It also has quite elaborate online documentation, which you can find at `https://seaborn.pydata.org/index.html`.

We will use two datasets to demonstrate most of the seaborn features. One dataset, `Wine Quality`, is already familiar to you, and we will introduce a new dataset containing *snack sales* data from a fictitious snack shop. Instead of reading these files many times in each of the recipes, we will describe both of them in this section, and subsequently we will just use them for plotting the graphs. This is a slight deviation from the approach we have taken so far in this book. Both these data files can be found in the code library for this chapter.

Snacks Sales dataset

This dataset (provided in the code library) contains information on the sales of various items for a given date, day of the week, whether it is a weekend, and whether there was promotion on that day. We have data for three years: 2015, 2016, and 2017. The first five rows of the dataset look as follows:

	Period	daywk	weekend	Date	Cakes	Pies	Cookies	Smoothies	Coffee	Promotion
0	1	Tuesday	N	1/1/2015	79	46	518	60	233	No
1	2	Wednesday	N	1/2/2015	91	50	539	161	427	No
2	3	Thursday	N	1/3/2015	47	60	222	166	347	No
3	4	Friday	N	1/4/2015	89	64	734	153	358	No
4	5	Saturday	Y	1/5/2015	112	73	764	240	392	No

Then, we will add two derived variables that help plot the required graphs: Month (1 to 12) and Quarter (1 to 4). After adding these variables, the first five rows look as follows:

	Period	daywk	weekend	Date	Cakes	Pies	Cookies	Smoothies	Coffee	Promotion	Month	Quarter
0	1	Tuesday	N	1/1/2015	79	46	518	60	233	No	1	1
1	2	Wednesday	N	1/2/2015	91	50	539	161	427	No	1	1
2	3	Thursday	N	1/3/2015	47	60	222	166	347	No	1	1
3	4	Friday	N	1/4/2015	89	64	734	153	358	No	1	1
4	5	Saturday	Y	1/5/2015	112	73	764	240	392	No	1	1

The following code block reads the Excel file and adds additional variables:

```
import pandas as pd
import numpy as np

snacks_sales = pd.read_csv('Snacks_Data.csv')
snacks_sales['Month'] = pd.DatetimeIndex(snacks_sales['Date']).month
Quarter_Mapping = {1:1, 2:1, 3:1, 4:2, 5:2, 6:2, 7:3, 8:3, 9:3, 10:4,
                   11:4, 12:4}
snacks_sales['Quarter'] = snacks_sales['Month'].map(Quarter_Mapping)
```

Wine Quality

This dataset has 11 attributes that influence the quality of the wine. The Quality rating varies from 3 to 8, and then we map 3 and 4 to Low, 5 and 6 to Med, and 7 and 8 to High to create a new variable: Quality.

The first five rows of the dataset looks as follows:

	fixed acidity	volatile acidity	citric acid	residual sugar	chlorides	free sulfur dioxide	total sulfur dioxide	density	pH	sulphates	alcohol	quality	Quality
0	7.4	0.70	0.00	1.9	0.076	11.0	34.0	0.9978	3.51	0.56	9.4	5	Med
1	7.8	0.88	0.00	2.6	0.098	25.0	67.0	0.9968	3.20	0.68	9.8	5	Med
2	7.8	0.76	0.04	2.3	0.092	15.0	54.0	0.9970	3.26	0.65	9.8	5	Med
3	11.2	0.28	0.56	1.9	0.075	17.0	60.0	0.9980	3.16	0.58	9.8	6	Med
4	7.4	0.70	0.00	1.9	0.076	11.0	34.0	0.9978	3.51	0.56	9.4	5	Med

We will also compute the correlation matrix for the Wine Quality dataset, which we will use in some of the plots.

The following is the code block to read and add additional variables to the `Wine Quality` dataset:

```
import pandas as pd

# Read the data from a csv file into pandas data frame
wine_quality = pd.read_csv('winequality.csv', delimiter=';')

# Map numeric Quality codes to "Low", "Med" and "High" qualitative
   ratings
quality_map = {3:'Low', 4: 'Low', 5:'Med', 6:'Med', 7:'High', 8:'High'}
wine_quality['Quality'] = wine_quality['quality'].map(quality_map)

# compute correlation matrix
corr = wine_quality.corr()

# Display the first 5 records of wine_quality dataset, and unique
   values of quality variable
wine_quality.head()
set(wine_quality.quality)
```

Semantic and facet variables

Apart from two variables whose relationship is plotted in a two-dimensional graph, seaborn allows the plotting of the influence of three additional variables on the relationship between the two main variables. These three variables are called **semantic** variables. They are referred to as hue, size, and style, which act as arguments to the given plot function.

For each unique value of hue, there will be one relationship plot; similarly, for each unique value of style, there will be one relationship plot. If there are two unique values in the hue variable (for example, Yes and No) and there are two unique values in the style variable (for example, s and D markers), then there will be 2 * 2 = 4 relationship plots (*Yes & s, Yes & D, No & s, No & D* combinations). Various hue values are plotted in different colors, and various style values are plotted in different line or marker styles.

Similarly, the size variable influences the size of the points being plotted for the two main variables. Unlike the Matplotlib scatter function, here, the size variable range is divided into multiple bins, and points are assigned to these bins. In the Matplotlib scatter function, each point is mapped to a different value in the size variable individually.

In addition to these three semantic variables, seaborn allows the adding of two more variables to `row` and `col`, where for each unique value of the row/col variable, there will be one plot (axes), and it will be arranged in row/col. These `row` and `col` variables are called **facet variables**, as they allow us to understand the influence of other facets on the two main variables being plotted.

These additional variables can be mapped to various dimensions on which data is to be analyzed, or the relationship between two variables is to be analyzed. In a typical sales analysis scenario, the two main variables could be sales (either units or $) or time (day, month, or quarter), and the dimensions could be business unit, product line, region/country, sales rep, promotions, currency, and so on.

Relational plots

Relational plots depict the relationship between two continuous variables. There is one common API in `seaborn`, `relplot()`, which is used for two types of plots: **line** and **scatter** plots. However, there are separate functions for each of these two types as well: `lineplot()` and `scatterplot()`. We can either use `relplot()` with an argument to plot a line plot or scatter plot, or directly use the `lineplot()` and `scatterplot()` functions.

Line plots with one-to-one and one-to-many relationships

In line plots, observations are connected to a line whose style can be customized. The relationship between x and y variables could be one-to-one, or at times it could be one-to-many. In our `Snack Sales` dataset, if we plot each item's sales against the date or period, it is a one-to-one relationship, as there is just one observation for each pair of dates/period and sales. However, if we take month and sales, then there are 30 observations (sales records) in each month, which is a one-to-many relationship.

Seaborn offers various options to plot both these types of relationships. In the main recipe, we will learn the one-to-one relationship and in the *There's More...* section, we will learn about the one-to-many relationship.

Getting ready

Import the required packages:

```
import matplotlib.pyplot as plt
import seaborn as sns
```

How to do it...

The following are the steps to plot four line plots with various options:

1. Set the background style:

```
sns.set(style='darkgrid')
```

2. Plot a line graph between `Period` and `Smoothies` sales with the title of the plot:

```
sns.relplot(x='Period', y='Smoothies',
            data=snacks_sales.query("Period < 300"), kind='line')
plt.title('line plot', size=20, color='g')
```

3. Plot a line graph between `Period` and `Smoothies` sales with the day of the week as hue:

```
day_order = ['Monday', 'Tuesday', 'Wednesday', 'Thursday',
'Friday',
             'Saturday', 'Sunday']
sns.relplot(x='Period', y='Smoothies', hue='daywk',
            hue_order=day_order,
            data=snacks_sales.query("Period < 300"), kind='line')
plt.title('line plot with hue=daywk', size=20, color='g')
```

4. Plot a line graph between `Period` and `Smoothies` sales with `Promotion` as the hue:

```
sns.relplot(x='Period', y='Smoothies', hue='Promotion', hue_order=
            ["Yes", "No"],
            data=snacks_sales.query("Period < 300"), kind='line')
plt.title('line plot with hue=Promotion', size=20, color='g')
```

5. Plot a line graph between `Period` and `Smoothies` sales with `Promotion` as the hue and `weekend` as the `style`:

```
sns.relplot(x='Period', y='Smoothies', hue='Promotion', hue_order=
            ["Yes", "No"], style='weekend',
            style_order=["Y", "N"], kind='line',
```

```
                    data=snacks_sales.query("Period < 300"))
        plt.title('line plot with hue and style', size=20, color='g')
```

How it works...

Here is the explanation of the code:

- `sns.set(style='darkgrid')` sets the background style for the plot. Seaborn provides five predefined styles: `dark`, `darkgrid`, `white`, `whitegrid`, and `ticks`
- `sns.relplot(x='Period', y='Smoothies', data=snacks_sales.query("Period < 300"), kind='line')` plots the relationship between the two main variables, specified by x and y:
    - `Period` and `Smoothies` are the names of two variables in the `Snacks Sales` dataset
    - `Snacks Sales` is the input dataset, and `query("Period < 300")` applies the filter on the dataset to plot only the first 300 observations (rows), since plotting the entire dataset gets too crowded
    - `kind='line'` means plot a line graph
- For the second plot, we will add `hue='daywk'` and `hue_order=day_order`
- `plt.title('line plot', size=20, color='g')` plots the title with a size of 20 points, and in *green*
- `day_order = ['Monday', 'Tuesday', 'Wednesday', 'Thursday', 'Friday', 'Saturday', 'Sunday']` specifies the order in which days of the week are to be plotted on the graph
- `hue='daywk'` means that plot the relationship between `Period` and `Smoothies` sales for each day of the week, and `hue_order=day_order` specifies that the day of the week should be printed in the order specified in the `day_order` list
- For the third plot, we will change `hue="Promotion"` and map `["Yes", "No"]` to `hue_order`
- For the fourth plot, we will add `style='weekend'` and `style_order=["Y", "N"]`

Upon executing the preceding code, you should see the following plots on your screen:

Line plot:

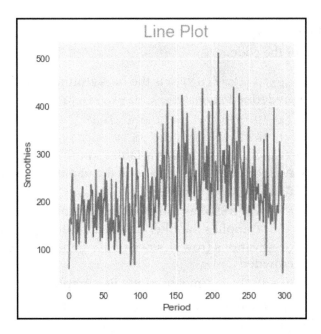

Line plot with hue as daywk:

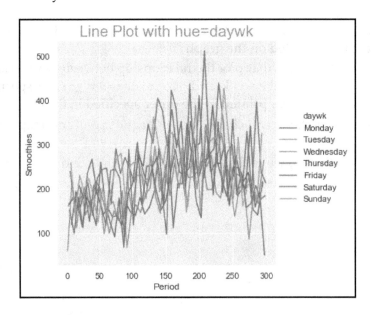

Line plot with hue as Promotion:

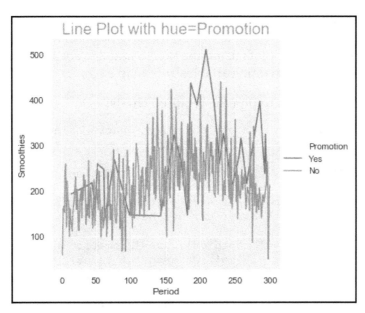

Line plot with hue and style:

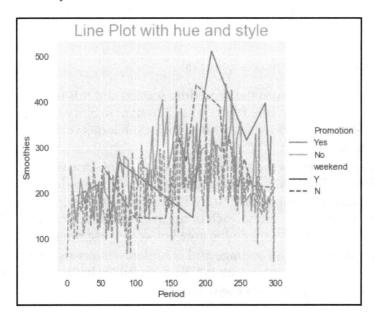

There's more...

In the preceding section, `Period` and `Smoothies` sales had one-to-one mapping. Now let's replace `Period` with the `Month` variable, where we have 30 observations (rows) for each month. We will again plot four plots using the `Month` and `Smoothies` sales variables. We will use the `hue` and `style` semantic variables and map `Promotion` and `weekend` to them.

The following is the code block to plot the required charts:

```
sns.relplot(x='Month', y='Smoothies', data=snacks_sales, kind='line')
plt.title('line plot', size=20, color='g')

sns.relplot(x='Month', y='Smoothies', hue='Promotion',
            data=snacks_sales, kind='line',
            err_style="bars", ci=68) # Standard Errors
plt.title('line plot with Error bar and hue', size=20, color='g')

sns.relplot(x='Month', y='Smoothies', hue='Promotion', style='weekend',
            kind='line', ci='sd', data=snacks_sales)
plt.title('line plot with hue and style', size=20, color='g')

sns.relplot(x='Month', y='Smoothies', hue='Promotion', style='weekend',
            dashes=False, markers=True,
            data=snacks_sales, kind='line', ci=None)
plt.title('line plot with hue and custom style', size=20, color='g')

plt.show();
```

Here is the explanation of how the code works:

- In the first plot, between the preceding section and this one, the only difference is the change of the variable from `Period` to `Month`. Since they have different relationships with `Smoothies` sales, the graph looks very different and provides different information.
- It basically computes the average sales of all 30 observations for a given month and plots the line graph for all such averages. It uses a default parameter, `ci=95`, which means to compute a 95% confidence interval around every average point and draw the range around each of the average points, connect all of them as a line graph, and finally shade the area between these ranges
- You can also switch off average and confidence intervals, by specifying `estimator=None` as an argument. Since variables have a one-to-many relationship, the plot takes a saw tooth pattern!

- In the second plot, we change the default line graph with an error plot, by specifying `err_style='bars'` and a confidence interval of 68%, `ci=68`. We also add `hue = 'Promotion'`.
- In the third plot, we change the confidence interval from a fixed value to a standard deviation of 30 values for each month, with `ci='sd'`, and add `style='weekend'`.
- In the fourth plot, we replace the default line styles of *solid* and *dashed* lines with default `markers`, by specifying `dashes=False` and `'markers=True'`. Instead of `markers=True`, we could have specified specific markers, such as `markers=['D', 's']`, to override default markers. We also specify `ci=None` to avoid plotting the confidence interval around average line plots.

Upon executing the preceding code, you should see the following graphs on your screen:

Line plot:

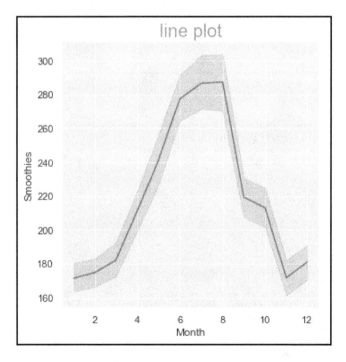

Line plot with error bar and hue:

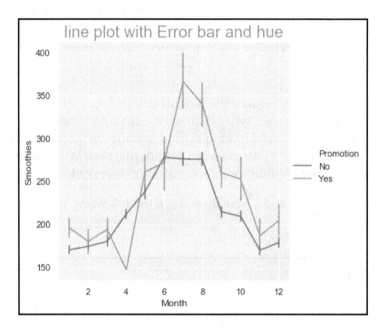

Line plot with hue and style:

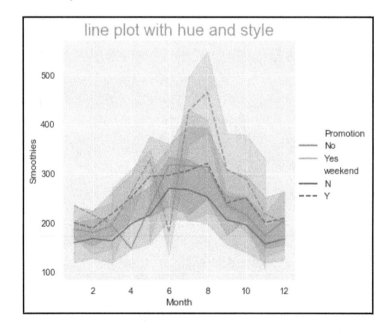

Line plot with hue and custom style:

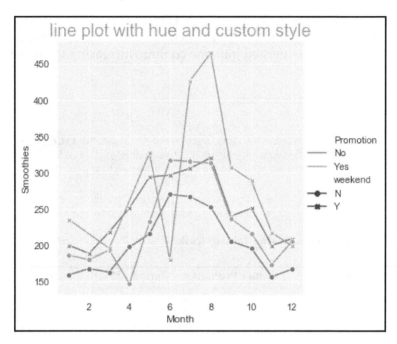

Line plots with a long-form dataset

In the previous recipe, we plotted the relationship between two variables as a single line graph and used other semantic variables to analyze them. The input dataset has the sales data for various items, such as `Pies`, `Cakes`, `Cookies`, `Coffee`, and `Smoothies`, and each of these items is a column in the dataset. However, if we want to plot a line graph for each of these items on the same axes/plot for relative sales analysis, we need to prepare the input data slightly differently, before passing it on to `relplot()`.

Getting ready

The input data in the current form is called **wide form**, as each item is represented in a column, increasing the width of the table. We need to create another dataset that is of a long format, where all the items are merged into one column, increasing the number of rows or the depth of the table.

The following is the code to achieve this:

```
# Create a long form DataFrame from wide form DF
long_sales = pd.melt(snacks_sales, var_name='Item', value_name='Sales',
                     id_vars=['daywk', 'weekend', 'Date', 'Promotion',
                     'Period', 'Month', 'Quarter'])

long_sales.shape          # dimensions, number of rows and columns
long_sales.sample(n=5)    # Display random 5 sample rows
```

Here is how five random rows in the dataset look:

	daywk	weekend	Date	Promotion	Period	Month	Quarter	Item	Sales
3899	Sunday	Y	9/7/2016	No	615	9	3	Smoothies	298
2689	Thursday	N	5/15/2016	Yes	500	5	2	Cookies	545
1193	Tuesday	N	4/9/2015	No	99	4	2	Pies	63
1274	Saturday	Y	6/29/2015	No	180	6	2	Pies	62
2884	Wednesday	N	11/26/2016	No	695	11	4	Cookies	558

How to do it...

We will plot two figures in this recipe. The first figure has four plots in it and the second one has one plot:

1. The first figure depicts sales of all five items in each plot using the hue variable, but each plot represents a combination of the weekend and Promotion variables, which are specified as row and col variables:

```
g = sns.relplot(x='Period', y='Sales', data=long_sales,
kind='line',
                hue='Item', row='weekend', col='Promotion')
```

2. The second figure depicts day-wise sales for 30 days in a month for all items, but includes only weekend sales, and when Promotion is ON and OFF:

```
# one line for each of Items
long_sales['Day'] = pd.DatetimeIndex(long_sales['Date']).day
sns.relplot(x='Day', y='Sales', hue='Promotion',
                data=long_sales.query("weekend =='Y'"), kind='line',
                units="Item", estimator=None, lw=1, height=6,
aspect=2);
```

How it works...

Here is the explanation of the preceding code:

- x, y, data, kind, and hue parameters are exactly the same as what we have seen in the previous recipe
- row='weekend' specifies that, for each unique value of weekend, plot a separate axes along the rows of the figure
- col='Promotion' specifies that for each unique value of Promotion, plot a separate axes along the columns of the figure
- When both row and col variables are specified, it plots the grid with a combination of both

The resulting figure looks like the following:

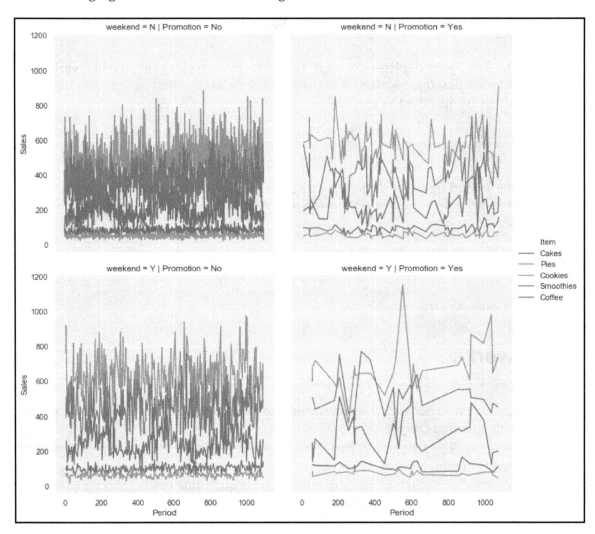

For the second figure, we first define a derived variable, Day, to store the day of the month value for each of the observations/rows and add it to the input dataset. Each day will have 12 sales observations in a year, representing each of the months in the year. We will plot day-wise sales in this figure:

- data=long_sales.query("weekend =='Y'") limits plotting the data to only for weekends.

- `units="Item"` specifies to plot a line graph for each unique value of `Item`.
- `estimator=None` switches off computing and plotting averages and confidence interval for each of the line plots
- `lw=1` specifies the width of the lines to be plotted
- `height=6` and `aspect=2` specify the size of the figure, with height as six inches and width as 12 inches (twice that of height)

The resulting figure looks as the following. One issue with it is that it is not clear which line plot belongs to which item! Currently, it does not allow us to plot labels in this case:

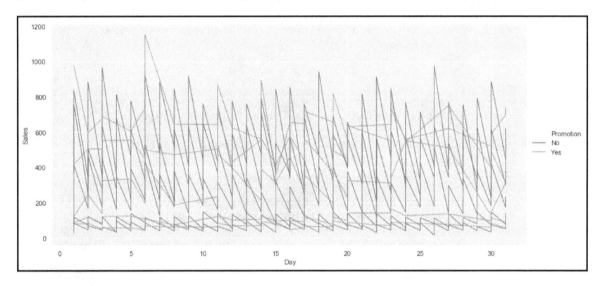

Scatter plots

Scatter plots plot the relationship between two variables as individual points, without connecting to each other. It helps visualize how these points spread across the x and y axes to find whether there are any patterns or clusters within the data. We will use the same `Snack Sales` dataset that we used in the preceding section, and we will use the same semantic variables in the main section, and `row` and `col` variables in the *There's more...* section.

Getting ready

Import the required libraries and set the background style to `dark`:

```
import matplotlib.pyplot as plt
import seaborn as sns
```

How to do it...

1. Plot a scatter plot between `Smoothies` sales and `Period`:

```
sns.relplot(x='Period', y='Smoothies', data=snacks_sales,
            kind='scatter')
plt.title('scatter plot', size=20, color='g')
```

2. Add `hue = 'Promotion'`:

```
sns.relplot(x='Period', y='Smoothies', hue='Promotion',
            data=snacks_sales)
plt.title('scatter plot with hue', size=20, color='g')
```

3. Add `style = 'weekend'`:

```
sns.relplot(x='Period', y='Smoothies', hue='Promotion',
            style='weekend', markers=['^', 'D'],
            data=snacks_sales)
plt.title('scatter plot with hue and style', size=20, color='g')
```

4. Add `size = 'Cookies'`:

```
sns.relplot(x='Period', y='Smoothies', hue='Promotion',
            style='weekend', size='Cookies',
            markers=['^', 'D'],data=snacks_sales)
plt.title('scatter plot with hue, size and style', size=20,
          color='g');
```

How it works...

The only difference between `lineplot()` and `scatterplot()` is to change `kind='line'` to `kind='scatter'`. In `relplot()`, `kind='scatter'` is the default, so you can omit this parameter, as we have done here for a few plots.

All the other parameters are exactly the same as in the preceding recipe.

Here are how the plots look:

Scatter plot:

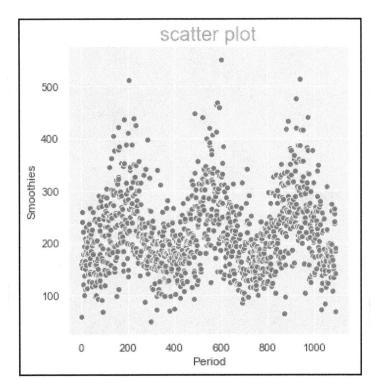

Scatter plot with hue:

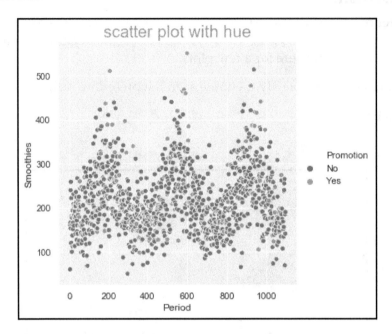

Scatter plot with hue and style:

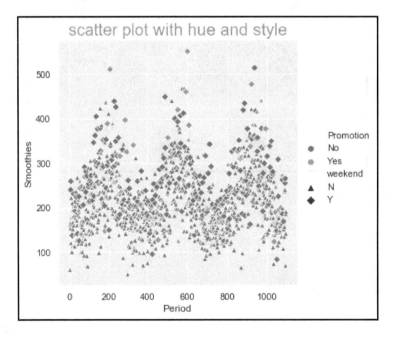

Scatter plot with hue, size, and style:

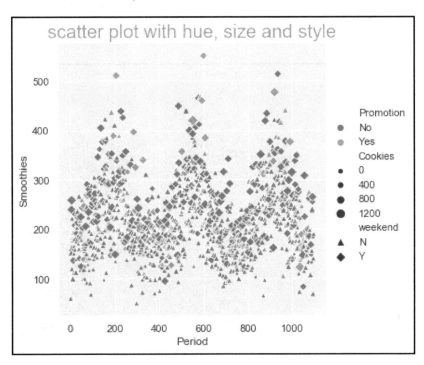

There's more...

In this section, we will use the row and col parameters, along with hue, to plot the same data.

Here is the code for this:

```
day_order = ['Monday', 'Tuesday', 'Wednesday', 'Thursday', 'Friday',
             'Saturday', 'Sunday']
sns.relplot(x='Period', y='Smoothies', hue='Promotion', col='daywk',
            col_wrap=3, col_order=day_order, data=snacks_sales,
            height=3)

sns.relplot(x='Period', y='Smoothies', col='daywk',
            col_order=day_order, row='Promotion', row_order=['Yes',
            'No'], data=snacks_sales, height=3)
plt.show();
```

`col_wrap=3` specifies to plot only three columns and after that, wrap it to the next row. When we use this option, we can't use the `row` parameter.

You should see the following figure on your screen:

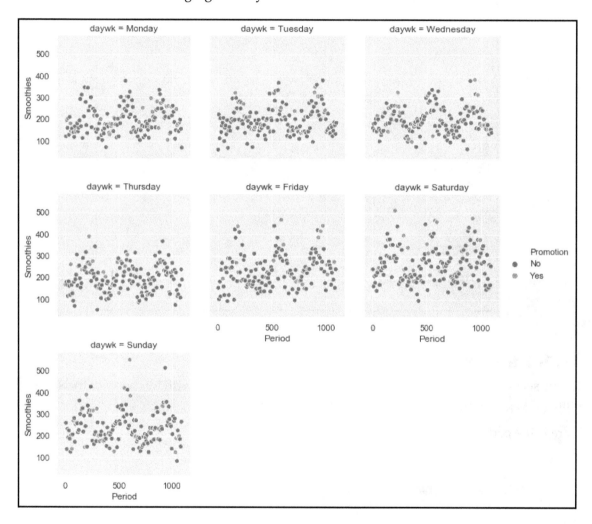

Similar to `hue_order` and `style_order`, we can also specify `row_order` and `col_order`.

The resulting figure looks like is:

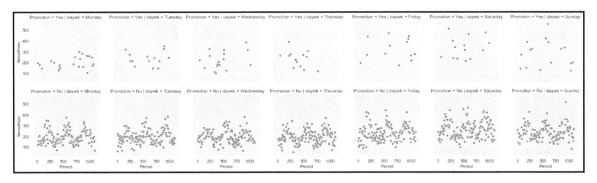

Categorical plots

A categorical plot is used when one of the two variables being plotted is categorical, instead of both being continuous. Seaborn enhances a few of the categorical plots provided by Matplotlib and also adds a few additional ones. We will cover five such groups of plots in this section.

Seaborn provides one common API, `catplot()`, to cover all such plots. This makes it easier to familiarize yourself with a common set of arguments that can be passed to plot all types of categorical plots. However, each of the different functions can be used directly, and at times some of them may offer unique features that are not common to all types of plots. Please refer to the documentation on each of the specific plots at `https://seaborn.pydata.org/api.html`.

Strip and swarm plots

Since one of the variables is categorical, all the values of the other variable for a given value of categorical variable fall in one straight line with many overlapping points, which makes it a bit hard to visualize. Strip and swarm plots allow these points to be plotted slightly away from the line, avoiding overlaps based on given parameters.

Getting ready

Import the required libraries, set the background style to `ticks`, and enable `color_codes` to be mapped to `seaborn` colors when specified in Matplotlib format:

```
import matplotlib.pyplot as plt
import seaborn as sns

sns.set(style="ticks", color_codes=True)
```

How to do it...

1. Plot a strip plot of sales of `Cookies` by day of the week, with `jitter=0.05` and `hue='Promotion'`:

```
day_order = ['Monday', 'Tuesday', 'Wednesday', 'Thursday',
'Friday',
             'Saturday', 'Sunday']
sns.catplot(x='daywk',y='Cookies', data=snacks_sales,
            hue='Promotion', order=day_order, jitter=0.05,
height=4,
            aspect=2, kind='strip')
plt.title('stripplot with jitter=0.05', size=20, color='g')
```

2. Plot a strip plot of sales of `Cookies` by the day of the week, except Thursday, with the default `jitter` and with a specified color palette:

```
sns.catplot(x='daywk',y='Cookies', data=snacks_sales.query("daywk
!=
            'Thursday'"), order=['Monday', 'Tuesday', 'Wednesday',
            'Friday', 'Saturday', 'Sunday'],palette='Set1',
            height=4, aspect=2); # jitter=False plots all the
points
                                 on one line similar to plt
plt.title('stripplot with default jitter', size=20, color='g')
```

3. Plot a swarm plot of sales of `Cookies` by the day of the week and `hue =` `'Promotion'`:

```
sns.catplot(x='daywk',y='Cookies', data=snacks_sales,
            order=day_order, hue='Promotion',
            kind='swarm',height=4, aspect=2)
plt.title('swarmplot', size=20, color='g');
```

How it works...

Here is the explanation of the preceding code:

- `order=day_order` specifies the order in which unique values of the categorical variable are to be plotted on the axis.
- `jitter=0.05` specifies the amount of jitter to be applied; the larger the value, the longer the range around the straight line.
- `kind='strip'` specifies the type of the plot, which in this case is `stripplot()`. However, this is the default type for `catplot()`, so it can be omitted as well.
- You can pass the `dodge=True` argument, if you want to plot `hue` variable values separately side by side, instead of both colors on the same strip. For `stripplot()`, `dodge=False` is the default, which is what we have used here.
- `data=snacks_sales.query("daywk != 'Thursday'")` filters input data to exclude all the observations for `Thursday`, so the plot includes only the remaining days of the week.
- `palette='Set1'` specifies the color palette to be applied. It is similar to the `cmap` of Matplotlib. We can use the `cmap` options provided by Matplotlib as well here.
- We use the default `jitter` for the second plot. The default is not a fixed amount of `jitter`, but varies based on the input data distribution.
- We can also switch off jitter by specifying `jitter=False`, in which case its output will be similar to that of Matplotlib.

- The third plot, `kind='swarm'`, specifies that a swam plot is to be plotted. Here, it uses a different algorithm to spread the points around the line to ensure that there are no overlapping points at all:

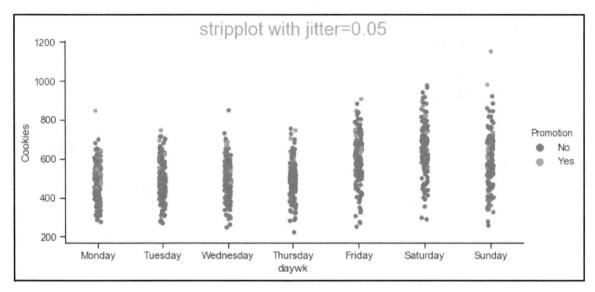

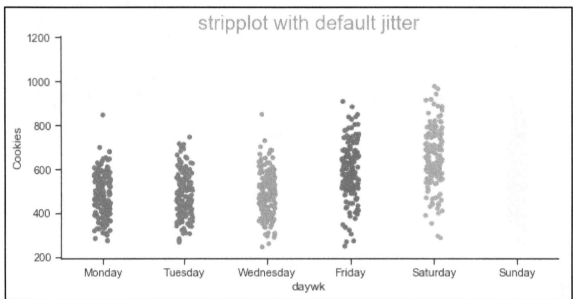

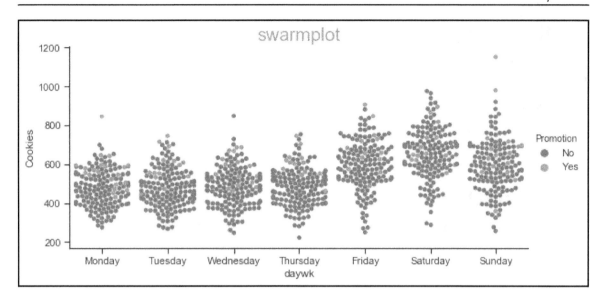

Box and boxn plots

`boxplot()` is similar to what we saw with Matplotlib, and `boxnplot()` is an extension by Seaborn to provide more details on the relationship.

`boxplot()` provides details of the median value (line inside the box), the first (bottom of the box), and the third quartiles (top of the box), whiskers at 1.5 IQR (1.5 times the size (height for vertical plots, width for horizontal plots) of the box) on top as well as the bottom, and outliers beyond the whiskers. This is quite enough for most cases, where the dataset size is small, say a few hundred observations.

However, when the dataset size is very large, then it does not provide adequate insights on the tail ends. `boxnplot()` addresses this limitation of `boxplot()` by providing multiple quartiles to cover the tail ends on both sides. For more details on this, please refer to the paper here: https://vita.had.co.nz/papers/letter-value-plot.html.

Getting ready

Import the required libraries, set the background style to `ticks`, and
enable `color_codes` to be mapped to seaborn colors when specified in Matplotlib format:

```
import matplotlib.pyplot as plt
import seaborn as sns

sns.set(style="ticks", color_codes=True)
```

How to do it...

Here, we will use a long form dataset and plot the sales of all the items:

1. Plot a `boxplot()` with the sales of various items:

    ```
    sns.catplot(x='Item', y='Sales', data=long_sales, kind='box',
                height=4, aspect=2);
    ```

2. Add `hue=Promotion` for the second plot:

    ```
    sns.catplot(x='Item', y='Sales', data=long_sales, kind='box',
                hue='Promotion', height=4, aspect=2);
    ```

3. Change hue to `hue=weekend` :

    ```
    sns.catplot(x='daywk', y='Sales', data=long_sales, kind='box',
                hue='weekend', order=day_order, height=4, aspect=2);
    ```

4. Repeat the last three steps with `boxnplot()`:

    ```
    sns.catplot(x='Item', y='Sales', data=long_sales, kind='boxen',
                height=4, aspect=2);
    sns.catplot(x='Item', y='Sales', data=long_sales, kind='boxen',
                hue='Promotion', height=4, aspect=2);
    sns.catplot(x='Sales', y='daywk', data=long_sales, kind='boxen',
                hue='weekend',
                order=day_order, height=4, aspect=2);
    ```

How it works...

Here is the explanation of the preceding code:

- `kind='box'` specifies that it is a `boxplot()`.
- `dodge=True` is the default for `boxplot()` as well as `boxnplot()`, so a separate plot will be drawn for each of the unique values of the hue variable by default. If we want to plot both on the same boxplot, then we have to pass on the `dodge=False` argument.
- `kind='boxen'` specifies to plot a boxn plot.

Upon execution of the preceding code, you should see the following plots on your screen:

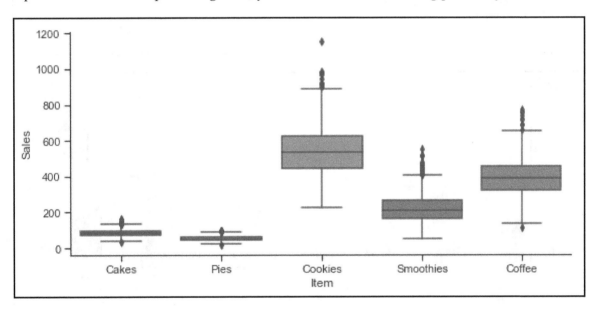

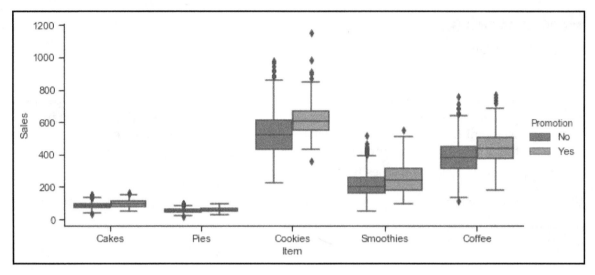

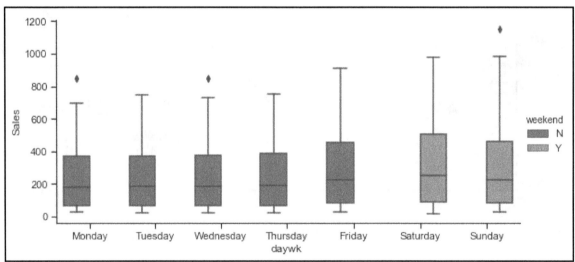

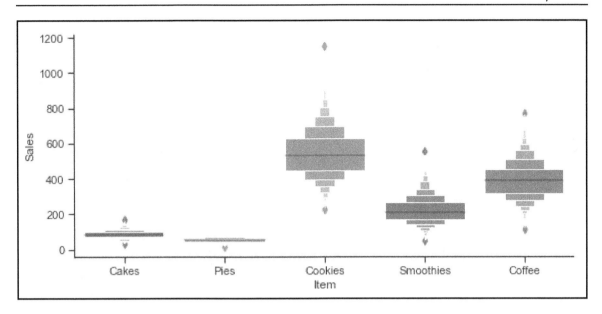

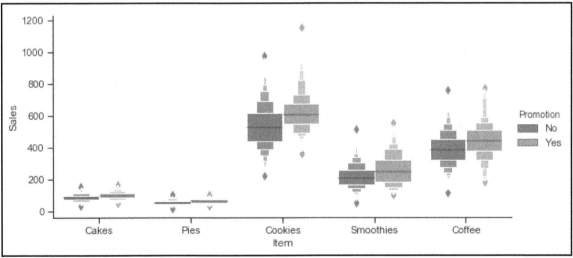

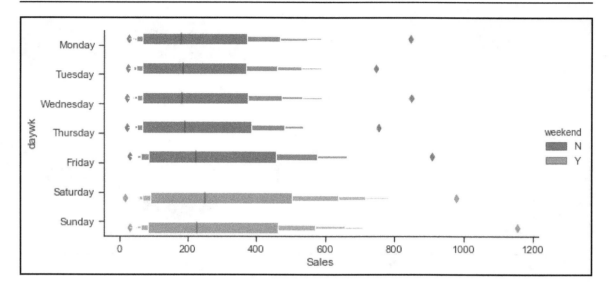

Bar and count plots

`barplot()` is similar to what we have seen in Matplotlib, but `countplot()` is an extension of seaborn. The height of the bar in `barplot()` represents the average value of all observations for a given category, whereas in `countplot()`, height represents the count of observations for a given category.

Getting ready

Import the required libraries, set the background style to `ticks`, and enable `color_codes` to be mapped to seaborn colors when specified in Matplotlib format:

```
import matplotlib.pyplot as plt
import seaborn as sns
from numpy import median

sns.set(style="ticks", color_codes=True)
```

How to do it...

We will plot four bar plots and three count plots using various different options:

1. Plot a `barplot()` using input data in the long data format, and annotate bars with the actual values on top:

```
plt.figure(figsize=(9,4))
b = sns.barplot(x='Item', y='Sales', data=long_sales,
estimator=sum,
                palette='husl')
b.set(yscale='log', ylim=[50000, 1000000])
sns.despine()
for bar in b.patches:
    b.annotate("{:,}".format(bar.get_height()),
               (bar.get_x()+bar.get_width()/2.,bar.get_height()),
             ha='center',va='center',xytext=
                          (0,10),textcoords='offset points',
                          color='b', weight='bold')
plt.title('Bar Plot: Long Data Format,value annotation &
          estimator=sum', size=15, color='g', weight='bold')
```

2. Plot a `barplot()` using input data in the wide data format to plot all numerical variables:

```
sns.catplot(data=snacks_sales, kind='bar', height=4, aspect=2, #
                                                      wide form
          order=['Cakes', 'Pies', 'Cookies', 'Smoothies',
                 'Coffee', 'weekday', 'Period'],
                 palette="Set1");
plt.title('Bar Plot: Wide Data Format,Plots all numerical
          variables', size=15, color='g', weight='bold')
```

3. Plot a `barplot()` using the long data format, estimator equals median, and a custom color palette:

```
sns.catplot(x='Item', y='Sales', data=long_sales, kind='bar',
          hue='Promotion', hue_order=['Yes','No'],
palette={"Yes":
          "r", "No": "indigo"},
          estimator=median, capsize=0.25, height=4, aspect=2);
plt.title('Bar Plot: Long Data Format, estimator=median and custom
          palette', size=15, color='g', weight='bold')
```

4. Plot a `barplot()` with `estimator=len/count`, a custom error width, and color:

```
day_order = ['Monday', 'Tuesday', 'Wednesday', 'Thursday',
'Friday',
            'Saturday', 'Sunday']
sns.catplot(x='daywk', y='Sales', data=long_sales, kind='bar',
            hue='Promotion', ci='sd',
            estimator=len, capsize=0.25, errcolor='m', errwidth=5,
            hue_order=['Yes','No'], palette="muted",
            order=day_order, height=4, aspect=2);
plt.title('Bar Plot, estimator=len(count), errwidth=5, errcolor=m',
            size=15, color='g', weight='bold')
```

5. Plot a `countplot()` with sales of all items:

```
sns.catplot(x='Item', data=long_sales, kind='count', height=4,
            aspect=2); # long form data frame
plt.title('Count Plot: Sales by Item', size=15, color='g',
            weight='bold')
```

6. Plot a `countplot()` with `hue` and a custom palette:

```
sns.catplot(x='Item', data=long_sales, kind='count',
            hue='Promotion', hue_order=['Yes','No'],
palette={"Yes":
            "r", "No": "indigo"}, height=4, aspect=2);
plt.title('Count Plot, hue=Promotion, custom palette', size=15,
            color='g', weight='bold')
```

7. Plot a `countplot()` with sales by day of the week:

```
day_order = ['Monday', 'Tuesday', 'Wednesday', 'Thursday',
'Friday',
            'Saturday', 'Sunday']
sns.catplot(x='daywk', data=long_sales, kind='count',
            hue='Promotion', hue_order=['Yes','No'],
palette="Set2",
            order=day_order, height=4, aspect=2);
plt.title('Count Plot: Sales by day of the week', size=15,
            color='g', weight='bold');
```

How it works...

Here is the explanation of the preceding code. This is the first plot:

- `catplot()` with `kind='bar'` does not give the flexibility to capture individual bars to be able to plot the value on top of each of the bars. Hence, for the first plot, we use `barplot()`, which is similar to the Matplotlib bar chart
- `b = sns.barplot(x='Item', y='Sales', data=long_sales, estimator=sum, palette='husl')` plots the bar plot:
  - `estimator=sum` specifies that instead of the default average value, plot the sum of all observations for a given item
  - `palette='husl'` specifies the color palette to be used
- `b.set(yscale='log', ylim=[50000, 1000000])` sets up the logarithmic scale on the *y* axis and sets the limits as provided
- `sns.despine()` makes the top and right spines invisible. If you want to make the left and bottom axis also invisible, you can pass the arguments `left=True` and `right=True`.
- `for bar in b.patches:` is a for loop that captures each of the bars and plots the value on top of it. It is the same as what we did in Chapter 2, *Getting Started with Basic Plots*, for the Matplotlib bar plot.
- `plt.title('Bar Plot: Long Data Format,value annotation & estimator=sum', size=15, color='g', weight='bold')` plots the title for the chart.

This is the second plot:

- We pass on the wide format dataset directly, without providing x and y variables as we have been doing so far. In such a case, it plots the bars for each of the numerical variables in the input dataset by default.
- However, we can prevent some of the numerical columns from being plotted, by not specifying those variables in the order list.
- `order=['Cakes', 'Pies', 'Cookies', 'Smoothies', 'Coffee', 'Period']`: We have included only `Period` in the order list, other than the actual items. Hence, it does not plot the `weekday`, `Month`, and `Quarter` variables, even though they are numeric variables.
- `palette="Set1"` sets the predefined color palette `Set1`.

This is the third plot:

- We go back to the long data format and specify x and y data variables.
- hue='Promotion' specifies to plot bars for each unique value of Promotion with different color mappings.
- hue_order=['Yes','No'] specifies the order in which the Promotion bars are to be plotted.
- palette={"Yes": "r", "No": "indigo"} specifies the custom-defined color palette dictionary.
- estimator=median specifies the statistic to be used to aggregate the value of observations for a given item. The default statistic is average; here, we are overriding it with the median. In this dataset, the mean and the median are very close to each other for all items, so we may not be able to observe the difference in the bar plots. Some functions sum, len are available in core Python, so there is no need to import them, whereas median is not available in Python, so we need to import it from NumPy.
- capsize=0.25 specifies the width of the error bar cap on the top and bottom of the error bar.

This is the fourth plot:

- estimator=len specifies to use length (count of observations) as the aggregate statistic.
- ci='sd' specifies to use standard deviation for the confidence interval instead of a fixed percentage value.
- errcolor='m' specifies the color of the error bar as *magenta*.
- errwidth=5 specifies the width of the color bar lines.

This is the fifth plot:

- kind='count' specifies that it should draw a count plot.
- Here, the height of the bars is the count of observations in each of the item categories. In this case, count is same for all items.

This is the sixth plot:

- We add hue="Promotion", so count is different for two values of Promotion.
- We use the custom color palette as we did for the third plot

This is the seventh plot:

- Replace `Item` with `daywk` for the *x* axis.
- `palette="Set2"` sets another predefined color palette.

Upon executing the preceding code, you should see the following seven plots on your screen:

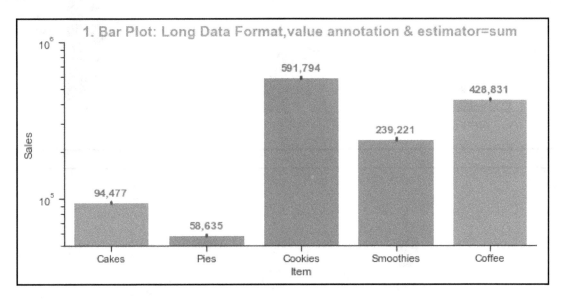

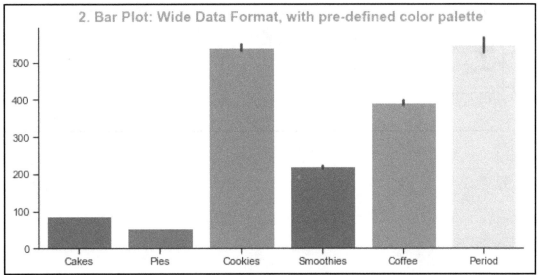

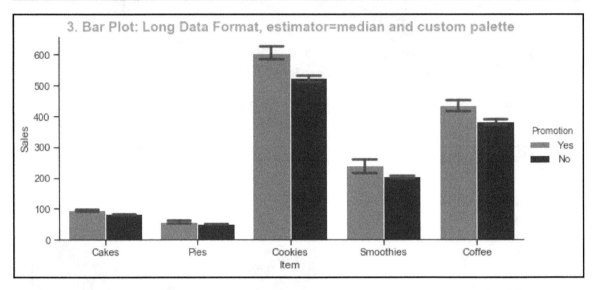

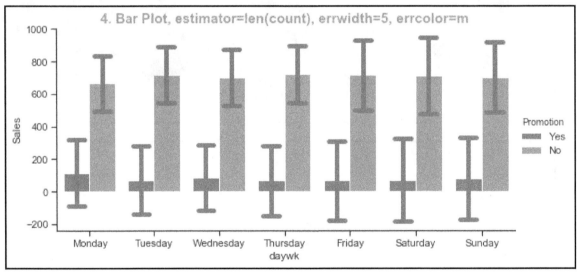

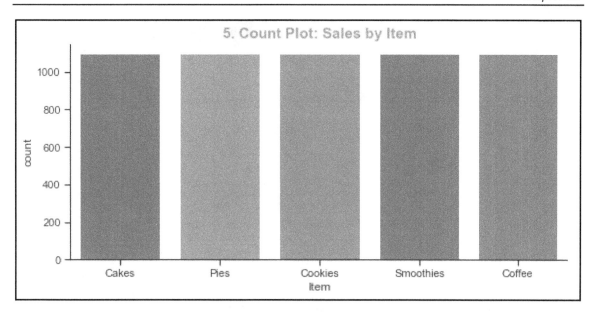

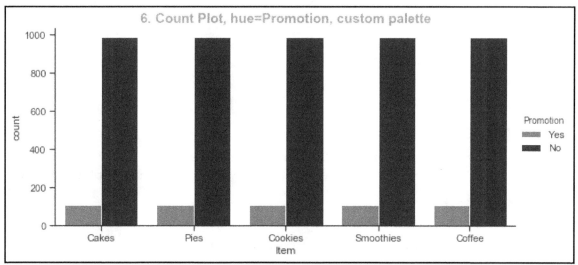

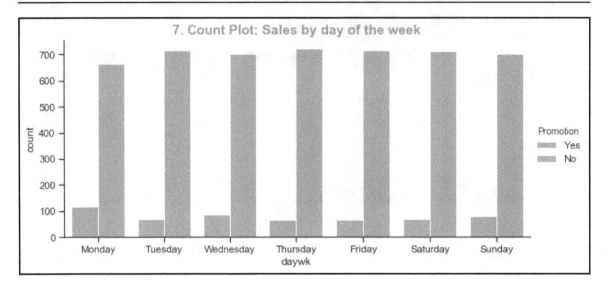

Violin plots

Seaborn has extended the violin plot functionality offered by Matplotlib to include different plots inside the violin plot. Unlike `boxplot`, which shows only summary statistics, violin plot even shows the distribution of data.

Getting ready

Import the required libraries, set the background style to `ticks`, and enable `color_codes` to be mapped to seaborn colors when specified in Matplotlib format:

```
import matplotlib.pyplot as plt
import seaborn as sns

sns.set(style="ticks", color_codes=True)
```

How to do it...

We will plot four violin plots with different options here:

1. Plot a horizontal violin plot with sales on the *x* axis and items on the *y* axis:

```
sns.catplot(x='Sales', y='Item', data=long_sales, kind='violin',
            height=6, aspect=1)
```

```
plt.title('1. Horizontal Violin Plot', size=15, color='g',
          weight='bold')
```

2. Plot a vertical violin plot with items on the *x* axis and sales on the *y* axis, add hue='Promotion', and fill the sides of the violin plot with different colors:

```
sns.catplot(x='Item', y='Sales', data=long_sales, kind='violin',
            hue='Promotion',
            hue_order=["Yes", "No"], split=True, height=4,
aspect=2)
plt.title('2. Vertical Violin Plot, hue=Promotion, split=True',
          size=15, color='g', weight='bold')
```

3. Plot a vertical violin plot with hue='Promotion' and fill each side of the violin with the actual distribution of the data:

```
day_order = ['Monday', 'Tuesday', 'Wednesday', 'Thursday',
'Friday',
             'Saturday', 'Sunday']
sns.catplot(x='daywk', y='Sales', data=long_sales, kind='violin',
            order=day_order, hue='Promotion',
            hue_order=["Yes", "No"], split=True, inner="stick",
            palette="pastel",height=4, aspect=2)
plt.title('3. Violin Plot, hue=Promotion, split=True, inner=stick',
          size=15, color='g', weight='bold')
```

4. Plot a vertical violin plot with hue='Promotion', fill the sides with a different color, and overlay a swarm plot:

```
g = sns.catplot(x='daywk', y='Sales', data=long_sales,
                kind='violin', order=day_order, hue='Promotion',
                hue_order=["Yes", "No"], split=True, inner=None,
                palette="pastel", height=4, aspect=2)
sns.catplot(x='daywk',y='Sales',
        data=long_sales[long_sales['Period'] < 50], order=day_order,
        color="k",  size=3, kind='swarm',height=4, aspect=2,
ax=g.ax)
g.ax.set_title('4. Violin Plot with overlay of swarm plot',
size=15,
               color='g', weight='bold');

plt.axis('off');  # remove unwanted empty axes
```

How it works...

Here is the explanation for the preceding code.

This is the first plot:

- x='Sales' and y='Item' specifies that the categorical variable is on the *y* axis and the continuous variable is on the *x* axis, resulting in a horizontal plot
- kind='violin' specifies that it is a violin plot
- height=6 specifies the height of the plot as 6 inches
- aspect=1 means the width of the plot is the same as the height

This is the second plot:

- x='Item', y='Sales' specifies a regular vertical plot.
- hue='Promotion' specifies the hue variable as Promotion.
- hue_order=["Yes", "No"] specifies the order in which Promotion values are to be plotted.
- split=True is applicable only when the hue variable is binary, and specifies that each side of the violin should be filled with a different color, representing the value of the hue variable.

This is the third plot:

- Replace the Item variable with the daywk variable on the *x* axis, and provide the order in which days are to be plotted.
- inner="stick" specifies to plot stick-like lines, representing the distribution of data on each side of the violin for two distinct values of the Promotion variable; this is applicable only when split=True, which in turn is applicable only when the hue variable is binary.
- palette="pastel" specifies the predefined color palette to be used.

This is the fourth plot:

- kind='violin' specifies to plot a violin plot.
- inner=None specifies not to plot anything on either side of the violin other than color mapping based on hue.

- `data=long_sales[long_sales['Period'] < 50]` limits plotting to only 50 observations to avoid clutter.
- `kind='swarm'` specifies that the overlay plot on top of `violinplot` is a `swarmplot`.
- `ax=g.ax` specifies the axes for the overlay plot, which are the same as the axes on which `violinplot` is plotted.

Upon execution of the preceding code, you should see the following four plots on your screen:

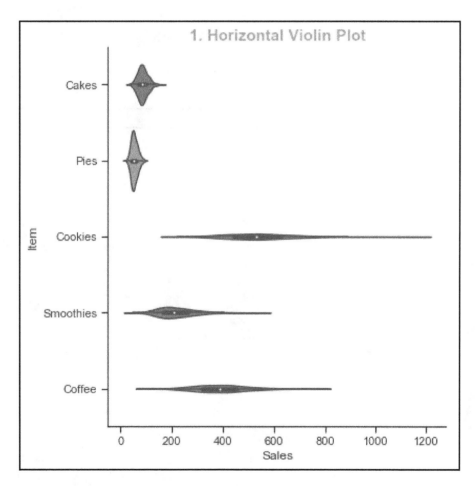

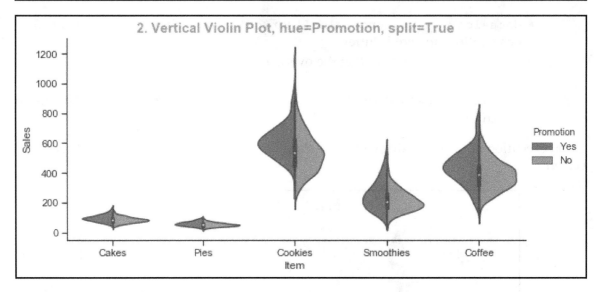

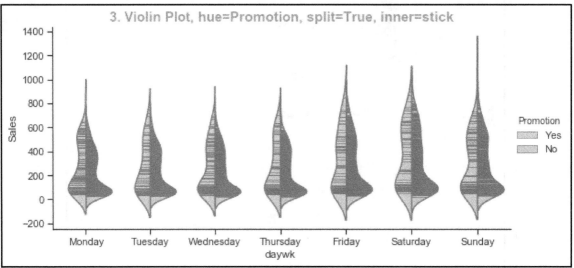

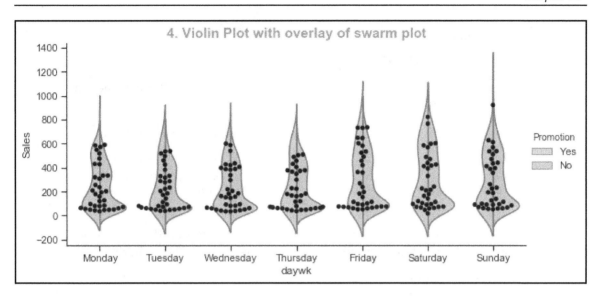

Point plots

Strip and swarm plots plot all the points that belong to a specific category in a non-overlapping manner; `box`, `boxn`, and `violin` plots depict summary statistics for a group of points for various categories; and, similarly, `bar` and `count` plots aggregate using some statistical metric and plot the bars accordingly. Finally, the `point` plot depicts the aggregate measure as a point in the graph, and all such points for various categories are connected with lines.

Getting ready

Import the required libraries, set the background style to `ticks`, and enable `color_codes` to be mapped to `seaborn` colors when specified in Matplotlib format:

```
import matplotlib.pyplot as plt
import seaborn as sns

sns.set(style="ticks", color_codes=True)
```

How to do it...

We will draw four point plots with different options:

1. Plot a `pointplot()` with the wide form dataset to plot all the numerical variables as listed in the order list:

```
sns.catplot(data=snacks_sales, kind='point', ci=99.99,
capsize=0.25,
            height=4, aspect=2, order=['Cakes', 'Pies', 'Cookies',
            'Smoothies', 'Coffee', 'weekday', 'Period'])
plt.title('1. Point Plot with wide form dataset', size=15,
          color='g', weight='bold');
```

2. Plot this `pointplot()` with the long form dataset to plot the item variable with s specified marker and standard deviation as the confidence interval:

```
sns.catplot(x='Item', y='Sales', data=long_sales, kind='point',
            markers='D', ci='sd', height=4, aspect=2) # long form
                                                    data frame
plt.title('2. Point Plot with diamond marker and std as ci',
          size=15, color='g', weight='bold');
```

3. Plot this `pointplot()` with additional `hue` and `col` variables, and a custom color palette:

```
sns.catplot(x='Item', y='Sales', data=long_sales, kind='point',
            hue='Promotion', hue_order=['Yes','No'],
palette={"Yes":
          "r", "No": "indigo"},
          markers=["^", "o"], linestyles=["-", "--"], ci=None,
          col='daywk', col_wrap=3,
          height=4, aspect=2, scale=1.5)
plt.suptitle("3. Point Plot, hue=Promotion, col='daywk'", size=15,
             color='g', weight='bold')
plt.tight_layout(pad=5,w_pad=0.25, h_pad=0.25);
```

4. Plot day-wise sales as a `pointplot()` with hue, and ensure that the line plots for two different values of `Promotion` don't overlap:

```
sns.catplot(x='daywk', y='Sales', data=long_sales, kind='point',
            hue='Promotion', dodge=True,
            hue_order=['Yes','No'], palette="Set2",
order=day_order,
            height=4, aspect=2)
plt.title('4. Point Plot of day wise sales with hue and dodge',
          size=15, color='g', weight='bold');
```

How it works...

Here is the explanation of the preceding code.

This is the first plot:

- `kind='point'` specifies that it is a `pointplot()`.
- `ci=99.99` specifies the confidence interval.
- `capsize=0.25` specifies the width of the cap on top of the error bar.
- `order=['Cakes', 'Pies', 'Cookies', 'Smoothies', 'Coffee', 'weekday', 'Period'])` specifies the order of the items on the axis.

This is the second plot:

- `markers='D'` specifies using a diamond marker in place of a circle.
- `ci='sd'` specifies using standard deviation for the confidence interval.

This is the third plot:

- `hue='Promotion'` specifies using the `Promotion` variable as hue.
- `hue_order=['Yes','No']` is the order in which hue values are plotted.
- `palette={"Yes": "r", "No": "indigo"}` is the custom color palette.
- `markers=["^", "o"]` specifies using these markers for each unique value of the `Promotion` variable.
- `linestyles=["-", "--"]` are the line styles for each of the line graphs.
- `ci=None` specifies not to plot the confidence interval range.
- `col='daywk'` specifies using the `daywk` variable to plot the columns.
- `col_wrap=3` specifies plotting only three plots in each row, and after that wrap into the next row.
- `scale=1.5` specifies the scaling factor on the sizes of objects on the plot over the default size.
- `plt.suptitle()` prints the title for the overall figure.
- `plt.tight_layout(pad=5, w_pad=0.25, h_pad=0.25);` adjusts the space between the plots and allows enough space on the top of the figure so that the title can fit in well.

This is the fourth plot:

- It is similar to the third plot, but doesn't use the col variable and applies `dodge=True` so that plots for two unique values of `Promotion` are set apart, instead of overlapping one over the other, as in the case of the third plot.

Upon executing the preceding code, you should see the following four plots on your screen:

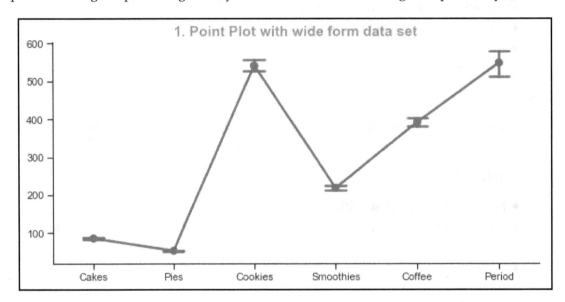

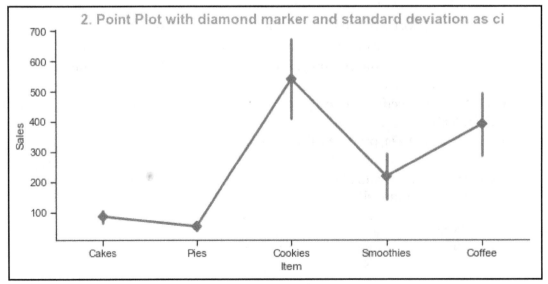

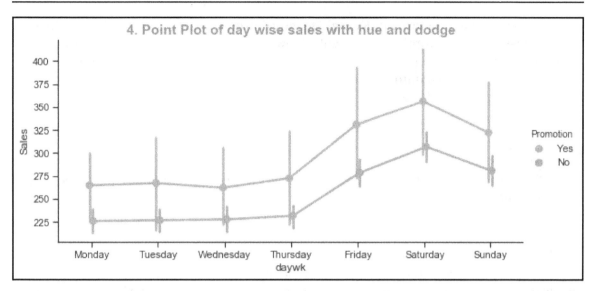

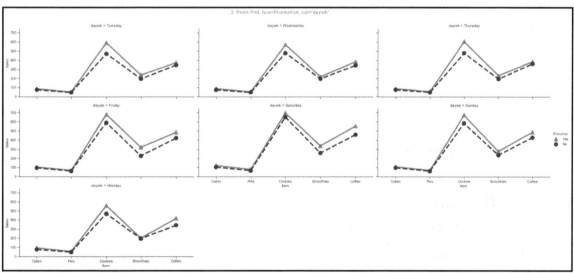

Distribution plots

Distribution Plots are used to visualize probability distributions of data. Seaborn provides three functions: `distplot()`, `kdeplot()`, and `rugplot()`.

distplot() can be used for both **Kernel Density Estimate** (**KDE**) and rug distributions as well, by passing the appropriate arguments. However, distplot() is limited to univariate distributions, whereas kdeplot() allows bivariate distributions as well. So, when a bivariate distribution is required, kdeplot() can be used, and for univariate distributions, distplot() can be used.

distplot()

We will plot three different distribution plots with various different options to demonstrate most of its features.

Getting ready

Import the required libraries, set the background style to white, and enable color_codes to be mapped to seaborn colors when specified in Matplotlib format:

```
import matplotlib.pyplot as plt
import seaborn as sns
from scipy.stats import norm, pareto, gamma

sns.set(style="whitegrid", color_codes=True)
```

scipy.stats is a scientific Python library containing various statistical functions, and norm, pareto, and gamma are different type of probability distribution functions. We will use them to fit the given dataset to see which distribution fits the data well.

How to do it...

Here are the steps to plot the required plots:

1. Plot the distribution of Coffee sales with a histogram, KDE, and rugplot:

```
sns.distplot(snacks_sales.Coffee, color='g', rug=True, rug_kws=
            {"color": 'm', "height": 0.1})
plt.title('1. Distribution Plot of Coffee Sales with rug=True',
          size=15, color='g', weight='bold')
plt.show();
```

2. Plot the horizontal distribution of Cookies sales with a step type histogram, shaded KDE, and legend:

```
sns.distplot(snacks_sales.Cookies, vertical=True,
             hist_kws={"histtype": "step", "linewidth": 3, "alpha":
             1, "color": "indigo", "label": "Histogram"},
             kde_kws={"shade": True, "color": "orange", "lw": 3,
                      "label": "KDE"})
plt.title('2. Horizontal Distribution Plot of Cookies Sales',
          size=15, color='g', weight='bold')
plt.show();
```

3. Plot the distribution of `Smoothies` sales and fit three different distributions to check which one fits the best for this data:

```
ax = sns.distplot(snacks_sales.Smoothies, fit=norm, kde=False,
                  rug=True, color='b',
                  fit_kws={"color": "b"}, label='normal')
sns.distplot(snacks_sales.Smoothies, hist=False, fit=pareto,
             kde=False, rug=True, color='g', label='pareto',
             fit_kws={"color": "g"}, ax=ax)
sns.distplot(snacks_sales.Smoothies, hist=False, fit=gamma,
             kde=False, color='r', label='gamma',
             fit_kws={"color": "r"}, ax=ax)
ax.legend()
plt.title('3. Distribution Plot - 3 different distribution
          functions', size=15, color='g', weight='bold')
plt.show();
```

How it works...

Here is the explanation for the preceding code:

This is the first plot:

- `sns.distplot(snacks_sales.Coffee, color='g', rug=True, rug_kws={"color": 'm', "height": 0.1})` plots. This is the required distribution plot.
- `snacks_sales.Coffee` is the coffee sales data whose distribution is to be plotted.
- `color='g'` specifies that the color of the histogram and KDE plots that are plotted by default is green.
- If you want to switch off the histogram or KDE plot, then pass the arguments `hist=False` and `kde=False`.

- `rug=True` specifies whether the rug plot should be plotted on this distribution plot. The default option is **False**, hence it is not plotted.
- `rug_kws={"color": 'm', "height": 0.1}` is the keyword dictionary to be used to format the rug plot. Here, we have used the color magenta, and the height of the sticks is `o.1` in the rug plot.
- `plt.show()` displays the plot on the screen, so that subsequent plots don't overlap on top of the first one.

This is the second plot:

- `vertical=True` specifies that the plot should be plotted on the vertical axis, which means a horizontal histogram plot. The default option is **False**, in which case it plots a vertical histogram plot, as can be seen in the first plot.
- `hist_kws={"histtype": "step", "linewidth": 3, "alpha": 0.7, "color": "indigo", "label": "Histogram"}` is the histogram keyword dictionary of parameters to be used for plotting the histogram:
  - `"histtype": "step"` specifies a staircase histogram, instead of a regular smooth ramp.
  - `"linewidth": 3` means the line width of the histogram is three points.
  - `"alpha": 0.7` specifies the transparency level of the histogram lines.
  - `"color": "indigo"` specifies the color of the histogram to be indigo.
  - `"label": "Histogram"` is the label that appears on the legend.
- `kde_kws={"shade": True, "color": "orange", "lw": 3, "label": "KDE"})` is the KDE plot keyword dictionary of parameters to be used for plotting the KDE plot:
  - `"shade": True` specifies that the area under the KDE plot should be shaded.
  - `"color": "orange"` specifies the color to be used for the KDE plot and shades the area under the KDE curve. Although we specify one color, it uses slightly different shades for the KDE curve and the shaded area under the curve to distinguish both of them.
  - `"lw": 3` specifies the width of the line to be plotted.
  - `"label": "KDE"` is the label that appears on the legend.

This is the third plot:

- In this plot, we are fitting three different curves for the same data to check which one fits the best. In reality, there are many continuous and discrete distributions; based on the nature of the data, we try couple of these distributions before picking the best one. We need to import the appropriate packages (`scipy.stats` is one good source) to load these distribution functions before using them in `distplot()`.
- `fit=norm` specifies to fit a normal distribution; similarly, `fit=pareto` and `fit=gamma` specify the `pareto` and `gamma` distribution functions to be used to fit the data we have.
- `kde=False` specifies not to plot the KDE curve, since we are fitting other distributions. If we want to compare the KDE curve with other distributions, we can keep it as well.
- `rug=True` specifies that we should also plot `rugplot()` for this data.
- `fit_kws={"color": "b"}` is the keyword dictionary to be used for fitting the given distribution function. It only specifies the color to be used for the distribution curve.

Upon execution of the preceding code, you should see the following three plots:

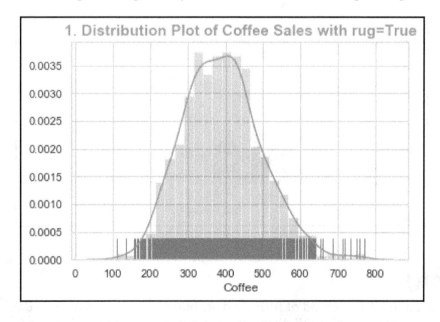

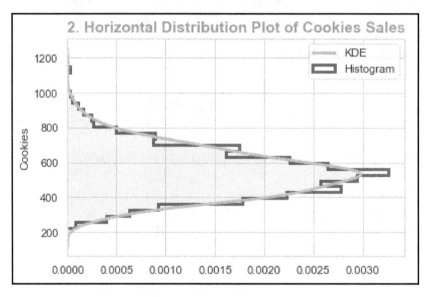

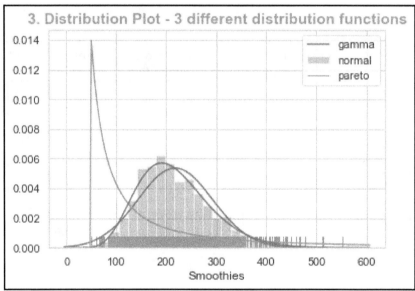

kdeplot()

KDE is a non-parametric method of fitting a distribution function to a given dataset. Hence, `kdeplot()` fits and plots the KDE distribution curve for the given univariate (single variable) or bivariate (two variables) data.

Getting ready

Import the required libraries, set the background style to `white`, and enable `color_codes` to be mapped to seaborn colors when specified in a Matplotlib format:

```
import matplotlib.pyplot as plt
import seaborn as sns
```

How to do it...

We will plot two bivariate KDE plots. In the second plot, we will plot two KDE plots with different sets of variables, on the same axes for comparison:

1. Plot the bivariate KDE plot with contours and a colorbar:

```
sns.kdeplot(snacks_sales.Smoothies, snacks_sales.Pies,
kernel='epa',
            n_levels=25, cmap='Reds', cbar=True)
plt.title('1. Bivariate KDE Plot', size=15, color='g',
          weight='bold');
plt.show();
```

2. Plot bivariate KDE plots for two sets of variables with a shaded area:

```
Cookies_temp = snacks_sales.Cookies + 500
ax=sns.kdeplot(snacks_sales.Period, snacks_sales.Coffee,
               kernel='gau',shade=True, shade_lowest=False,
               cmap='Purples_d')
sns.kdeplot(snacks_sales.Period, Cookies_temp, kernel='cos',
            shade=True, shade_lowest=False, cmap='Blues')
ax.set_ylabel('Sales')
ax.text(0, 1400, 'Cookies', color='b', weight='bold')
ax.text(0, 650, 'Coffee', color='purple', weight='bold')
plt.title('2. Bivariate KDE Plot - 2 sets of variables', size=15,
          color='g', weight='bold')
plt.show();
```

How it works...

Here is the explanation of the code.

This is the first plot:

- `snacks_sales.Smoothies` and `snacks_sales.Pies` are the variables to be plotted.
- `kernel='epa'` specifies the kernel method (Epanechnikov) to be used to fit the KDE. Other available options are `gau` (Gaussian/normal), `cos` (cosine), `biw` (biweight), `triw` (triweight), and `tri` (triangular). For more details, please refer to `http://homepages.inf.ed.ac.uk/rbf/CVonline/LOCAL_COPIES/AV0405/MISHRA/kde.html`.
- `n_levels=25` specifies the number of contours to be plotted.
- `cmap='Reds'` specifies the colormap to be used.
- `cbar=True` specifies to plot the colorbar.

This is the second plot:

- `Cookies_temp = snacks_sales.Cookies + 500` increases the values of all observations by 500, so that these values do not overlap with other variable values that we will be plotting on the same axes.
- `ax=sns.kdeplot(snacks_sales.Period, snacks_sales.Coffee, kernel='gau',shade=True, shade_lowest=False, cmap='Purples_d')` plots the first KDE plot on the `ax` axes.
- `kernel='gau'`, uses the Gaussian kernel method `shade=True` and fills the area within the contours.
- `shade_lowest=False` is applicable only when `shade=True`, which is applicable only for bivariate KDE plots. It forces it not to fill the outermost contour, which covers the whole area of the axes outside the contours. If we don't set this to *false*, we may see the entire axes area filled with the color of the outermost contour.
- `ax.set_ylabel('Sales')` overwrites the default *y* axis label picked up from the data variable name.
- `ax.text(0, 1400, 'Cookies', color='b', weight='bold')` and `ax.text(0, 650, 'Coffee', color='purple', weight='bold')` insert the label for the KDE plots:
  - The `'label'` option available in `kdeplot()` works only for univariate plots. Hence, we have used the `text` option here.

Upon executing the preceding code, you should see the following two plots on your screen:

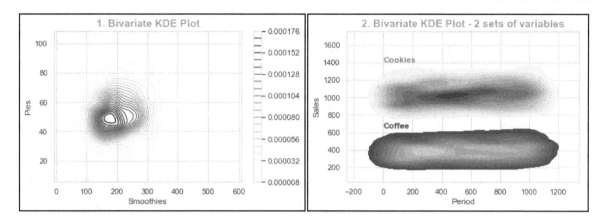

Regression plots

Regression plots help in fit two-dimensional data in to a linear or polynomial curve. This helps in visualizing the relationship between two variables to understand how closely it fits a linear or polynomial of order n. Seaborn provides three functions for this purpose: `regplot()`, `residplot()`, and `lmplot()`. Both `regplot()` as well as `lmplot()` serve the same purpose of fitting two-dimensional data to a linear or polynomial of order n, but `regplot()` is an axes-level function, whereas `lmplot()` is a figure-level function, which enables it to use the `row` and `col` semantic variables to draw multiple regression plots in a single figure. `residplot()` helps fitting the curve and plotting the residuals to understand the quality of the fit.

regplot() and residplot()

We will plot two regression plots and one residual plot to demonstrate the various options available in these functions.

Getting ready

Import the required libraries, set the background style to `dark`, and enable `color_codes` to be mapped to seaborn colors when specified in Matplotlib format:

```
import matplotlib.pyplot as plt
import seaborn as sns
from scipy.stats import pearsonr

sns.set(style="dark", color_codes=True)
```

How to do it...

Here are the steps to plot the required plots:

1. Plot a linear regression plot, with R^2 and the *p-value* annotation:

```
R, p = pearsonr(wine_quality['fixed acidity'], wine_quality.pH)
g1 = sns.regplot(x='fixed acidity', y='pH', data=wine_quality,
                 truncate=True, ci=99,
                 marker='D', scatter_kws={'color': 'r'});
textstr =
'$\mathrm{pearson}\hspace{0.5}\mathrm{R}^2=%.2f$\n$\mathrm{pval}=%.
    2e$' % (R**2, p)
props = dict(boxstyle='round', facecolor='wheat', alpha=0.5)
g1.text(0.55, 0.95, textstr, transform=ax.transAxes, fontsize=14,
        va='top', bbox=props)
plt.title('1. Linear Regression', size=15, color='g',
weight='bold')
```

2. Plot a polynomial regression curve of order 2:

```
g2 = sns.regplot(x='fixed acidity', y='pH', data=wine_quality,
                 order=2, ci=None,
                 marker='s', scatter_kws={'color': 'skyblue'},
                 line_kws={'color': 'red'});
plt.title('2. Non Linear Regression of order 2', size=15,
color='g',
            weight='bold')
```

3. Plot a logistic regression curve:

```
wine_quality['Q'] = wine_quality['Quality'].map({'Low': 0, 'Med':
0,
                                                 'High':1})
g2 = sns.regplot(x='fixed acidity', y='Q', logistic=True,
                 n_boot=750, y_jitter=.03, data=wine_quality,
                 line_kws={'color': 'r'})
plt.show();
```

4. Plot a residual plot:

```
g3 = sns.residplot(x='fixed acidity', y='density', order=2,
                   data=wine_quality, scatter_kws={'color': 'b',
                   'alpha': 0.5});
plt.show();
```

How it works...

Here is the explanation of the code.

This is the first plot:

- `R, p = pearsonr(wine_quality['fixed acidity'], wine_quality.pH)` computes `R` and `p` values for the given data distribution. R^2 and p values indicate the quality of the fit to the data.
- `g1=sns.regplot()` plots the regression curve along with a scatter plot of the original data points:
  - `truncate=True` specifies to fit the curve only till the available data points. The default is to extend it to both ends of the axes.
  - `ci=99` specifies to plot a 99% confidence interval around the linear curve.
  - `marker='D'` plots the points in a diamond shape, instead of the default circles.
  - `scatter_kws={'color': 'r'}` is the scatter plot keyword dictionary with properties to be used. Plot the points in red.
  - `textstr` in rich text format specifies the text to be plotted on the curve.
  - `props` specifies the properties of the box around the text string to be plotted on the curve.
  - `g1.text()` prints the text at the specified location.

This is the second plot:

- `g2 = sns.regplot()` plots the scatter plot with a second order polynomial.
  - `order=2` specifies fitting the polynomial of order two.
  - `ci=None` doesn't plot the confidence interval around the fitted curve.
  - `marker='s'` plots the points in a square shape, instead of the default circles.
  - `scatter_kws={'color': 'skyblue'}` specifies the color for the scatter points.
  - `line_kws={'color': 'red'}` specifies color for the regression line.

This is the third plot:

- `wine_quality['Q'] = wine_quality['Quality'].map({'Low': 0, 'Med': 0, 'High':1})` derives a new quality variable that only has a binary value of '0' or '1' by mapping `Low` and `Med` to 0, and `High` to 1. This is required to fit a logistic regression curve.
- `g3 = sns.regplot()` plots a scatter plot and fits a logistic regression curve:
  - `logistic=True` specifies to fit a logistic regression curve.
  - `n_boot=750` specifies the number of resamples to be used to estimate the confidence interval.
  - `y_jitter=.03` specifies the amount of deviation to be added so that points don't get overlapped too much. This affects only the visualization, and gets added after fitting the curve and before plotting.
  - `line_kws={'color': 'r'}`, plots the fitted curve in red.

This is the fourth plot:

- `g4 = sns.residplot()` plots the scatter plot of residuals and a dotted line around the 0 residual.
- `scatter_kws={'color': 'b', 'alpha': 0.5}` plots the residual points in blue with a transparency level of 0.5.

Upon executing the preceding code, you should see the following four plots on your screen:

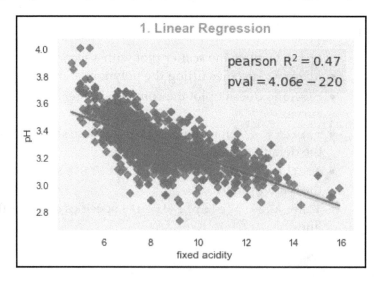

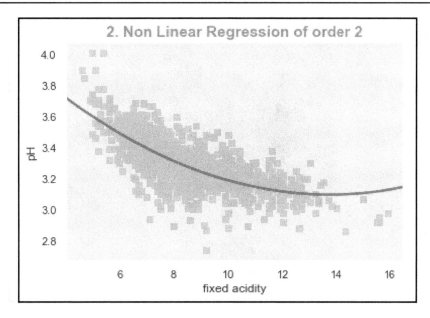

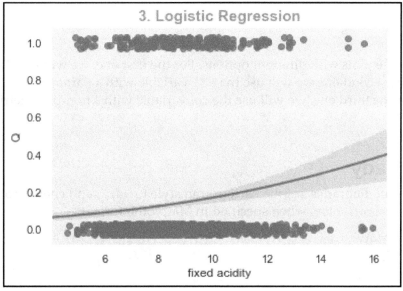

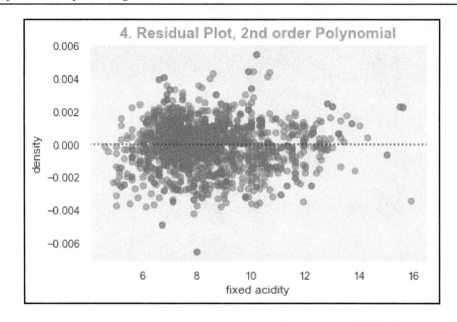

Implot()

We will plot three plots with different options. For the first one, we will use the `hue` variable, for the second one we will use the `col` variable with a parametric regression model, and for the third one, we will use the col variable with a non-parametric regression model.

Getting ready

Import the required libraries, set the background style to `dark`, and enable `color_codes` to be mapped to seaborn colors when specified in Matplotlib format:

```
import matplotlib.pyplot as plt
import seaborn as sns

sns.set(style="dark", color_codes=True)
```

How to do it...

Here are the steps to plot the required plots:

1. Plot a linear regression plot with `Quality` as the `hue` variable:

```
g1 = sns.lmplot(x='fixed acidity', y='pH', hue='Quality',
hue_order=
                ['Low', 'Med', 'High'], logx=True,
                data=wine_quality, height=4, aspect=2, ci=None)
```

2. Plot a parametric regression plot with `Quality` as the `col` variable, and customize the labels, ticks, and axis limits:

```
g2 = sns.lmplot(x='fixed acidity', y='pH', data=wine_quality,
ci=99,
                col='Quality', col_order=['Low', 'Med', 'High'],
                height=3, robust=True, scatter_kws={'color': 'g'})
g2 = g2.set_axis_labels("Fixed Acidity", "pH")
g2.set(xlim=(0, 20), ylim=(2.4, 4.0), xticks=[5, 10, 15, 20],
        yticks=[2.5, 3.0, 3.5, 4.0])
```

3. Plot a non-parametric regression plot with `Quality` as the `col` variable:

```
g3 = sns.lmplot(x='fixed acidity', y='density',
                data=wine_quality, lowess=True, markers='s',
                col='Quality', col_order=['Low', 'Med', 'High'],
                height=3, line_kws={'color': 'g'})

plt.show();
```

How it works...

Here is the explanation of the code.

This is the first plot:

- `hue='Quality'` specifies `Quality` as the `hue` variable, so that for each unique value of the `Quality` variable, it plots a regression plot with a different color.
- `hue_order=['Low', 'Med', 'High']` is the order of hue variable values to be plotted.
- `logx=True` specifies to fit a curve of the form $y = log(x)$.
- `ci=None` specifies not to plot the confidence interval around the curve.

The resulting plot looks as follows:

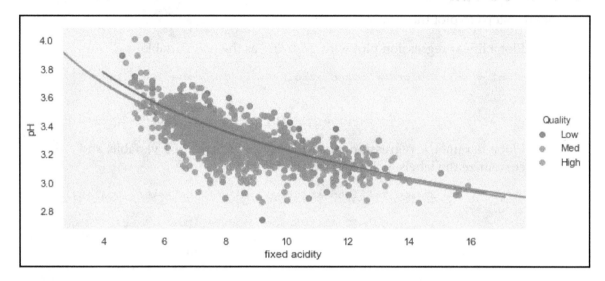

This is the second plot:

- `ci=99` specifies to plot a 99% confidence interval.
- `col='Quality'` specifies `Quality` as the column variable so that for each unique value of Quality, it plots a regression plot along the columns of the figure.
- `col_order=['Low', 'Med', 'High']` specifies the order in which plots are placed on the figure.
- `robust=True` specifies to mitigate the influence of outliers on fitting the curve to data.
- `scatter_kws={'color': 'g'}` specifies to plot the points in green.
- `g2 = g2.set_axis_labels("Fixed Acidity", "pH")` overrides the default axis labels with user-defined labels.
- `g2.set(xlim=(0, 20), ylim=(2.4, 4.0), xticks=[5, 10, 15, 20], yticks=[2.5, 3.0, 3.5, 4.0])` overrides the default axis limits and ticks.

The resulting plot looks like the following:

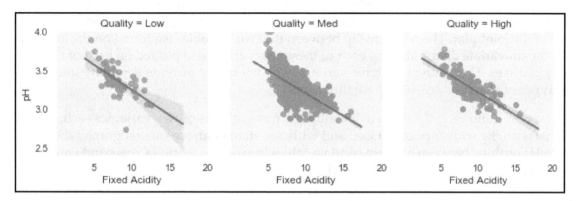

This is the third plot:

- `lowess=True` specifies fitting a non-parametric regression model
- `markers='s'` plots the points in squares with the default color
- `line_kws={'color': 'g'}` plots the fitted curve in green

The resulting plot looks like the one shown here:

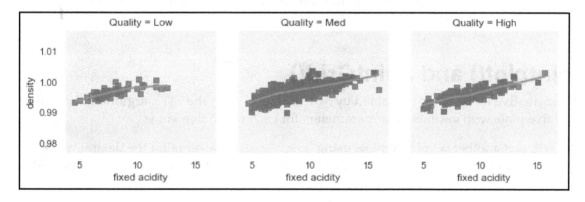

Multi-plot grids

We have already seen some types of multi-plot grids, when we used the `row` and `col` variables for various facets of visualization in the *Line plots with long form dataset* and *Point plot* recipes earlier in the chapter. However, seaborn provides three sets of predefined grids for different purposes.

`jointplot()` and `JointGrid()` enable the creation of three axes/plots as one figure. The main axes is called the **joint plot**, and the other two are called **marginal axes**. One of the marginal axes is on top of the joint plot, and the second marginal axes is on the right side of the joint plot. The relationship between the two variables is plotted on the joint plot, and the univariate distribution of each of these two variables is plotted on each of the marginal axes. These functions have various parameters that provide flexibility in choosing the types of graphs on each of these three axes.

`pairplot()` and `PairGrid()` enable multiple plots in pairs of two variables each. We can just pass on the wide format dataset, and with one statement, we can get graphs showing the relationships between all numerical variables in pairs, as a grid of rows and columns. Here again, there are many options to choose different types of graphs.

The difference between `jointplot()` and `JointGrid()`, as well as `pairplot()` and `PairGrid()`, is the flexibility in choosing various parameters and types of graphs offered by each. `jointplot()` and `pairplot()` have less flexibility, but are easy to use and get quick plots. `JointGrid()` and `PairGrid()` offer more flexibility, with many parameters to choose from.

`FacetGrid()` is the third category of multi plot grid. This is used for multi-dimensional analysis with a combination of `hue`, `style`, `size`, `row`, and `col` variables. We have already seen these in the context of relational and categorical plots. They internally use `FacetGrid()`; here, we will access it directly.

jointplot() and JointGrid()

There are five kinds of plots enabled by `jointplot()` with the `kind` argument. We will plot five plots with various other parameters for each of the five kinds.

We will plot another set of five plots using `JointGrid()`, leveraging the flexibility offered by it to control the type and style of plots that can be plotted in the three axes of the grid.

Getting ready

This part is common for both `jointplot()` and `JointGrid()`, whereas the *How to do it...* and *How it works...* sections will be repeated for each of them separately.

Import the required libraries:

```
import matplotlib.pyplot as plt
import numpy as np
import seaborn as sns

from scipy.stats import norm
from itertools import chain # chain enables iteration of multiple lists
                              in loops such as for loop.

# The following parameters are set in rc configuration file, so they
  will be applicable for the entire session
# font_scale factor is the multiplier of default font size(instead of
  absolute size, it is relative size)
sns.set(rc={"axes.linewidth": 1, "xtick.major.width": 1,
            "ytick.major.width": 1,
            "xtick.major.size": 5, "ytick.major.size": 5},
            style="ticks", context="paper", font_scale=1.25)
```

jointplot()

We will plot five plots for the five different kinds of plots supported by jointplot().

How to do it...

Here are the steps to plot the required graphs:

1. Plot the regression plot:

```
g1 = sns.jointplot(x='Pies', y='Smoothies', data=snacks_sales,
                   kind='reg',
                   marginal_kws=dict(bins=15, fit=norm, rug=True,
                   color='darkblue'),
                   space=0.1, color='g')
g1.ax_marg_x.set_title('1. Regression Plot - Histogram, KDE,
Normal,
                        Rug', size=20, color='g')
```

2. Plot the scatter plot:

```
g2 = sns.jointplot(x='Cookies', y='Smoothies', data=snacks_sales,
                   s=100, marginal_kws=dict(kde=True, rug=True,
                   hist=False, color='orange'), space=0.1,
                   color='g', edgecolor="blue", alpha=0.6)
g2.ax_marg_x.set_title('2. Scatter Plot - KDE, Rug', size=20,
                   color='g')
```

3. Plot the KDE plot:

```
g3 = sns.jointplot(x='Period', y='Smoothies', data=snacks_sales,
                   kind='kde', space=0, color='indigo')
g3.ax_marg_x.set_title('3. KDE Plots', size=20, color='g');
```

4. Plot the Hexbin plot:

```
g4 = sns.jointplot(x='Quarter', y='Pies', data=snacks_sales,
                kind='hex', space=0, color='violet');
g4.ax_marg_x.set_title('4. Hexbin Plot - Histograms', size=20,
                color='g');
```

5. Plot the residual plot:

```
g5 = sns.jointplot(x='Cakes', y='Smoothies', data=snacks_sales,
                   kind='resid', space=0, color='c')
g5.ax_marg_x.set_title('5. Residual Plot - Histogram, Normal',
                   size=20, color='g');
```

How it works...

Here is the explanation of the code.

This is the first plot:

- `g = sns.jointplot()` plots the required joint plot of the three graphs.
- `kind='reg'` specifies to plot a regression plot.

- `marginal_kws=dict(bins=15, fit=norm, rug=True, color='darkblue')` is the dictionary of parameters to be applied to the marginal axes graphs. They are applicable to both the top and right marginal axes, but not related to joint plot objects:
    - `bins=15` is the number of bins for the histogram to be plotted; by default, a histogram is plotted.
    - `fit=norm` specifies to fit a `normal` distribution curve for the given data.
    - `rug=True`, plots the rug plot for the given data.
    - `color='darkblue'` is the color to be used for all the elements of both marginal axes.
    - `space=0.1` specifies the amount of space between the joint plot and marginal axes. *Zero* means they are connected tightly without any gap between them.
    - `color='g'` specifies the color for joint plot objects.
    - The KDE curve will be fitted to the data by default. If we don't want to plot it, we should set it to *false*. In this case, we will have both the KDE curve and the `normal` distribution curve.
- `g1.ax_marg_x.set_title('1. Regression Plot - Histogram, KDE, Normal, Rug', size=20, color='g')` plots the title for the plot:
    - `ax_marg_x` is the marginal axis on the top. `jointplot()` internally calls `JointGrid()`, which gives us access to the joint plot and two marginal axes. We will learn more about it in the *JointGrid()* recipe covered next.
    - `size=20` is the font size of the title, and `color='g'` sets the color of the title to green.

This is the second plot:

- We have not provided the kind argument, since `kind='scatter'` is the default. Hence, it plots a scatter plot.
- `s=100` specifies the size of each of the dots to be plotted.
- `kde=True` fits a KDE curve to the given data.
- `rug=True` plots a rug plot of sticks.
- `hist=False` doesn't plot the histogram.

- `color='orange'` is the color for the marginal axes objects.
- `space=0.1` is the amount of space between the joint axes and marginal axes.
- `color='g'` applies a green color to joint plot objects.
- `edgecolor="blue"` is the color of the edges of the circles.
- `alpha=0.6` is the level of transparency of the scatter points.

Upon execution, these two plots should look as follows:

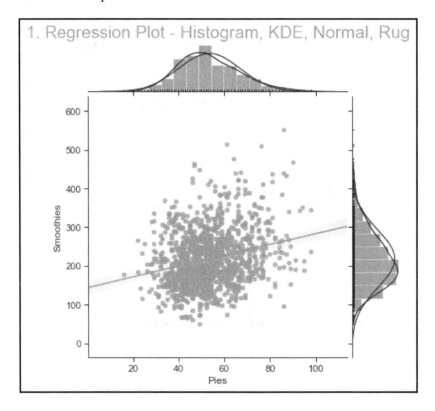

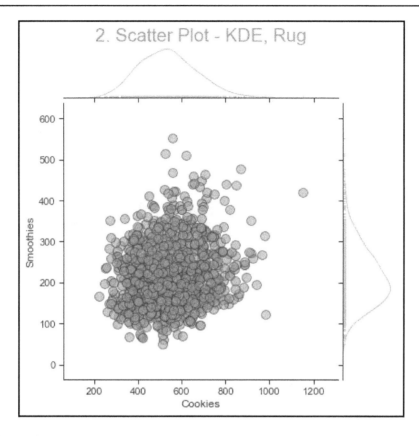

This is the third plot:

- `kind='kde'` is a bivariate KDE plot
- `space=0` specifies no space between the joint axes and marginal axes
- `color='indigo'` is the color for all the objects; since we have not supplied `marginal_kws`, it uses the same for the marginal axes objects also

This is the fourth plot:

- `kind='hex'` plots the Hexbin plot
- `space=0` means no space between joint axes and marginal axes
- `color='violet'` is the color for all objects

Upon execution of the code, the third and fourth plots should look as follows:

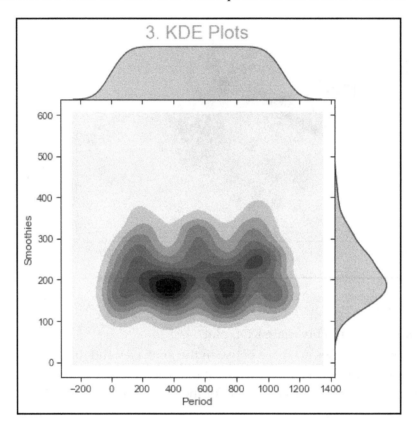

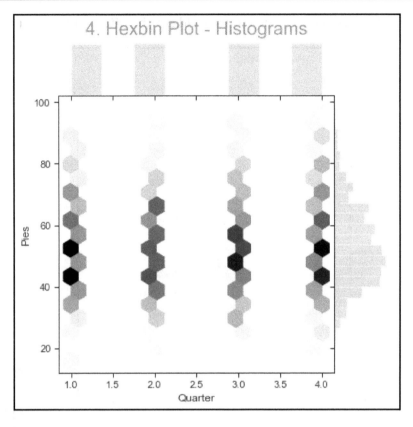

This is the fifth plot:

- `kind='resid'` plots the residual plot
- `space=0` means no space between the joint axes and marginal axes
- `color='c'` use a cyan color for all objects

Upon execution of the preceding code, you should see the fifth plot as shown here:

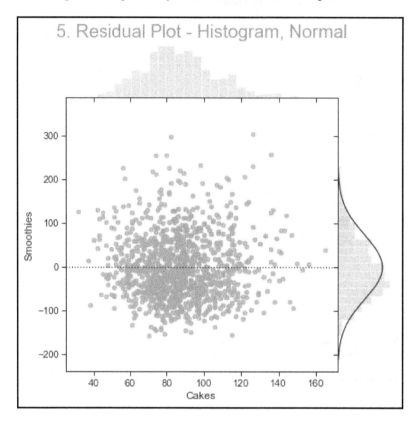

JointGrid()

We will plot five plots using `JointGrid()` and various parameters to demonstrate most of the features available.

How to do it...

Here are the steps to plot the required plots:

1. Create a simple `JointGrid` with default parameters, and axes-level customization:

```
g1 = sns.JointGrid(x='Coffee', y='Cookies', data=snacks_sales,
                   space=0.1, height=6, ratio=2)
g1 = g1.plot(sns.regplot, sns.kdeplot)
```

```
#g = g.plot(plt.scatter, sns.distplot);

g1.ax_joint.set_xlabel('Coffee', color='g', size=20, weight='bold')
g1.ax_joint.set_ylabel('Cookies', color='g', size=20,
weight='bold')

plt.setp(g1.ax_marg_x.get_yticklabels(), visible=True)
plt.setp(g1.ax_marg_x.get_xticklabels(), visible=True)
plt.setp(g1.ax_marg_y.get_xticklabels(), visible=True)
plt.setp(g1.ax_marg_y.get_yticklabels(), visible=True)

g1.ax_marg_x.set_facecolor('wheat')
g1.ax_marg_y.set_facecolor('wheat')

for l in chain(g1.ax_marg_x.axes.lines, g1.ax_marg_y.axes.lines):
    l.set_linestyle('--')
    l.set_lw(3)
    l.set_color('red')
g1.ax_marg_x.set_title('1. Regression Plot - KDE on marginals',
                        size=20, color='g')
```

2. Separate the *joint* and *marginal* plots with their respective parameters:

```
g2 = sns.JointGrid(x='Pies', y='Smoothies', data=snacks_sales,
                    space=0, ratio=2)
g2 = g2.plot_joint(sns.regplot, color="g", order=3, ci=68 )
g2 = g2.plot_marginals(sns.distplot, kde=False, rug=True, fit=norm,
                    color="#1EAFCD23")
g2.ax_marg_x.set_title('2. Regression Plot - Histogram, Normal,
                    Rug', size=20, color='g')
```

3. Separate the joint, *marginal* x, and *marginal* y plots with independent controls on each:

```
g3 = sns.JointGrid(x='Pies', y='Smoothies', data=snacks_sales,
                    space=0, ratio=2)
g3 = g3.plot_joint(sns.regplot, color="g", order=3, ci=68)
g3.ax_marg_x.hist(snacks_sales['Pies'], color="b", alpha=.6,
                bins=np.arange(0, 100, 5))
g3.ax_marg_y.boxplot(snacks_sales['Smoothies'], 1, 'gD')
g3.ax_marg_x.set_title('3. Regression Plot - Histogram, Boxplot',
                    size=20, color='g');
```

4. Implement hue on JointGrid:

```
g4 = sns.JointGrid("Cookies", "Smoothies", snacks_sales, space=0,
                    ratio=2)
i=1
```

```
for quarter, sales in snacks_sales.groupby('Quarter'):
 sns.kdeplot(sales["Cookies"], ax=g4.ax_marg_x, label='Q'+str(i));
 sns.kdeplot(sales["Smoothies"], ax=g4.ax_marg_y, vertical=True,
           label='Q'+str(i));
 g4.ax_joint.plot(sales["Cookies"], sales["Smoothies"], "D", ms=5)
 i +=1
g4.ax_marg_x.set_title('4. Scatter Plot - Histogram with hue, KDE
on
                   marginals', size=20, color='g')
```

5. Use a user-defined joint and marginal plots:

```
g5 = sns.JointGrid("Cookies", "Coffee", snacks_sales, space=0.5,
              ratio=6)

def marginal_boxplot(a, vertical=False, **kws):
    g = sns.boxplot(x="Promotion", y="Coffee", orient="v", **kws)
if
                vertical \
              else sns.boxplot(x="Cookies", y="Promotion",
                                orient="h", **kws)
    g.set_ylabel("")
    g.set_xlabel("")

g5.plot_marginals(marginal_boxplot, palette={"Yes": "#ff000088",
"No": "#00aa007e" }, data=snacks_sales,
              linewidth=1, fliersize=10,notch=True)

sns.regplot(x="Cookies", y="Coffee",
data=snacks_sales.query("Promotion == 'Yes'"), color="#ff000088",
           truncate=True, label='Promotion: Yes', marker='D',
           ax=g5.ax_joint,
           scatter_kws={"s": 100, "edgecolor": "k", "linewidth":
           .5, "alpha": .8})
sns.regplot(x="Cookies", y="Coffee",
data=snacks_sales.query("Promotion == 'No'"),
           color="#00aa007e", marker='^', label='Promotion: No',
           scatter_kws={"s": 50, "edgecolor": "k", "linewidth":
.5,
           "alpha": .4},
           line_kws={"linewidth": 2}, ax=g5.ax_joint)

g5.ax_marg_x.set_title('5. Regression Plot with hue - Boxplots on
                       marginals', size=20, color='g')
g5.ax_joint.legend(loc=4)

plt.show();
```

How it works...

Here is the explanation of the code:

This is the first plot:

- `g1 = sns.JointGrid()` sets up the grid:
  - `space=0.1` is the amount of gap between the joint plot and marginal plots.
  - `height=6` is the height of the plot in inches.
  - `ratio=2` is the ratio of joint plot height and marginal plot height.
- `g1 = g.plot(sns.regplot, sns.kdeplot)` specifies the type of plot for the joint plot and both of the marginal plots. Other compatible plots such as `plt.scatter` and `sns.distplot` can also be used, instead of `sns.regplot` and `sns.kdeplot`.
- `g.plot()` does not give any flexibility to supply various parameters, it just uses all default parameters of the supplied plot types. However, axes-level customization is possible, as follows:
  - `g1.ax_joint.set_xlabel('Coffee', color='g', size=20, weight='bold')` overrides the default *x* axis label of the joint axes. "`ax_joint`" is the axes name of the joint plot.
  - `g1.ax_joint.set_ylabel('Cookies', color='g', size=20, weight='bold')` overrides the default *y* axis label of the joint axes.
  - Make the marginal axes tick labels visible:
    - `plt.setp(g1.ax_marg_x.get_yticklabels(), visible=True)`
    - `plt.setp(g1.ax_marg_x.get_xticklabels(), visible=True)`
    - `plt.setp(g1.ax_marg_y.get_xticklabels(), visible=True)`
    - `plt.setp(g1.ax_marg_y.get_yticklabels(), visible=True)`
    - `ax_marg_x` and `ax_marg_y` are the names of the top and right marginal axes

- `g1.ax_marg_x.set_facecolor('wheat')` sets the face color of the marginal *x* axes (top plot).
- `g1.ax_marg_y.set_facecolor('wheat')` sets the face color of the marginal *y* axes (right plot).
- `for l in chain(g1.ax_marg_x.axes.lines,` `g1.ax_marg_y.axes.lines)`: is a loop to customize line plots on both marginal axes:
    - `l.set_linestyle('--')` is the line style to be used.
    - `l.set_lw(3)` is the line width.
    - `l.set_color('red')` is the color of the line.
- `g1.ax_marg_x.set_title('1. Regression Plot - KDE on marginals', size=20, color='g')` plots the title for the figure. `ax_marg_x` is the top marginal axes, and title gets printed on top of it. This is the same for all other plots in this section.

This is the second plot:

- Here, we get to plot the joint plot and marginal plots separately, and can pass on appropriate attributes to customize them.
- `g2 = sns.JointGrid(x='Pies', y='Smoothies', data=snacks_sales, space=0, ratio=2)` sets up the grid with the required data, as in the first plot.
- `g2 = g2.plot_joint(sns.regplot, color="g", order=3, ci=68 )` plots a regression plot on the joint axes:
    - we can pass all the parameters applicable to `sns.regplot()`.
    - `color="g"` specifies to use green.
    - `order=3`, specifies to fit a third-order polynomial curve for the data supplied.
    - `ci=68` specifies the confidence interval to be plotted around the fitted curve.

- `g2 = g2.plot_marginals(sns.distplot, kde=False, rug=True, fit=norm, color="#1EAFCD23")` plots a distribution plot on both marginal axes, and the supplied parameters are applicable for both:
  - `kde=False` doesn't plot the KDE curve.
  - `rug=True` plots the rug sticks.
  - `fit=norm` fits a normal curve.
  - `color="#1EAFCD23"` uses the color specified in hexadecimal form.

Upon execution of preceding code, you should see following two plots on the screen:

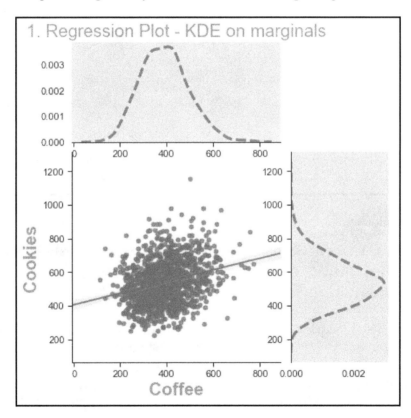

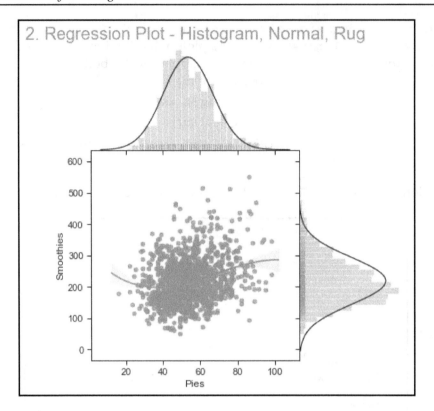

This is the third plot:

- Here, we get the flexibility to plot different type of plots on both marginal axes.
- `g3 = sns.JointGrid()` creates the grid as in the first two plots.
- `g3 = g3.plot_joint(sns.regplot, color="g", order=3, ci=68)` is the same as in the second plot.
- `g3.ax_marg_x.hist(snacks_sales['Pies'], color="b", alpha=.6, bins=np.arange(0, 100, 5))` plots a histogram on the top marginal axes.
- Essentially, `g3.ax_marg_x` acts like a standard matplotlib axes on which we can plot anything, using any of the Matplotlib plots. Here, we are plotting a histogram and the parameters passed are from the Matplotlib histogram.

- `g3.ax_marg_y.boxplot(snacks_sales['Smoothies'], 1, 'gD')` plots a boxplot on the right marginal axes. Again, it is a Matplotlib `boxplot` and the arguments passed are from the Matplotlib `boxplot`.
- `1` specifies to use the notch, the default of `0` is without the notch, a rectangular box.
- `'gD'` specifies the color and marker for outliers, which in this case are green and diamond.

This is the fourth plot:

- In this plot, we get to implement `hue` on `JointGrid`, and also plot seaborn plots on marginal axes. In the third plot, we used Matplotlib plots.
- `g4 = sns.JointGrid("Cookies", "Smoothies", snacks_sales, space=0, ratio=2)` is the same as usual for all JointGrid plots.
- `i=1` initializes the index to 1.
- `for quarter, sales in snacks_sales.groupby('Quarter'):` is a for loop to group sales data by quarter so that they can be plotted on marginal axes, while the bivariate data can be plotted on the joint axes:
    - `sns.kdeplot(sales["Cookies"], ax=g4.ax_marg_x, label='Q'+str(i))` plots KDE plot on the top marginal axes with the labels Q1, Q2, Q3, and Q4, one in each iteration of the for loop
    - `sns.kdeplot(sales["Smoothies"], ax=g4.ax_marg_y, vertical=True, label='Q'+str(i))` plots another KDE plot on the right marginal axes with similar labels as in the top axes:
        - `vertical=True` specifies plotting it with a horizontal orientation.
    - `g4.ax_joint.plot(sales["Cookies"], sales["Smoothies"], "D", ms=5)` plots a scatter plot on the joint plot:
        - `"D"` is to use diamond marker
        - `ms=5` is the marker size

Upon execution of the preceding code, you should see the following two plots on your screen:

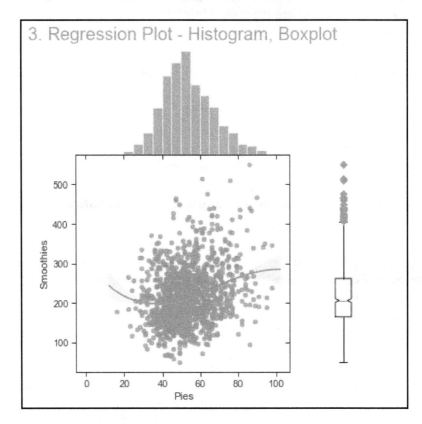

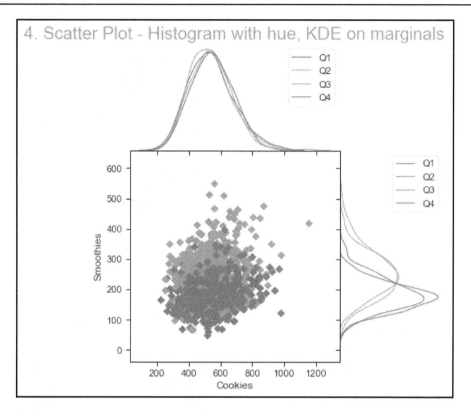

This is the fifth plot:

- Here, we use user-defined functions for plotting on the joint axes and both marginal axes. We will continue to have a hue effect.
- `g5 = sns.JointGrid("Cookies", "Coffee", snacks_sales, space=0.5, ratio=6)` creates the grid as usual.

- `def marginal_boxplot(a, vertical=False, **kws):` is the function to plot the boxplot on the marginal axes:
  - `g5 = sns.boxplot(x="Promotion", y="Coffee", orient="v", **kws) if vertical\else sns.boxplot(x="Cookies", y="Promotion", orient="h", **kws)`
    - We are not calling this function, but passing it on to the `sns.plot_marginals()` function, which will set the `vertical` flag to **True** or **False**, depending on which axes it is plotting, and the previous statement checks the status of this flag, and maps the data and orientation parameters appropriately.
    - `g5.set_ylabel("")` and `g5.set_xlabel("")` removes the default labels from the axes.
- `g5.plot_marginals(marginal_boxplot, palette={"Yes": "#ff000088", "No": "#00aa007e" }, data=snacks_sales,linewidth=1, fliersize=10,notch=True)` plots boxplot graphs on marginal axes:
  - `marginal_boxplot` is the function we have defined to plot boxplot graphs on the marginal axes.
  - `palette` specifies the color codes for the different values of the `Promotion` variable, which is being used as a hue variable.
  - `linewidth=1` specifies the width of lines plotted in boxplots.
  - `fliersize=10` specifies the size of outliers beyond the whiskers.
  - `notch=True` specifies to plot the box with the notch, instead of a rectangular box.
- `sns.regplot()` plots a regression plot on the joint axes once for `Promotion=Yes` data, and a second time with `Promotion=No`. All the parameters were discussed in regression plots (`lmplot()` and `regplot()`) in detail. So, we re not repeating that here.
- `g5.ax_joint.legend(loc=4)` plots the legend on the bottom-right corner of the joint axes.

Upon executing the preceding code block, you should see the fifth plot on your screen, as shown here:

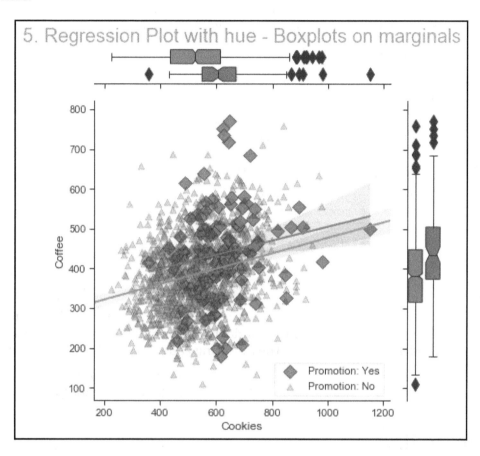

pairplot() and PairGrid()

`pairplot()` and `PairGrid()` enable plotting all numerical variables in the dataset as pairs of two in one statement. This is a quick way of understanding the high-level relationships and correlations that exist among the variables in the entire dataset. This speeds up the feature-engineering process of machine-learning projects. `pairplot()` has only two options for bivariate plotting, scatter and regression. `PairGrid()` does not have any such limitation.

Getting ready

This part is common for both `pairplot()` and `PairGrid()`, whereas the *How to do it...* and *How it works...* sections will be repeated for each of them separately.

Import the required libraries:

```
import matplotlib.pyplot as plt
import seaborn as sns

# The following parameters are set in rc configuration file, so they
  will be applicable for the entire session
# font_scale factor is the multiplier of default font size(instead of
  absolute size, it is relative size)
sns.set(rc={"axes.linewidth": 1, "xtick.major.width": 1,
            "ytick.major.width": 1,
            "xtick.major.size": 5, "ytick.major.size": 5},
            style="ticks", context="paper",
            font_scale=1.25)
```

pairplot()

We will take the only subset of our `Snacks Sales` dataset to avoid cluttering plots with too many variables to plot. We will only include five items and the promotion variable, which will be used as the hue variable. The following code extracts the required subset:

```
snacks_sales_items = snacks_sales.loc[:,['Cakes', 'Cookies', 'Pies',
                                          'Smoothies','Coffee','Promotion']]
```

How to do it...

There are three ways of specifying what types of grids we want to plot using `pairplot()`. Let's plot all three formats and see the difference:

1. Plot all the numeric variables in the supplied dataset:

    ```
    sns.pairplot(snacks_sales_items, hue='Promotion', kind='reg')
    plt.show();
    ```

2. Plot select variables from the supplied dataset:

```
sns.pairplot(snacks_sales, vars=['Coffee', 'Pies'],
hue='Promotion',
             kind='reg')
plt.show();
```

3. Plot selected variables from the supplied dataset in a row and col grid, similar to the facet variables we used earlier:

```
g = sns.pairplot(snacks_sales, x_vars=['Coffee', 'Pies', 'Cakes'],
                 y_vars=['Cookies', 'Smoothies'],
                 hue='Promotion', kind='scatter')
g.fig.subplots_adjust(wspace=.02, hspace=.02);
plt.show();
```

How it works...

Here is the explanation of the preceding code.

This is the first plot:

- `sns.pairplot(snacks_sales_items, hue='Promotion', kind='reg')` creates and plots the required grid:
    - `snacks_sales_items` is the dataset we have just created for this recipe.
    - `hue='Promotion'` specifies the hue variable.
    - `kind='reg'` specifies that a regression plot should be plotted for all bivariate plots.
    - On the diagonal, it plots the univariate `kdeplot()` by default.

Upon execution, you should see the following plot on your screen:

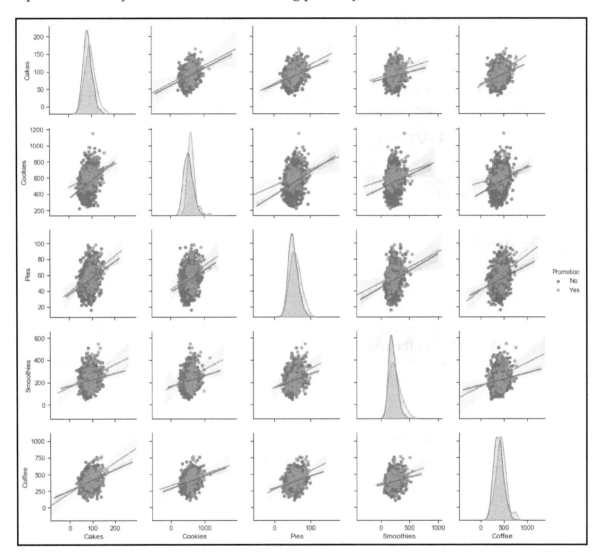

This is the second plot:

- `sns.pairplot(snacks_sales_items, vars=['Coffee', 'Pies'],hue='Promotion', kind='reg')` plots only two variables: `Coffee` and `Pies`.
- The other parameters are same as in the first plot.

Upon execution, you should see the following plot on your screen:

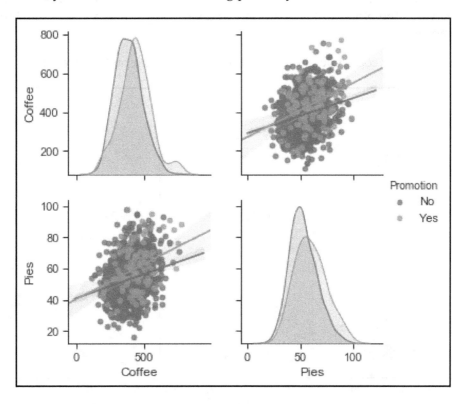

This is the third plot:

- `g = sns.pairplot(snacks_sales_items, x_vars=['Coffee', 'Pies', 'Cakes'], y_vars=['Cookies', 'Smoothies', hue='Promotion', kind='scatter')` will create a 3 x 2 grid and plots x_vars in rows and y_vars in columns.
- `kind='scatter'`, plots bivariate scatter plots.
- `g.fig.subplots_adjust(wspace=.02, hspace=.02)`, adjusts the space between the plots both horizontally and vertically. This can be applied to the first and second plots as well.

Upon execution of the code, you should see the following plot on the screen:

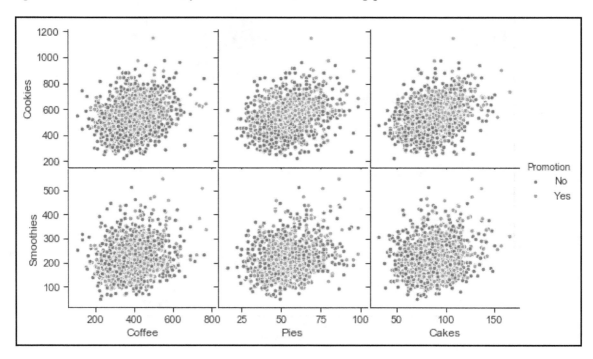

PairGrid()

`PairGrid()` works very similarly to `pairplot()`, but gives additional flexibility to use any type of plot for diagonal, off-diagonal, or even lower and upper diagonal plots separately. However, a row and col matrix grid of `pairplot()` is not supported in `PairGrid()`, since it uses **univariate** plots along the diagonal, whereas a row and col grid has only **bivariate** plots.

How to do it...

Apart from a full dataset and a selected list of variables, it also has three ways of specifying specific type of plots in the grid:

1. Using the same type of plot for all the cells/axes in the grid:

```
g = sns.PairGrid(snacks_sales_items, hue='Promotion', hue_kws=
                {"marker": ["^", "D"]},
                palette={'Yes': 'blue', 'No': '#00a99f05'})
g.map(plt.scatter, edgecolor='k', s=50)
g.add_legend()
g.fig.subplots_adjust(wspace=.02, hspace=.02);
```

2. Using one type of univariate plot for diagonal, and another bivariate type for off-diagonal plots:

```
g = sns.PairGrid(snacks_sales_items, vars=['Coffee', 'Pies',
                'Smoothies'], hue='Promotion', palette={'Yes':
                'Orange', 'No': 'g'})
g.map_diag(plt.hist, histtype="step", linewidth=2)
g.map_offdiag(sns.kdeplot, n_levels=25, cmap="coolwarm")
g.add_legend()
g.fig.subplots_adjust(wspace=.02, hspace=.02);
```

3. Using one type of univariate for the diagonal, one bivariate type for the upper diagonal, and another bivariate type for lower diagonal plots:

```
g = sns.PairGrid(snacks_sales_items, vars=['Cakes', 'Pies',
                'Cookies'], hue='Promotion',
                palette={'Yes': 'darkblue', 'No': 'r'})
g.map_diag(sns.stripplot, jitter=True)
g.map_upper(sns.regplot, order=2, ci=90)
g.map_lower(sns.residplot, order=2, lowess=True)
g.add_legend();
```

How it works...

Here is the explanation for the preceding code:

This is the first plot:

- `g = sns.PairGrid(snacks_sales_items, hue='Promotion', hue_kws={"marker": ["^", "D"]},palette={'Yes': 'blue', 'No': '#00a99f05'})` creates the grid for all the variables in the dataset:
    - `hue_kws={"marker": ["^", "D"]}` specifies the markers to be used for *Yes* and *No* values of the `hue` variable `Promotion`
    - `palette={'Yes': 'blue', 'No': '#00a99f05'}` specifies the color codes to be used for the hue variable unique values
- `g.map(plt.scatter, edgecolor='k', s=50)` plots scatter plot on each of the plots on the grid:
    - `edgecolor='k'` specifies black for the edges of points on the scatter plot.
    - `s=50` specifies the size of the points/markers on the scatter plot.
- `g.add_legend()` adds the legend to the figure. For some reason, `seaborn` does not add it automatically, as is the case of all other types of plots!
- `g.fig.subplots_adjust(wspace=.02, hspace=.02)`, adjusts the space between the plots horizontally and vertically.

Upon execution of the code, you should see the following plot on your screen:

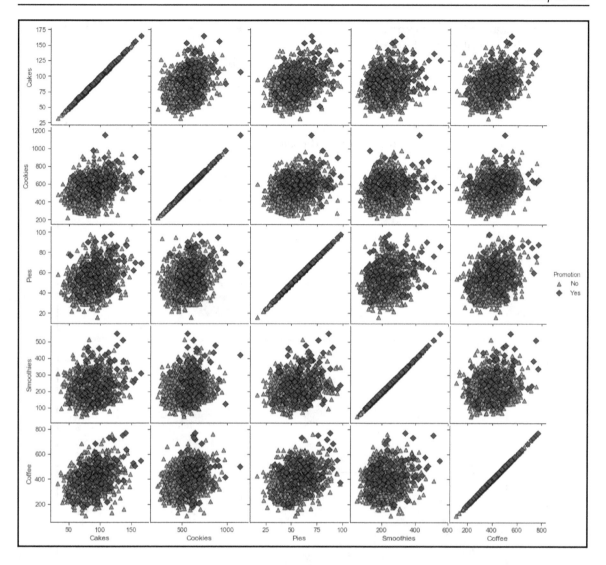

This is the second plot:

- g = sns.PairGrid() creates the grid as before, with the standard parameters
- g.map_diag(plt.hist, histtype="step", linewidth=2) specifies to plot a histogram on all diagonal boxes:
  - histtype="step" is a staircase instead of smooth curve.
  - linewidth=2 is the width of the line of the histogram.

- `g.map_offdiag(sns.kdeplot, n_levels=25, cmap="coolwarm")` plots the kde plot on all off-diagonal boxes:
    - `n_levels=25` specifies the number of contours to plot.
    - `cmap='coolwarm'` is the color map to be used to plot contours.
    - `g.add_legend()` adds the legend.
    - `g.fig.subplots_adjust(wspace=.02, hspace=.02)` adjusts the space between the plots.

Upon execution of the code, you should see the following plot on your screen:

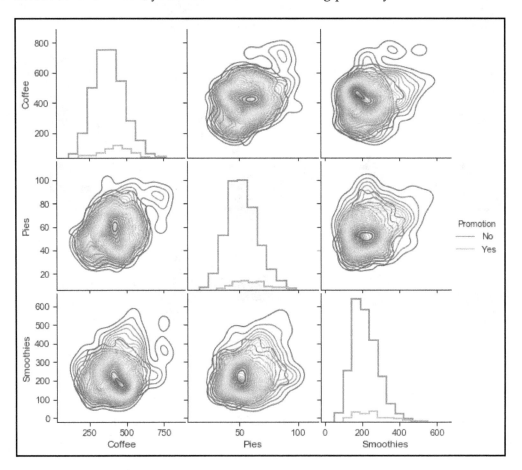

This is the third plot:

- `g = sns.PairGrid()` creates the grid for a selected set of variables in the dataset.

- `g.map_diag(sns.stripplot, jitter=True)` plots the strip plot on diagonal cells, with jitter set on so that all the points don't fall on one straight line.
- The `g.map_upper(sns.regplot, order=2, ci=90)` regression plot is plotted in the upper diagonal cells:
  - `order=2` specifies to fit a second-order polynomial to the given data.
  - `ci=90` plots a 90% confidence interval around the fitted polynomial.

Upon execution of the code, you should see the following plot on your screen:

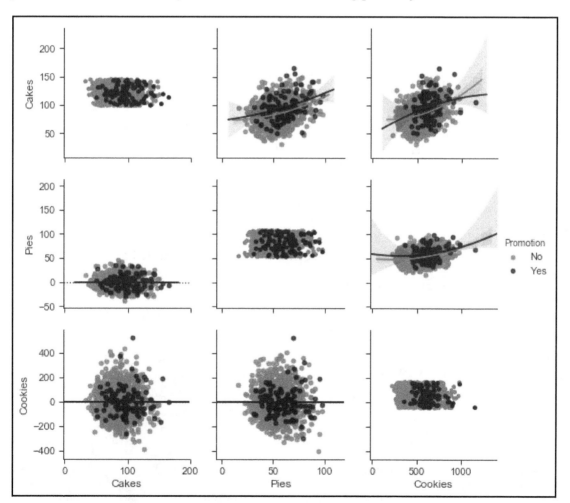

FacetGrid()

As explained earlier, `FacetGrid()` is used to perform multi-dimensional analysis using the semantic variables `hue`, `style`, and `size`, and the facet variables `row` and `col`. We have already used these features indirectly when we learned about relational and categorical plots.

Getting ready

Import the required libraries:

```
import matplotlib.pyplot as plt
import seaborn as sns

# The following parameters are set in rc configuration file, so they
  will be applicable for the entire session
# font_scale factor is the multiplier of default font size(instead of
  absolute size, it is relative size)
sns.set(rc={"axes.linewidth": 1, "xtick.major.width": 1,
            "ytick.major.width": 1,
            "xtick.major.size": 5, "ytick.major.size": 5},
         style="ticks", context="paper",
         font_scale=1.25)
```

How to do it...

Here are the steps to plot various `FacetGrid()` plots to demonstrate its features:

1. Plot a univariate histogram:

   ```
   g = sns.FacetGrid(snacks_sales, col="Promotion", row="weekend",
                     height=3)
   g = g.map(plt.hist, "Cookies", bins=10, color='m')
   ```

2. Plot a bivariate swarm plot:

   ```
   g = sns.FacetGrid(snacks_sales, col="Promotion", row="weekend",
                     height=3, margin_titles=True)
   g = g.map(sns.swarmplot, "Quarter","Smoothies", order=[1, 2, 3, 4],
             color='g')
   ```

3. Plot a bivariate regression plot:

   ```
   g = sns.FacetGrid(snacks_sales, col="Quarter", row="weekend",
                     hue="Promotion",hue_order=['Yes', 'No'],
   ```

```
                          height=3, margin_titles=True, palette="Set2",
                          hue_kws=dict(marker=["^", "v"]))
       g = g.map(sns.regplot, "Cookies","Coffee")
       g.set(xlim=(200, 900), ylim=(100,800))
       g.add_legend();
```

4. Plot a bivariate point plot:

```
       day_order = ['Monday', 'Tuesday', 'Wednesday', 'Thursday',
       'Friday',
                     'Saturday', 'Sunday']
       item_order = ['Coffee', 'Cakes', 'Pies', 'Cookies', 'Smoothies']
       g = sns.FacetGrid(long_sales, col="daywk",col_wrap=3,
                     col_order=day_order, hue="Promotion",
                     hue_order=['Yes', 'No'], palette="Set1",
       height=3,
                     legend_out=False,
                     aspect=1.5, margin_titles=True)
       g = g.map(sns.pointplot, "Item","Sales",
             order=item_order).set_titles("{col_name}").add_legend()
       g = g.fig.subplots_adjust(wspace=.05, hspace=.15);
```

How it works...

Here is the explanation for the preceding code:

This is the first plot:

- `g = sns.FacetGrid(snacks_sales, col="Promotion", row="weekend", height=3)` creates the grid:
    - `snacks_sales` is the input DataFrame.
    - `col="Promotion"` specifies `Promotion` as the column variable.
    - `row="weekend"` specifies `weekend` as the row variable.
    - `height=3` specifies the height of each of the plots in the grid.
    - A default aspect ratio of 1 is used, which means width is same as height.
- `g = g.map(plt.hist, "Cookies", bins=10, color='m')` plots a histogram on all plots of the grid:
    - `bins=10,` specifies the number of bins in the histogram.
    - `color='m',` specifies to use magenta as the color.

This is the second plot:

- `g = sns.FacetGrid(snacks_sales, col="Promotion", row="weekend", height=3, margin_titles=True)` creates the grid:
  - `margin_titles=True` specifies the titles of the row variables are plotted to the right of the last column.
- `g = g.map(sns.swarmplot, "Quarter","Smoothies", order=[1, 2, 3, 4], color='g')` plots a swarm plot of quarter-wise sales of `Smoothies`.
- `order=[1, 2, 3, 4]` specifies the order in which quarters are to be plotted on the x axis; since it is a numerical value, it can automatically take an ascending order.
- `color='g'` colors the points on the plot green.

Upon execution of the code for these two plots, you should see the following plots on the screen:

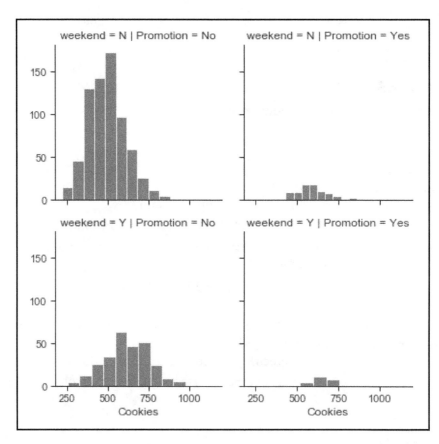

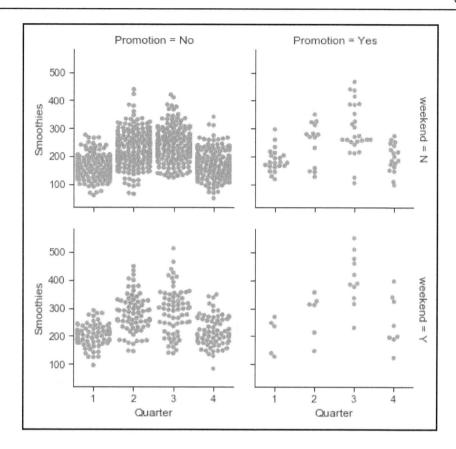

This is the third plot:

- `g = sns.FacetGrid()` creates the required grid:
    - `col="Quarter"` maps `Quarter` to the column variable.
    - `row="weekend"` maps `weekend` to the row variable.
    - `hue="Promotion"` maps `Promotion` to the hue variable.
    - `hue_order=['Yes', 'No']` is the order in which they should be plotted.
    - `height=3` sets the height of each plot to be three inches.
    - `margin_titles=True` sets the titles of the row variable to be plotted to the right of the last column.
    - `palette="Set2"` uses a predefined color palette.
    - `hue_kws=dict(marker=["^", "v"])` specifies to use these markers for unique values of the `Promotion` variable.

- `g = g.map(sns.regplot, "Cookies","Coffee")` plots a regression plot of the `Cookies` and `Coffee` variables
- `g.set(xlim=(200, 900), ylim=(100,800))`, sets the *x* and *y* axis limits
- `g.add_legend()` means that since the hue variable is now added, we can plot the legend.

Upon execution of the preceding code, you should see the following plot on the screen:

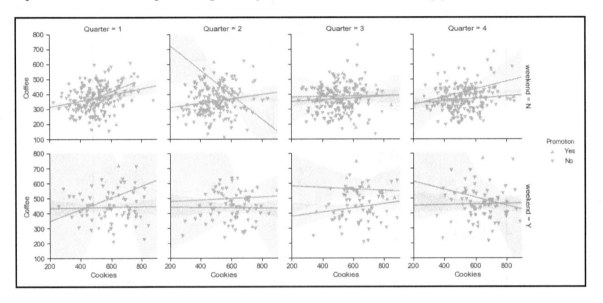

This is the fourth plot:

- `day_order` is the list specifying the order in which weekdays are to be plotted
- `item_order` is the list specifying the order in which items are to be plotted
- `g = sns.FacetGrid()` creates the grid with the following attributes:
    - `long_sales` is the long form DataFrame containing the data to be plotted.
    - `col="daywk"` maps the `daywk` variable to a column.
    - `col_wrap=3`, specifies to wrap subsequent plots into rows, after every three columns.

- `col_order=day_order`, specifies the order in which days of the week are to be plotted.
- `hue="Promotion"` is the `Promotion` variable mapped to `hue`.
- `hue_order=['Yes', 'No']` is the order in which `Promotion` values are to be plotted.
- `palette="Set1"` is the color palette to be used.
- `height=3` is the height of each of the plots.
- `aspect=1.5` is the width of each plot in the grid, which should be `1.5` times the height.
- `legend_out=False` specifies not to push the legend outside the plot on the right side. Then, it chooses the best location within the plot to print. The default is to plot it outside the plot area, right of center.
- `margin_titles=True` means the titles of the row variable are plotted to the right of the last column.
- `g = g.map(sns.pointplot, "Item","Sales", order=item_order).set_titles("{col_name}").add_legend()`:
  - Plots a point plot of item and sales.
  - `order=item_order` *items* are plotted in this order.
  - `set_titles("{col_name}")` sets the title with the `col_name` of corresponding plot, instead of using the default title.
  - `add_legend()` adds the legend to the figure.
- `g = g.fig.subplots_adjust(wspace=.05, hspace=.15)`, adjusts the space between the plots.

Upon execution of the preceding code, you should see the following plot on the screen:

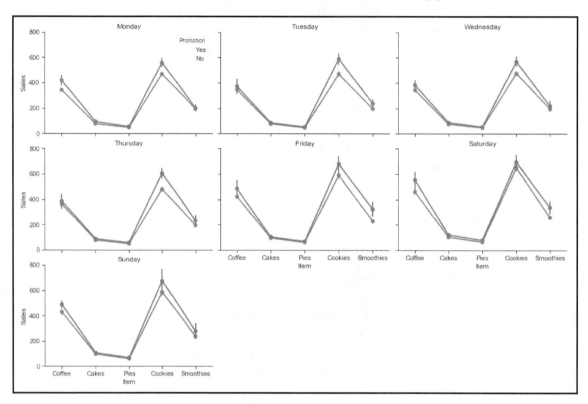

Matrix plots

While `pairplot()` and `PariGrid()` enable plotting relationships between many variables in a grid of two variables each, matrix plots enable this in matrix format, using an aggregated metric relating the variables, such as correlation, covariance, or it could be normal business data such as finance, sales, or operations related to the two variables.

Seaborn provides two matrix plots, `heatmap()` and `clustermap()`.

`Heatmap()` provides a colored representation of numbers to understand increasing, decreasing, diverging, or converging trends, which may not be easy to capture with numbers directly, especially when the numbers are too small or too large.

`Clustermap()` uses hierarchical clustering methods and plots the resulting dendrogram.

Heatmaps

Heatmaps represent numbers in colors by using colormaps, so that our eyes catch the relative strength of various variables in the data.

Getting ready

Import the required libraries. Set the background style and prepare the data required for plotting the graphs.

We will use the same long format DataFrame as input, group by `Item` and `Quarter` to get quarter-wise sales of various items, and create a pivot table out of it, still in the DataFrame format, which can be fed to the Seaborn plots:

```
import matplotlib.pyplot as plt
import seaborn as sns

sns.set(style='white')

# Prepare the data in matrix format with Quartes on rows and Items in
  columns
sales = pd.DataFrame(long_sales.groupby(["Item",
                                         "Quarter"]).Sales.mean())
sales = sales.reset_index()
sales = sales.pivot('Quarter','Item', 'Sales')
sales.head()
```

How to do it...

Here are the steps to plot the required graphs. We will plot three figures, one after the other. The first figure will have three plots, the second figure one plot, and the third figure two plots:

1. Define the first figure object and define the axes objects on which we will plot the seaborn plots:

```
fig, (ax1, ax2, ax3) = plt.subplots(1,3, figsize=(15,5))
```

2. Plot a heatmap with a predefined colormap:

```
sns.heatmap(sales, annot=True, fmt='.0f', linewidths=.5,
            cmap="YlGnBu", ax=ax1)
ax1.set_title('Using pre-defined Colorbar')
```

3. Plot a heatmap with a colormap centered at a specific value:

```
sns.heatmap(sales, annot=True, fmt='.0f',linewidths=.5,
robust=True,
                cmap="YlGnBu", center=sales.loc[3, 'Cookies'],
                yticklabels=False, ax=ax2)
ax2.set_title("Colorbar Centered at [3, 'Cookies']")
```

4. Plot a heatmap with set limits for the colormap:

```
sns.heatmap(sales, annot=True, fmt='.0f',linewidths=.5,
robust=True,
                vmin=200, vmax=600,
                cmap="YlGnBu", yticklabels=False, ax=ax3)
ax3.set(title='Colorbar range(200, 600)', ylabel='')
```

5. Adjust the space between the plots and display the figure on the screen:

```
plt.tight_layout()
plt.show();
```

6. Define the second figure object and plot the heatmap and colorbar on separate axes, with a horizontal colorbar:

```
grid_kws = {"height_ratios": (.9, .05), "hspace": .4}
f, (plot_ax, cbar_ax) = plt.subplots(2, gridspec_kw=grid_kws)
ax = sns.heatmap(sales, ax=plot_ax, cmap="Set1", annot=True,
                fmt='.0f',linewidths=.5,
                cbar_ax=cbar_ax, cbar_kws={"orientation":
                "horizontal"});
```

7. Define the third figure and plot a heatmap of the wine_quality correlation matrix:

```
fig, (ax1, ax2) = plt.subplots(1,2, figsize=(16,6))
sns.heatmap(corr, annot=True, fmt='.2f',linewidths=.5,
                cmap="inferno", ax=ax1)
```

8. Plot a heatmap of a partial correlation matrix on the third figure defined in the previous step:

```
mask = np.zeros_like(corr)
mask[np.triu_indices_from(mask)] = True
sns.heatmap(corr, mask=mask, vmax=.3, annot=True, fmt='.2f',
                cmap="inferno", ax=ax2)
```

9. Display the figure on the screen:

```
plt.show();
```

How it works...

Here is the explanation of the preceding code.

This is the first figure:

- `fig, (ax1, ax2, ax3) = plt.subplots(1,3, figsize=(15,5))` defines the figure and three axes in a row.
- `sns.heatmap(sales, annot=True, fmt='.0f',linewidths=.5, cmap="YlGnBu", ax=ax1)` plots the heatmap:
    - `sales` is the quarter and item sales data frame.
    - `annot=True` specifies to display the actual numbers on the plot.
    - `fmt='.0f'` specifies that the numbers should be displayed in integer format without any decimal values.
    - `linewidths=0.5` specifies that all the rows and columns should be plotted with lines of this width.
    - `cmap=" YlGnBu"` specifies the predefined colormap.
    - `ax=ax1` specifies the axes on which this graph is to be plotted.
- `ax1.set_title('Using pre-defined Colorbar')` plots the title for the first plot.
- `sns.heatmap(sales, annot=True, fmt='.0f',linewidths=.5, robust=True, cmap="YlGnBu", center=sales.loc[3, 'Cookies'], yticklabels=False, ax=ax2)` plots the second heatmap, which centers the colormap at the specified value:
    - `robust=True`: When the `vmin` and `vmax` range is not specified, the colormap range is derived by down-weighting the outliers.
    - `center=sales.loc[3, 'Cookies']` sets the center color of the colormap at this value, and adjusts the color bar to the range of data being plotted. If the chosen value is on either extreme of the range of data, then only half of the original colormap gets used for the new colorbar.
    - `yticklabels=False` switches off the tick labels of the Y axis for this plot.
    - `ax=ax2` is the axis where this graph is plotted.

- `sns.heatmap(sales, annot=True, fmt='.0f',linewidths=.5,` `robust=True, vmin=200, vmax=600, cmap="YlGnBu",` `yticklabels=False, ax=ax3)` plots one more heatmap with limits set on the colorbar:

  - `vmin=200` is the lower limit and `vmax=600` is the upper limit. All the numbers in the data below the lower limit are colored at the lower extreme of the colorbar, and the numbers above the upper limit will be colored with the upper extreme color.

- `ax3.set(title='Colorbar range(200, 600)', ylabel='')` prints the title and switches off the *y* axis label.

- `plt.tight_layout()` adjusts the space between the plots so that there are no overlaps.

Upon execution of the preceding code, you should see the following plot on the screen:

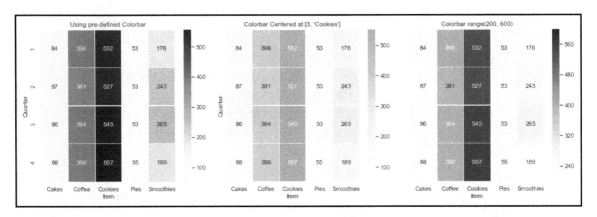

This is the second figure:

- `f, (plot_ax, cbar_ax) = plt.subplots(2, gridspec_kw=grid_kws)` defines the figure and two axes in a column.

- `grid_kws = {"height_ratios": (.9, .05), "hspace": .4}` is the dictionary of parameters for the grid. The heights of the two axes are in the ratio of 0.9:0.05, so that the colorbar axes' heights ares very short compared to the plot's height. The horizontal space between the two axes is 0.4.

- `ax = sns.heatmap(sales, ax=plot_ax, cmap="Set1", annot=True, fmt='.0f',linewidths=.5, cbar_ax=cbar_ax, cbar_kws={"orientation": "horizontal"})` plots the heatmap:
  - `sales` is the data to be plotted.
  - `ax=plot_ax` specifies the axes on which the plot is to be placed.
  - `cmap= "Set1"` is another predefined colormap.
  - `annot=True` displays the numbers on the plot.
  - `fmt='.0f'` numbers are to be displayed without decimal values.
  - `linewidths=0.5` lines are drawn in the matrix with a width of 0.5.
  - `cbar_ax=cbar_ax` specifies the colorbar axes.
  - `cbar_kws={"orientation": "horizontal"})` plots a horizontal colorbar.

Upon execution of the preceding code, you should see the following plot on the screen:

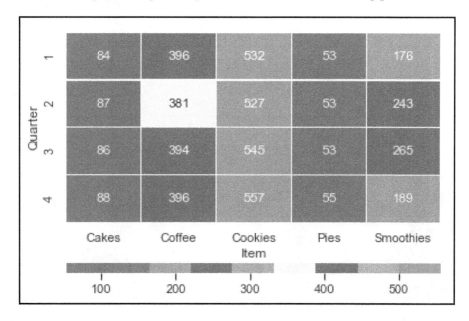

This is the third figure:

- `fig, (ax1, ax2) = plt.subplots(1,2, figsize=(16,6))` defines the third figure, with two axes in a row.

- `sns.heatmap(corr, annot=True, fmt='.2f',linewidths=.5, cmap="inferno", ax=ax1)` plots the heat map of the correlation matrix for the `wine_quality` data. All the parameters were already explained in the last two figures.
- For the second plot, `mask = np.zeros_like(corr)` creates a mask with the same dimensions as the corr matrix, and fills it with zeros.
- `mask[np.triu_indices_from(mask)] = True` sets all the elements in the upper diagonal to *true*, and others (diagonal and lower diagonal cells) will remain `False(0)`.
- `sns.heatmap(corr, mask=mask, vmax=.3, annot=True, fmt='.2f', cmap="inferno", ax=ax2)` plots the heatmap:
  - `mask=mask` specifies the mask to be applied on the overall matrix. It displays only the entries that are set to `Zero(False)` and hides those that are set to `True(1)`. It matches the indices in the *mask* matrix with those in the *corr* matrix.
  - `vmax = 0.3`, sets the limit for the color bar at 0.3. All the values above 0.3 will be colored with the color on top of the colorbar.
  - `cmap="inferno"` sets another predefined colormap to be used here.

Upon execution of the preceding code, you should see the following plot on the screen:

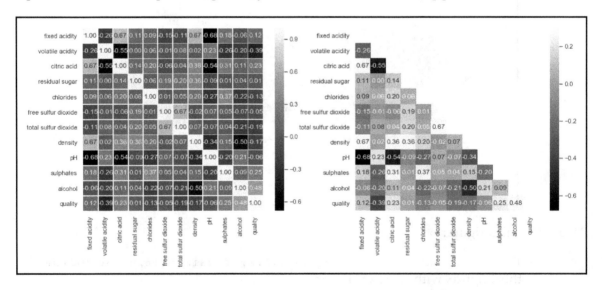

Clustermaps

`clustermap()`, as the name indicates, clusters various variables in the dataset using hierarchical clustering methods and plots the resulting dendrogram.

Getting ready

Import the required libraries:

```
import matplotlib.pyplot as plt
import numpy as np
import seaborn as sns

sns.set(style='white')
```

How to do it...

Here are the steps to plot two cluster maps, one with raw data in the `Wine Quality` dataset, and the other with the associated correlation matrix:

1. Plot the clustermap of the `Wine Quality` dataset:

```
row_colors =
wine_quality["Quality"].map(dict(zip(wine_quality["Quality"].unique
                        (), "rbg")))
g = sns.clustermap(wine_quality.drop('Quality',axis=1),
                standard_scale=1, robust=True,
                row_colors=row_colors, cmap='viridis')
```

2. Plot the clustermap of the correlation matrix of the `Wine Quality` dataset:

```
g = sns.clustermap(corr, figsize=(10,8),  z_score=1, cbar_kws={"label":
                                        "color bar"})
```

How it works...

Here is the explanation of the code:

The `Quality` variable in the `Wine Quality` dataset has `Low`, `Med`, and `High` values, with `63`, `1319`, and `217` counts respectively. We want to highlight which observations in the cluster belong to which quality rating. So, we extract these three unique values and assign three colors, red, green, and blue, to them so that the corresponding observations are colored accordingly:

- `row_colors = wine_quality["Quality"].map(dict(zip(wine_quality["Quality"].unique(), "rbg")))` gets the indices of all observations and assigns the appropriate color code, corresponding to `Low` (green), `Med` (blue), and `High` (red) values.

- `g = sns.clustermap(wine_quality.drop('Quality',axis=1), standard_scale=1, robust=True, row_colors=row_colors, cmap='viridis')` plots the clustermap:
  - `wine_quality.drop('Quality',axis=1)` drops the `Quality` variable from the cluster map, since it is being used as hue.
  - `standard_scale=1`, specifies to standardize all the variables in the dataset. This can be done row-wise or column-wise. We are doing it column-wise, as we want to standardize the variables organized in columns. Essentially, it computes the minimum and maximum values of the variable, and subtracts the minimum value from each value, then divides the result by the maximum value. This helps in improving the performance of the model.
  - `row_colors=row_colors` specifies the color codes for the observations to be displayed on the clustermap.
  - `cmap='viridis'` specifies the colormap to be used.
  - We could try different methods of linkage to assign clusters using the `method` parameter, and different distance metrics using the `metric` parameter. Please refer https://docs.scipy.org/doc/scipy/reference/generated/scipy.spatial.distance.pdist.html for more details.
  - We can get the sequence of the row and col indices of clusters using `g.dendrogram_row.reordered_ind` and `g.dendrogram_col.reordered_ind` respectively, where `g` is the clustermap object.

Upon execution of the preceding code, you should see the following plot on the screen:

Upon execution of the preceding code, you should see the following plot on the screen:

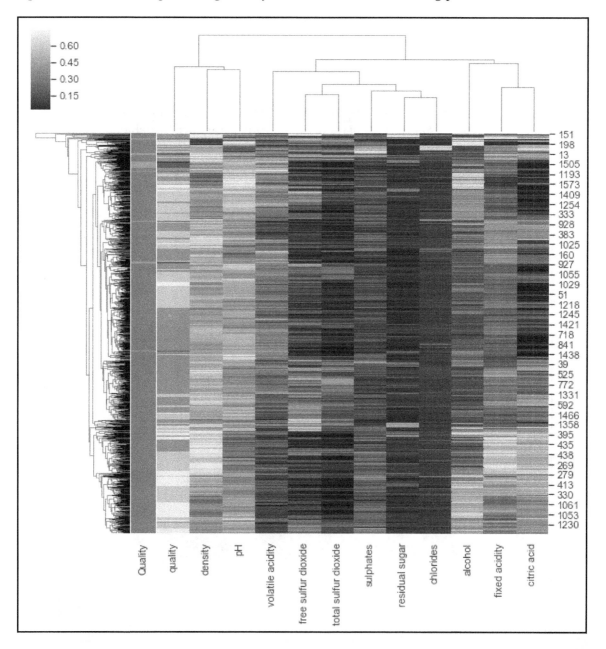

Further explanation is as follows:

- `g = sns.clustermap(corr, figsize=(10,8), z_score=1, cbar_kws={"label": "color bar"})` plots the cluster map of the correlation matrix of the `Wine Quality` dataset:
  - `figsize=(10,8)` specifies the size of the figure in which the clustermap is to be plotted.
  - `z_score=1` is another standardization method, where mean and standard deviation are computed for each variable, mean is subtracted from each element, and then it is divided by the standard deviation so that the resulting variable distribution will have a mean of zero and a standard deviation/variance of 1.

Upon execution of the preceding code, you should see the following plot on the screen:

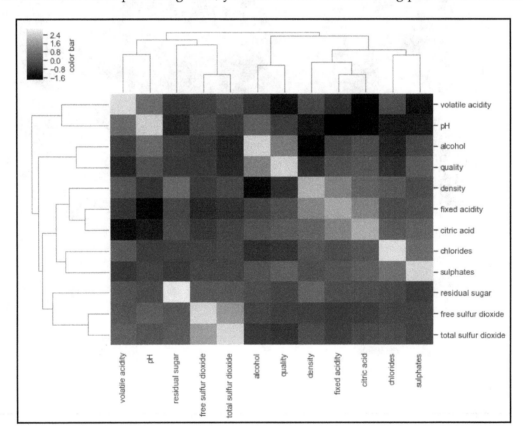

Other Books You May Enjoy

If you enjoyed this book, you may be interested in these other books by Packt:

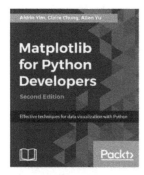

Matplotlib for Python Developers - Second Edition
Aldrin Yim

ISBN: 9781788625173

- Create 2D and 3D static plots such as bar charts, heat maps, and scatter plots
- Get acquainted with GTK+3, Qt5, and wxWidgets to understand the UI backend of Matplotlib
- Develop advanced static plots with third-party packages such as Pandas, GeoPandas, and Seaborn
- Create interactive plots with real-time updates
- Develop web-based, Matplotlib-powered graph visualizations with third-party packages such as Django
- Write data visualization code that is readily expandable on the cloud platform

Matplotlib 2.x By Example
Allen Yu

ISBN: 9781788295260

- Familiarize with the latest features in Matplotlib 2.x
- Create data visualizations on 2D and 3D charts in the form of bar charts, bubble charts, heat maps, histograms, scatter plots, stacked area charts, swarm plots and many more.
- Make clear and appealing figures for scientific publications.
- Create interactive charts and animation.
- Extend the functionalities of Matplotlib with third-party packages, such as Basemap, GeoPandas, Mplot3d, Pandas, Scikit-learn, and Seaborn.
- Design intuitive infographics for effective storytelling.

Leave a review - let other readers know what you think

Please share your thoughts on this book with others by leaving a review on the site that you bought it from. If you purchased the book from Amazon, please leave us an honest review on this book's Amazon page. This is vital so that other potential readers can see and use your unbiased opinion to make purchasing decisions, we can understand what our customers think about our products, and our authors can see your feedback on the title that they have worked with Packt to create. It will only take a few minutes of your time, but is valuable to other potential customers, our authors, and Packt. Thank you!

Index

buttons
  using 308, 311

C

callbacks 275
cartopy
  used, for plotting country maps 510, 513
categorical plots
  about 553
  bar plot 562
  box plot 557
  boxn plot 557
  count plot 562
  point plot 575
  strip plot 553
  swarm plots 553
  violin plot 570
check buttons
  using 314, 317
clustermaps 639, 642
co-ordinates
  displaying, by data co-ordinates transformation
    176, 180
collections
  plotting, object-oriented API used 164
color
  specifying 104, 108
constrained layout 198, 200
contour plot
  about 65, 401, 404
  using 66, 68
  working 403
correlation matrix
  plotting, pyplot and object-oriented APIs used
    156
count plot 562, 566
country maps
  plotting, cartopy used 510, 513
  plotting, GeoPandas used 510, 513
  plotting, with political boundaries 503, 507, 510
cursor
  using 306
curvilinear grids
  defining, in rectangular boxes 429, 430, 432

D

data co-ordinate system
  transforming, for co-ordinates display 176, 180
  using 183
decision tree (DT) 80, 318
default environment variables
  modifying 21, 23
  resetting 21, 23
distplot()
  using 580, 583
distribution plots
  about 579
  distplot(), using 580
  kdeplot(), using 584

E

events 275
exception
  handling 275, 277
extent arguments
  using, for image orientation 204, 206
external files
  reading from 17

F

facet variables 534
FacetGrid() 626, 630
False Positive Rate (FPR) 80
figure elements
  axes 10
  axis 10
  grid 11
  label 10
  legend 10
  spines 11
  ticklabels 11
  title 10
figure enter event
  capturing 297
figure leave event
  capturing 297
figure
  anatomy 9
  elements 8